Mexico, Central, and South America:
New Perspectives

Volume 5
Race and Ethnicity

Series Content

Mexico, Central, and South America:
New Perspectives

Volume 5
Race and Ethnicity

Edited with introductions by

Jorge I. Domínguez
Harvard University

ROUTLEDGE
New York/London

Published in 2001 by

Routledge
29 West 35th Street
New York, NY 10001

Published in Great Britain by
Routledge
11 New Fetter Lane
London EC4P 4EE

Routledge is an Imprint of Taylor & Francis Books, Inc.
Copyright © 2001 by Routledge

Printed in the United States of America on acid-free paper.

10 9 8 7 6 5 4 3 2 1

Library of Congress Cataloging-in-Publication Data

Democracy in Latin America in the 1990s / edited with introductions by Jorge I. Domínguez.
    p. cm. -- (Mexico, Central and South America : the scholarly literature of the 1990s ;
   v. 2)
  Includes bibliographical references.
  ISBN 0-8153-3692-6 (set : alk. paper) -- ISBN 0-8153-3694-2 (v. 2 : alk. paper)
   1. Latin America--Politics and government--1980- 2. Democracy--Latin
America--History--20th century. I. Domínguez, Jorge I., 1945- II. Mexico, Central and
South America ; v. 2.

F1414.2 .D4317 2001
320.98--dc21

                                              2001524240

ISBN 0-8153-3692-6 (set)
ISBN 0-8153-3693-4 (v.1)
ISBN 0-8153-3694-2 (v.2)
ISBN 0-8153-3695-0 (v.3)
ISBN 0-8153-3696-9 (v.4)
ISBN 0-8153-3697-7 (v.5)

Contents

Introduction

Latin America remains the only region of the world where societies are racially and ethnically heterogeneous and overt national conflict has been rare among political parties and social movements organized on the basis of race and ethnicity. In the 1990s, however, such conflict became more frequent. The essays in this volume explore the dimensions of greater contestation over race and ethnicity in a number of Latin American countries. Nine articles focus on indigenous peoples in the Andean subregion, Mexico, and Guatemala, and four articles study racial issues in Brazil.

Deborah Yashar provides a general account of the impact of democratization and state reform on the development of indigenous movements in several Latin American countries with large indigenous populations. She focuses on Bolivia, Ecuador, Guatemala, Mexico, and Peru. She argues that democratization legalized the right to organize and lowered the barriers of repression. The freedom to express opinions publicly, distribute information, hold assemblies, and organize across communities had practical consequences. But the incentive to use these rights stemmed from the impact of the reform of the state on indigenous communities. Before the 1990s, government policies induced indigenous peoples to identify as "peasants" by making available to them both material resources and specialized means of clientelist or corporatist representation. In the name of budget balancing, many agricultural subsidies were cut; in the name of efficiency, clientelist patronage practices to benefit the poor were curtailed; and in the name of both efficiency and liberty, corporatism and the special protections of some indigenous communities were dismantled. The liberal state freed indigenous peoples to organize in terms of identity, not just social class. The state's neoliberal economic policies provoked them to do so. And the preexisting networks among indigenous peoples enabled them to act.

Another vehicle for activating these long-latent racial and ethnic cleavages has been the internationalization of social movements that involve Latin America's indigenous peoples, a topic that Alison Brysk explores. To face powerful states in order to claim rights to land, language, and religion, indigenous social movements reached out to partners beyond state boundaries to obtain funds, learn about strategies and tactics, and raise barriers against state repression. International actors, in turn, put local groups in contact with each other and gave them material and symbolic incentives to cooperate, strengthening within-country networks. Indigenous rights movements remain weak, however, and thus often have few tools other than effective image projection and political theater, relying on the mass media to generate public support worldwide. Postmodern instruments have empowered peoples that remain premodern in many ways.

Why bother organizing movements based on language, culture, and other features of identity at the close of the twentieth century? To a significant extent, indigenous peoples have lacked the opportunity to choose whether or not to emphasize their identity. Rather, discrimination on the basis of their ethnicity has been thrust on them. Two articles explore ethnic-based labor-market discrimination.

Barry Chiswick, Harry Patrinos, and Michael Hurst examine some dimensions of the problem in Bolivia. They find that Spanish monolinguals are more likely to be younger people, active labor-market participants, and residents of cities. Indigenous monolinguals are more likely to be older women, born in rural areas, with several children. Among men and especially women, indigenous monolinguals participate in the labor force more than bilinguals, who in turn participate more than Spanish monolinguals. Language use has a dramatic impact on income. Spanish monolinguals earn about 25 percent more than bilinguals. All indigenous monolinguals earn less than bilinguals, but women indigenous monolinguals earn about 25 percent less than bilinguals. Clearly, the ethnic penalties are very expensive.

Donna MacIsaac and Harry Patrinos explore similar issues in Peru. The earnings of indigenous workers are less than half those of nonindigenous workers, a finding rather similar to those from the Bolivian data. Nonindigenous workers dominate better-paying occupations. Returns to schooling for Spanish-speaking workers are higher than for indigenous workers; university education is the only significant educational factor to increase earnings for indigenous men in Peru, but only 3 percent of the indigenous workforce has some university education.

To address and reverse their subordinate circumstances, indigenous peoples have organized in their communities, in labor markets, and in politics. Four articles illustrate various strategies that combine cultural resources with other forms of activity.

Lynn Stephen notes that the production of indigenous crafts for tourist and export markets depends on the commodification of indigenous culture. In the two previous articles, wage discrimination in the labor market was burdensome. Stephen's article analyzes a different domain for economic activity: a strategy of entrepreneurship that successfully employs ethnicity as an economic resource. In some instances craft production has resulted in self-managed economic development that strengthens local cultural institutions, as among the Otavalan Quechua speakers in Ecuador, the Nahua and the Zapotec in Mexico, and the Kuna in Panama. In these cases indigenous producers used a significant part of their income to reinvest in community institutions. These outcomes obtained provided communities had preserved a significant land base, had engaged in commercial production since Spanish colonial times, had a history of locally controlled marketing and distribution through local and regional networks, and had maintained ethnic institutions responsible for fostering social, cultural, and religious practices and high participation in traditional community systems of governance. These communities participate today in international and domestic markets to control their own economic growth and to defend their culture precisely because they are the inheritors of a pattern of opposition to past attempts at cultural assimilation.

Tanya Korovkin also studies the Otavalos in Ecuador. She assesses the theory of everyday forms of peasant resistance or hidden ethnic and class war, developed elsewhere for comparative analyses, as yet another strategy in the tool kit of some indigenous peoples. She highlights the importance of paying attention to long periods of apparent political calm, when peasants may successfully encroach on landlord property and power. She details how the Otavalos gradually induced and coerced hacienda owners to subdivide and sell their land to their workers and surrounding communities. In the 1970s and 1980s, responding to opportunities created by a government-sponsored land reform and especially by democratization (as Yashar's article also emphasizes), Otavalan resistance evolved into overt political protest through land seizures and participation in Ecuador's Confederation of Indigenous Nationalities (CONAIE). In 1990 the latter caught national and international attention when it organized a national indigenous uprising— a pattern repeated in the years that followed.

Donna Lee Van Cott explores a third strategy for the advancement of the interests of indigenous peoples: the efforts in Bolivia and Colombia to implement constitutionally mandated regimes of legal pluralism. What, she asks, has been the result of efforts to incorporate the practice of customary law, that is, the mostly unwritten forms of dispute resolution and social control practiced by ethnic communities or language groups? The Colombian constitution recognized legal pluralism in 1991, and Bolivia followed suit in 1994 in its constitutional revision in terms remarkably similar to Colombia's. And yet, Van Cott shows, implementation has varied significantly between the two countries. Indigenous communities in Bolivia have been more autonomous than in Colombia because the Bolivian government and courts are less capable and less knowledgeable about indigenous issues or customary law. Legal pluralism succeeded in Bolivia thanks to neglect on the part of state institutions. In Colombia, in contrast, indigenous communities are much less likely to be isolated; their members are more accustomed to making use of regular courts, and there is much greater professionally assertive engagement by Colombia's courts.

Revolt is, of course, a fourth strategy. June Nash analyzes long-term Mayan responses to state intervention in Chiapas, Mexico, in part to understand the 1 January 1994 uprising of the Zapatista National Liberation Army (EZLN). She argues that both economic and cultural issues have been at stake in Chiapas. Land, schools, and medical services are key EZLN demands, but EZLN rebels are well aware that they have been excluded from access to better things in life because of their ethnicity. Nash also argues, however, that the distinctive histories of the Chiapas Maya work against the possibilities of pan-indigenous movements. Leaders of highland Mayan communities often aligned with the ruling Institutional Revolutionary Party (PRI) in order to strengthen control over their own people and secure public funds; as a result, they sowed the seeds for intense class conflict and eventual support for the left-wing Party of the Democratic Revolution (PRD). Highland Maya continued to prefer individual farming, however, and found the art of association more difficult. Lowland Mayan communities, in contrast, were more likely to participate in regional associations independent of the PRI, confront local landlords, and adopt and adapt communalist forms of work. Support for the EZLN was stronger at first among the lowland Maya. Although their strategies differed, these two Mayan communities engaged in forms of ethnic reassertion. Highland Maya sought to reinforce strategies embedded in their ethnic traditions protected by the state; lowland Maya fought powerful agro-industrial interests in the name of justice and identity.

Concern over the rights and opportunities of indigenous peoples invites reflection about the racial, class, and gender characteristics of prevailing ideologies within and outside indigenous communities. This is Carol Smith's subject. Her study traces continuities and changes among Guatemalan Maya. As recently as the 1970s, she notes, the Maya, like other Guatemalans, accepted an essentialist construct of the bases of ethnic identity. They believed that the Maya formed distinct peoples descended from local community-specific ancestors and that they obtained their identities and social positions in their communities through descent or biology. Community endogamy was extremely high. There were community-specific forms of language and dress; women more than men bore the burden of maintaining these markers of Mayan identity. Mayan communities resisted the Guatemalan state and the domination of national economic elites by retaining a relatively autonomous economic existence, refusing proletarianization; they maintained their separatist, anti-assimilationist cultural and political stance by keeping their women outside the national marriage pool. From the late 1970s to the early 1990s many Maya joined a Marxist-Leninist revolutionary movement to topple the Guatemalan government. And yet Mayan women and men who joined the revolutionary movement continued to oppose the attempts by non-Mayan revolutionary leaders to establish a unified, rather than community-based, political agenda and were dismayed by the revolutionaries' sexual beliefs and disrespect for Mayan traditions. Even in a revolutionary situation, most Maya remained unwilling to forgo the strongest props for community-specific forms of ethnic identity: community endogamy and the gender code necessary to support it. The community's rights to survival took precedence over individuals' rights to sexual freedom.

Race relations in Brazil differ, of course, from the racial and ethnic patterns that prevail in Indo-America. Afro-Brazilians speak the Portuguese language, as do other Brazilians. Afro-Brazilian religions draw a disproportionate number of believers from the Afro-Brazilian population, but most of these religions do not exclude believers on the basis of skin color; many whites believe in these religions as well. Nor is the problem of access to and retention of land the same for Afro-Brazilians as it is for indigenous peoples. Afro-Brazilian concern about land issues is typically related to social class and economic resources, not to the cultural meanings of ancestral land, as might be the case with some indigenous peoples (the property rights of descendants of the relatively few Maroon communities are an exception).

Peter Fry explains the origins and significance of the "myth of racial democracy" in Brazil. There has long been a strong and widely shared belief in Brazil that there is no racial problem in the country, that Brazilians do not discriminate on the basis of racial categories, and that miscegenation is the key to this less contentious relationship. Between the 1950s and the 1970s scholars demonstrated that there is, on the contrary, ample evidence of persistent prejudice and discrimination against people of color in Brazil. Fry then considers the debate about the myth in the 1990s among those who wish to expose and eradicate the ideological fraud, those who believe that racism will endure and so Afro-Brazilians must construct their own means for identity and collective action, and those who wish to build on the myth as a goal for what a liberal society free from racism ought to be. The debate rages concerning the appropriateness of affirmative action, because it goes to the heart of Brazilian ideas of nationhood: Are we one people? Should Brazil emphasize individual or group rights?

In any event, there should be no doubt that Afro-Brazilians are severely disadvantaged. The next two articles call attention to some dimensions of the problem. George Reid Andrews explores the Afro-Brazilian disadvantage by comparing Brazil and the United States, the two largest multi-racial societies in the Americas, using statistical evidence. As he notes, there is a long history of making such comparisons; for some decades that result was often favorable to Brazil. Race relations in Brazil "felt" less contentious and were less repressive of peoples of color. Brazilian society seemed to offer greater opportunities for black upward mobility when compared with rigid racial segregation patterns in the United States. Andrews shows that until 1960 racial differentials in the United States exceeded racial differentials in Brazil on almost every indicator for which data are available. The earlier scholarship that had called attention to the "better" pattern in Brazil was not incorrect in comparative terms. In the years that followed, however, in the United States much changed about race relations; in Brazil, little did. By 1980 the statistical comparison of racial differences in the two countries no longer favored Brazil; the United States had become the more racially equal of the two societies. Interestingly, however, Brazil remained less racially unequal than the United States on some dimensions at the heart of Brazil's myth of racial democracy: marriage patterns, family structure, and urban residential distribution. Afro-Brazilians suffered much tougher conditions than Afro-Americans but experienced better interpersonal relations with people of different skin pigmentation. The latter was the sturdy pillar on which the myth of racial democracy still rested; it was both soothing comfort to Afro-Brazilians and, paradoxically, an obstacle to the urge to seek justice.

Michael Mitchell and Charles Wood analyze the practical significance of skin color in the relations between Brazilian citizens and representatives of state authority. Afro-Brazilians are more likely than whites to be the victims of assault, and they are more likely to be assaulted by the police. The data distinguish between whites, browns, and blacks. There are not statistically significant differences in victimization rates between whites and browns, but there are between them and blacks. Therefore, the key divide for this more extreme form of disadvantage is not between whites and nonwhites but between blacks and nonblacks.

Afro-Brazilians have responded to the country's realities in various ways. One of them has been participation in politics. Ollie Johnston analyzes Afro-Brazilian membership in the national Congress and the behavior of Afro-Brazilian deputies and senators. He shows that Afro-Brazilians typically held about 3 percent of the seats in Congress in the 1980s and 1990s, a woeful underrepresentation of their share of the population. The Brazilian Workers Party has elected the largest number of Afro-Brazilians to Congress. Afro-Brazilian deputies and senators have proposed legislation to penalize acts of racial discrimination, to modify the curriculum in public schools, and to institute affirmative-action programs, among other measures, but they have had little success, in part because their numbers are so small.

Latin America's future will require a greater engagement of the region's people of color in order to consolidate the rights of all citizens, address long-standing injustices, and realize genuine equal opportunity for all. The Indo-American and Afro-Latin experiences illustrate the persistence of conditions that every human being should deem unacceptable and take steps to redress.

Contesting Citizenship

Indigenous Movements and Democracy in Latin America

Deborah J. Yashar

The most recent round of democratization in Latin America has coincided with a wave of political organizing across indigenous communities. Indigenous communities have formed national and international peasant confederations, law centers, cultural centers, and, more recently, political parties and platforms. Challenging the historical image of Indians as a submissive, backward, and anachronistic group, these newly formed organizations have declared, embraced, and mobilized around their indigenous identity. Their demands have included territorial autonomy, respect for customary law, new forms of political representation, and bicultural education. While the specific characteristics of organizations and agendas vary, they have commonly demanded that constitutional, democratic, individual rights be respected and that collective indigenous rights be granted. Consequently, they are contesting the practice and terms of citizenship in Latin America's new democracies.

The emergence of indigenous organizations, politicization of indigenous identities, and demand for indigenous rights over the past two decades challenge historical norms and scholarly conclusions about the politicization of ethnic cleavages in Latin America. The historical record suggests that in the twentieth century indigenous communities have rarely initiated or sustained social movements that proclaimed an indigenous identity and demanded indigenous rights. To the contrary, active rural organizing within and between indigenous communities has traditionally been the reserve of peasant unions, political parties, churches, and revolutionaries. These movements have historically attempted to mobilize Indians to forge class, partisan, religious and/or revolutionary identities over, and often against, indigenous ones. Accordingly, scholars have generally underscored the weak politicization of ethnic cleavages in Latin America and concluded that ethnicity in Latin America has had comparatively little explicit impact on political organizing, party platforms, debates, and conflict, in sharp contrast to other regions in the world. [1]

The emergence of indigenous organizations that proclaim and promote indigenous identity and rights, therefore, constitutes a new phenomenon that merits explanation.[2] This article addresses why indigenous identity has become a more salient basis of political organizing and source of political claims in Latin America by comparing rural politics since 1945 in Bolivia, Ecuador, Guatemala, Mexico, and Peru.

23

Indigenous identity has become increasingly politicized over the past three decades in the first four cases, but its politicization is limited in the fifth. By exploring the marked but uneven politicization of ethnic cleavages in these five cases, I both explain why indigenous organizing has emerged in the contemporary period and why significant indigenous organizations have emerged in Bolivia, Ecuador, Guatemala, and Mexico but not Peru.

I propose a historically grounded comparative analysis that underscores the different ways in which state reforms have combined with political liberalization and preexisting networks to forge Latin America's new indigenous movements. I argue that indigenous movements have emerged to challenge the Latin American state and the disadvantageous terms of contemporary citizenship. As political liberalization legalizes the right to organize, state reforms have restricted access to state resources and jeopardized pockets of local political, material, and cultural autonomy that indigenous communities had carved out. Excluded from national political circles and challenged at the local level, indigenous communities have mobilized around their indigenous identity. Politicized indigenous identity, however, has found organized expression as an indigenous movement only where communities have been able to draw upon preexisting networks. These networks constructed autonomous spheres for transforming identity and creating organizational capacity. Where they already existed, these networks unwittingly provided the basis for broader movements and subsequently for mobilization of the communities connected by them.

This historical comparative argument is predicated on a relational and contingent understanding of contemporary state formation, citizenship, and social movements. While state formation and citizenship are most commonly described as unitary processes with clear institutional ends, this article does not assume that the most recent round of democratization and state reforms necessarily engenders more democratic states, practices, or citizenship. As O'Donnell, Fox, Cohen and Arato, and Tilly have argued in their work on citizenship, many contemporary states have implemented reforms that have initiated an incomplete (at times contradictory) process of democratization; while democratization has expanded political opportunities for the development of civil society, weak and/or nondemocratic state institutions have often restricted political access, participation, and local autonomy, particularly for historically marginalized groups.[3] Social movements have emerged in this context to contest the institutional boundaries and practice of citizenship.

The Cases

Bolivia, Guatemala, Peru, Ecuador, and Mexico are home to ninety percent of Latin America's estimated 35–40 million indigenous peoples and have the highest indigenous to nonindigenous ratio.[4] While Mexico's indigenous population constitutes a

24

relatively smaller percentage of the country's total population, at over an estimated ten million persons it is absolutely the largest (29 percent of Latin America's total indigenous population). Indigenous populations in the rest of the region's countries are significantly smaller both relatively and absolutely, constituting 10 percent or less of each country's total population.

Significant indigenous movements have emerged in Ecuador, Bolivia, Guatemala, and Mexico.[5] In these countries, indigenous peoples have mobilized beyond the local level to forge moderate to strong regional/subnational and national organizations (where strength is defined in terms of mobilizational capacity and organizational endurance) that have assumed a significant place in national policy debates. While each case is different, the following sketch highlights broad similarities in the emergence of indigenous movements in Ecuador, Bolivia, Guatemala, and Mexico, particularly when contrasted with Peru.

The Ecuadorian indigenous movement has transformed rural organizing and shaped state policy on bicultural education, agrarian reform, and territorial autonomy.[6] With its origins in disparate organizations, the Ecuadorian movement developed two significant regional federations, ECUARUNARI in the Andes and CONFENAIE in the Amazon, that subsequently founded the national confederation CONAIE in the 1980s. Among other indigenous confederations, CONAIE has become the prominent interlocutor of Ecuador's indigenous peoples, particularly following its organization of a weeklong indigenous civic strike in 1990 that shut down roads and cut off commerce. It has sustained this protest capacity, although in less dramatic ways, throughout the 1990s, contesting government policies and proposing alternatives. In 1996, following internal debates, indigenous organizations entered the electoral arena as part of a larger coalition and successfully fielded Andean and Amazonian legislative candidates.

Bolivia's contemporary indigenous movement can be traced to a heterogeneous movement in the late 1960s and early 1970s that sought to reclaim indigenous voices and autonomy in the Andean-based peasant movement and universities.[7] They called themselves Kataristas to commemorate Túpaj Katari, an eighteenth century Aymaran hero. By 1979 Kataristas assumed control of the military-dominated peasant organization, asserted greater independence from the national labor federation, and challenged the military-peasant pact. While Katarismo as an organizational force did not sustain political momentum or unity, it has had a lasting impact on union and electoral politics, illustrated by the election of Katarista Víctor Hugo Cárdenas as vice president in 1993. The Bolivian Amazon has since 1990 become an active site of indigenous organizing, especially of the regional confederation, CIDOB. In the 1990s these regional organizations have sustained a prominent national role in debating and negotiating territorial autonomy and land reform proposals as well as proposing candidates for national and local elections.

The Guatemalan indigenous movement emerged with the organization and coor-

25

dination of the Second Continental Meeting of Indigenous and Popular Resistance in 1991.[8] Newly founded Mayan organizations, such as Majawil Q'ij, CONIC, and COMG, proclaimed the centrality of indigenous identity for their political work. They challenged the predominantly class-based discourse and goals of Guatemala's popular movements and sought to create organizations more responsive to indigenous communities and concerns. During negotiations to end Guatemala's civil war, these diverse and often competitive organizations participated through national forums in the peace process; their efforts culminated in 1995 in the Accord on Identity and Rights of Indigenous Peoples and in 1996 in the Final Peace Accord. Indigenous popular organizations also formed an electoral coalition, Nukuj Ajpop, and a number of its municipal and legislative candidates was successful in the 1995 election.

Mexico's indigenous movements gained national and international attention with the rebellion by the Zapatistas (EZLN) in Chiapas, initiated on January 1, 1994.[9] Efforts to organize and promote indigenous organizing predate the Zapatistas. Nonetheless, the historically and comparatively limited capacity of Mexico's Indian communities to constitute a significant and independent national movement led scholars to remark on the historically minor role that indigenous organizations had played in Mexico. The Zapatistas challenged this pattern. Their largely indigenous army mobilized significant support and compelled the Mexican government to engage in negotiations. The EZLN's agenda includes indigenous autonomy and cultural respect alongside democratization. The EZLN has engineered a political opening for Mexico's indigenous peoples by simultaneously promoting discussions between indigenous communities and negotiations with the Mexican state. While it remains subnational in origin and one among many localized indigenous movements in Mexico, the EZLN has had an obvious national impact, as with the original Zapatistas in the 1910s.

In contrast, the Peruvian indigenous movement barely exists.[10] This low level of organizing is ironic in light of Víctor Raúl Haya de la Torre and José Carlos Martiátegui's early twentieth century arguments about Peru's indigenous core. Nonetheless, it is widely observed that, "in Peru, there is no Indian movement. The political proposal to organize specifically around indigenous identity is a profound failure in the country."[11] Organizing in the countryside has developed along different lines. On the one hand, *Sendero Luminoso* has until recently organized quite effectively throughout much of the Peruvian countryside. Although this movement organizes indigenous peasants, it rejects demands or agendas emanating from an indigenous identity. I therefore exclude it from the indigenous movements discussed here. On the other hand, *rondas campesinas* have emerged. These peasant organizations play a role in the adjudication and enforcement of justice as well as in the oversight of public works. The *rondas campesinas*, however, have remained localized in nature and do not focus specifically on indigenous concerns. Indeed, the emergence of

26

Sendero Luminoso and the *rondas campesinas* highlights the limited role of indigenous identity as a basis for political mobilization and claims in Peru. The exception is smaller Amazonian-based organizations like AIDESEP, which remain marginalized from national politics.

In short, ethnic cleavages have become significantly more politicized in recent years in Ecuador, Bolivia, Guatemala, and Mexico. In Ecuador indigenous organizations have developed one national confederation that speaks on behalf of various regional federations. In Bolivia indigenous communities have developed strong regional federations. In Guatemala competitive national organizations have gained a voice in national forums. In Mexico moderately strong regional organizations have gained a significant voice in contemporary political debates. All these organizations share a commitment to organize and defend Indians as Indians. They fundamentally demand both that the promise of democracy to respect the individual rights of indigenous men and women be fulfilled and that the state legally recognize the rights of indigenous communities to land and local forms of governance. These movements have assumed an indigenous identity and focus that is not prevalent in Peru's rural organizations. Ethnic cleavages in Peru are politically overshadowed by class-based organizing and protest. Organizing occurs within indigenous communities but is local in scope, weak in outreach, and marginalized from political debates. An explanation of the rising political salience of indigenous organizing, therefore, requires not only that we explain why it has developed recently in Ecuador, Bolivia, Guatemala, and Mexico, but also why it has remained so weak in Peru.

Prevailing Explanations

The emergence of indigenous protest and organizing in Latin America has challenged those who assumed that indigenous cultural and political identities were anachronistic and ephemeral. In particular, it has questioned the universal and teleological assumptions of orthodox forms of Marxism and liberalism about primary identities and directions of change. It has also opened up the field to competing explanations of indigenous collective action.

Primordialism[12]   Primordialists assume that ethnic identities are deeply rooted affective ties that shape primary loyalties and affinities. While they do not assume that all ethnic identities lead to conflict, they assume that all actors possess a strong sense of ethnic or racial identity that primarily shapes their actions and world-view. Accordingly, individuals and communities commonly advance and/or defend ethnically derived concerns, particularly when they perceive a disadvantage. The emergence of indigenous organizations and protest are therefore understood as a natural expression of integral ethnic identities.

27

5

Primordial arguments have found their greatest renaissance among chroniclers of the former Soviet Union, former Yugoslavia, Burundi, Rwanda, and Israel/Palestine. In the first two, it is argued that the regimes suppressed a deeply rooted sense of national identity; the subsequent breakdown of repressive political institutions enabled submerged ethnic identities to resurface. In the latter three, the ongoing conflict is analyzed as a consequence of historic antagonisms within or between states.

Yet primordial arguments generally fall short. First, they can not be empirically sustained; they sidestep the issue why these identities emerge as a central axis of action in some cases but not in others. Ethnic identities and conflicts are not everywhere reclaimed, even when there are moments of political opening. Latin America is most instructive here. Earlier rounds of democratization did not lead to the emergence of indigenous organizations or ethnic conflict, even when indigenous identities were clearly significant at the local level. Indeed, indigenous politicization is a new phenomenon in the region. Second, ethnic identities do not everywhere become a salient political identity. Hence, even if democratization allows for the greater expression of ethnic identity, individuals will not necessarily assume an ethnic political identity. Finally, even if ethnic loyalties are given, unchanging, and deeply rooted (an extremely dubious assumption), primordialist arguments provide little insight into why, when, or how they translate into political organizing and action in some cases and not others. Even if ethnicity is the primary identity that affects where one lives, how one votes, and where one spends money, individuals will not necessarily join ethnic political organizations and mobilize on behalf of their ethnic group. In short, the emergence of ethnic movements and conflicts speaks to the existence of deeply rooted identities, but primordial arguments fail to problematize the conditions under which they become politically salient and engender political organizations.

Instrumentalism[13]   Challenging primordial identity-oriented explanations, instrumentalist or rational choice analyses assume that individuals have (generally political and material) preferences, are goal oriented, act intentionally, and engage in utility-maximizing behavior. These assumptions lead instrumentalists to question why individuals choose to act collectively, particularly if in the absence of doing so they can still enjoy collective benefits. To explain this dilemma instrumentalists address the costs and benefits alongside the positive and negative incentives associated with collective action.

While instrumentalist explanations of collective ethnic action vary widely, they have thus far tended to shift the question away from why ethnicity becomes salient to how political entrepreneurs mobilize and politicize ethnic groups to pursue (personal) political and/or economic ends. In this scenario, the politicization of ethnicity is largely instrumental in achieving other goals; the ethnic card is one tool among many. The conditions under which ethnicity becomes politicized are less relevant than modeling and predicting the utility of and capacity for collective action.

28

Yet this redefinition of the problem sidesteps the question why ethnic loyalties become the basis for political action at one time rather than another. Studies have provided little insight into how one arrives at utility functions (particularly if actors are not acting in their economic self-interest) without making post hoc arguments, why actors occasionally act in ways that appear detrimental to their material interests, and when and why ethnicity (as opposed to other categories) becomes politicized. To answer these central questions, one needs to move away from rational choice's trademark parsimony to historically grounded determinations of preferences and institutional boundaries. In short, rational choice theory explains oganization building and maintenance better than it does the conditions under which ethnic identity becomes politically salient.[14] Accordingly, Cohen has distinguished between social movement theorizing that privileges strategy (discussed here) and identity (discussed next).[15]

Poststructuralism   Poststructural approaches, despite their diversity, commonly assume that identities are not given or ordered but are socially constructed and evolving.[16] Individuals do not necessarily identify with or act according to structurally defined positions, for structural conditions do not determine or define actors in any kind of uniform, unitary, or teleological fashion. Individuals are plural subjects, and power is diffuse. As subjects, they can assume a role in fashioning and reconstituting their identities (as Indians, workers, or women, for example), although there is no agreement over the degree of choice that actors have vis-à-vis these diffused power relations.

Poststructuralism allows ethnic identities to be seen as primary and purposive without arguing that they are primordial or instrumental in nature. By challenging structural and teleological explanations, it problematizes identity rather than assuming it. By refocusing on the local, analyzing discourse, and highlighting identity as a social construction, poststructural studies have heightened our sense of context, complexity, and the dynamic process by which agents (re)negotiate their identities. Indigenous identity is, from this perspective, both constituted by social conditions and renegotiated by individuals.

This article draws on poststructural assumptions that individuals are plural subjects with multiply configured identities and that these identities are socially constructed and transmutable. But it also assumes that very real structural conditions of poverty and authoritarian rule can impede the unencumbered expression of identities and pursuit of collective action just as they can shape needs as preferences. Given the structural conditions faced by Latin America's indigenous peoples, I do not singlemindedly subscribe to the literary method that pushes scholarship in a discursive and relativist direction. Discursive analyses can not speak to the comparative questions raised in this article; while problematizing ethnicity, poststructural approaches can neither explain why it becomes assumed as a salient political identity across

29

cases nor delineate the conditions under which people are likely or able to organize around it. Many poststructural theorists would argue that these questions wrongly presuppose universal explanations where none exist. Ultimately, poststructural distancing from generalized explanations begs the question why indigenous movements have emerged throughout the Americas in the past decades.

In general, the ahistoricity of these three approaches limits their ability to explain the contemporary salience of indigenous identity in political organizing in Latin America. The primordialists view identity as a constant, therefore negating the possibility of change over time; instrumentalists assume utility functions for individuals, therefore placing historical context outside the model; and poststructuralists challenge historical master narratives and see identity and identity-related action as largely contingent and nongeneralizable. Yet one can not explain the identity and organizational dimensions of Latin America's new indigenous movements without situating the contemporary period in a historical context.

The primordialist, instrumentalist, and poststructuralist approaches can not individually explain the politicization of and organization around indigenous identity. However, they can not be summarily dismissed. Balancing primordialists against poststructuralists, I acknowledge the power of ethnic ties without assuming that they are primary or unchanging. Confronting instrumentalists' concern for organization building and strategy, I evaluate the conditions in which actors can and do join organizations. To integrate a concern for identity and organizations, I situate these questions historically.

The Argument

I argue for a historically grounded, multilevel approach that is sensitive to the politics of identity, the politics of organizational capacity, and the comparative politics of opportunities. Why have indigenous identities become more politically salient in the region? How have these identities been successfully translated into indigenous social movements, particularly given their localization? What conditions have enabled the formation of new indigenous movements in Ecuador, Bolivia, Guatemala, and Mexico but not in Peru?

The comparative historical approach advocated here links the politicization of identity and movement building to state formation.[17] State formation institutionalizes formal political power by defining citizenship, delimiting civil society, and delivering political resources. It shapes political opportunities during regime change. It politicizes the identity of political actors. In allocating goods it affects organizational capacity. State formation, however, is a contested and contingent process. While political elites define institutions, other social actors often subvert them by contesting the terms and practice of citizenship. Indigenous movements in Latin

America have subverted them by struggling for inclusion and autonomy in the face of shallow national democratic institutions.[18] In situating social movements vis-à-vis state formation and analyzing political opportunities, organizational capacity, and the politicization of identity, I draw explicitly on the integrative comparative framework developed by Tarrow and his colleagues.[19]

In contemporary Latin American indigenous movements, the political liberalization of the 1980s provided the macropolitical opportunity for organizing, as states demilitarized and legalized freedoms of associations and speech. But the incentive to organize as Indians lay in state reforms that left Indians politically marginalized as individual citizens, disempowered as corporatist peasant actors, and confronted with a challenge to local, political, and material autonomy.[20] The capacity to organize as Indians, however, has depended on transcommunity networks previously constructed by the state and other social actors (see Table 1).

Table 1 Emergence of Indigenous Movements in Latin America: Overview of Argument and Cases

	Opportunity: Political Liberalization	Incentive: State Reforms Challenge Local Autonomy For Peasants	For Amazon	Capacity: Pre-Existing Networks	Outcome: Indigenous Movements
Ecuador	Opening 1978 on	Dismantling of rural state programs, 1980s-1990s	State development programs, 1960s on	Peasant unions & church networks	Significant national movement: CONAIE
Bolivia	Opening 1978/1982 on	Dismantling of rural state programs, 1980s-1990s	State development programs, 1960s on	Peasant unions, church networks, & NGOs	Significant regional movements: Kataristas & CIDOB
Mexico	Partial opening 1988 on	Dismantling of rural state programs, 1980s-1990s	-------	Peasant unions & church networks	Significant regional movements: i.e., EZLN
Guatemala	Uneven opening 1985 on	Dismantling of rural state programs after 1954 coup	-------	Peasant union is repressed; churches create new networks	Significant national movements: i.e., Majawil Q'ij, CONIC, COMG
Peru	Growing restrictions, 1980-1992; 1992 autogolpe	Dismantling of rural state programs after 1975 coup	State development programs, 1960s on	Fragmented peasant unions; fragmented church networks	Weak regional movements in Amazon: i.e., AIDESEP

Changing Macropolitical Opportunities: Political Liberalization[21]   Political liberalization, understood as increased freedoms of association, expression, and the press, provided a changing political opportunity for legal popular movement organizing in the late 1970s and 1980s. With declining repression and increasing respect for civil rights citizens in Ecuador, Bolivia, Guatemala, and Mexico confronted fewer constraints on expressing opinions publicly, distributing information, organizing across communities, and holding public assemblies. Hence political liberalization enabled the potential development of civil society and the politics of identity.

31

In interviews in 1995, 1996, and 1997, indigenous leaders generally stated that political liberalization had created a more conducive context for organizing. While they often qualified their comments by emphasizing ongoing human rights violations, unfulfilled promises, and serious political constraints, they acknowledged that in the absence of political liberalization it would have been difficult to organize legal social movements. Indeed, the establishment and growth of legal indigenous movements largely coincide with or follow the current round of political liberalization (see Table 1).

Political liberalization is nonetheless insufficient in explaining either movement or identity questions. Political liberalization does not always result in the organizing of social movements. Indeed, in the most recent round of political liberalization political parties have eclipsed many urban social movements. Moreover, indigenous identity has not been politicized in every liberalization. To explain why indigenous identity becomes the basis for political mobilization at some times and not others, one must distinguish the most recent round of political liberalization from others. What has motivated people to organize for indigenous rights and has provided them the capacity to do so?

Incentives to Organize: State Reforms, National Access, and Local Autonomy
The current round of political liberalization has disadvantaged indigenous communities. State reforms that reversed prior modes of rural incorporation have diminished hopes of gaining access to political institutions just as they have jeopardized local indigenous autonomy. Confronted with vanishing entry points for participation, representation, and resources, with individual democratic rights breached, historically constructed corporatist rights dismantled, and local indigenous community institutions jeopardized, these state reforms are perceived as displacing Indians at all levels. The final challenge to local institutions, in particular, has catalyzed Indians to mobilize as Indians to demand citizenship rights that include individual alongside community rights. Comparison of earlier state reforms with recent ones supports this. argument.

Prior democratic (and some authoritarian) regimes expanded the role of the developmental state as part of populist and/or corporatist coalitions. While they rarely respected individual democratic rights within indigenous communities, they often promised at least one of two goods: the promotion of social and economic policies, targeting peasants as a corporatist sector, and the institutionalization of corporatist forms of interest intermediation that offered access to the state. These reforms constituted a form of peasant incorporation in Mexico (1934–1940), Guatemala (1944–1954), Bolivia (1952–1964), Ecuador (1964–1966, 1973–1978), and Peru (1968–1975).

The populist reforms in each case had a multifold effect. First, they resulted in greater state penetration and patronage in agricultural rural areas. The reforms forged new state institutions for social provision, increased access to social services, and supported the growth of peasant institutions, for example, opening the possibility of access to resources and of (limited) political expression before the state. With the formation of development agencies and Indian institutes that distributed land, extended agricultural credits, and provided agricultural subsidies, indigenous peoples developed a new relationship with the state, that subordinated them to official channels in exchange for clientelistic rewards. While the actual implementation of these reforms was quite uneven within and across countries, they generated allegiance among those rural sectors that gained (or hoped to gain) access to land and the state. Even after the Mexican, Bolivian, Ecuadorian, and Peruvian states reformulated rural development policy to the advantage of agricultural elites, they kept the older legislation on the books and maintained institutional ties with the peasantry, fostering the rural poor's dependence on the state for (piecemeal) access to land, credit, and services.[22]

Second, these reforms obliged Indians to define themselves as peasants, particularly if they hoped to gain access to state resources. Official political discourse promoted assimilation into mestizo culture and extended resources to rural citizens insofar as they identified and organized as peasants.

Finally, these state reforms unintentionally created greater local political and economic autonomy. Greater state penetration, land reforms, and freedom of movement often increased indigenous peasant independence from local landlords and enabled indigenous communities to strengthen and (re)construct local public spaces for community authority structures and customary law.[23] Even if states did not respect indigenous jurisdiction in these communities, indigenous communities often did.

In short, as a result of this redefinition and nominal protection of rural property rights, rural men and women assumed a peasant status before the state and practiced an indigenous identity derived from and structured by local practices. Local communal practices were shielded and national access to the state at least nominally extended. These clientelist and corporatist arrangements were most advanced in Mexico and Bolivia, followed by Ecuador; their broad outlines endured in these three countries until the 1980s. Short-lived state efforts to incorporate the peasantry also occurred in Guatemala (1944–1954) and Peru (1968–1975). While abruptly reversed, these populist policies left an enduring impression on memories about rights and options.

The most recent round of political liberalization and democratization is distinct from earlier ones. It still breaches individual rights in the countryside. But it has occurred following or in tandem with the contraction of state policies that had historically benefited peasants and small farmers and gave them a semblance of national political representation and local autonomy. In essence, recent state reforms have forged a different kind of state, in some ways more technocratic and lean, in others less capable of acting as a political authority, particularly in rural areas. As the "rewards" for controlled participation have been withdrawn, the terms of interaction

33

with official politics have become more contested, and indigenous peasants have both gained and used greater autonomy to contest the terms and practice of citizenship. In this changing institutional and social context, indigenous movements have emerged to (re)gain access to the state and to secure local autonomy.

In Guatemala and Peru this changing set of state-society relations originates with counterreform coups in 1954 and 1975, respectively. Militaries reversed state programs, dismantled state institutions, and suppressed peasant unions. With political liberalization in the 1980s and 1990s, civil administrations have made no significant effort to revive or promote populist programs for the peasantry; to the contrary, they have announced support for neoliberalism and used this doctrine to legitimate limits on state-run rural programs, except for targeted safety net programs.

In Ecuador, Bolivia, and Mexico rural programs have been weakened most clearly in the 1980s and 1990s, in tandem with the process of political liberalization. Jettisoning populist discourse once in office, governments in these three countries have advanced neoliberal reforms. Stabilization and structural adjustment have resulted in reduced budgets for agriculture, social services, and economic programs, including protection of peasant lands, access to credit, and agricultural subsidies. Real wages in the agricultural sector declined steadily declined from the 1980s and by 1992 fell by thirty percent in Latin America as a whole.[24]

The dismantling of rural programs associated with state-oriented developmental policies has increased uncertainty about property regimes. Liberalizing states have made it clear that they will not reestablish (in Guatemala and Peru) or maintain (in Mexico, Ecuador, and Bolivia) special forms of property rights, credit, and subsidies for peasants. Consequently, the poor face diminishing access to the state and its resources. In all five countries, peasant status provides limited political purchase, as peasant programs are officially dismantled and peasant organizations weakened. With no promise of state-backed access to land, credit, and subsidies, many indigenous peasants have come to fear that their economic situation will deteriorate even further. Rural organizing and protest respond to the material uncertainty raised by indebtedness, declining incomes, and the loss of land.

The indigenous character of the contemporary movements, however, extends beyond material concerns for land as a productive resource. The potential loss of land also affects the viability and autonomy of local indigenous political institutions that operate in and assume a relatively well-defined and stable geographic space. The Bolivian and Ecuadorian states' removal of controls on agricultural products in the mid 1980s and the Ecuadorian state's suspension of agrarian reform, for example, insert instability into local property regimes and therefore pose a challenge to the material security and local political autonomy of Andean indigenous communities.[25] In Guatemala and Peru local autonomy was challenged not only by the reversal of state reforms but also by civil wars that ravaged the countryside in both countries throughout the 1980s and part of the 1990s.

34

This state challenge to local autonomy is perhaps clearest in the Mexican case. The Mexican constitution legally protected communally owned lands, or *ejidos*, and laid the framework for subsequent rounds of land reform. Following the land reform of the 1930s, many Indian communities regained title to land, and in Chiapas 54 percent of the land came to be held as *ejidos*. In the 1970s the state once again invested heavily in agriculture, overseeing further land distribution, social programs, and food distribution and purchasing projects. While often plagued by corruption, these state policies provided resources and promises of support. In the 1990s, by contrast, the state reversed both policy and discourse. The decision of Salinas' administration in 1991 to dismantle constitutional protection for this corporately held land catapulted many indigenous communities and the Zapatista army to protest.

Seen comparatively, the Latin American state of the 1980s played a less prominent role in social provision and decreased the entry points for peasants to gain access to the state. But it did not replace declining corporatist access with the individual representation and mediation theoretically characteristic of the liberal state. In the absence of viable and responsive democratic institutions to process their individual claims and confronted with diminishing corporate protection, Indians have had to turn to local forms of political identity and participation. State reforms that privatize property relations, however, have also created instability and raised challenges to the previously more secure local community spaces in which indigenous authority, practices, and material production had been institutionalized.

The Bolivian, Ecuadorian, and Peruvian Amazon followed a different historical course than the pattern just outlined. Yet the apparent Amazonian exception demonstrates the significance of state challenges to local political and material autonomy for indigenous movements. In the Amazon the state has historically been weak and has had limited impact on policy, social services, infrastructure, government access, and institutions. Populist and corporatist policies did not find significant institutional expression in the Amazon. While the state expanded in the three decades after World War II in the Andes, the Amazon remained relatively marginalized from contemporary politics, the market, and the state's role in both. From the 1960s to 1980s, however, the state increasingly penetrated the Amazon; it constructed development agencies that encouraged colonization by Andean peasants (indigenous and nonindigenous) and the expansion of cattle ranching, logging operations, and oil exploration. Together, these developments challenged indigenous communities in the Amazon that had remained relatively independent from the state and sustained political and economic control over vast land areas. Indigenous movements have emerged to challenge these developments.

Thus, in agricultural areas the state has supported the dismantling of corporatist forms of representation, agricultural subsidies, and protection of communally and individually held lands. In the Amazon it has increased its presence and promoted colonization by Andean nationals and foreign companies. In both its challenge to

35

land tenure and use has threatened material livelihoods and indigenous forms of local governance, both of which had depended on more stable property relations.

Ironically, the argument developed thus far draws in unintended ways from the liberal and Marxist arguments that were earlier rejected. Although the teleological assumptions of liberal and Marxist approaches about identity, change, and progress have proven problematic, the simultaneous failure of democratic regimes to uphold liberal conceptions of the individual and the state's challenge to corporate (class and community) identities created the political opportunity and impetus for indigenous communities to secure old and new political institutions.

Latin American indigenous communities have commonly voiced their opposition to these state reforms with political symbols that frame needs (land) and designate targets (neoliberalism).[26] Land demands are the symbolic glue that enables communities with diverse needs (including redistribution, titling, and territorial autonomy) to mobilize behind a common cause, most clearly illustrated by CONAIE's capacity to merge Andean demands for land redistribution with Amazonian demands for territorial autonomy. These diverse land demands, however, do not just refer to land as a productive resource but increasingly refer to the state's obligation to respect the jurisdiction of indigenous authorities and customary law over geographic space.

If land is the symbolic glue, neoliberalism is the symbolic target. Indigenous movements often denounce neoliberal state reforms for their deleterious impact on indigenous communities. The EZLN's "Encounter against Neoliberalism and for Humanity" in 1996 is but one example of the antineoliberal discourse prevalent in indigenous movement marches, conferences, and pamphlets. This antineoliberal rallying cry provides a common political target and is prevalent even where the impact of neoliberalism is unclear. Neoliberalism, therefore, has become synonymous with the culpable state and has enabled indigenous movements to target the state for retribution, justice, and guarantees.

Capacity: Organizational Networks   Movements do not emerge mechanically as new political opportunities, needs, and symbols present themselves, particularly in the case of indigenous identities, which are often more clearly defined by and embedded in the local community. Indigenous movements require the construction of transcommunity networks. The state, unions, churches, and nongovernmental organizations have played a crucial role in constructing networks. While pursuing their respective missions, they (unwittingly) provided institutional links that allowed the forging of translocal indigenous identities and movements.

The state attempted to mobilize support and control rebellions within peasant communities as part of its developmental policies. With the passage of land reforms, states attempted to construct a loyal national peasantry, to weaken more localized ethnic identities, and to forge a nation-state. In Mexico and Bolivia, where these processes were most advanced, peasant unions were linked to corporatist state-parties that promised access to land, economic support, and social services. In Ecuador the state agrarian reform program promoted rural organizing, significantly increasing the registration of rural *comunas*, cooperatives, and associations. This state-sanctioned rural organizing in Mexico, Bolivia, and Ecuador engendered cross-community networks and crystallized the state as the locus of power and therefore the target of organizing.

Guatemala's democratic regime (1944–1954) and Peru's military reform government (1968–1975) also passed land reforms and encouraged peasant organizing, but subsequent counterreform governments in Guatemala (1954) and in Peru (1975) undermined their accomplishments. Consequently, the Guatemalan and Peruvian peasantry in the 1980s and 1990s has not sustained transcommunity peasant networks through patron-client ties with the state, as in Mexico, Bolivia, and Ecuador. The Guatemalan and Peruvian states have been hostile to peasant demands and have attempted to localize, disarticulate, and suppress rural organizing efforts. Peru has never established or sustained a national peasant network, except perhaps briefly during Velasco's government (1968–1975).[27] Without sustained political liberalization and a sustained developmentalist state in the countryside, it has been difficult to construct a national peasant movement. And without peasant networks, it has been difficult to construct indigenous identity and organization that transcends their localized referent. Guatemala, unlike Peru, later organized an opposition peasant movement based on networks constructed by the Catholic church.[28]

Churches have helped to construct and strengthen rural networks between communities in Mexico, Guatemala, Bolivia, and Ecuador.[29] They often provided the means of communication, locus of interaction, and literacy skills that linked one community to another. So, too, church leaders inspired by liberation theology created Christian base communities that encouraged activism and created lay leaders that could travel between communities to address local and national problems.

In Guatemala many post-Vatican II clerics and lay persons organized Christian base communities in the countryside. Many of their members subsequently forged a new peasant movement and used the base communities to reconstruct intercommunity networks that had been suppressed by the military. Catholic and Protestant churches also played a crucial role in constructing networks in Chiapas, Mexico. Bishop Samuel Ruiz, for example, organized indigenous forums, brought resources to indigenous communities, and encouraged more active local organizing. In Bolivia and Ecuador a more heterogeneous church presence, including Salesians, Franciscans, Protestants, and a summer institute for linguistics, also played a particularly important role in the Amazon in bridging significant differences between communities, addressing literacy, providing radio services, and organizing against land invasions.

In short, states, unions, churches, and more recently nongovernmental organizations (particularly in Bolivia) have provided networks that enabled indigenous com-

37

munities to transcend localized identities and to identify commonly trusted leaders. They provided literacy skills that enabled indigenous leaders to gain access to outside information and resources to communicate with the state. As rural-state relations threatened property relations and local autonomy from the 1970s to the 1990s, these networks provided a basis for indigenous mobilizing. They enabled communities to transcend localized identities and to mobilize in the political liberalization of the 1980s and 1990s to protect property relations that would secure material needs and lay the geographical basis for political autonomy.

Indigenous movements—CONAIE in Ecuador, CIDOB in Bolivia, COMG in Guatemala, and the EZLN in Mexico—emerged in this context. Where sustained, national networks did not exist, as in Peru, and where networks did not exist in Mexico, Bolivia, Ecuador, and Guatemala, indigenous peoples did not mobilize to the same extent or on the same scale.

Concluding with Democracy

A comparative, historical institutional approach can illuminate the intersection of ethnic politics and indigenous movements in Latin America. State formation has reframed rural citizenship and unwittingly created mobilizational networks through which indigenous movements have emerged. Latin America's indigenous movements are primarily a response to incomplete political liberalization and state reforms. Political liberalization in the 1980s provided greater space for the public expression of ethnic identities, demands, and conflicts. Nonetheless, indigenous communities have experienced a new stage of political disenfranchisement, as states still disregard individual rights associated with liberal democracy and economic reforms dismantle state institutions that previously extended de facto or de jure corporatist class rights and community autonomy. Building on social networks left in place by prior rounds of political and religious organizing, indigenous groups have mobilized across communities to demand rights and resources denied them as Indians. They have mobilized around land rights as a means to achieve material survival with local political autonomy.

This argument hinges on a more nuanced understanding of Latin America's democratic institutions. Recent literature on democratization has analyzed largely urban, elite, and institutional transactions, including elite accommodations, pact making, institution building, agenda setting, and party systems. By focusing on national political institutions, forms of representation, and agenda setting, it has underscored the different types of democracy that urban politicians can construct. Newly constructed institutions are important not least because they provide a clear set of rules and regulations for ordering political interaction and making politics more transparent and predictable, freeze power relations and institutionalize compro-

38

mise, and create a new set of vested interests. State institutions therefore determine the locus and direction of political interaction.

But the story told here suggests that studies of democratization disaggregate their treatment of institutions to account for local politics, channels of representation, and the countryside. The literature on democratization has assumed a unitary process of institutional engineering. Yet state structures are not homogeneous in scope, presence, or capacity. One can not simply effect national institutional changes and expect them to have similar results, particularly given cross-national variations in local state institutions, practices, and social relations. Latin America's indigenous movements reflect the weak process of democratization and state building in the countryside and the deleterious affects that the current transition has had on indigenous communities.

As indigenous organizations demand autonomy and respect for local forms of governance, they also challenge liberal democratic assumptions. Rather than delineate a single relationship between the state and its citizens, indigenous organizations demand multiple types of citizenship with boundaries that guarantee equal rights and representation at the national level and recognize corporate indigenous authority structures in the indigenous territory. They challenge policymakers and states to recognize both individual and communal rights in an ideologically meaningful, practically feasible, enduring way. Such recognition requires that the law be configured on the basis of universal claims to citizenship and differentiated claims to difference. This problem is not just philosophical but also practical, as politicians struggle to consolidate Latin America's tenuous democracies.

NOTES

A longer version of this article appeared as Kellogg Institute Working Paper No. 238 (South Bend: University of Notre Dame, June 1997). For their insightful comments on an earlier draft I thank David Collier, Michael Coppedge, Jorge I. Domínguez, Jonathan Fox, John Gershman, Doug Imig, Gerardo Munck, Guillermo O'Donnell, Elisabeth Wood, and three anonymous reviewers. Research was supported by the Kellogg Institute, the United States Institute of Peace, the Joint Committee on Latin American Studies of the Social Science Research Council and the American Council of Learned Societies, and Harvard University's Center for International Affairs and David Rockefeller Center for Latin American Studies.

1. See Crawford Young, *The Politics of Cultural Pluralism* (Madison: University of Wisconsin Press, 1976), ch. 11; Donald L. Horowitz, *Ethnic Groups in Conflict* (Berkeley: University of California Press, 1985); Samuel P. Huntington and Jorge I. Domínguez, "Political Development," in Fred I. Greenstein and Nelson W. Polsby, eds., *Handbook of Political Science*, vol. 3 (1975), pp. 1–114; Ted Robert Gurr with Barbara Harff, Monty G. Marshall, and James R. Scarritt, *Minorities at Risk: A Global View of Ethnopolitical Conflicts* (Washington, D.C.: United States Institute of Peace Press, 1993).

2. I do not claim that organizing in the countryside is new. I also do not explain the emergence of new indigenous identities at the individual or community level; identities have existed to varying degrees and in various forms over time and space. I focus on the translation of local identities into regional and national political and organizational ones. I do not claim that all Indians live in nonurban areas, although I

39

restrict my focus to rural indigenous organizing. Finally, I do not judge the "trueness" of an organization's indigenous identity. I do not exclude groups because self-proclaimed indigenous organizations have some nonindigenous leaders and do not include organizations that mobilize indigenous communities for other ends.

3. Guillermo O'Donnell, "On the State, Democratization and Some Conceptual Problems: A Latin American View with Glances at Some Postcommunist Countries," *World Development*, 21 (August 1993), 1355–69; Guillermo O'Donnell, "Delegative Democracy?," *Journal of Democracy*, 5 (January 1994), 55–69; Jonathan Fox, "The Difficult Transition from Clientelism to Citizenship: Lessons from Mexico," *World Politics*, 46 (January 1994), 151–84; Jonathan Fox, "Latin America's Emerging Local Politics," *Journal of Democracy*, 5 (April 1994), 105–16; Jean Cohen and Andrew Arato, *Civil Society and Political Theory* (Cambridge, Mass.: MIT Press, 1992); Charles Tilly, ed., Citizenship, Identity and Social History," *International Review of Social History*, Supplement 3 (1995).

4. Bolivia, 71.2 percent; Guatemala, 60.3 percent; Peru, 38.6 percent; Ecuador, 37.5 percent; and Mexico, 12.4 percent. Deborah J. Yashar, "Indigenous Protest and Democracy in Latin America," in Jorge I. Domínguez and Abraham Lowenthal, eds., *Constructing Democratic Governance: Latin America and the Caribbean in the 1990s, Themes and Issues* (Baltimore: The Johns Hopkins University Press, 1996), p. 92.

5. Rodolfo Stavenhagen, "Challenging the Nation-State in Latin America," *Journal of International Affairs*, 45 (Winter 1992), 421–40; Richard Chase Smith, "A Search for Unity within Diversity: Peasant Unions, Ethnic Federations, and Indianist Movements in the Andean Republics," in Theodore McDonald, Jr., ed., *Native Peoples and Economic Development* (Cambridge: Cultural Survival, Inc., 1985); Florencia E. Mallon, "Indian Communities, Political Cultures, and the State in Latin America, 1780–1990," *Journal of Latin American Studies*, 24, Quincentenary Supplement (1992), 35–53; Alberto Adrianzén et al., *Democracia, etnicidad y violencia política en los países andinos* (Lima: Instituto de Estudios Peruanos and Instituto Francés de Estudios Andinos, 1993); Enrique Mayer, "Reflexiones sobre los derechos individuales y colectivos: Los derechos étnicos," in Eric Hershberg and Elizabeth Jelin, eds., *Construir la democracia: Derechos humanos, ciudadanía y sociedad en América Latina* (Caracas; Nueva Sociedad, 1996), pp. 171–78; Donna Lee Van Cott, ed., *Indigenous Peoples and Democracy in Latin America* (New York: St. Martin's Press, 1994); Yashar, "Indigenous Protest."

6. León Zámosc, "Agrarian Protest and the Indian Movement in the Ecuadorian Highlands," *Latin American Research Review*, 29 (1994), 37–68; Melina H. Selverston, "The Politics of Culture: Indigenous Peoples and the State in Ecuador," in Van Cott, ed., pp. 131–52; Jorge León Trujillo, *De campesinos a ciudadanos diferentes: El levantamiento indígena* (Quito: Cedime and Abya-Yala, 1994); Ileana Almeida et al., *Indios: Una reflexión sobre el levantamiento indígena de 1990* (Quito: Ediciones Abya-Yala, 1992); Confederación de Organizaciones Indígenas del Ecuador, *1992: 500 Años de resistencia india: Las nacionalidades indígenas en el Ecuador: Nuestro proceso organizativo* (Quito: Ediciones Tinkui, 1989).

7. Silvia Rivera Cusicanqui, *Oprimidos pero no vencidos: Luchas del campesinado aymara y qhechwa de Bolivia, 1900–1980* (La Paz: HISBOL-CUSTCB, 1984); Kitula Libermann and Armando Godínez, eds., *Territorio y dignidad: Pueblos indígenas y medio ambiente en Bolivia* (La Paz: ILDIS and Editorial Nueva Sociedad, 1992); Xavier Albó, "And from Kataristas to MNRistas? The Surprising and Bold Alliance between Aymaras and Neoliberals in Bolivia," in Van Cott, ed., pp. 55–82; Esteban Ticona A., Gonzalo Rojas O., and Xavier Albó C., *Votos y Wiphalas: Campesinos y pueblos orginarios en democracia* (La Paz: Fundación Milenio and CIPCA, 1995).

8. Santiago Bastos and Manuela Camus, *Quebrando el Silencio: Organizaciones del Pueblo Maya y sus Demandas (1986–1992)*, 2nd ed. (Guatemala: FLACSO, 1993); Santiago Bastos and Manuela Camus, *Abriendo Caminos: Las organizaciones mayas desde el Nobel hasta el acuerdo de derechos indígenas* (Guatemala: FLACSO, 1995); and Carol A. Smith, *Guatemalan Indians and the State, 1540 to 1988* (Austin: University of Texas Press, 1990).

9. George A. Collier with Elizabeth Lowery Quaratiello, *Basta! Land and the Zapatista Rebellion in*

Chiapas (Oakland: The Institute for Food and Development Policy, 1994); Neil Harvey, Luis Navarro Hernández, and Jeffrey Rubin," *Transformation of Rural Mexico*, 5 (La Jolla: Center for U.S.-Mexican Studies, 1994); and Neil Harvey, "Impact of Reforms to Article 27 on Chiapas: Peasant Resistance in the Neoliberal Sphere," in Laura Randall, ed., *Reforming Mexico's Agrarian Reform* (Armonk: M. E. Sharpe, 1996).

10.   Julio Cotler and Felipe Portocarrero, "Peru: Peasant Organizations," in Henry A. Landsberger, ed., *Latin American Peasant Movements* (Ithaca: Cornell University Press, 1969); Howard Handelman, *Struggle in the Andes: Peasant Mobilization in Peru* (Austin: University of Texas Press, 1975); Cynthia McClintock, *Peasant Cooperatives and Political Change in Peru* (Princeton: Princeton University Press, 1981); Cynthia McClintock, "Peru's Sendero Luminoso: Origins and Trajectories," in Susan Eckstein, ed., *Power and Popular Protest: Latin American Social Movements* (Berkeley: University of California Press, 1989); Orin Starn, "'I Dreamed of Foxes and Hawks': Reflections of Peasant Protest, New Social Movements and the Rondas Campesinas of Northern Peru," in Arturo Escobar and Sonia Alvarez, eds., *The Making of Social Movements in Latin America: Identity, Strategy, and Democracy* (Boulder: Westview, 1992); Linda J. Seligmann, *Between Reform and Revolution: Political Struggles in the Peruvian Andes, 1969–1991* (Stanford: Stanford University Press, 1995).

11.   Mayer, "Reflexiones," p. 175.

12.   Clifford Geertz, "The Integrative Revolution: Primordial Sentiments and Civil Politics in the New States," in *Old Societies and New States*, 3rd ed. (New York: The Free Press, 1967); Harold R. Isaacs, "Basic Group Identity: The Idols of the Tribe," in Nathan Glazer and Daniel P. Moynihan, eds., *Ethnicity: Theory and Experience* (Cambridge, Mass.: Harvard University Press, 1975); John Stack, *The Primordial Challenge: Ethnicity in the Contemporary World* (New York: Greenwood Press, 1986); Pierre Van den Berghe, *The Ethnic Phenomena* (New York: Elsevier, 1981).

13.   Alvin Rabushka and Kenneth A. Shepsle, *Politics in Plural Societies: A Theory of Democratic Instability* (Columbus: Charles E. Merrill Publishing Company, 1972); Robert Bates and Barry Weingast, "A New Comparative Politics: Integrating Rational Choice and Interpretivist Perspectives," paper presented at the Annual Meetings of the American Political Science Association, August 31–September 3, 1995. For sympathetic but critical elaborations see Russell Hardin, *One for All: The Logic of Group Conflict* (Princeton: Princeton University Press, 1995); and David D. Laitin, *Hegemony and Culture: Politics and Religious Change among the Yoruba* (Chicago: University of Chicago Press, 1986).

14.   Laitin; Ashutosh Varshney, "Ethnic Conflict and Rational Choice: A Theoretical Engagement," Working Paper No. 95-11 (Cambridge, Mass.: Center for International Affairs, Harvard University, 1995).

15.   Jean L. Cohen, "Strategy or Identity: New Theoretical Paradigms and Contemporary Social Movements," *Social Research*, 52 (Winter 1985), 663–716.

16.   Michel Foucault, *Power/Knowledge* (New York: Pantheon Books, 1980); Ernesto Laclau and Chantal Mouffe, *Hegemony and Socialist Strategy: Towards a Radical Democratic Politics* (London: Verso, 1985); Alain Touraine, *The Return of the Actor: Social Theory in Postindustrial Society* (Minneapolis: University of Minnesota Press, 1988); Alberto Melucci, *Nomads of the Present: Social Movements and Individual Needs in Contemporary Society* (Philadelphia: Temple University Press, 1989).

17.   Charles Tilly, *From Mobilization to Revolution* (Reading: Addison-Wesley, 1978); Charles Bright and Susan Harding, eds,. *Statemaking and Social Movements: Essays in History and Theory* (Ann Arbor: University of Michigan Press, 1984); Laitin; Sidney Tarrow, *Power in Movement: Social Movements, Collective Action and Politics* (Cambridge: Cambridge University Press, 1994); Joe Foweraker, *Theorizing Social Movements* (London: Pluto Press, 1995); Joane Nagel, "The Political Construction of Ethnicity," in Susan Olzak and Joane Nagel, eds., *Competitive Ethnic Relations* (Orlando: Academic Press, 1986); and Paul R. Brass, "Ethnic Groups and the State," in Paul R. Brass, ed., *Ethnic Groups and the State* (London: Croom Helm, 1985).

18.   Cohen and Arato, pp. 502–16; Tilly, pp. 5–6.

19.   See Tarrow, *Power in Movement*; and Doug McAdam, John D. McCarthy, and Mayer N. Zald, eds.,

41

Comparative Perspectives on Social Movements: Political Opportunities, Mobilizing Structures, and Cultural Framings (Cambridge; Cambridge University Press, 1996).

20. The terms "corporate" and "corporatist" refer to state-designated forms of political representation and mediation between the state and social groups. They do not presume that indigenous communities are closed. See Eric Wolfe, "Closed Corporate Peasant Communities in Mesoamerica and Central Java," *Southwestern Journal of Anthropology*, 13 (1957), 1–18.

21. See Doug McAdam, "Conceptual Problems, Future Directions," in McAdam, McCarthy, and Zald, eds., p. 27. McAdam lays out four dimensions of political opportunity structures: degree of political opening, elite alignments, presence of elite allies, and the state's capacity and propensity to use repression. In Latin America's indigenous movements elite alignments and access to elite allies do not uniformly play a role in movement formation even if they affect policy success. I emphasize the first and fourth dimensions.

22. Merilee S. Grindle, *State and Countryside: Development Policy and Agrarian Politics in Latin America* (Baltimore: The Johns Hopkins University Press, 1986) pp. 113–15, 137, 158.

23. Andrés Guerrero, "De sujetos indios a ciudadanos-étnicos: De la manifestación de 1961 al levantamiento de 1990," in Adrianzén et al., eds., pp. 83–101; Carlos Iván Degregori, "Identidad étnica: Movimientos sociales y participación política en el Perú," in Adrianzén et al., eds., pp. 113–33; Deborah J. Yashar, *Demanding Democracy: Reform and Reaction in Costa Rica and Guatemala, 1870s–1950s* (Stanford: Stanford University Press, 1997), chs. 2, 4, 5; Ticona, Rojas, and Albó; Juliana Ströbele-Gregor, "Culture and Political Practice of the Aymara and Quechua in Bolivia: Autonomous Forms of Modernity in the Andes," *Latin American Perspectives*, 23 (Spring 1996), 72–91; and Jan Rus, "The Comunidad Revolucionaria Institucional: The Subversion of Native Government in Highland Chiapas, 1936–1968," in Gilbert M. Joseph and Daniel Nugent, eds., *Everyday Forms of State Formation: Revolution and the Negotiation of Rule in Modern Mexico* (Durham: Duke University Press, 1994), esp., pp. 284, 287.

24. James W. Wilkie, Carlos Alberto Contreras, and Katherine Komisaruk, eds., *Statistical Abstract of Latin America*, vol. 31 (Los Angeles: UCLA Latin American Center Publications, 1995), Table 3107, p. 990; Catherine M. Conaghan and James M. Malloy, *Unsettling Statecraft: Democracy and Neoliberalism in the Central Andes* (Pittsburgh: University of Pittsburgh Press, 1994); Miguel Urioste Fernández de Córdova, *Fortalecer las comunidades: Una utopía subversiva, democrática...y posible* (La Paz: AIPE/PROCOM/TIERRA, 1992), pp.109–34; Nora Lustig, *Coping with Austerity: Poverty and Inequality in Latin America* (Washington, D.C.: The Brookings Institution, 1995); Alain de Janvry et al., "Ecuador," in Alain de Janvry et al., *The Political Feasibility of Adjustment in Ecuador and Venezuela* (Paris: OECD, 1994); Samuel A. Morley, *Poverty and Inequality in Latin America: The Impact of Adjustment and Recovery in the 1980s* (Baltimore: The Johns Hopkins University Press, 1995).

25. Stroëbele-Gregor; Conaghan and Malloy, p. 140; Zámosc; and Selverston, p. 145.

26. For a suggestive discussion, see Alison Brysk, "Hearts and Minds: Bringing Symbolic Politics Back In," *Polity*, 27 (Summer 1995), 559–85.

27. Cotler and Portocarrero; Handelman, ch. 6; McClintock, *Peasant Cooperatives*; and Seligmann.

28. See Milagros Peña, *Theologies and Liberation in Peru: The Role of Ideas in Social Movements* (Philadelphia: Temple University Press, 1995). Little has been written on the impact of liberation theology and theologians in the Peruvian countryside.

29. See Ruth J. Chojnacki, "Indigenous Apostles: Notes on Maya Catechists Working the Word and Working the Land in Highland Chiapas," paper presented at the Annual Meeting of the Latin American Studies Association, Washington, D.C., September 28–30, 1995; Charlene Floyd, "Catalysts of Democracy: Maya Catechists as Political Actors in Chiapas," paper presented at the Annual Meeting of the Latin American Studies Association, Washington, D.C., September 28–30, 1995; Michael F. Brown, "Facing the State, Facing the World: Amazonia's Native Leaders and the New Politics of Identity," *L'Homme*, 126–128 (April-December 1993), 307–26; Roberto Santana, *Ciudadanos en la etnicidad: Los indios en la política o la política de los indios* (Quito: Ediciones Abya-Yala), chs. 6–7.

Race-Class-Gender Ideology in Guatemala: Modern and Anti-Modern Forms

CAROL A. SMITH

University of California, Davis

More often than not, women bear the burden of displaying the identifying symbols of their ethnic identity to the outside world, whether these be items of dress, aspects of language, or distinctive behavior. Men of the same ethnic group, especially when filling lower-order positions in the local division of labor, usually appear indistinguishable from men of a different ethnicity but in similar class positions.[1] Thus in Guatemala, for example, one readily identifies a Maya Indian woman by her distinctive and colorful dress, her tendency to speak only the local dialect of a Maya language, and her modest demeanor when in public settings, especially those involving non-Maya. Most Maya men, in contrast, are not so easily distinguished from non-Maya (that is, Ladino[2]) men of equivalent class in Guatemala.[3]

I am especially grateful to Charles R. Hale, Suad Joseph, and G. William Skinner, who discussed with me many of the issues involved as I worked out these arguments—others should be so lucky to have such colleagues. Since I did not always take their good advice, they cannot be blamed for my views. Different versions of this essay have been delivered to several different audiences (anthropological, feminist, and Latin Americanist) at the University of California, Davis; Stanford University; the University of Texas, Austin; and the University of Wisconsin, Madison. I would like to thank members of the audiences for useful comments, questions, and challenges. I would also like to thank Nora England, Diane Nelson and Abigail Adams for suggesting that I historicize my discussion of contemporary Maya Guatemalans.

[1] It appears, however, that when an ethnic minority is not at or near the bottom of the local status hierarchy—as in the case of the Hasidic Jews of New York—men are as likely as women to be labeled with a special ethnic marker. Why this should be so will be apparent as the argument unfolds.

[2] The meaning of Ladino in Guatemala is very specific to the nation of Guatemala. People who are currently classified Ladinos are any people who are non-European or non-Maya; but the identity of people categorized as Ladinos has changed over time (see Gould 1994). I more fully explain the meaning of the term Ladino as I describe the historical particulars of Guatemala.

[3] In several dozen Maya communities where women still weave the bulk of the clothing, some men continue to wear ethnically distinctive clothing; even in these communities, however, younger men wear general rustic clothing indistinguishable from that of rural non-Mayans, especially when away from their community. Virtually all Maya women, in contrast, maintain community-distinctive dress as a moral commitment, even when they do not weave it themselves (see Otzoy 1988, 1992). For a sophisticated discussion of class, ethnic, and gender specific cultural patterns in another indigenous area of Latin America, see Gill (1993) and de la Cadena (1991).

0010-4175/95/4414-0162 $7.50 + .10 © 1995 Society for Comparative Study of Society and History

In this essay, I attempt to explain why women, rather than men, carry the emblems of the stigmatized position of a lower-order ethnic group in places that the West has colonized by examining the gender politics of this behavior in Guatemala, where the pattern is especially pronounced. I also attempt to show how ideologies of descent and rules of marriage operate in such systems, in ways that both parochialize women and conflate beliefs about race,[4] class, and culture. For this purpose I contrast the subordinate Maya belief system about identity with the dominant non-Maya or Ladino belief system—which differs on some propositions about race, class, and gender, but shares others. Finally, I consider how these two different belief systems, as they were first articulated into a race-class-gender ideology[5] and then reformulated within a revolutionary context, affect the construction of ethnic and national identity. In addressing this latter question, I offer some suggestions for why ethnic nationalists are more resistant than others to liberating or modernist ideologies, whether revolutionary or feminist.

I beg more questions than I can fully address by raising so many questions simultaneously, but there is a certain logic to this method. Ultimately I want to argue that race, class, and gender are conjoined systems of belief about identity and inequality in much of the contemporary world and that they are linked by certain assumptions about descent and inheritance and by certain social practices that enact these beliefs. If this is so, it will be useful to trace out the ways in which various beliefs and practices concerning social identity (that is, race, class, gender, ethnicity, nation, and individual subject) interact with and constrain one another in two interactive cultural systems, one part of the dominant national ideology, the other, not. As this wording implies, I do not want to separate out and juxtapose one form of social identity, such as race, to another, such as gender. Instead, I want to consider several different ways in which social categories are linked to social practices in the general realm of identity construction.

The particular cultural matrix from which I work is that of modernity, which I assume to be linked to European colonial expansion and capitalism. In my view the hierarchies of race, class, and gender associated with capital-

---

[4] Throughout this essay I mean by race the conflation of social origin (Europe, Africa, native America) and color (or general phenotype) that is embedded in North American and Latin American racial and racist discourse. Naturally, I repudiate the idea that race is a scientific biological category.

[5] When I create words joined by hyphens (as in race-class-gender) throughout this essay, I am highlighting the fact that the elements in the series are discursively joined. For example, race, class, and gender (in either ideology or social practice) are conjoined systems of oppression in which the social construction of each element powerfully affects the nature of the other elements: The social construction of race (often derived from phenotype, which is taken to be the marker of a biological or descent category) is affected by the class and gender of the person; the social construction of class is also affected by race (or phenotype) and gender; and the social construction of gender is affected by race (or phenotype) and class. These linked forms of social construction are especially prominent in modernity when the individual is not fully enmeshed in relatively permanent communities which carry the weight of social position.

ism are not necessary or even logical outcomes of capitalism but are based on the cultural baggage that came along with the way in which the material world of capitalism was historically constructed: for example, with particular kinds of racialized, gendered, free and unfree labor, as they were constituted by Western categories and institutions. With the expansion of Western culture through capitalism, the systems of race, class, and gender were no longer separate, competitive forms of oppression but came to be linked and mutually reinforcing in practice and through Western cultural precepts about race-class-gender hierarchies.

I begin by trying to make the case for the general social and ideological links between race, class, and gender, first in Western culture generally and then in modern nation-states of the West, as others have constructed the case. I conclude by attempting to reformulate the meaning of modernity for race-class-gender systems in social relations that involve colonialism, nationalism, and ethnicity, as well as ideologies of modern liberation. I illustrate my argument with the case of contemporary Guatemala, an interesting historical mix of modern and anti-modern elements,[6] some congruent with each other, most deeply contradictory. Guatemala makes an interesting and complex case because it was colonized by the West in the sixteenth century (during which a premodern symbolics of blood became dominant among the colonists); it separated in the late nineteenth century into two competing national potentials (hispanicized Ladinos and culturally resistant Maya); and it has been pulled since then in three different directions: the creation of a modern authoritarian state ruled by elite white men, the creation of a modern revolutionary state representing the mixed blood of the proletariat, and an anti-modern multi-cultural state comprising the diverse Maya communities.

IDEOLOGICAL LINKS AMONG RACE, CLASS, AND GENDER IN THE WEST

Throughout Western history, people who assumed powerful positions in class society defended their class privileges in terms of their blood—a descent ideology that was implicitly racialist. Michel Foucault (1980) describes the premodern system as a "symbolics of blood" upon which an emerging bourgeoisie erected the more directly biologist, racist system of modernity. As he sees it, the "blood relation" remained a significant ideological precept[7]

---

[6] I take the idea of "anti-modern" from a recent article by Joel Kahn (1990), who depicts peasants as anti-capitalist rather than non-capitalist or precapitalist. I use the term anti-modern rather than anti-capitalist in order to extend the idea that peasants are resisting assumptions of the modern nation-state as well as capitalism.

[7] By the term ideological precept, I mean essentially what Brackette Williams means, that is, "rules and standards, often expressed in principles, maxims, or proverbs, which declare the world to be of a certain composition and to work in a certain way. Precepts become ideological when they are linked to politically privileged interpretations of human experiences which ignore or consider irrelevant information that contradicts the logic of these rules and standards" (1993:184).

in "modern mechanisms of power, its manifestations, and its rituals" (1980:148). In "blood regimes," the value of descent lines are predominant, and blood constitutes one of the fundamental signifiers of position in a society. Systems of marital and political alliance are linked and based on blood status ("blue blood"); the political legitimacy of the sovereign is based on blood lines; and society is differentiated into orders and castes on the basis of blood descent (Foucault 1980:147–8). Later (that is, under capitalism), "the symbolic function" of blood comes to predominate:

Beginning in the second half of the nineteenth century, the thematics of blood was sometimes called on to lend its entire historical weight toward revitalizing the type of political power that was exercised [in a new disciplinary form]. Racism took shape at this point (racism in its modern, "biologizing," statist form). . . . Nazism was doubtless the most cunning and the most naive . . . combination of the fantasies of blood and the paroxysms of a disciplinary power (Foucault 1980:149).

Other scholars have described the significance of Western "blood regimes" for women's reproductive and sexual roles. Jack Goody (1976:41–65), for example, described how monogamous European marriage systems, organized as heir-producing devices, institutionalized class distinctions in the West. Only the certified wife (the rank of whose blood lines were equivalent to those of her husband) produced a legitimate heir; the offspring of (lower-class) concubines would remain distinct and propertyless. Goody developed a contrast between Eurasia and Africa, noting that in Africa, where polygyny prevailed (and all wives were of equivalent marital status), the blood lines of the upper classes were not so clearly distinguished. Goody only implicitly notes the difference in sexual standards between men and women of the upper classes in regimes of blood. But from his descriptions it is clear that social expectations concerning the sexual behavior of an upper-class woman were very different from those concerning the upper-class man.

Gerda Lerner (1986) theorizes the linkage between sexual standards and race-class-gender hierarchies. She argues that the Western caste-like system of stratification that arose with the Western patriarchal state required that women's bodies and social freedoms be controlled because women had been construed as the biological "repositories" of descent systems (blood regimes) that ideologically and materially bolstered Western class systems. Thus, differences in blood explained differences between genders as well as those between races and classes because blood differences could only be maintained through the control of women's sexuality and ultimately their social freedoms. In this way, class and race oppression based itself upon the control over women's sexuality and socially constructed differences put in biological terms to such an extent that race, class, and gender were seen to be linked.

Lerner then goes on to explain how Western regimes of blood required the sexual purity and ideological complicity of upper-class women. Elite women could retain their status and reproduce themselves (in both class and biolog-

24

ical terms) only through their sexual conduct: They had to remain virgin until marriage, monogamous after marriage, and socially protected throughout their lives from even the suspicion of improper sexual behavior. Only by controlling elite women's sexuality could the upper classes (both men and women) proclaim that their progeny were of pure or legitimate blood. Those elite women who violated the rules of sexual conduct could lose their class status to become, like lower-class women, the concubines, prostitutes, and sexual playthings of elites; they could even become mates for the lower classes. Elite men faced no such restrictions on their sexual behavior—they had access to many women of many ranks throughout their lives, some of whom became their legal wives, others of whom became their irregular concubines. In this way, Lerner argues, the ideological foundations for class reproduction in the West were as much rooted in the control and oppression of women as in biologism (or racism).[8]

Verena Stolcke (1981), the best source on the intersection of marriage with race and class in historical Latin America, suggests how the Western "symbolics of blood" shifted under capitalism to create an even more virulent form of racism (see also Hobsbawm 1975), together with a greater concern with the sexual conduct of upper-class women. Stolcke argues that the ideology of capitalism attacked at one level the aristocratic ideas in Europe that pure blood lines should define and limit political and economic rights. Bourgeois society espoused the ideology that all men are created equal and that the best of them will win out in fair market competition; yet, the rising bourgeoisie wanted to maintain their holdings or family property over time. In order to rationalize existing and continuing class inequalities and to reproduce a class system over time, bourgeois society explained the maintenance of classes over generations with a notion of the survival of the fittest.[9] Fitness, of course, was assumed to be based on inherited qualities and required even greater concern with elim-

---

[8] Irene Silverblatt (1988) assures us that the reproductive (gender) kernel of class and race domination in the West, which required control over women's sexuality and reproduction, is not a functional prerequisite of class society everywhere. Her own work on the Inca (1987) describes an alternative sexual-reproductive system associated with class stratification and the state. Jack Goody, in a large number of publications (see especially 1976), must be credited with showing that this linkage is not universal in all social systems with class stratification. Developing a contrast between African and Eurasian systems of stratification, Goody shows that African class systems are based on entirely different rules and beliefs concerning proper marriages, inheritance, sexual conduct, and the like.

[9] Hobsbawm, in noting the difficulty the bourgeoisie had in justifying its own success by the rules of "freedom, opportunity, the cash nexus and the pursuit of individual profit," makes a similar observation:

Hence the growing importance of the alternative theories of biological class superiority, which pervade so much of the nineteenth-century Weltanschauung. Superiority was the result of natural selection, genetically transmitted. The bourgeoisie was, if not a different species, then at least the member of a superior race, a higher state of human evolution, distinct from the lower orders which remained in the historical or cultural equivalent of childhood or at most adolescence (1975:247–8).

25

inating the non-fit (that is, those thought to have inferior blood) from competition in the market.[10] Stolcke, who terms this new ideology "scientific naturalism," explains its paradoxical development in the following way:

The age of the French and American revolutions not only proclaimed the ideas of freedom, equality, and tolerance, but also saw the birth of racial classifications and hierarchies. The crucial issue was how to reconcile freedom and equality of all men with perceived inequalities. Racial classifications from the start collapsed phenotypical, cultural, and social traits and were applied not only to the "savages" abroad but also to differences at home. . . . If the self-determining individual seemed to prove incapable of making the most of the opportunities society appeared to offer him, it must be due to some essential inherent natural defect which was hereditary. The result was a sociopolitical and cultural elitism grounded in theories of biological class superiority (Stolcke n.d.: 2).

Stolcke goes on to argue that scientific naturalism found its fullest expression in Nazi Germany as well as in the white-ruled colonies of the West. It resulted in systematic forms of racism (often apartheid, sometimes genocide) and increased concern for women's purity as reproducers of the biologically fit. She makes clear, however, that the ideology of scientific naturalism was not an imperialist mutant but, rather, was basic to social life under Western capitalism, remaining a "diffuse social sentiment" today (1981:38).

THE IMPACT OF NATIONALISM AND COLONIALISM ON RACE/CLASS/GENDER IDEOLOGY

The European assumptions that conflate race, class, and culture diffused throughout the world not simply as a cultural accompaniment to capitalism but also as elements in the widespread ideological construction of modern nations—a political and cultural effect of capitalism's European origins.[11] Thus, in the third world and in Europe, national sovereignty was proclaimed everywhere and came to be justified by certain identical ideological claims which logically integrated notions of territoriality, biological purity, cultural homogeneity, and status stratification, indicating how earlier notions of nation as blood group remain tied to the formation of the state as a political unit (see B. Williams 1990, 1993). Partha Chatterjee (1986) suggests how this might have happened in non-Western cultural contexts in his study of Indian nationalism. Indian nationalists such as Bankinchandra, Gandhi, and Nehru were all anti-colonialists united mainly in an attempt to create an autonomous national state and culture. They were doomed to fail in this enterprise because they

[10] Given the link between capitalism and imperialism, the notion of fit races made a lot of sense to both lower and upper classes in the centers of the very unequal capitalist world-economy, which came into being upon the production of basic commodities with the labor of African slaves, New World Indians, and other non-white serfs all over the world.

[11] The belief that all classes within a nation shared the same basic culture, if not blood, is now widely acknowledged to be a modern or nineteenth-century invention; such a belief was not at all typical of early archaic states made up of a mosaic of different peoples (see, for example, Anderson [1983], Gellner [1983]).

were forced to derive the cultural meaning of what they were attempting to construct (a single and homogeneous state, nation, and culture) from Western discourse about them. He summarizes this argument in a later article:

[Indian] nationalism located its own subjectivity in the spiritual domain of culture, where it considered itself superior to the West and hence undominated and sovereign. . . . [The] formation of a hegemonic "national culture" was *necessarily* built upon the privileging of an "essential tradition" [in which 'women' and 'home' were not to be 'modernized' or Westernized], which in turn was defined by a system of exclusions [of women, ethnic minorities, lower classes]. . . . [This] went hand in hand with a set of dichotomies that systematically excluded from the new life of the nation the vast masses of people [for example, women, minorities, lower classes] whom the dominant elite would represent and lead. . . . In the confrontation between colonialist and nationalist discourses, the dichotomies of spiritual/material, home/world, feminine/masculine, while enabling the production of a nationalist discourse *different* from that of colonialism, nonetheless remain trapped within its framework of false essentialisms (Chatterjee 1989:631–2).

As Chatterjee sees it, then, the adoption of Western nationalist discourse by Indian nationalists led to a homogenized and essentialized cultural self-representation—a "derivative discourse" on the Indian state, nation, and culture—necessarily couched in Western terms. Thus, Indian nationalists, even as they struggled against a colonial discourse on gender, began to see the relation of gender to the nation in a Western way. They also began to exclude their ethnic minorities and lower classes from their conception of the nation in a Western way. In this fashion anti-colonial precepts came to embody Western precepts about the nation—and about the links between the nation, race, class, and culture. In this way, too, gender played a pivotal role in essentializing the spirit of the nation.

Chatterjee's argument suggests that in modern nationalist ideologies, whether European or non-European, the female will always come to stand for the spirit of the nation and the site of its reproduction because the female is (always?) the "essentialized" homebodied Other. In my view, however, Western beliefs about inheritance (in its material, biological, and cultural senses)[12] provide the key ideological element linking race, class, culture, and nation to gender. In Western ideology, a person's race, class, and culture are thought to be more clearly inherited from women than from men because it is assumed that women's uncontrolled sexual lusts will make paternity muddy or uncertain. Europeans institutionalized these concerns about patrilineal inheritance with particular kinds of sexual controls and marital arrangements. As Goody

---

[12] It is noteworthy that the Western term inheritance means not only "(4) the act of inheriting property," but also "(2) genetic characters transmitted from parent to offspring" and "(1) the acquisition of a possession, condition, or trait from past; something that is or may be inherited; property passing at the owner's death to the heir or those entitled to succeed; legacy (*Random House Webster's New Collegiate Dictionary* [New York: Random House, 1992]).

27

(1976) points out, they created separate roles for wives and concubines, controlling the sexuality of each (and the progeny of each) in different ways. As colonialists, moreover, Europeans linked different marriage and mating patterns to women of different classes, races, and national origins in such a way as to maintain separate hierarchies for different races, classes, and cultures (see also Martinez-Alier 1974; Stoler 1991). Women thus became the key icons around which a modern nation or culture would be built in cultural, biological, and material terms. And reproductive control over women—control of their sexuality—became the instrumental means by which economic, political, and cultural dominance of the elite in a new nation was assured. While obtaining such reproductive control over women is not a necessary or universal pattern to instituting a modern nation state, it is certainly predominant in those nation-states that were former European colonies. In this way the formation of different and unequal forms of marriage and concubinage became a pervasive feature of modernity.

THE COLONIAL CONSTRUCTION OF A GUATEMALAN "SYMBOLICS OF BLOOD"

Different colonial powers of the West created the political and cultural conditions by which new nations would interpret race, class, and gender in distinctive ways.[13] As mentioned earlier, Stolcke is the best source on the intersection of marriage and kinship with race and class in historical Latin America.[14] In a recent article, Stolcke (1991) suggested, in a summary of her work, how the Spanish conquest of indigenous and African slave women and the institutionalization of different and unequal kinds of marriage patterns between people of different social origins (African, American, European) affected race-class-gender ideology in the Hispanic parts of the New World:

> When social position is attributed to inherent, natural, racial, and therefore hereditary qualities, the elite's control of the procreative capacity of their women is essential for them to preserve their social preeminence. As a nineteenth-century Spanish jurist argued, only women can bring bastards into the family. By institutionalizing the metaphysical notion of blood as the carrier of family prestige and as the ideological instrument to guarantee the social hierarchy, the state, in alliance with families that were pure of blood, subjected their women to renewed control of their sexuality while their sons took their pleasure with those women who lacked social status without having to assume any responsibility for it (Stolcke 1991:28).

---

[13] Ann Stoler has described the patterns institutionalized during the nineteenth and twentieth centuries in colonial Southeast Asia (1992). These patterns bear a general resemblance to those institutionalized much earlier in Latin America.

[14] Stolcke's first major work was written on Cuba under Martinez-Alier (1974). Since then her ideas on the relationship between race, class, and gender in the Americas have been taken up by others, most prominently Arrom (1985) and Seed (1988), who treat colonial and post-colonial Mexico. See also Lavrin (1989) on colonial Latin America and C. A. Smith (n.d.) on the pattern throughout the Americas in the post-colonial period.

The mestizo and mulatto population multiplied as a result of the ubiquitous concubinage between white men and Indian or black women . . . and inspired deep distrust because they . . . placed in doubt or actively threatened the emerging racial hierarchy. . . . For the elites and for those who sought to get close to them, legitimate birth from a legitimate married couple thus acquired new importance as the only proof of purity of blood. Illegitimate birth, on the other hand, was a sign of "infamy, stain and defect" stemming from the mixture of races. The only guarantee of racial purity, hence social prestige, was marriage between racial [and class] equals (Stolcke 1991:26–27).

In this way, a "dual marital strategy"[15] was produced throughout colonial Latin America, wherein men of European descent established legal monogamous marriages with women of their own race and class, whose offspring became their legitimate heirs, while engaging in irregular liaisons, frequently by force, with non-European women, rarely recognizing those offspring. At the same time elite men felt the need to safeguard vigorously the purity of women they considered theirs from men other than their legitimate spouses, especially from men of lower-ranking social origins.

Severo Martínez Pelaez (1973), the foremost Guatemalan historian of the colonial period, recapitulates the importance of these assumptions in understanding the positions of the white (Spanish) elite in Guatemala (whom he terms *creoles*) and Ladinos (who are people of non-legitimate lineage in the eyes of creoles). His understanding about the linkage between race, lineage, and class is exceptionally keen; his understanding of gender only implicit. I quote him at length here because his exposition of Guatemalan ideology has clarity and specificity concerning race, class, and gender:

The (male) Spaniard—as well as the hispanic creole—carried out very different acts when he copulated with a Spanish woman and when he copulated with an Indian one. . . . [H]e took the Spanish woman, or had to take her, to the Church and there, in a ceremony to which the assembled attributed transcendental meaning, he committed himself to live with her in everlasting union, to protect and educate his children, and to make them, and eventually her too, heirs to his goods. These children received certain material goods as well as a certain capacity to conserve and expand them. They entered a group [to which] their parents and other families belonged which also had something to conserve, inherit, and expand. They became part of the dominant class.

. . . The Indian woman was not simply fertilized by the Spaniard or the creole. Whether she was raped, deceived, bribed, seduced, or persuaded . . . the fundamental condition of the relationship that occurred between Spanish men and Indian women was, after all, the superiority of the colonizer over the native—not only the pretention of superiority but effective superiority in terms of economic and social advantage. . . . [The important point is that] the Indian woman was not the wife of the Spaniard or the creole who occasionally or regularly possessed her. She was rather his Indian concubine (his *barragana* in the judicial lexicon of the era), which in this context meant his extramarital servant supplying the commodity of sex.

---

[15] R. T. Smith (1984, 1992) defines and describes a dual-marriage strategy as one in which upper-class men typically maintain both legitimate and "outside" wives or concubines. Smith has worked mainly on the pattern in the Caribbean but notes that the strategy is also common to Latin America.

No law, no moral code obligated the colonial gentleman to his Indian concubine, nor to the children he procreated with her. Inheritance of blood equalled inheritance of power. The protection of wealth within a small European nucleus of heirs of the conquest demanded that the nucleus remain closed and its racial "character" protected—a racial character to which was attributed from the beginning a false significance as a source of distinction in every sense. . . . [S]ocial opinion was not bothered by concubine relations and spurious children—common happenings in colonial life—as long as the man's conduct left it clearly understood that these were escapades that did not threaten the structure nor the patrimony of the legitimate [creole] family. The colonial aristocracy, the creole class . . . remained closed to the people of mixed blood and to the Indians during the respectable lapse of three centuries.

Let us understand, then, that the initial *mestizaje* (the creation of mixed-blood offspring) was an act realized in the context of and as a consequence of the social inferiority and disadvantage of a woman from the dominated class facing a man from the dominant class. It was the result of a biological union based on profound human disunion and inequality—of fornication as an act of veiled domination or, in many cases, simple and open rape. The children of these unions, the original *mestizos,* were what they were—workers without patrimony . . .—as a consequence of their parents belonging to two antagonistic classes. Neither could give them a place without bringing harm to their class or themselves.

The secondary mestizaje, the multiplication of mestizos combining among themselves and with various other groups—including of course the Spaniards and creoles themselves—could not be anything other than the prolongation and compilation of what resulted from the initial mestizaje. From the multiplication of beings who were born outside the wealthy dominant class and outside the servile Indian group was a proliferation of individuals in search of middle-level and inferior vacant positions and occupations. Individuals without inherited property, or authority, or Indian servants, had to make themselves useful in order to survive. The need for free workers acted as a mold into which the human stream of mestizos was poured [thus was born the Guatemalan Ladino] (Martínez 1973:355–60, my translation).

In the post-colonial, nationalist context of Latin America in the nineteenth and twentieth centuries, according to Stolcke, "scientific racism came to replace the metaphysics of purity of blood" (1991:28); but the kinship, marital, and sexual patterns institutionalized in the colonial period remained essentially the same (for documentation of this, see Arrom 1985; Stepan 1991). The major shift that occurred in the post-colonial period throughout Latin America is that the ruling class tended to become more mestizo and less white. Color distinctions among mestizos remained important, however, and extremely gendered (see C. A. Smith n.d.)

In post-colonial Guatemala, for example, some Ladinos rose to positions of wealth and prominence, while others remained the disenfranchised workers to whom Martínez alludes. Upwardly mobile Ladinos, however, took on the beliefs and kinship practices of the white creoles, who remained Guatemala's true ruling class—and the producers of the hegemonic national and race-class-gender ideology (Martínez 1973; Casaus Arzú 1992). After Independence, lower-class Ladino women were more likely to be preyed upon by upper-class males than Indian women, leading to what Martínez terms secondary *mestizaje*. Ortmayr (1991) documents that the marital practices of upwardly mobile Ladinos began to resemble those of the creole elite in the nineteenth century.[16] And McCreery (1986) observes that virtually no prostitutes in late-nineteenth-century Guatemala were Indian; most were lower-class Ladino women. In this little-studied period, Maya beliefs concerning race, class, and gender also reformulated themselves; and sexual (reproductive) contact between self-identified Maya and Ladinos seems to have diminished considerably.

Few anthropologists have followed up on Stolcke's pioneering work on historical Latin American race-class-gender relations and their impact on contemporary marriage and kinship systems, though she has been extremely influential in the Caribbean literature (see, for example, R. T. Smith 1984, 1992). I find her arguments for contemporary Guatemala generally persuasive, though incomplete. As formulated, her arguments do not treat the contemporary or nationalist periods, nor do they consider the impact of colonizing ideologies on colonized peoples, such as the Maya. In addition, she pays relatively little attention to the strategies of oppressed women and their complicity, or resistance to a masculinist elite ideology. Despite the advantage of those in power to impose on others their new institutions, beliefs, and sentiments through persuasion or force, we would be perpetuating elite delusions of omnipotence to confuse their race-class-gender metaphors and evaluations with those of society as a whole. The problem, then, is to discover or suggest if and how colonial elite race-class-gender ideology has been accepted, resisted, or reformulated by the oppressed races, classes, and genders. I explore this notion further by examining Guatemalan race-class-gender ideologies in the contemporary period, concentrating on the beliefs and behaviors of Maya women, who are the triply oppressed in terms of race, class, and gender. I begin, however, with the dominant ideology held by the elites and Ladinos of modern Guatemala.

RACE/CLASS IDEOLOGY AMONG MODERN GUATEMALAN ELITES

Class in Guatemala is inextricably bound up with constructions of race and blood in ways that we might suspect from the above.[17] Guatemalan elites still consider themselves white in race (though few are without some non-white

---

[16] According to Ortmayr (1991), who treats marriage and society in nineteenth-century Guatemala, the rate of marriage for Ladino women rose substantially between 1850 and 1950. Ortmayr, however, makes no distinctions by class, so he is really documenting the upward mobility of some Ladinos in cultural and class terms. As Ladino economic and political fortunes rose with independence from Spain, they become more closely identified with Spanish creoles and eventually assume most creole cultural patterns. This is not true of lower-class Ladinos, however, whose marital and other cultural patterns remained different from that of creoles. Silvia Arrom (1985) makes this argument much more clearly for nineteenth-century Mexico City.

[17] See, for example, Brintnall 1979; Smith 1990; Knight 1990. There has been a long and misleading debate on the matter (described in Brintnall 1979) among anthropologists, which is only now being rectified.

admixture) and European in culture (Casaus Arzú 1992). They attempt to maintain both their racial purity and their legitimacy as the main power holders in Guatemala by maintaining their cultural and marriage ties to the whiter and more dominant parts of the world, namely, Europe and the United States. This makes it virtually impossible for them to create a unified Guatemalan nation. On what basis—other than a racist ideology—can a white, basically non-Guatemalan elite claim to have the right to rule all of Guatemala, which is more than half Mayan? And if persuasive, does not this racist ideology impugn even the rights of white Guatemalans, who are assumed to be less racially pure than the white foreigners they emulate? This problem has forced Guatemala's white anti-colonial nationalists to do a lot of soul searching and hand wringing, even though it has caused surprisingly few of them to challenge the underlying assumptions about their own right to rule over Guatemala. The assumption that creoles (those of European descent) should rule in Guatemala has rarely been challenged, even to the present day.[18] Although those of more clearly mixed descent have been "invited into history" by changes in ethnic and racial labels which no longer distinguish between Ladinos and creoles (both groups now being labeled Ladinos), Guatemalans of predominantly European ancestry clearly remain Guatemala's ruling class and continue to make distinctions between themselves and those of mixed ancestry (Casaus Arzú 1992; Gould 1994).

There is little question that Guatemala's middle- and lower-class Ladinos, whose class and race position is considered intermediate between that of Guatemala's elites and Maya Indians, support the elite ideology, even though they are exploited by it. The class position of most Ladinos is that of salaried workers and petty bureaucrats, which in the context of an economy that is not fully capitalist puts them in the middle, rather than lower, class rungs of the system. Lower positions are reserved for Indian peasants and artisans who bear the burden of absolute, rather than relative, class exploitation. Because Ladino race and class position is thought to be intermediate between that of Indians and creoles, the two systems, race and class, bolster each other in the actual material organization of Guatemala's economy. The Ladino proletariat is happy to accept a system that basically exploits them, not only because salaried work is better paid and more secure than non-proletarian forms of labor but because it allows them to identify with creoles vis-à-vis Guatemala's Maya Indians and, thus, to more easily exploit Guatemala's Maya majority, who are less fully proletarianized (C. A. Smith 1990).

As in much of Latin America, race is largely defined through culture rather than through descent (for an especially good depiction of this complexity, see Stutzman 1981). A person who is publically recognized as Ladino can be

---

[18] In this regard, Guatemala is more conservative than Mexico (though see Knight 1990); on Guatemala, see Martínez Pelaez (1973), C. A. Smith (1990).

virtually any biological mixture—from all Mayan to all European—but must acquiesce to the dominant national culture, sever kinship ties with indigenous community members, and speak Spanish. In fact, state policy in Guatemala since independence from Spain has promoted the cultural assimilation of Maya, accepting assimilated individuals as Ladino citizens with the full political rights that unassimilated Maya do not have. At the same time, however, lighter and more Europeanized Ladinos are more highly evaluated by other Ladinos, especially as marriage partners, than darker, more Mayan, individuals. Color, education, and connections to Europe and or North America are as important as class in positioning different Ladinos opposite the creole power elite.

SEX AND MARRIAGE AMONG GUATEMALA'S LADINOS

Ladino sexual and marital patterns in Guatemala, which I consider modern, if somewhat more traditional than most, are similar to those found throughout Latin America. Class position has a much more dramatic impact on the sexual and marital options available to Ladino women than to Ladino men. There are three statuses for women descended from the white elite, based on their sexual activity: virgins, legitimate wives, and prostitutes. (Women whose sexual activities violate the elite sexual standard are labeled prostitutes, which effectively declasses them.) These statuses reinforce the class-race-gender system as follows. Legitimate wives in Guatemala mostly come from the same race and class background as the men they marry. Legitimacy in marital status, following upon virginity, is especially important to upper-class white women. Laurel Bossen describes the sexual status of elite women in the mid-1970s in the following terms:

The . . . woman who produces children without a contract of paternal recognition (legal marriage) from a man of her class jeopardizes her membership in the class. She must be able socially to "prove" the paternity of children in order to maintain class privilege. Social proof generally consists of the absence of any evidence or insinuation of independent interaction with males other than a woman's kin or husband. She must be above suspicion. Hence, virginity for unmarried women and the appearance of absolute sexual monogamy for married women are means by which legally married parents of middle or upper socioeconomic status ensure the right of their children to inherit their class status and privileges (Bossen 1984:294–5).

Even though birth control and abortion are now widely available to these women, most have internalized what we would consider a Victorian notion of their sexuality. A twenty-one-year-old unmarried woman, member of the creole elite, described sexual differences between men and women to Bossen as follows:

I think sex is more important for a man. Men want to demonstrate their *hombría* (manliness). A woman can reserve herself. She must deny sexuality. If she did not do so, she would be like the prostitutes. In my environment, there are some girls who are freer for love, but later, it is thrown in their face (Bossen 1984:292).

This woman, like most members of the elite, thus reduces women of her class into the three groups described above: unmarried virgins (like herself), legitimate wives (whose sexual-reproductive activity is reserved for their husbands), and prostitutes (who can no longer reproduce elite status).

The reduction of elite women to race and class reproducers is reflected in their high birth rates within legal marriage, together with their low employment and divorce rates (Bossen 1984:288–95). Elite women with children rarely work outside of the home. Indeed, until recently Guatemala's Civil Code allowed men to restrict their wife's employment:

The husband can oppose the wife's dedication to activities outside the home, as long as he supplies what is necessary for the support of the same. . . . Once procreation starts with the birth of the first child, the woman must understand that her mission is in the home, and except for very special circumstances she must not neglect her children under the pretext of personal necessities or the desire to aid her husband (Código Civil Dto. Ley 106, Articulo 114, cited in Bossen 1984:274).

Some women interviewed by Bossen resisted this restriction in various ways, but few questioned male authority in this domain. Most reasoned that men forbade women to work outside the home out of (appropriate) sexual jealousy or to protect the reputation of the family—both the man as breadwinner and the woman as sexually circumspect.

Upper-class women's views about work and marriage help explain the contradictory position of lower-class Ladino women on both of those topics. Lower-class Ladino women would also prefer legal (civil) marriage but rarely attain it. Roughly two-thirds of the lower-class Ladino women interviewed by Bossen (half in an urban squatter settlement, half in a rural plantation area) were not legally married, and most had had more than one sexual partner. Because these women worked, mostly outside the home, they were sexually suspect. Those few women who were legally married were mostly wedded to men who had stable employment; these men could (and did) "demand a high degree of control over their wives' activities, typically seen in a curtailment of sexual freedoms and social relationships outside the family" (Bossen 1984:167). Even so, married women were not immune to being abandoned by their husbands. As Bossen saw it, lower-class Ladino women faced strong competition from other women for men who had stable jobs or good incomes:

While alcoholism and male peer groups may be contributing factors, wives generally perceive their real competition to be other women: prostitutes in town who are interested in a worker's paycheck and local women . . . who may hope to establish a permanent support relationship. An insecure wife is reluctant to jeopardize her position by directly attacking her husband when he wrongs her [which] would challenge his authority or drive him even more surely to the comforts of a new partner. Instead, women who feel severely threatened are prone to attack the competition. While such attacks may begin with verbal abuse, they may well culminate in physical violence (Bossen 1984:154).

Where possible, lower-class Ladino women would exchange a poor provider for a better one—for example, substituting the role of wife to a poor man for the role of concubine to a richer man. This was not a major sacrifice, for, in severely reduced economic circumstances, there is not a great deal of separation between legitimate wives (who can legally make certain property claims for themselves and their children) and concubines (who can make no such claims). It seems fairly clear, in fact, that people in the upper classes saw most lower-class Ladino women in that light as sexual objects who could be either prostitutes or concubines, that is, women who could not press property claims for themselves or their children.

Lower-class Ladino women who possess some form of social capital (lighter skin, education, personal connections) can sometimes marry up—mostly to darker, richer men.[19] But more frequently lower-class women form nonlegitimate liaisons with higher-class men—the *casa chica*, or kept woman, phenomenon. Women who make such liaisons cannot expect much in the way of day-to-day assistance or companionship from their higher-status mates—something not easily obtainable from same-status mates either. But they can expect greater social and sexual freedom than is possible in a relationship with a same-status Ladino man.[20] Because of this option for lower-status Ladino women (who in this respect have options that upper-class Ladino women lack), there is a scarcity of women at the bottom rungs of society. Richer and more powerful Ladino men have more than one woman, leaving poorer, less powerful men with less than one. Little else distinguishes upper- and lower-class Ladino men with respect to marital and sexual options.

TRADITIONAL MAYA BELIEFS ABOUT RACE AND GENDER

How do Ladino sexual and marital patterns affect Maya women in Guatemala? Do Maya women marry up by making liaisons with the darker, poorer Ladinos? My evidence suggests that they do not—or that they do so only rarely. The reasons they do not, moreover, enhance and solidify Maya ethnic identity. Let me try to explain this phenomenon beginning with a discussion of the main symbols of Maya ethnic identity to traditional Maya: These symbols include local community descent, language, women's dress, gender roles, and rules of sexual conduct within the community.[21]

---

[19] Alan Knight (1990) observes that no Mexican president has ever married a woman "darker" than himself. He notes the racism, but not the sexism, involved in such practices.

[20] Martínez-Alier (1974) argues that this factor more than any other was responsible for the high rate of concubinage among mulattos in nineteenth-century Cuba. It may also be a major factor in mestizo Latin America, about which less is known.

[21] The Maya of whom I speak here are traditional community-centered Maya—still the vast majority of Maya in Guatemala—rather than those Maya who emerged in the 1980s and 1990s identified with a broader pan-Mayan community, a community with some classic nationalist characteristics (see C. A. Smith 1991).

In the 1970s the Maya, like all other Guatemalans, accepted an essentialist construct of the bases of ethnic identity. They believed that the Maya formed distinct peoples descended from local community-specific ancestors and that they obtained both their identities and social positions in their communities through descent or biology (see Warren 1989; Watanabe 1992). Identity was community specific, based upon an extremely high rate of community endogamy.[22] All Maya were expected to marry within the community, and virtually all of them did so. Particular Maya communities were thought to have existed as separate social entities since time began. They were marked as particular in two main ways: community-specific forms of language and of dress. These differences distinguished Maya communities from each other as well as from non-Maya communities. The community of most Maya women, unlike most Maya men, could be immediately classified by both language and dress, that is, Maya women spoke mainly the local Maya dialect and dressed in a community distinctive form. Women, then, bore the burden of maintaining the main markers of Maya ethnic identity. While there were significant pre-conquest elements in the Maya local identity pattern, traditional Maya culture in the twentieth century (which included Maya gender relations, marriage, and kinship patterns) was clearly a product of Maya interaction with Spanish colonial precepts, like most other cultural elements identified as traditional Maya today (see Wolf 1959; Warren 1989; C. A. Smith 1990).

The maintenance of Maya women's parochialism (through dress and language) helped to maintain Maya women as marital partners for Maya men in community-specific ways. Most Maya women married local men at a fairly young age and then were expected to bear and nurture as many children as possible, imbuing those children (especially daughters) with community-specific Maya values. Thus, Maya women were seen to be (and were) the reproducers of the Maya community, both culturally and biologically. On these grounds, one could argue that ethnic identity and Maya community solidarity was based on the reproductive control of traditional Maya women. But before reaching this conclusion too hastily, let us look more closely at gender roles and rules of conduct within various Maya communities.

Until very recently, the rate of male migration from Maya communities far outstripped that of female migration (Demarest and Paul 1981). This provided a strong contrast to the Ladino migration pattern, in which women found it easier than men to position themselves in urban areas as servants, as traders, and as sexual partners for Ladino men. It also suggests that Maya women, who could easily have been accepted as Ladinos in urban areas, did not feel confined within their communities.[23] Previous sexual experience or marital

---

[22] The Maya rate of in-marriage is about 90 to 95 percent in communities now averaging about 10,000 individuals, one of the highest rates of community in-marriage in the world (Adams and Kasakoff 1975).

[23] See Chaney and Garcia Castro (1989) for a discussion of female migration patterns in Latin

failure did not jeopardize the chances of remarriage for either women or men. There were no prostitutes or concubines within Maya communities, and virginity was not highly prized.[24] Maya men would occasionally have more than one wife but made no distinctions among their wives—all wives (whose status of wife was achieved simply by taking up domestic relations with a Maya man) could make equal economic claims for themselves and their children. "[Maya] women also form[ed] sexual and exchange relationships with more than one man simultaneously, although with greater discretion" (Bossen 1984:122). Bossen provides an example:

[A Maya woman] Maria Lazaro, roughly 60 years old, is married to Efrain [of the same community] who is about the same age. Both have been married twice previously. Efrain's first wife ran away with another man after she had had two children with Efrain. [Such a woman would be socially recognized as the "legitimate wife" of her second mate, once the relationship was securely established, as long as he was a member of the same community.] His second wife bore more children and died, leaving him with young dependents. Maria Lazaro had also been widowed, first, and then separated from her second husband. She was in her mid-50s and living with her father when Efrain came to ask for her. She had never had any children and at any rate was beyond childbearing age when Efrain came to ask for her. He officially petitioned her father, although it is understood that the father cannot command a grown daughter, only a young one (Bossen 1984:117).

Maria Lazaro was married to her third husband by Maya custom (a small bride price was paid for her), despite the fact that she had earlier been widowed, had married a second time, was abandoned by her second husband, and was now well past the age of bearing children.

Maya women, unlike other Guatemalan women, were relatively autonomous subjects (socially and economically) within their communities. They inherited their own land, usually had their own sources of income, and were relatively free to move about (within the community). Maya women, moreover, could seek divorce, mediation, or redress from the community if mistreated by their husbands and were more or less guaranteed a relatively secure place in the community, with or without their original husbands, if they followed the local rules of cultural and sexual conduct. The rules of sexual conduct did not require them to abstain from social contact with men other than kin in the community, to be virgins at marriage, or to risk abandonment by kin and community if discovered in sexual relations with men in the community other than their husbands—unlike the demands made of legiti-

America. In most areas the number of women migrants far outstrips that of men because they are more easily employed in urban areas then men.

[24] Evidence from more remote and traditional Maya communities (such as Chiapas, Mexico) make this clear (see, for example, Collier 1973, 1974; and Rosenbaum 1993). But in certain Maya areas of Guatemala, where contact with the Catholic Church and with Ladino sexual and marital mores has been relatively strong, there is greater concern for female virginity (see Ehlers 1990, 1991).

mate wives in the rest of Guatemalan society. Instead, Maya women were mainly required to wear the emblems of their community identity, marry local men, and bear and nurture children of the community.

There was one other requirement, a product of colonialism: Maya women were expected to avoid contact with men outside the community, especially Ladinos, and were expected to conduct themselves modestly, which is not the perceived behavior of Ladino women.[25] While a Maya woman raped by a Ladino would not be repudiated by her community (nor would the child of such a union), a woman who voluntarily left her community for a mating arrangement with a Ladino (usually in the process adopting Ladino identity) would not be welcomed back into her community. In Totonicapán, the Maya community where I lived in the 1970s, women who changed to Ladino dress (which was interpreted as a public announcement that they were seeking a relationship with a Ladino man) were called whores and rarely married within the community.[26] Those women who took up employment as domestics in Ladino households—where they were often sexually abused— were able to contract marriages with Maya men from their community but appeared to contract less advantageous marriages than women who did not take up such employment. In this sense, Maya women appeared to be stamped as community property, if not individual male property, in a sexual sense.

As I see it, then, Maya women exchanged the freedom to abandon their communities (socially, culturally, sexually, and reproductively) for a certain personal security within their communities—a security that no other Guatemalan women had. By following the rules of cultural and sexual conduct, the Maya woman, at least traditionally, could expect community support against abandonment or mistreatment by her husband. Because of her economic autonomy and value, a Maya woman who was abandoned or who wished to repudiate her marriage could return home, remarry,or live independently with her children. It should be noted that Maya women were no more likely to be abandoned than Maya men, for most Maya men also eschewed Ladino norms of sexual and social conduct (that is, machismo and promiscuity), if not other patriarchal rights. In order to find legitimate spouses within their communities, Maya men were expected to be as hard working, respons-

[25] For discussions of the code of conduct for both Maya and Ladino women that support this argument, see Rigoberta Menchú's autobiography (Burgos-Debray 1984), Laurel Bossen (1984), Rosenbaum (1993). I am not so sure any sanctions are applied to Maya women who marry Maya men of other communities. In precolonial times, elite Maya did marry across communities.

[26] I cannot claim that this is common to all Maya communities. Women in some communities have changed their dress as a group without major repercussions or without losing community identity (Ehlers 1990). The highly politicized nature of this labeling of non-traditional women in Totonicapán, where I worked, may reflect particular sexual or ethnic tensions in that community.

ible, and non-promiscuous as Maya women.[27] Maya men were given much wider sexual latitude than Maya women, however.

Given that male sexual and cultural behavior outside of their community was not as closely circumscribed as female sexual and cultural behavior, were not Maya women still oppressed when compared to Maya men? And did not their conduct reproduce, though in a different form, the dominant race-class-gender ideology of Guatemala—making both Maya and Ladino women icons of race and class identity? As a feminist I would have to say yes to both questions, but I would also have to say, as those few other students of Maya women have also said, that Maya women were freer than any other Guatemalan women in this regard. Their actions, moreover, challenged certain elements in the dominant ideology. By exchanging what was assumed to be their essential position in reproducing Maya culture at a community level for basic protections by the community, protections that no other Guatemalan women had, Maya women put certain conditions on the sexual and marital conduct of Maya men. We should not be surprised, then, that Maya women basically supported the limits placed on them which produced the community solidarity that confined but protected them. Maya women were, in fact, mostly proud to produce and wear the symbolic emblems of their stigmatized status as Maya and as women.

GENDER, RACE, AND ETHNIC NATIONALISM IN REVOLUTIONARY POLITICS

Let us now look at the implications of traditional Maya beliefs about race, class, and gender for reproducing ethnic nationalism in Guatemala and for creating certain contradictions within it. The dominant race-class-gender ideology is based on the expectation that everyone plays by the same rules, that is, that everyone competitively strives for individual position in society by accepting the same norms, by assimilating to national culture and belief systems, and by making the most advantageous marriages possible. Thus, since independence in 1821, the dominant classes in Guatemala have attempted to draw Maya into the Guatemalan (Ladino) nation by getting them to take on Ladino norms of language, dress, and sexual conduct—not in order to accept them as equals but to deal with them as part of the overall race-class-gender hierarchy rather than as a separate cultural system.

The existence of distinct beliefs about race, class, and gender within Maya

---

[27] This pattern may be changing somewhat for the Maya who are part of the pan-Maya nationalist movement. At the same time Maya nationalists are attempting to challenge Ladino nationalist discourse, they may be appropriating certain assumptions about the world (see C. A. Smith 1991), as much as about appropriate masculine and feminine behavior. If this becomes a clear pattern in succeeding years, Partha Chatterjee's argument about "derived" modernist discourses (1986) gains further support.

communities clearly conflicted with this expectation. Traditional Maya neither accepted nor rejected their position in the national race and class hierarchy: They operated by a different set of principles. Rather than competing in the national hierarchical system, they attempted to remain separate from it in economic and ideological terms. By retaining a relatively autonomous economic existence (refusing proletarianization), Maya communities managed to remain separate from the national class system (see C. A. Smith 1990). And by keeping their women out of the national marriage pool, Maya communities maintained their separatist (anti-assimilationist) cultural and political stance against the Ladino nation.

The particular form that Maya resistance took to the national race-class-gender hierarchies required the Maya to remain divided as separate communities rather than united as a (potentially) revolutionary or ethnic-nationalist force. Most Maya, both consciously and unconsciously, refused to stand as a separate nation within Guatemala: They stood as separate nations or communities, united only by the same basic principles that divided them as a political force. Gender politics in Maya communities played a key role in defining separatist Maya ethnic-national politics. To substantiate this claim, let me briefly describe two distinct moments—one in 1979 and one in 1989—in Maya resistance to incorporation in a revolutionary national race-class-gender system. These moments depict changing Maya stances toward the revolutionary ideology which shared many cultural precepts with the nationally dominant (Ladino) ideology on matters concerning race and gender. The main point on which the revolutionary ideology differed on gender was its belief that all Guatemalan women, Ladino and Maya alike, should be free to deploy their sexuality as they wished.[28]

Between 1978 and 1979, for a variety of reasons that cannot be fully explored here, significant numbers of Maya men and women joined a Marxist–Leninist revolutionary movement intended to topple Guatemala's corrupt, repressive military-state regime that Ladinos had always exclusively controlled.[29] By that time, the revolutionary movement was perceived to be of, and for, the Maya, even though it was clearly led by Ladino commanders. Those Maya who became active participants in the revolutionary movement were subjected by the Ladino leadership to an intense barrage of revolutionary rhetoric designed to break down the parochial bases for their grievances against the state and unite them (with lower-class Ladino cadre) into a national liberation movement against the state in which they would be unified by the

[28] On the parallels between dominant and revolutionary ideology concerning ethnicity, or the necessity of assimilating Maya into the Ladino nation, see C. A. Smith (1990, 1991, 1992). On the revolutionary position concerning "the women's question," see *Women's International Resource Exchange* (1983) on Guatemala.

[29] The most useful discussions of Maya participation in the revolutionary struggle, from my perspective, can be found in Burgos-Debray (Rigoberta Menchú) (1984), Carmack (1988), Manz (1988), C. A. Smith (1990), and Wilson (1991).

40

grievances of all oppressed, that is, all workers, whether Indian or Ladino, presumably also whether women or men. The revolutionary language was Spanish; the revolutionary dress was military (for both men and women); and a primary revolutionary goal was to end the divided, exploited, and assumed marginal existence of Maya communities. The presence of large numbers of Maya in this revolutionary movement forced the revolutionary leadership to at least consider certain separate Maya issues and thus a number of revolutionary position papers on what was termed "the Indian question" were produced. Symptomatic of deeper problems in the Ladino-led revolutionary project, none of these papers was able to address adequately the issue of Maya autonomy in the revolutionary project (C. A. Smith 1992). By 1984, many Maya had left the revolutionary fold (see C. A. Smith 1990; Wilson 1991; Jonas 1991), having become quite disillusioned about the revolutionary agenda.

In discussions with these dissidents in 1988 and 1989, I found to my considerable surprise that race and sexuality had become key issues to them, leading many Maya to renounce the vanguardist politics of Ladino revolutionaries and to support more traditional forms of Maya resistance.[30] Most of the Maya I interviewed complained about Ladino dominance of revolutionary rhetoric and goals and were disturbed by Ladino insistence on a unified, as opposed to a particularized (community-based), political agenda for the Maya. Almost all of them pointed out that Ladino revolutionaries had no understanding of or respect for Maya traditions and women's dress codes. Many hinted at their dismay about revolutionary sexual beliefs and conduct that required Maya women to deal with unacceptable sexual practices. The people who complained were women as often as men.

Had I heard these stories of revolutionary disillusionment among Maya cadre in 1979, I probably would have concluded that the Maya were simply unable to accept the universalizing modernist message basic to a revolutionary movement. I would have agreed with Ladino revolutionaries that the Maya, for both economic and cultural reasons, remained too parochial for revolution. By 1989, however (partly because of discussions I was having with Maya cultural nationalists), I saw Maya complaints about revolutionary unity in a somewhat different light. The demands of revolutionary unity would, in a sense, destroy the structural props of Maya ethnic identity—the main revolutionary goal of most Maya and one for which they had been willing to fight and die.

The experience of Guatemalan (Marxist–Leninist) revolutionaries among the Maya suggests some of the limits to revolutionary recruitment among community-based peasants. Revolution requires that local (parochial) communities be destroyed for the purpose of meeting the higher goal of creating a

---

[30] These traditional forms of resistance have now been described by a small group of Maya intellectuals who call for recognition that "Guatemala is a multi-cultural nation" (see C. A. Smith 1991). These intellectuals appear to be unaware of the gender politics that grounds their multicultural nationalism.

larger "imagined community" (*cf.* Anderson 1983) or some other utopian set of social relationships. In the practice of revolutionary struggle, most Maya found that they were unwilling to substitute a utopian community for their real community bases, which were rooted in a particular pattern of sexual and gender conduct. It may be worth noting that few women in traditional agrarian societies have been attracted to the revolutionary promise of sexual autonomy. This suggests that they recognize, as traditional Maya women did, that sexual autonomy without family or community support is more of a burden than a liberation (see M. Wolf 1985; Molyneux 1985).

The evidence also seems clear about the relation between ethnic identity and traditional Maya beliefs about race, class, and gender. The strongest material prop to community-specific forms of ethnic identity among Guatemala's Maya Indians was community endogamy or in-marriage and the kind of sexual conduct that supported and reproduced it. It now seems clear to me that the complex set of beliefs and social relations that underwrote Maya practices concerning race and gender was that which preserved community-specific ethnic identity in Guatemala. The retention of non-capitalist social relations within these communities was also important, to be sure—as most of my other writings have emphasized. But I now doubt that the economic autonomy of Maya communities could have been preserved without the support of the Maya marital and sexual practices described here, especially insofar as the particular economic system of Maya communities (artisanal production) required a willing household labor force that was not lured away by the promise of better jobs or higher status outside the community. The only people who did leave Maya communities in significant numbers before the 1980s were unmarried youths (Demerest and Paul 1981). Being properly married within a Maya community meant that one's Maya identity was relatively fixed. Many traditional Maya beliefs and practices concerning community, class, and gender appear to be transforming rapidly in the post-revolutionary period, but they are not going in the directions desired or expected by conservative Ladino elites or Ladino revolutionaries.[31]

I cannot claim that a complex of beliefs and practices similar to that described for the Maya operates in most other cases of ethnic resistance to homogenizing nationalist appeals. Not all ethnic groups are as anxious as the

---

[31] The significant changes that are occurring in the post-revolutionary period have much to do with the development of a pan-Maya movement in Guatemala, led by intellectuals whose sense of identity is no longer community-based. One indication of this change relevant to the thesis presented here is that Maya women who are part of this movement typically wear Maya clothing from many different communities (thus proclaiming their pan-Mayanism). While Maya women who are part of the movement can associate with Ladinos (though usually only in a group context), they are still much more strongly sanctioned than Maya men for marrying Ladinos. As could be expected, both men and women who are part of the pan-Maya movement are much more likely to marry outside of their community of birth than traditional Maya.

Maya to retain multiple, locally based, ethnic communities. Yet, there appear to be some aspects of ethnic resistance important in this case that are more generally significant. Most obvious is that ethnic groups typically construct themselves around ideologies of common descent, which politically motivates and mobilizes people in terms of rules of marriage and sexual conduct. Without defining a line across which marriage or sexual (reproductive) relations are forbidden, it is very difficult to make an imagined ethnic community appear real to people. Feminists have often observed that feminist mobilization is very difficult in cases where ethnic mobilization is already a strong social force. The intertwined sets of relationships described above may help explain why.

MODERN AND ANTI-MODERN RACE-CLASS-GENDER IDEOLOGIES

To deal with some of the more difficult issues of nationalism, as well as with the difference between modern and non-modern ideologies, let me refer to an apparently very different case that Claudia Koonz (1987) examined. Koonz depicts the race-class-gender ideology of Nazi Germany as "anti-modern" because it rested upon the total rejection of modernizing freedoms—of sexuality, of the individual, of social mobility, of strong elements in civil society such as organizations for workers and for feminists—that characterized the Weimar republic and erected in their place folk notions of family, traditional gender roles, security, and commitment to ideals of community. It was an "imagined community," to be sure, that was completely subservient to the demands of a militarist state; but its founding premise was reconstructing Germany as a "natural" (racially pure) community. Control over women was key to constructing what the Nazis deemed a racially pure German community. Concentrating on middle-class women in Nazi Germany, Koonz documents their complicity in their own and other women's subjugation as well as in the horrors perpetrated by the Nazi state.

Yet modernity was not erected anywhere in the world on Weimar-like freedoms for women. As I argued above, most modern class systems and most forms of modern nationalism, whether anti-colonial or not, rest upon a Western folk ideology of descent or biological inheritance. That is, they rest upon biological explanations for the social relations created by humans, bolstering the kinds of racist ideologies and racism that found expression among the Nazis. All of us who want to immortalize and perpetuate ourselves through descendants of our own blood buy into this ideology to some extent. It is, as Verena Stolcke observes, a "naturalized" belief and thus natural in Western society. In this way, kinship cemented in blood relations—which can include ever-larger communities up to the nation—appears to us to be a natural part of the human condition. Although the modernist impulse of capitalism works against it, human beings have resisted the creation of alienated individuals who are totally without ties to and claims on blood kin.

Marxist–Leninist revolutionaries, such as those who led Guatemala's recent revolutionary movement, are more likely than regular modernists to support Weimar-style freedoms—of sexuality, of the individual, of status mobility, and of strong elements in civil society such as organizations for workers and for feminists. But as Stacey (1983) and M. Wolf (1985) have argued for revolutionary China and as Molyneux (1985) and Randall (1992) have shown for revolutionary Nicaragua, the sexual and marital freedoms of revolutionary society are largely illusory. Just like the conservative modern (Ladino) race-class-gender ideology, revolutionary ideology appears to offer women the possibility of using their sexuality and reproductive potential as they will, even though the free woman is likely to reap dire consequences for her actions, should she actually break the rules of appropriate sexual and reproductive conduct. Truly anti-modern belief systems (which the Maya had, but the Nazis did not), on the other hand, reject that illusion. That is, they more clearly deny to individual women the possibility of sexual (reproductive) freedom. More important, however, they substitute for that freedom the security provided by some kind of protective and real, rather than totally imagined, community. Both systems are socially supported by the reproductive woman's extreme social vulnerability.

Almost all kinds of nationalism build upon our attachment to the supports and claims that we can make of blood ties, kinship, and family. (In the words of many nationalist ideologues, "the family is the microcosm of the nation.") This is as true of Ladino Guatemalan nationalism, with its modern race-class-gender system, as it is of Nazi nationalism. The various attempts that Guatemalans have made to create a nation, contradictory as they have been, required the incorporation of Maya into the Guatemalan family—which to the Maya has meant the death of their own cultures, nations, and kinship systems. When it appeared to Ladino Guatemalans, erroneously as it turned out, that all Maya were united in an attempt to claim the nation, they did not hesitate to consider a "final solution" that required for Guatemala, as for Nazi Germany, the eradication of those unfit or unwilling to become part of the Ladino Guatemalan nation. In the early 1980s, the Guatemalan military chased over half of the Maya from their homes in a campaign of terror specifically directed against Indians—a campaign that involved the death and torture of more than 100,000 Maya—with the implicit consent of most ordinary Ladino Guatemalans.

How could ordinary Guatemalans, most of them at least partially descended from the Maya, support this campaign? I believe they could do so because they accepted the idea that Maya (revolutionary) nationalism would destroy the foundations of their own nation, together with the blood and kinship supports they had constructed within that nation. The Ladino Guatemalan is inscribed in a modern race-class-gender system that promises individual freedom and mobility, but the complex of beliefs that undergird it is still rooted in non-modern blood sentiments which mainly circumscribe women and minorities. These non-modern sentiments, which are part of all modern nationalist ideologies, were readily mobilized by the Guatemalan military state. It remains a major question how readily they can be mobilized in any modern nationalist conflict.

The differences between these different ideological systems—modern, anti-modern, and revolutionary—I conclude, are only ones in degree, not in kind. A truly different kind of system would have to base itself outside of blood ties, requiring an end to kinship and marriage as we know it. Until we construct a different kind of system—a system that disempowers the sentiments of blood and descent—we will have to live with the consequences of racism and sexism and to guard against the very real possibilities of the sort of ethnic holocaust recently enacted in Guatemala.

REFERENCES

Adams, John W.; and Alice B. Kasakoff. 1975. "Factors Underlying Endogamous Group Size," in *Regional Analysis, vol. II, of Social Systems*, C. A. Smith, ed. New York: Academic Press.

Anderson, Benedict. 1983. *Imagined Communities: Reflections on the Origin and Spread of Nationalism*. London: Verso.

Arrom, Silvia Marina. 1985. *The Women of Mexico City, 1790–1857*. Stanford: Stanford University Press.

Bossen, Laurel. 1984. *The Redivision of Labor: Women and Economic Choice in Four Guatemalan Communities*. Albany: State University of New York Press.

Burgos-Debray, Elizabeth, ed. 1984. *I, Rigoberta Menchú: An Indian Woman in Guatemala*. London: Verso.

Brintnall, Douglas. 1979. "Race Relations in the Southeastern Highlands of Mesoamerica." *American Ethnologist*, 6:4, 638–52.

de la Cadena, Marisol. 1991. "'Las mujeres son más indias': etnicidad y género en una comunidad del Cusco." *Revista Andino*, 9:7–47.

Carmack, Robert, ed. 1988. *Harvest of Violence: The Mayan Indians and the Guatemalan Crisis*. Norman, OK: University of Oklahoma Press.

Casaus Arzú, Marta. 1992. *Guatemala: Linaje y racismo*. San José, Costa Rica: Facultad Latinoamericana de Ciencias Sociales (FLASCO).

Chaney, Elsa; and Mary Garcia Castro, eds. 1989. *Muchachas No More: Household Workers in Latin America and the Caribbean*. Philadelphia: Temple University Press.

Chatterjee, Partha. 1986. *Nationalist Thought and the Colonial World: A Derivative Discourse?* London: Zed Books.

———. 1989. "Colonialism, Nationalism and Colonialized Women: The Contest in India." *American Ethnologist*, 16:4, 622–33.

Collier, Jane. 1973. *Law and Social Change in Zinacantan*. Stanford: Stanford University Press.

———. 1974. "Women in Politics," in *Woman, Culture, and Society*, M. Rosaldo and L. Lamphere, eds. Stanford: Stanford University Press.

Demarest, W. J.; and B. D. Paul. 1981. "Mayan Migrants in Guatemala City." *Anthropology UCLA*, 11:1–2, 43–73.

Ehlers, Tracy. 1990. *Silent Looms: Women and Production in a Guatemalan Town.* Boulder, CO: Westview Press.
————. 1991. "Debunking Marianismo: Economic Vulnerability and Survival Strategies among Guatemalan Wives." *Ethnology,* 30:1, 1–16.
Foucault, Michel. 1980. *The History of Sexuality,* vol. I. New York: Vintage Books.
Gellner, Ernest. 1983. *Nations and Nationalism.* Oxford: Basil Blackwell.
Gill, Lesley. 1993. "'Proper Women' and City Pleasures: Gender, Class, and Contested Meanings in La Paz." *American Ethnologist,* 20:1, 72–88.
Goody, Jack. 1976. *Production and Reproduction: A Comparative Study of the Domestic Domain.* New York: Cambridge University Press.
Gould, Jeffrey L. 1994. "What's in a Name? From Ladino to Mestizo in Central America." Paper presented at the Eighteenth International Congress of the Latin American Studies Association, Atlanta, Georgia.
Hobsbawm, Eric. 1975. *The Age of Capital.* London: Weidenfeld and Nicolson.
Jonas, Suzanne. 1991. *The Battle for Guatemala: Rebels, Death Squads, and US Power.* Boulder, CO: Westview Press.
Kahn, Joel. 1990. "Towards a History of the Critique of Economism: The Nineteenth-Century German Origins of the Ethnographer's Dilemma." *Man (N.S.),* 25:230–49.
Knight, Alan. 1990. "Racism, Revolution, and Indigenismo: Mexico, 1910–1940," in *The Idea of Race in Latin America, 1870–1940,* Richard Graham, ed. Austin: University of Texas Press.
Koonz, Claudià. 1987. *Mothers in the Fatherland.* Rutgers, NJ: Rutgers University Press.
Lavrin, Asunción, ed. 1989. *Sexuality and Marriage in Colonial Latin America.* Lincoln, NE: University of Nebraska Press.
Lerner, Gerda. 1986. *The Creation of Patriarchy.* New York: Oxford University Press.
Manz, Beatriz. 1988. *Refugees of a Hidden War: The Aftermath of Counterinsurgency in Guatemala.* Albany: State University of New York Press.
Martínez-Alier, Verena. 1974. *Marriage, Class and Colour in Nineteenth-Century Cuba.* London: Cambridge University Press.
Martínez Pelaez, Severo. 1973. *La patria del criollo.* Guatemala: Editorial Universitaria.
McCreery, David. 1986. "Female Prostitution in Guatemala City, 1880–1920." *Journal of Latin American Studies,* 18:333–53.
Molyneux, Maxine. 1985. "Mobilization without Emancipation? Women's Interests, the State, and Revolution in Nicaragua." *Feminist Studies,* 11:2, 227–54.
Ortmayr, Norbert. 1991. *Matrimonio, estado y sociedad en Guatemala (siglo XIX y XX).* Guatemala: Ediciones CEUR, Universidad de San Carlos.
Otzoy, Irma. 1988. "Identity and Higher Education among Mayan Women." M. A. Thesis, Anthropology, University of Iowa.
————. 1992. "Identidad y trajes mayas." *Mesoamérica,* 23 (June), 95–112.
Randall, Margaret. 1992. *Gathering Rage: The Failure of Twentieth Century Revolutions to Develop a Feminist Agenda.* New York: Monthly Review Press.
Rosenbaum, Brenda. 1993. *With Our Heads Bowed: The Dynamics of Gender in a Maya Community.* Austin: University of Texas Press.
Stanford Central America Action Network, eds. 1983. *Revolution in Central America.* Boulder, CO: Westview Press.
Seed, Patricia. 1988. *To Love, Honor, and Obey in Colonial Mexico: Conflict over Marriage Choice, 1574–1821.* Stanford: Stanford University Press.

46

Silverblatt, Irene. 1987. *Moon Sun, and Witches: Gender Ideologies and Class in Inca and Colonial Peru.* Princeton: Princeton University Press.

―――. 1988. "Women in States." *Annual Review in Anthropology,* no. 17:427–60.

Smith, Carol A. 1990. *Guatemalan Indians and the State, 1540–1988.* Austin: University of Texas Press.

―――. 1991. "Maya Nationalism." *Report on the Americas,* 25:29–33.

―――. 1992. "Marxists on Class and Culture in Guatemala," in *1492–1992: Five Centuries of Imperialism and Resistance,* Ron Bourgeault *et al.,* eds. Halifax, Nova Scotia: Fernwood Press.

―――. n.d. "The Symbolics of Blood: Mestizaje in the Americas." Forthcoming in *Identities.*

Smith, R. T. 1984. "Introduction," in *Kinship Ideology and Practice in Latin America,* R. T. Smith, ed. Chapel Hill, NC: University of North Carolina Press.

―――. 1992. "Race, Class, and Gender in the transition to freedom," in *The Meaning of Freedom,* F. McGlynn and S. Drescher, eds. Pittsburgh: University of Pittsburgh Press.

Stacey, Judith. 1983. *Patriarchy and Socialist Revolution in China.* Berkeley: University of California Press.

Stepan, Nancy Leys. 1991. *"The Hour of Eugenics": Race, Gender, and Nation in Latin America.* Ithaca: Cornell University Press.

Stolcke, Verena. 1981. "The Naturalizations of Social Inequality and Women's Subordination," in *Of Marriage and the Market,* Kate Young *et al.,* eds. London: CSE Books.

―――. 1991. "Conquered Women." *Report on the Americas,* 24 (February), 23–49.

―――. n.d. "The Individual between Culture and Nature." Unpublished manuscript.

Stoler, Ann. 1991. "Carnal Knowledge and Imperial Power," in *Gender at the Crossroads of Knowledge,* M. diLeonardo, ed. Berkeley: University of California Press.

―――. 1992. "Sexual Affronts and Racial Frontiers: European Identities and the Cultural Politics of Exclusion in Colonial Southeast Asia." *Comparative Studies in Society and History,* 34:3, 514–551.

Stutzman, Ronald. 1981. "El mestizaje: An All-Inclusive Ideology of Exclusion," in *Cultural Transformations and Ethnicity in Modern Ecuador,* N. E. Whitten, ed. Urbana: University of Illinois Press.

Warren, Kay. 1989. *The Symbolism of Surbordination: Indian Identity in a Guatemalan Town,* 2nd ed. Austin: University of Texas Press.

Watanabe, John. 1992. *Maya Saints and Souls in a Changing World.* Austin: University of Texas Press.

Williams, Brackette. 1990. *Stains on My Name, War in My Veins: Guyana and the Politics of Cultural Struggle.* Durham, NC: Duke University Press.

―――. 1993. "The Impact of the Precepts of Nationalism on the Concept of Culture: Making Grasshoppers Out of Naked Apes." *Cultural Critique,* 24 (Spring), 143–91.

Wilson, Richard. 1991. "Machine Guns and Mountain Spirits: The Cultural Effects of State Repression among the Q'eqchi' of Guatemala." *Critique of Anthropology,* 11:1, 33–61.

Wolf, Eric. 1959. *Sons of the Shaking Earth.* Chicago: University of Chicago Press.

Wolf, Margery. 1985. *Revolution Postponed: Women in Modern China.* Stanford: Stanford University Press.

Women's International Resource Exchange. 1983. *We Continue Forever: Sorrow and Strength of Guatemalan Women.* New York: Ragged Edge Press.

Peter Fry

Politics, Nationality, and the Meanings of "Race" in Brazil

G IVEN THAT BRAZIL has "imported" people and ideas through-out its history and celebrated its "anthropophagous" absorption of them, it becomes particularly interesting to know why just a few outside ideas seem so indigestible. After all, however much Robert Schwarz might argue that liberal democracy was an "idea out of place" in the late nineteenth century of Machado de Assis,[1] it has nevertheless been appro-priated as a central element of Brazilian nationalism together with its ancillary "racial democracy."

Indeed, it is in the name of the "imported" ideology of liber-alism that so many other Brazilians now reject affirmative action, especially in its most categorical form of quotas. When some ideas from outside have been eaten and digested, they seem to lead to a kind of nausea in relation to other ideas that enter into contradiction with them. Quotas are nauseous to many not only because they appear to contradict racial democ-racy and liberal democracy *tout court*, but also because they seem to threaten the very idea of "anthropophagy" itself. It is as if once Brazil had eaten formalized affirmative action, other foods it held dear became increasingly unpalatable.

In a recent article on what they term "cultural imperialism," Pierre Bourdieu and Loïc Wacquant argue that a "number of topics which result directly from intellectual confrontations

Peter Fry is professor of anthropology at the Institute of Philosophy and Social Sciences at the Federal University of Rio de Janeiro and a member of the Interdis-ciplinary Nucleus for the Study of Inequality (NIED).

83

related to the social specificity of American society and American universities are being imposed in what appear to be de-historicized forms on the totality of the planet."² Thus, "multiculturalism" and "neo-liberalism"—concepts developed in the specific context of the United States—are transformed into "natural," universal, and taken-for-granted truths, except, they note, when ridiculed as "political correctness" and "para-doxically utilized, within French intellectual circles, as an in-strument of reprobation and of repression against all manner of subversive impulses [*velléités*], notably feminist or homosexual ones. . . ."³

Noting that the debate on "race" and "identity" has also been subject to "similar ethnocentric intrusions," they turn to Brazil to illustrate their argument.

> An historical representation, born of the fact that the American tradition arbitrarily imposed a dichotomy between Whites and Blacks on an infinitely more complex reality, can even impose itself in these countries where the principles of vision and division, codified or practical, of ethnic differences are completely different, and which, as in Brazil, were until recently held as a counter example to the "American model."⁴

This "symbolic violence" derives, they argue, from the use of American racial categories to describe Brazil and from the power of the United States to obtain the "collaboration, con-scious or not, directly or indirectly out of interest, of all the 'purveyors' and importers of cultural products with or without a griffe," such as editors, directors of cultural institutions, operas, museums, galleries, magazines, and the like. They also single out the role of the great American philanthropic and research foundations in "the diffusion of the North-American racial doxa in the heart of Brazilian universities at the level of representations and practices."⁵

The irony of invoking Brazil in this context is that since the days of slavery, well before modern globalization, "race rela-tions," real and imagined, in Brazil and the United States, have been held as contrasting models that in a sense have come to define for many the two national identities.

In this essay, I will argue that Bourdieu and Wacquant have presented an interpretative model, which only partially does justice to the facts as I see them. While it is true that many North American intellectuals consider that Brazil's ideology of "racial democracy" is, or should be, a dead letter, claiming that Brazil's only claim to specificity is the particularly insidious racism it engenders, and while it is also true that North American philanthropic organizations provide financial and intellectual support for research on "race" and for black activist groups, it is also true that many of their staff, together with a sizeable number of Brazilian academics and activists, are reluctant to abandon a commitment to the *idea* that "race" or physical appearance should not be invoked to discriminate in any way. By the same token, while many activists and intellectuals perceive "race relations" in Brazil as a contest between two categories of people—whites and people of color—others continue to celebrate the virtues of "mixture," of both genes and cultures. Still others hold a combination of these ideas and invoke them depending on the situation. That one set of ideas has become identified with Brazil and another with the United States results from metonymic associations and metaphorical contrasts that are part of the politics of nation-building and a concern for national "authenticities."

The mechanism of personifying nations and then attributing to them cultural homogeneity and purposeful projects for hegemony can obfuscate the issues that are really at stake, that are endogenous to all modern societies: namely, the conflict between the post-Boasian position that "race" is not a biological reality but rather a historical and social artifact and the persistently lingering and increasingly powerful presence of "race" as a guiding principle for the formation of meaningful social categories and groups. This mechanism, of course, also ignores the way in which distinct individuals, groups, and categories present in "subaltern" societies understand and react to the messages they receive in terms of their own cultural categories and political agendas.

As the ethnographic record shows, and in spite of Gananath Obeyesekere's counterposition, Captain Cook was killed because the people of Hawaii thought he was their God Lono.[6] I will suggest that if Brazilian society has any specificity at all as far as these issues are concerned, it lies in the original ways in which this conflict of ideas is made manifest in public debate, and in the myriad forms in which Brazilians cope with "race" and "racism." And this specificity, again in contrast with the United States, lies in one of the few objective facts in this field so beset with subjectivism: the law. In Brazil, racial discrimination is and has been illegal since the inauguration of the republican regime in 1890.[7] In the United States, "race" was, until the civil rights movement of the 1960s, a legal construct that divided the population along "racial" lines in all spheres of social life. Since then it has continued to be as powerful as ever either to justify prejudice or to counter it. Affirmative action was relatively easy to introduce in the United States because it was built on shared premises of "racial" difference. In Brazil, it is a far more thorny issue since it runs counter to the notion of racial democracy. But, as Bourdieu and Wacquant note, the irony lies in the fact that as pressure mounts in the United States to question affirmative action and the easy dichotomy of blacks and whites, so too in Brazil pressure mounts in the opposite direction.

THE DEVELOPMENT OF THE IDEA OF MIXTURE AND RACIAL DEMOCRACY IN BRAZIL

In 1859, Count Joseph Arthur de Gobineau arrived in Rio de Janeiro to spend one year as French ambassador to the court of Emperor Dom Pedro II, with whom he soon established a firm friendship. Four years later, Gobineau, the author of *Essai sur l'inégalité des races humaines*,[8] which was later to inspire the most pernicious of twentieth-century "scientific racism," published an article about Brazil that extolled the natural wealth and beauty of the country but was less sanguine about the human beings who inhabited it. Observing the formidable mixture of "races" in Brazil and claiming that mulattos "do not reproduce themselves beyond a limited number of generations," he concluded on the basis of an analysis of available census data that the population of Brazil would have "disappeared completely, to the last man," within 270 years at the maximum or 200 years at the minimum.[9] To avoid such a catastrophe, he advocated more valuable alliances with "European races." By so doing, "the race would become re-established, public health would improve, moral values recharged and felicitous changes would be introduced into this admirable country."[10] There is little doubt that Gobineau's distaste for mixture reflected deep concerns for the future of his native country, which, since the French Revolution, had experienced the waning of the "racial purity" and political control of an elite of supposedly German descent to which he himself claimed to belong. His efforts could well be interpreted as an attempt to universalize the reaction to the French Revolution.

Brazilian scholars imagined other outcomes for Brazil as they contemplated its multicolored population, which Gobineau and other proponents of "scientific racism" considered nonviable.[11] Nina Raymundo Rodrigues devised a complex racial classification and predicted that the population would tend toward three basic types—whites, mulattos, and blacks—that could be defined not by genealogical criteria as much as by appearance. Inspired by the Italian school of criminal anthropology, Rodrigues argued that each of these groups possessed its own moral system and went so far as to suggest that separate penal codes should be developed for each of them.[12] His ideas, however, fell on stony ground, at least where formal legislation is concerned. Since the abolition of slavery in 1888 and the inauguration of the republic in 1890, Brazilian constitutions and legislation have not discriminated on the basis of "race" or "color," even if immigration policies revealed the racial thinking of the times. By importing white people from Europe, it was hoped gradually to "whiten" the population, as the superiority and strength of white "blood" gradually eliminated African and Amerindian physical and cultural traits.[13] João Batista de Lacerda, director of the National Museum, argued in 1911 that within a hundred years the population would become not so much white as "Latin."[14] The irony of the Brazilian position in contrast to that of the United States is that whereas in the former white was supposed to subsume black, in the latter the opposite was thought to occur. To this day the "one-drop rule" may be invoked to classify any person with at least one African ancestor or ancestress as African-American without regard to physical appearance.

In 1933, Gilberto Freyre published *Casa Grande e Senzala*, in which he argued that "miscegenation" and the mixing of cultures was not Brazil's damnation but rather its salvation. In the preface to the first edition of the book, in the same paragraph in which he recognized his intellectual debt to Franz Boas under whom he had studied in the United States, he recalled having observed a "band of Brazilian sailors—*mulatos* and *cafuzos*" leaving ship in Brooklyn. "They gave me the impression of human caricatures.... Miscegenation had resulted in that. What was missing was the presence of someone who, like Roquette Pinto talking to the 'Arianists' of the 1929 Brazilian Eugenics Congress, could tell me that these individuals whom I imagined representatives of Brazil were not simply *mulatos* or *cafuzos,* but *cafuzos* and *mulatos* who were sick."[15]

Casa Grande e Senzala was Freyre's vindication of Brazilian miscegenation. Pulling together a vast array of documentation on colonial and imperial Brazil as well as his own reminiscences as the son of a Northeastern landed family, and embellishing his text with considerable poetic license, he described Brazil as a hybrid society in which Africans, Amerindians, and Europeans (especially the Portuguese) had intermingled through the interchange of genes and cultures. Freyre described a society founded on a series of what he called cultural and economic antagonisms, based on "profound traditional realities," between "sadists and masochists, the learned and the illiterate, individuals of predominantly European culture and others of principally African or Amerindian culture."[16] He argued that this duality was not entirely "prejudicial" and that a certain equilibrium existed between the "spontaneity and freshness of imagination and emotion of the great majority and . . . the contact between the elites with science, technology and with the advanced thinking of Europe."[17] But above all, the antagonisms were "harmonized" by "conditions of fraternization and social mobility specific to Brazil: miscegenation, the dispersion of inheritances, easy and frequent changes of employment and residence, the easy and frequent access of mulattos and natural children to elevated social and political positions, lyrical Portuguese Catholicism, moral tolerance, hospitality to foreigners and inter-communication between the different parts of the country."[18]

Freyre, like his predecessors, was concerned as much with describing Brazil as identifying its specificity in relation to other countries, in particular the United States. *Casa Grande e Senzala* was as much an exercise in nation-building as historical ethnography. In this regard it is not without significance that Freyre's analysis of Brazil became an important part of Boas's cross-cultural critique of "race."

> Race feeling between Whites, Negroes, and Indians in Brazil seems to be quite different from what it is among ourselves. On the coast there is a large Negro population. The admixture of Indian is also quite marked. The discrimination between these three races is very much less than it is among ourselves, and the social obstacles for race mixture or for social advancement are not marked. Similar conditions prevail on the island of Santo Domingo where Spaniards and Negroes have intermarried. Perhaps it would be too much to claim that in these cases race consciousness is nonexistent; it is certainly much less pronounced than among ourselves.[19]

As Célia Azevedo has argued, the notion that the relations between masters and slaves were more harmonious in Brazil than in the United States had grown apace throughout the nineteenth century as abolitionists in both countries "constructed little by little the image of Brazil as a society immune to racial violence."[20] Even Nina Rodrigues had adhered to this idea.

> Whether it be the influence of our Portuguese origin, and the tendency of the Iberians to cross [sic] with the inferior races; whether it is a special virtue of our white population, which I don't believe; or whether it might be finally one more influence of the character of the Brazilian people, indolent, apathetic, incapable of strong passions, the truth is that color prejudices, which certainly exist among us, are little defined and intolerant on the part of the white race. In any event, much less than it is said that they are in North America.[21]

But in an important way, Freyre did part company with the past, in particular with a wholly negative image of Amerindian and African cultures. Although he never completely abandoned the neo-Lamarckianism of associating culture with descent,[22] he did emphasize the positive contribution each had lent to Brazilian society as a whole. All Brazilians, he claimed, regardless of their genealogical affiliation, were *culturally* African, Amerindian, and European. In Freyre's sociology the three "races" were *imagined* as cultural clusters that in combination allowed for the imagination of a racially and culturally hybrid Brazil. In the absence of "racial" segregation, "races" were not so much sociological realities as somehow present in various degrees of cultural and biological combination in each *individual*, where they are fused.[23]

RACIAL DEMOCRACY UNDER ATTACK

Up to the 1940s, this image of Brazil was widely accepted both in Brazil and elsewhere. Indeed, there are good reasons to suppose that the idea of "racial democracy" was consolidated by activists, writers, and intellectuals looking at Brazil from lands where racial segregation was the rule. Blacks from the United States, for example, who visited Brazil, returned full of praise. Leaders such as Booker T. Washington and W. E. B. DuBois wrote positively of the black experience in Brazil while black nationalist Henry McNeal Turner and radical journalist Cyril Biggs went so far as to advocate emigration to Brazil as a refuge from oppression in the United States.[24] In 1944, the Jewish writer Stefan Zweig found Brazil to be the least racially bigoted society he had visited.[25] In DuBois's time, then, Brazil was widely held to be a "racial democracy" where relations between people of diverse colors were fundamentally harmonious.

As the world took full stock of the horrors of Nazi racism in the years following World War II, UNESCO agreed, on the suggestion of Brazilian anthropologist Arthur Ramos, to sponsor a pilot research project in Brazil with the aim of studying "the problems of different racial and ethnic groups living in a common social environment."[26] Brazil was chosen not only because it appeared to represent a viable alternative to racial segregation and conflict but also because UNESCO had at this time shown considerable sensitivity to the specific problems of the developing world.[27]

Verena Stolcke notes that "within Brazil concern was voiced, as it turned out prophetically, that a systematic scrutiny into the nature of the country's race relations might open the Pandora's box of 'racial democracy.'"[28] The North American, French, and Brazilian anthropologists who worked on the project did indeed provide evidence of massive inequality and prejudice throughout the country. And yet, as Marcos Chor Maio has shown, the research results did not deny the importance of the myth of racial democracy.[29] What they did was to reveal the tensions between the myth and Brazilian-style racism, a tension that had already been enunciated by black and white intellectuals and activists, in particular by Abdias do Nascimento and Guerreiro Ramos.[30]

Although the UNESCO-funded researchers documented severe racial discrimination in Brazil, they continued to perceive "race relations" as distinct from those in the United States. Florestan Fernandes, for example, felt that racial discrimination and the inequality between whites and people of color were largely the result of the legacy of slavery and the difficulty Brazilian blacks had experienced in adapting to capitalism. He predicted that with their integration into the economy, inequality and discrimination would fade away.[31] Fernandes's work talks about "blacks and whites," which was the terminology used by his black activist friends and informants to classify themselves and others. Other writers, however, singled out what they saw as Brazil's specific way of classifying the population. Instead of classifying according to the simple dichotomous taxonomy used in the United States, Brazilians categorized on the basis of a complex taxonomy of terms. Furthermore, they did so on the premise not of descent but of "appearance."

The statistical documentation of racial inequality entered into a new era of sophistication with the publication in 1979 of sociologist Carlos Hasenbalg's *Discriminação e Desigualdades Raciais no Brasil*.[32] Controlling his data carefully to eliminate the effects of class, Hasenbalg was able to argue, against those who claim that discrimination is directed more toward the poor than to people of color, that "race" was significantly related to poverty. He concluded that such inequality could not be attributed to the legacy of slavery but only to persistent prejudice and discrimination against people of color, an argument that had in fact already been put forward by UNESCO project researcher Luis de Aguiar Costa Pinto.[33] Subsequent research has confirmed his findings. Demographers have established a higher infant mortality rate for nonwhites than for whites (105 as against 77 in 1980) and a lower life expectancy for nonwhites than for whites (59.4 years as against 66.1 years). In education, nonwhites complete fewer years of study than whites, even controlling for income and family background. In 1990, 11.8 percent of whites had completed 12 years of education as against 2.9 percent of nonwhites. As Hasenbalg notes, these educational differences obviously affect the subsequent careers of nonwhites and whites. The average income of blacks and mestizoes is a little less than half that of whites. Research on social mobility indicates that nonwhite members of the middle and upper classes experience less social mobility than similarly placed whites, and that they have more difficulty in transmitting their new status to their children. All these studies suggest, then, that racial discrimination has the effect of forcing nonwhites into the least privileged niches of Brazilian society.

While people of color in Brazil generally fare badly in education and in the workplace, they are most vulnerable in relation to the criminal justice system. Paulo Sérgio Pinheiro found that of 330 people killed by the police in São Paulo in 1982, no less than 128 (38.8 percent) were black.[34] Moema Teixeira notes that in 1988, 70 percent of the prison population of Rio de Janeiro was composed of "blacks" and "browns." In São Paulo, the situation is little different. Quoting a 1985–1986 survey, Teixeira notes that the percentage of "blacks" and "browns" in the prison population (52 percent) was almost twice as much as in the São Paulo population as a whole (22.5 percent).[35]

In a study of the criminal justice system of São Paulo, Sérgio Adorno found that of those arrested and accused of theft, drug trafficking, rape, and armed robbery in São Paulo in 1990, blacks lost out at each step of the system: 58 percent of blacks accused were arrested in the act of committing a crime as opposed to only 46 percent of whites. Similarly, a greater proportion of whites (27 percent) awaits trial on bail than blacks (15.5 percent). When finally brought to trial, "the proportion of Blacks who are condemned is higher than their proportion in the racial distribution of the population of the municipality of Sao Paulo."[36]

Carlos Antonio Costa Ribeiro's findings based on crimes brought to trial by jury in the city of Rio de Janeiro from 1890 to 1930 are similar, and he concludes that "[t]he blackness of the defendant increases the probability of conviction more than any other characteristic."[37] Costa Ribeiro argues that discrimination against people of color was related during the period in question to the strength of the proponents of "criminal anthropology," of the "positive school" of thought that was established in Brazil by Nina Rodrigues. Although Rodrigues had been unsuccessful in establishing distinct penal codes for blacks, mulattos, and whites, the association of African physical traits with a propensity for crime was ritualized in the obligatory measurements of color and physiognomy in the Office for Criminal Identification of Rio de Janeiro until 1942.[38] Despite having fallen into disrepute in forensic science, these same ideas inform police practice and most of public opinion in Brazil to this day.

Adriano Maurício provides particularly poignant evidence of the entrenchment of these ideas in his remarkable study of public transport in Rio de Janeiro.[39] The young Mozambican began to notice that hardly anyone ever sat next to him on the bus that brought him from his house in the suburbs to the university in the center of town. Having read an article on Aimée Césaire's conversion to negritude on a tram in Paris where he suddenly discovered that he was looking at a rather disheveled black woman with the same disgust as the white passengers,[40] Maurício embarked on a systematic study of seating patterns on a number of bus routes and interviewed black and white passengers on their seating preferences. In his extremely delicate and careful ethnography he was able to demonstrate that the order of seating preferences of white passengers was first, white women, second, women of color, third, older men of color, and last, younger men of color. He concluded that these seating patterns were related to the common assumption that the people most likely to conduct assaults on buses are young black males. At the same time, however, he perceived that the buses were not racially segregated as such. The patterns he observed were the result of implicit rather than explicit assumptions about the salience or nonsalience of "race" in public places.

The demonstration and recognition of the existence of racism pointed to the chasm between Brazil's ideology of "racial democracy" and sociological reality. On this point, few would disagree. Indeed, public opinion polls show quite clearly that the majority of Brazilians (not just academics and black activists) are well aware of discrimination. In 1995, a survey conducted by the São Paulo newspaper *A Folha de São Paulo* revealed that almost 90 percent of the population acknowledged the presence of racial discrimination in Brazil.[41] A survey carried out in Rio de Janeiro in 1996 showed that 68.2 percent of the inhabitants of Rio de Janeiro agree that "blacks" suffer more than "whites" from the "rigors of the law."[42] At the same time, however, both surveys revealed that most Brazilians adhere to an ideal of "racial democracy" and deny having any prejudice themselves. As many as 87 percent of respondents who classified themselves as white and 91 percent of those who defined themselves as brown claimed to have no prejudice against blacks, while 87 percent of the blacks interviewed denied having any prejudice against whites. Even more surprisingly, 64 percent of the blacks and 84 percent of the browns denied having themselves suffered from racial prejudice. It is as if Brazilians are prejudiced against racial prejudice, as a white informant told Florestan Fernandes and Roger Bastide many years ago.[43]

Whereas most agree that the myth of racial democracy coexists with prejudice and discrimination, interpretations differ. The interpretation that has fired the imagination, above all of Brazil's black activists, is that the myth does more than merely deny true racial democracy. It has the powerful function of masking discrimination and prejudice and of impeding the formation of a large-scale black protest movement. Under this interpretation, Brazilian racism becomes the more insidious because it is officially denied. Michael George Hanchard presents this argument in its most sophisticated form in his analysis of the black movement in Brazil. What he calls a "racial hegemony" in Brazil neutralizes racial identification among non-whites, promoting racial discrimination while simultaneously denying its existence. By the same token, the myriad color categories present in Brazil, in particular the differentiation of mulattos from blacks and whites, also has a "function."[44] As Degler would have it, the mulattos are the "escape hatch" that dissipates possible racial polarizations and animosities.[45] For these authors, what began as Brazil's glory is now its damnation.

This new version of the Brazilian nation was constructed, like that of Freyre's, on an explicit comparison with the United States. This time, however, Brazil does not represent a superior alternative, but rather an archaic and obscurantist system that must give way in time to the "reality" of clearly defined "races."

Talcott Parsons argued some years ago that racial polarization was a necessary and welcome feature of "modernity."

> Relatively sharper polarization clearly favors conflict and antagonism in the first instance. Providing, however, other conditions are fulfilled, sharp polarization seems in the longer run to be more favorable to effective inclusion than is a complex grading of the differences between components, perhaps particularly where gradations are arranged on a superiority-inferiority hierarchy. To put cases immediately in point, I take the position that the race relations problem has a better prospect of resolution in the United States than in Brazil, partly because the line between white and Negro has been so rigidly drawn in the United States and because the system has been sharply polarized.[46]

Writing much more recently, Michael Hanchard expresses a similar opinion. "Conflicts between dominant and subordinate racial groups, the politics of race, help constitute modernity and the process of modernization throughout the world. They utilize racial phenotypes to evaluate and judge persons as citizens and non-citizens. . . . This is the politics of race between whites and blacks at the end of the twentieth century, and Brazil is no exception."[47] And Angela Gilliam, a black North American social scientist, has proclaimed: "Much of the thrust of conscious Africanization in Brazil must come from the United States. American black people must start to realize that even some of the conceptualizations and solutions towards an *Afri-*

can Africa will come from our efforts. The struggle is *one*."[48] In comparison with the "normality" and "modernity" of the United States, Brazil, then, must be declared wanting: for not having polarized "races;" for defining a person's "race" by appearance rather than genealogy;[49] for not having produced a strong mass black movement; for not having been the stage for racial confrontation; and for officially subordinating the specificity of races to class inequality. The "myth of racial democracy" is interpreted as a functional element, somehow outside Brazil's "race" arrangements, which impedes Brazil from its "natural" destiny. And just as "racial democracy" was once a dominant symbol of Brazilian nationalism, it has now become demonized in certain academic and activist circles as an ideology largely responsible for Brazil's most insidious racism. As Suely Carneiro, executive coordinator of Geledês Instituto da Mulher Negra (Geledês Black Women's Institute) of São Paulo, said at a recent seminar on citizenship and diversity funded by the United States Information Service, "there exists an attempt to disqualify the advances obtained by the black movement in this fight against racism through . . . a neoracial democracy, which aims to thwart [*esvaziar*] the growing consciousness and capacity for making demands of descendants of Africans, especially the younger ones, and to impede that racial conflict might become explicit with its radical demands for social change."[50]

Bourdieu and Wacquant argue that this swing of the tide results from cultural imperialism, pointing to the influence of American funding, American activists and intellectuals, and the media in general. In a sense, they are right, for there can be no doubt about the importance of organizations such as the Ford and MacArthur Foundations, to name the two most prominent, in the funding of research and black activism. But then one must ask why it was that these ideas found such resonance among Brazilian intellectuals and black activists, unless we are to assume that they have all in one way or another been transformed, unwittingly or not, into "collaborators."

This particular interpretation of Brazil has become increasingly powerful over recent years not only because of the influence of North American scholarship and the utilization of "racial" categories, which were developed to describe North

American "races" and "race relations,"[51] but also because of the parallel growth of an articulate black movement that has been generally strongly allied to academic researchers. A case in point is Florestan Fernandes, who in his monumental *A Integração do Negro na Sociedade de Classes* utilized the terms *"negro"* and *"branco"* in accordance with the desire of his black activist informants.[52] While there is no doubt that Brazilian black activism was inspired by movements in the United States and South Africa (how could it be otherwise? I would even venture the guess that the heroic status in Brazil of Martin Luther King and Nelson Mandela is greater than the Brazilian Zumbi), their very existence suggested that Brazilians should not be seen as a continuum of "colors" but rather as "blacks" and "whites." And while such a dichotomy is clearly redolent of the "American model," it had indeed always been latent in Brazil and is most clearly expressed in the term *pessoa de cor* (person of color) and in the popular adage "quem passa de branco preto é" ("He/she who is not white is black"). Perhaps, therefore, one should understand the social and historical construction of race in Brazil as lying in a tension between one taxonomy and another.

But the interpretation of the myth of racial democracy as crafty deceit has problems. First, it shows a hearty disrespect for all those (the majority of the population) who profess a belief in it. Second, it carries with it the generic defects of all functional interpretations. If one takes the "myth of racial democracy" from a more anthropological point of view, either as a charter for social action or as an ordered system of social thought that enshrines and expresses fundamental understandings about society, then it can be understood not so much as an "impediment" to racial consciousness but as the foundation of what "race" still actually means to most Brazilians. Political scientist Jessé Souza, for example, has conducted research in Brasília on the distribution of prejudice. He found that while prejudice against homosexuals, women, the poor, or people from the Northeast was common in all levels of society, if slightly less evident in higher income groups than in lower income groups, racism was the only prejudice that the vast majority of his informants from all income groups explicitly condemned. He goes so far as to suggest that antiracism is "one of the few values that is shared without restriction by all social strata."[53]

It seems, then, that some academics tend to side with the black movement while others claim to invoke what they variously term Brazilian society or Brazilian culture. Needless to say, each lends his or her "authority" to one of two principal sides in the political battles that now rage over the racial issue. And there is nothing strange in this, since, as Marisa Peirano has pointed out, the boundary between social activism and academic life in Brazil has always been blurred.[54]

POLITICAL ACTION

During the discussions leading to the 1988 Constitution, the black movement and its academic allies armed themselves to try to bring the racial issue into sharper constitutional focus. As a consequence, the new constitution gave stronger teeth to the Afonso Arinos Law, which had been introduced in 1951 to punish racial discrimination by redefining racist practice as a crime rather than a mere misdemeanor.[55] The Afro-Brazilian Federal Deputy Carlos Alberto Caó later presented new legislation that, in accordance with the new constitution, denied bail to those accused of "crimes resulting from racial or color prejudice" and stipulated prison sentences from one to five years for those found guilty. This harsh law also states that crimes arising from racial or color prejudice cannot lapse because of the passage of time (*imprescritíveis*).[56]

The novelty of the new constitution was that it recognized the property rights of descendants of maroon (*quilombo*) communities who continue to occupy their lands.[57] For the first time, the special status of certain black communities was recognized in an affirmative sense, giving them legal rights similar to those that have long been available to Indian communities but not to other "nonethnic" rural populations. Consequently, numerous researchers and activists have started to map these communities, many of which now enjoy legal title. But this is not without a cost, for to establish their "authenticity," the communities in question are obliged to prove their status to the technician (usually an anthropologist or historian) responsible for producing the official report (*laudo*). The process of recognition of the very existence of these communities is having, I would argue, an important effect on the way in which the race question is thought of in Brazil. The effects of the process of identification are both practical and symbolic: practical because land tenure is secured; symbolic because Brazil is confronted with a "reality" that challenges the self-image of a mixed-up society and replaces it with one in which there are "racial" authenticities. A similar effect is produced by the Africa-inspired carnival groups in Salvador and elsewhere. By imagining a multiracial and multicultural Brazil rather than a Brazil of inextricable mixture, they effectively produce it in the manner of the self-fulfilling prophecy described by Robert Merton.

The same arguments mapped out by the academics and activists have also led to changes in governmental attitudes toward "race" in Brazil. During the military dictatorship, the suggestion that there was racism in Brazil could lead to accusations of subversion. Government activity was restricted to the support of cultural events, later through the Palmares Foundation in the Ministry of Culture, which administered a minuscule and unpredictable fund for that purpose. The Fernando Henrique Cardoso government, however, which came to power in 1994, extended its concern for Afro-Brazilian issues from the Ministry of Culture to the Ministries of Labor and Justice.[58] In 1995, the government launched its National Human Rights Program, which contained a series of planned activities in the interests of the "black community." These included "the inter-ministerial working group—created by Presidential Decree on November 20, 1995—for drawing up activities and policies to recognize the value of the black population," and a "Working Group for the Elimination of Discrimination in the Workplace and in Careers" within the Ministry of Labor. All these measures can be classified as "antidiscriminatory." They are used to strengthen individual rights and freedoms as established by the federal constitution. As attempts at combating racism and racialism, they represent no marked change in policy and are in consonance with the ideals of "racial democracy."

However, the National Human Rights Program goes beyond this goal to propose interventions that aim to strengthen a bipolar definition of race in Brazil and to implement specific policies in favor of black Brazilians. For example, the program suggests bringing the Brazilian system of racial classification in line with that of the United States, "instruct[ing] the Brazilian Institute for Geography and Statistics (IBGE) [responsible for collecting official census data] to adopt the criterion of considering mulattos, browns and blacks [*os mulatos, os pardos e os pretos*] as members of the black population [*integrantes do contingente da população negra*]." In addition, the program suggests providing "support for private enterprises which undertake affirmative action [*discriminação positiva*]," developing "affirmative action to increase the access of blacks to professional courses, the university and areas of state of the art technology," and "formulating compensatory policies to promote the black community economically."

These actions are, of course, radically distinct from the deracializing strategies of combating racism. Instead of denying the significance of "race," they celebrate the recognition and formalization of "race" as a criterion for defining and targeting policy. For the first time since the abolition of slavery the Brazilian government has not only recognized the existence and iniquity of racism, but has chosen to contemplate the passing of legislation that recognizes the existence and importance of distinct "racial communities" in Brazil. Fernando Henrique Cardoso, whose academic career as a sociologist began with research on race relations as a spin-off of the UNESCO project,[59] announced in his presidential speech on Independence Day in 1995: "We wish to affirm, and truly with considerable pride, our condition as a *multi-racial society* and that we have great satisfaction in being able to enjoy the privilege of having *distinct races* [*raças distintas*] and distinct cultural traditions also. In these days, such diversity makes for the wealth of a country."[60] What could be further from the concept of distinct races than the *mixture* idealized by Freyre? And what, to give greater credence to Bourdieu and Wacquant, could be closer to the dominant ideology of "progressive" thought in the United States?

In July of 1996, soon after the president's speech, the Brazilian government sponsored a seminar in Brasília on "Affirmative Action and Multiculturalism," at which a number of Brazilian and U.S. academics discussed the issue of affirmative action in Brazil. What is interesting about this seminar is that it at once attests to the propriety of Bourdieu and Wacquant's analysis and also challenges it. While the event was surely held to promote affirmative action in Brazil, powerful cautionary arguments were also advanced in the name of "liberal democracy" or "sociological intelligence."

Political scientist Fábio Wanderley Reis argues that affirmative action runs contrary to the precepts of liberal democracy, which is based on individualism as a fundamental value. "We want," he suggests, "a society where an individual's racial characteristics are irrelevant, that is, where opportunities of all types are not related to individuals on the basis of their belonging to one or another racial group. . . . We desire a society which does not discriminate, or perceive races, which is blind to the racial characteristics of its members."[61] He recognizes that although the notion of racial democracy does not correspond to the facts of racism in Brazil, it is an "irreplaceable goal," exactly because it affirms the irrelevance of racial characteristics. As such, it is clearly important because it imagines a society that avoids the "militant affirmation of distinct racial identities."[62] He concludes with the suggestion that government should do everything in its power to redress the negative stereotypes associated with people of color through education, the media, and so on, but that it should apply affirmative action as such "socially" rather than "racially," concentrating on reducing poverty. Since color and class run together in Brazil, he argues, such a policy would respect liberal democratic values while at the same time assuaging "racial" inequality.

Anthropologist Roberto da Matta has other objections. His argument is based not so much on the importance of liberal ideals as on Brazil's distinct "sociological intelligence." For him the classificatory issue cannot be put aside as merely a "technical problem." On the contrary, it lies at the very center of the debate. Comparing the one-drop rule in the United States and the Brazilian penchant for multiple categories, da Matta concludes that while the United States pursues the distinction and compartmentalization of ethnic groups in self-contained, contrasting units in a constant attempt to avoid ambiguity, the Brazilian classificatory system actually celebrates ambiguity and compromise, functioning on the basis of a finely graded hierarchy.[63] Like Reis he asks how one could possibly create the kind of binary classification that is necessitated by affirmative action (i.e., either you are eligible or you are not). He also draws attention to the consequences of affirmative action in the United States, where, he argues, the increased social mobility of many blacks has been brought about at the expense of strengthening racial prejudice and segregation. Like Reis, he suggests an educational campaign to explain the way racial discrimination works in Brazil and to exalt the idea of racial democracy.[64]

The argument in favor of affirmative action in Brazil was most clearly advanced by sociologist Antonio Sérgio Guimarães. He asserts that a "nonreified" and temporary program of affirmative action is compatible with individualism and equality of opportunity because it is a way of promoting equity and social integration.[65] His recommendation is that affirmative action be applied not to the mass of the population where "universalistic" policies should prevail, but rather to secure the formation of a multiracial elite. To do this, he suggests quotas for black university staff and student applicants, arguing that this is the only way to "'deracialize' meritocratic economic and intellectual elites."[66] Guimarães brushes aside the thorny classificatory issue by asking, rhetorically: "who would want to be black to get into the universities other than those who are blacks?"[67] (He does not ask how many people defined as blacks would prefer to enter the university merely as citizens.) To avoid fraud, he suggests that color be reintroduced into identity cards: "If being black is really such a stigma, who would want to be classified as *'negro'* who wasn't one?"

But what most clearly distinguishes Guimarães's position from that of Reis and da Matta is his defense of the celebration of "racial identities." For Guimarães this is one of the positive results of affirmative-action policies. He argues that the differences that are the cause of inequality should not disappear (that would be impossible) but should be "transformed into the opposite, a source of compensation and reparation."[68] Consistent with this point of view, Guimarães has also recently argued for reintroducing the concept of "race" into analytic discourse.[69]

Guimarães's position is similar to that of Hanchard and to that of an important sector of the black movement in Brazil, in that the Brazil he imagines for the future is a society not of ambiguity and mediation but of clearly marked racial and sexual identities, which, since he believes they should be "strengthened," he assumes exist. There are those who would argue, and I am one of them, that the policy of cultural integration effected with such diligence and even violence in Brazil has been so successful that the identities that Guimarães would like to see valued have first to be constructed. And this is indeed what the ethnographic record suggests. The history of the black movement in Brazil has largely been the history of not-resoundingly-successful attempts to construct a black identity to which people of color would feel impelled to adhere.[70]

The issues at stake at the Brasília seminar on multiculturalism, as I see them, reveal serious contradictions that lie at the root of Brazilian society. On one side is a strong commitment to "liberal democracy," which, however much contradicted by the realities of patronage, corruption, nepotism, prejudice, and sheer violent power, remains an ideal to which many still aspire. On another, not so different from the first, is an appeal to "tradition," to "Brazilian sociological intelligence," which evokes the specificity of Brazilian society caught between the "ideals" of democracy and the "tradition" of hierarchy and ambiguity. And on yet another is a demand for radical change, a casting off of "tradition," the formal recognition of distinct "races" and the introduction of temporary measures to alleviate the inequalities between them. While there can be no doubt that the debate was provoked by the American experience of affirmative action (a number of North Americans were invited to recall that experience), it reveals quite clearly that the "American model" has by no means become hegemonic in Brazil. Furthermore, the issues at stake, although appearing under national banners, are really of a more general nature, for they go to the very heart of the question of humanity and its diversity in the modern world.

SOCIAL ACTION

With race issues brought to the fore in the Human Rights Program and interministerial working groups established, myriad initiatives aimed at addressing inequality and discrimination have mushroomed around the country. Most are funded by the government, international foundations, churches, or combinations of these. The range of initiatives reflects the range of opinions present in the academic debate. Some have chosen to explore options made possible by the laws against racism, bringing cases before the courts. Others concentrate on building self-esteem and a black identity, while others demand quota systems for blacks in public service and universities. Still others prefer hybrid solutions that simultaneously address issues of "racial" inequality and poverty in general by providing pre-university training courses for "blacks and the underprivileged" (*negros* e *carentes*). A few initiatives are promoted by transnational companies, a few are embedded in commercial enterprises, and a small number survive that are self-financing. There is not space here to discuss all these initiatives or to do justice to the complexity of this field. I choose just a few to illustrate the range of activities presently underway.

A number of organizations have concentrated their efforts to bring racism before the courts under the Caó law and under state and municipal legislation that has been complied by Hédio Silva, Jr., of the Center for the Study of Labor Relations and Inequalities (CEERT).[71] Notable are CEERT, the Center for the Articulation of Marginalized Populations (CEAP) in Rio de Janeiro, and Geledês, a São Paulo black women's organization.[72] Although it is extremely difficult to prove racist practice and even more difficult to bring miscreants to conviction given the extremely harsh penalties the law demands, a number of exemplary cases have been won.[73]

Traditionally, Brazilian black movements have placed the greatest emphasis on establishing a specific black identity.[74] Like academics, they felt that Brazil's complex and finely graded system of "racial" classification, as part of the "myth of racial democracy," was responsible for masking the true bipolar division of Brazilians into whites and blacks, *brancos* and *negros*.

Besides, as I argued earlier, to be able to exist at all, the movement was obliged to argue for a black identity in Brazil that would include all those who were not white. As John Burdick has so brilliantly shown, this particular affront to what da Matta called Brazilian sociological intelligence alienated many people who were sympathetic to the antiracist cause but reluctant to abandon their identities as Brazilians or as *morenos* for what appeared to them to be the exclusiveness of blackness.[75] Furthermore, it has always been difficult for black groups to establish diacritical emblems of black culture, because, under the canopy of racial democracy, many cultural touchstones, such as *feijoada* (Brazil's national dish based on black beans and pork), *samba*, and *capoeira* (a balletic martial art), that can be traced back to Africa have become symbols of Brazilian nationality.[76] Perhaps that is why the symbols of black identity were frequently taken from outside Brazil, such as reggae in Maranhão,[77] hip-hop in Rio de Janeiro and São Paulo, and, finally, Africa itself, especially in Bahia, where "Afro" carnival groups, in particular Ilê Aiyê, have, since the early 1980s, brought African-inspired themes to the Carnival parade and restricted their membership to people with very dark skin. Out of this experience, a musical style, Axê music and its derivatives, developed and became almost a national obsession.[78] Very recently, however, and I think related to these initiatives, a strong movement has emerged to celebrate exactly what Nogueira had noted marks "race" in Brazil, namely, appearance. The commercial success of the magazine *Raça Brasil*, which is now in its fourth year, surely lies in its emphasis on the aesthetics of blackness. Another example of celebrating a black aesthetic and trying to improve access of black Brazilians to the labor market is the Brazilian Center for Information and Documentation of the Black Artist (CIDAN), founded by actress Zézé Motta to promote black artists through a catalog that is now available on the Internet (www.cidan.org.br).

At a recent seminar on blacks and the labor market at the Federal University of Rio de Janeiro, psychologist Maria Aparecida Silva Bento, a longtime black activist and presently general coordinator of CEERT, affirmed that to suggest quotas for blacks is always interpreted as a "provocation," to the extent that in her knowledge no such program exists in Brazil. Even those transnational corporations whose headquarters are in the United States and who conduct "diversity" programs in Brazil avoid any mention of quotas, concentrating their efforts on cultural events and support for poor communities. The Xerox Corporation funds the Vila Olímpica, where young athletes from the Rio shantytown of Mangueira receive training, while BankBoston has teamed up with Geledês to support promising black high-school students.

Where quotas have been proposed, opposition has been virulent. For example, a bill introduced by veteran black movement leader Abdias Nascimento, mandating a 20 percent quota for the hiring of blacks into the civil service, found no support in the Senate, where arguments similar to those of Reis were advanced to suggest the bill's unconstitutionality.[79] Likewise, a bill introduced into the Rio de Janeiro Legislative Assembly by "Green" deputy Carlos Minc by which 10 percent of places in public universities and technical colleges would be reserved for "historically discriminated ethno-racial sectors" and a further 20 percent for the "needy" (*carentes*) has met with no greater success. A group of students at the University of São Paulo who proposed a quota system for black candidates for university places and a complex system for deciding who fits into that category has also run into heavy opposition so far, even though it has led the university administration to appoint a Commission on Public Policy for the Black Population in 1999. The Commission has been charged with conducting research to discover the demand, access, and success rates of black students at the university and to propose measures to reduce whatever difficulties they identify and to increase the enrollment of black students. Conversations with members of the Commission reveal yet again the dilemma of meeting the demands for black advancement without offending the sensibilities of those who reject quotas.

While the building of a "racial" identity continues to inspire many organizations, there has been a growing emphasis on addressing the concrete issues of inequality in the workplace, in the educational system, in relation to health, and in religious organizations. As a result, black caucuses have emerged in trade unions, preuniversity courses for young blacks and other disadvantaged people have been organized countrywide, special efforts have been made to reach black women concerning their reproductive health, and black priests and pastors have organized to fight racism within the Catholic and Protestant Evangelical churches.[80] With a reduction of an exclusive emphasis on forging identity, parts of the movement have also become more inclusive, seeking alliances beyond the small core of black activists (*militantes negros*) and recognizing that not all Brazilians favor forgoing their complex system of racial classification for the bipolar model.[81] As I have argued elsewhere, the very movement itself seems unable to ritualize its own desire.[82] On November 20, 1995, not long after Louis Farrakhan's March on Washington, various black organizations in Brazil organized a "March on Brasília" to celebrate the anniversary of the death of the maroon leader and national hero Zumbi and to protest racial discrimination. Two students who participated in the march returned with the clear sensation that they had participated in a very "Brazilian" affair. In contrast to the besuited masculine seriousness of the Washington march, the Brazilian version consisted of men *and* women of all possible colors, who *danced* their way to the center of power *dressed in the brightest garb*, rather in the manner of a carnival samba school (*escola de samba*). The students commented that it was as if Brazil had refused to accept a racial division within social and political life, even when it came to the issue of racism itself.[83]

In these ways, and by avoiding a head-on collision with the ideals of mixture and "racial democracy," the movement has been able to attract more support and achieve greater credibility. A particularly interesting example of this response to the demands for "racial" equality without total racialization is the Movimento Pré-Vestibular para Negros e Carentes (MPVNC), whose successful students are given scholarships to the Pontifical Catholic University of Rio de Janeiro (PUC). As its name suggests, this movement organizes courses to prepare students who are black, poor, or both for the university entrance exams (*vestibulares*). Those who pass the entrance exam to the Catholic University of Rio automatically win scholarships on the basis of an agreement signed between the two organizations in 1994.

The name of the movement reflects the dilemmas that confront Brazilian activists who feel the need for affirmative action but who recognize that "particularistic" initiatives tend to run up against opposition from the "liberals" and from those who believe Brazil to be "different." The decision to include "*negros*" and "*carentes*" in the name of the organization represents a compromise between the two positions. There are a number of reasons for this. In the first place, the Catholic Church itself is averse to racial distinction, and a number of white Catholic teachers participate in the course.[84] Second, the organizers of the course recognize that exclusion from educational opportunity is not a monopoly of black Brazilians. But it may also be that the decision simply reflects the diplomacy of cordiality. Regardless of the reasons for the choice of name, the movement has been enormously successful, and the number of nuclei and students grows apace.

The course itself is similar to the many other *pre-vestibular* courses in Rio de Janeiro. What makes it different is that the teachers give their own time and students contribute with an almost symbolic payment of about $10 per month as compared with the commercial courses that cost up to $500 per month. It refuses all outside funding. In addition, a weekly class on civics in which the racial issue is addressed is added to the standard curriculum.

Anthropologist Yvonne Maggie suggests that the great success of the movement may lie in its ability to allow for the coexistence of various positions on the racial question within the movement itself. "Far from trying to give priority to candidates for places who are activist members of the black movement, the Movement chose a different strategy, attracting students of diverse colors and with diverse views about the race issue."[85] Thus, students who define themselves as "*negros*" study side by side with students who define themselves as "Flicts," after the hero of a children's book written by the humorist Ziraldo. (The word "Flicts" in this context indicates both all colors and none.) Finally, Maggie and her team have found that the vast majority of students and teachers, excepting part of the leadership of the movement, are not in favor of quotas for black university applicants but rather show a strong commitment to individualism as defined by Reis. Although they work together in study groups and although the entire movement is based on generous solidarity, the belief that students ultimately enter the university on the basis of their own hard work and dedication is dominant.

Yet the Catholic University's involvement with the MPVNC has not gone without criticism among a certain sector of the student population. In November of 1997, a student newspaper, significantly called *The Individual* (*O Indivíduo*), published an article entitled "The Black Night of Consciousness." In this article, Pedro Sette Câmara launched a violent critique of the "Week of Black Consciousness" that took place to commemorate the black hero Zumbi, the leader of the Quilombo of Palmares, the best-known maroon community localized in Alagoas in the seventeenth century. He argued that it was obviously inspired by "the North American notion of political correctness" and was a clear example of cultural colonialism, and ventured the opinion that such events are themselves racist. "Nobody would like it if we had the week of white consciousness," he wrote. "Whenever you exalt a race it is racism."[86]

The following year, during elections for the students' union, one faction, "PUC Diversity," accused another, "PUC 2000," of being "prejudiced" and "segregationist." A PUC Diversity literature student was quoted as saying: "Three years ago, the entry of students from the pre-university course for blacks and the needy (*negros e carentes*) ended up changing the social landscape of the PUC, a school which is traditionally seen as elite.... This group which won the elections is prejudiced and it discriminates and segregates. Diversity of social classes is healthy." Another member of PUC Diversity claimed that one of their members who lives in the North Zone of Rio and studies on a scholarship was told that he should not be studying at the PUC because he was poor, while yet another complained that PUC 2000 had accused PUC Diversity of providing a base for "poor people, blacks and pot smokers." Walter de Sá Cavalcante, a law student and member of PUC 2000, countered the accusation: "The Students' Union is mixed [*mesclado*]. The difference is that [PUC Diversity] cannot understand that the world has changed and that the students' movement must modernize. We are doers, while they still believe in the armed struggle." He went on to describe PUC Diversity as "the PT crowd" in an alliance with "neo-hippies."[87]

This social drama reveals yet again the contradictory premises upon which "racial politics" are built in Brazil. As Monica Grin, who is conducting research on events at the PUC, has noted, all of the actors prefer to talk about social class rather than race.[88] When they do get around to the issue of "race," each side accuses the other of being segregationist, as if neither were prepared to forgo the "mixture" that PUC 2000 identifies with Brazilian culture. Ironically, the accusation of "cultural colonialism" and "the North American notion of political correctness," normally made by the Left against the "neo-liberals," moves in the opposite direction in the debate arising from the celebration of black identity at the Catholic University. Once again, the "American model" is invoked as Brazil's nemesis.

This drama brings me back to the questions I raised earlier. PUC 2000 could be interpreted as paradoxically using American "political correctness" as an effective accusation designed to repress the positive "subversion" of PUC Diversity. But who decides what is positively subversive and what is not? Are Bourdieu and Wacquant having their cake and eating it too? Are they characterizing "political correctness" as an accusation made by conservatives against "subversives" in some situations and as the ethnocentric imposition of alien ideas in others? In the drama of the PUC, I find it difficult to understand the attitude of the rector and those who supported him (only 40 percent of the student body, according to Grin) in judging the opinions of the authors of the essay published in *The Individual* sufficiently abhorrent to discount the right to freedom of expression, which is guaranteed by the Constitution. I find it especially difficult to understand given the fact that the PUC was the target of massive repression, above all of the freedom of expression, during the years of the military regime.[89] But then, in all fairness, the debate over the "racial" issue, whether in France, Brazil, or the United States, is, as I hope I have shown, founded on doubt and contradiction, above all because the issues at stake are so intimately intermingled with questions of national and personal identity and projects. I find it difficult not to side with those who resent attempts to interpret the "Brazilian model" or "Brazilian sociological intelligence" as fundamentally erroneous. To do otherwise would be to renege on the tenets of my discipline and succumb to pressures to capitulate to the inevitability of the "racialization" of the world. And yet, taking such a position, contrary to the dominant views of so many of my friends and colleagues, including those in the thick of the antiracist struggle in Brazil, is painful, bringing, as it does, accusations of "neo-Freyreanism," representing white privilege or even of a lack of concern for racism and "racial" inequality. For however particular and specific the "American model" may be, it has the political and epistemological advantage of simplicity and consistency. As such, the "Brazilian model," with all its ambiguity and internal contradiction, is far more difficult to grasp intellectually, let alone as a base for political action.

CONCLUSION

The events I have described persuade me that the idea of affirmative action has gone to the heart of the most potent of Brazilian nationalisms. The hybrid ideas and institutions that have begun to emerge over the issue of affirmative action, combining concerns for the inequality between people of different colors and between people of different social classes, are testimony to the potency of the desire to maintain primacy of the individual over his or her "nature," as it were; of what Brazilians call *jeitinho* over rigorous classificatory discipline.[90]

Even so, although tempers run high between the backers of diversity and the stalwarts of individualism, as is the case between PUC Diversity and PUC 2000, the debate is at least out in the open, probably far more so than in those parts of the world that have emerged from a tradition of legal racial segregation and where the mere suggestion of "integration" raises many eyebrows. Furthermore, the appropriation of "affirmative action" in the concrete case of the MPVNC is a good example of the way "foreign" ideas are interpreted in local terms, acquiring in the process new meanings and considerable symbolic and practical efficacy. As a result, more poorer and darker people are entering Brazilian universities, but not at the expense of the values of democracy, racial or otherwise. To end on a positive note, and to return to the specificity of Brazil, I suggest that the situation at present is one that allows for multiple forms of expression and myriad forms of social action as the old ideal of racial democracy, which is still shared by most Brazilians of all colors, meets increasingly cogent demands for equity and the elimination of prejudice and discrimination.

ACKNOWLEDGMENTS

I would like to thank the other authors in this issue of *Dædalus* for their important suggestions. I would also like to thank Yvonne Maggie, Olívia Cunha, Monica Grin, and the researchers of the Núcleo da Cor of the Institute for commenting on earlier versions of the paper. To Marcos Chor Maio of the Oswaldo Cruz Foundation, I owe special thanks for correcting errors of fact and for guiding me through a recent bibliography. Needless to say, I hold none of them responsible for the opinions expressed in this essay.

ENDNOTES

[1] Robert Schwarz, *Ao vencedor as batatas: forma literária e processo social nos inícios do romance brasileiro* (São Paulo: Livraria Duas Cidades, 1971).

[2] "le pouvoir d'universaliser les particularismes liés à une tradition historique singulière en les faisant méconaître comme tels." Pierre Bourdieu and Loïc Wacquant, "Les Ruses de la Raison Impérialiste," *Actes de la Recherche en Sciences Sociale* 121–122 (1998): 109.

[3] Ibid., 111.

[4] Ibid., 112.

[5] Ibid., 113. In particular, they cite my own university, where, they claim, the Rockefeller Foundation, which funded a project on race and ethnicity, made it a condition of funding that the research team be recruited on the basis of the American criteria of affirmative action. And, as it so happens, the example they cite runs counter to their own argument, since the Rockefeller Foundation did not in fact impose any conditions for funding the race and ethnicity program at the Federal University of Rio de Janeiro, which brought to our university scholars from all over the world (including Loïc Wacquant) with

the express purpose of putting the "American model" in cross-cultural perspective. For us, and for many others, a blind "imposition" of the "American model" would bring about consequences far more pernicious than "symbolic violence." We knew, from our understanding of the effects of imperialism and colonialism *tout court*, that impositions of this type that run counter to local understandings might be at best inefficacious and at worst painful. In this case, then, at least one Brazilian university was funded by a great American foundation to put the American experience in its due place, as just one historically specific way of construing race, institutionalizing racism, and then combating it.

[6]Marshall Sahlins, *How "Natives" Think: About Captain Cook, for example* (Chicago and London: The University of Chicago Press, 1995).

[7]This is not to deny, of course, the various attempts to bring race issues to public policy, in particular the encouragement of "white" immigration (see G. Seyferth, "A assimilação dos imigrantes como questão nacional," *Mana—Estudos de Antropologia Social* 3 [1997]) and the invocation of race as a primary concern of criminal investigation (see Olívia Gomes da Cunha, "Intenção e Gesto: Política de identificação e repressão à vadiagem no Rio," doctoral thesis, Museu Nacional, Universidade Federal do Rio de Janeiro, 1998).

[8]Arthur de Gobineau, *Essai sur l'inégalité des races humains* (Pairs: Libraire de Paris, 1855).

[9]Gobineau, quoted in Georges Raeders, *O Inimigo Cordial do Brasil: O Conde de Gobineau no Brasil* (São Paulo: Paz e Terra, 1988), 241.

[10]Ibid., 242.

[11]Lilia Moritz Schwarcz, *O Espetáculo das Raças* (São Paulo: Companhia das Letras, 1993); Thomas Skidmore, *Black into White: Race and Nationality in Brazilian Thought* (Durham: Duke University Press, 1993 [1974]).

[12]Raymundo Nina Rodrigues, *As Raças Humanas e a Responsabilidade Penal no Brasil* (Rio de Janeiro: Livraria Progresso Editora, 1957 [1894]).

[13]Oliveira Viana, *Raça e Assimilação* (São Paulo: Editora Nacional, 1934).

[14]Giralda Seyferth, "A antropologia e a teoria do branqueamento da raça no Brasil: a tese de João Batista de Lacerda," *Revista do Museu Paulista* (1985): 81–98.

[15]Gilberto Freyre, *Casa Grande e Senzala* (Rio de Janeiro: Maia & Schmidt, 1933), 17–18. Marcos Chor Maio has observed that Freyre was also indebted to the Brazilian anthropologist Roquette Pinto, who in the First Brazilian Eugenics Congress argued that "the number of somatically deficient individuals in some regions of the country is quite marked. This, however, is not due to any racial factor but rather pathological causes which have nothing to do with anthropology. It is a question of educational and sanitary policy." Marcos Chor Maio, "'Estoque semita': a presença dos judeus em *Casa-Grande & Senzala*," *Luso-Brazilian Review* 36 (1999): 95–110.

[16]Freyre, *Casa Grande e Senzala*, 168.

114   Peter Fry

[17]Ibid.

[18]Ibid., 171.

[19]Franz Boas, *Anthropology and Modern Life* (New York: Dover Publications, Inc., 1986), 65. I am grateful to Yvonne Maggie for this reference.

[20]Célia Azevedo, "O abolicionismo transatlântico e a memória do paraíso racial," *Estudos Afro-Asiáticos* 30 (1996): 152.

[21]Rodrigues, *As Raças Humanas e a Responsabilidade Penal no Brasil*, 149–150.

[22]Ricardo Benzaquen de Araújo, *Guerra e Paz: Casa-Grande & Senzala e a Obra de Gilberto Freyre nos anos 30* (Rio de Janeiro: Editora 34, 1994).

[23]I owe this interpretation to Olívia Gomes da Cunha, who, on the basis of her work in the Office of Criminal Identification in Rio de Janeiro, argues that individuals were identified and classified according to the singular combination of "racial" characteristics that their measured bodies betrayed. Olívia Gomes da Cunha,"Intenção e Gesto: Política de Identificação e Repressão à Vadiagem no Rio de Janeiro," postgraduate program in social anthropology, doctoral thesis, Museu Nacional, Universidade Federal do Rio de Janeiro, 1998.

[24]Michael George Hanchard, *Orpheus and Power: The Movimento Negro of Rio de Janeiro and São Paulo, Brazil, 1945–1988* (Princeton: Princeton University Press, 1994).

[25]Leo Spitzer, *Lives in Between: Assimilation and Marginality in Austria, Brasil, West Africa, 1780–1945* (Cambridge: Cambridge University Press, 1989); Stefan Zweig, *Brasil, País do Futuro* (Rio de Janeiro: Civilização Brasileira, 1960).

[26]Verena Stolcke, "Brasil: Uma nação vista através da vidraça da 'raça,'" *Revista de Cultura Brasileña* 1 (1997): 207–222.

[27]Marcos Chor Maio, "O Brasil no concerto das nações: a luta contra o racismo nos primórdios da Unesco," *História, Ciências, Saúde* V (1998): 375–413.

[28]Verena Stolcke, "A Nation Between Races and Class: A Transatlantic Perspective," unpublished paper presented to the Race and Ethnicity Program, Institute of Philosophy and Social Sciences, Universidade Federal do Rio de Janeiro, 1996, 3.

[29]Marcos Chor Maio, "A história do Projeto Unesco: estudos raciais e ciências sociais no Brasil," Universidade de Rio de Janeiro Institute for Research (IUPERJ), 1997.

[30]Abdias do Nascimento, ed., *O Negro Revoltado* (Rio de Janeiro: Nova Fronteira, 1982); A. Guerreiro Ramos, "A Unesco e as relações de raça," in ibid.

[31]Florestan Fernandes, *A Integração do negro na Sociedade de Classes*, vol. 1/2, ensaios 34 (São Paulo: Editora Ática, 1978).

[32]Carlos A. Hasenbalg, *Discriminação e Desigualdades Raciais no Brasil* (Rio de Janeiro: Graal, 1979).

[33]Luis de Aguiar Costa Pinto, *O negro no Rio de Janeiro: relações de raça numa sociedade em mudança* (São Paulo: Companhia Editora Nacional, 1953).

[34]Paulo Sérgio Pinheiro, *Escritos Indignados* (São Paulo: Brasiliense, 1984).

[35]Moema Teixeira, "Raça e Crime: Orientação para uma Leitura Crítica do Censo Penitenciário do Rio de Janeiro," *Cadernos do ICHF* (Universidade Federal Fluminense) 64 (1994): 1–15.

[36]Sérgio Adorno, "Discriminação Racial e Justiça Criminal em São Paulo," *Novos Estudos CEBRAP* (1995): 59.

[37]Carlos Antonio Costa Ribeiro, *Cor e Criminalidade: Estudo e Análise da justiça no Rio de Janeiro (1900–1930)* (Rio de Janeiro: Editora UFRJ, 1995), 72.

[38]Cunha, "Intenção e Gesto."

[39]Adriano Maurício, "Medo de Assalto: a democraci racial em questão no ônibus público na cidade do Rio de Janeiro," masters thesis, Universidade Federal do Rio de Janeiro, 1998.

[40]Michael Lambert, "From Citizenship to Négritude: 'Making a Difference' in an Elite of Colonized Francophone West Africa," *Comparative Studies in Society and History* 35 (1993).

[41]Cleusa Turra and Gustavo Venturi, eds., *Racismo Cordial: A Mais completa análise sobre o preconceito de cor no Brasil* (São Paulo: Editora Ática, 1995).

[42]CPDOC-FGV/ISER, *Lei Justiça e Cidadania* (Rio de Janeiro: CPDOC-FGV/ISER, 1997).

[43]"'We Brazilians,' said a white person, 'have a prejudice against having prejudice.'" Roger Bastide and Florestan Fernandes, *Brancos e Negros em São Paulo*, 3d ed. (São Paulo: Anhembi, 1971), 148.

[44]Hanchard, *Orpheus and Power.*

[45]Carl Degler, *Neither Black nor White: Slavery and Race Relations in Brazil and the United States* (Madison: University of Wisconsin Press, 1986).

[46]Talcott Parsons, "The Problem of Polarization on the Axis of Color," in *Color and Race*, ed. John Hope Franklin (Boston: Beacon Press, 1969), 352–353.

[47]Hanchard, *Orpheus and Power*, 182–183.

[48]Angela Gilliam, "From Roxbury to Rio—and Back in a Hurry," in *African-American Reflections on Brazil's Racial Paradise*, ed. David J. Hellwig (Philadelphia: Temple University Press, 1992), 180.

[49]Oracy Nogueira, "Preconceito Racial de Marca e Preconceito Racial de Origem," in *Tanto Preto quanto Branco: Estudos de Relações Raciais* (São Paulo: T. A. Queiroz, 1985), 67–94.

[50]Jamari França, "Um modelo que exclui a maioria negra," *Jornal do Brasil* (1998): 4.

[51]I have analyzed this elsewhere. See Peter Fry, "O que a Cinderela Negra tem a Dizer sobre a 'Política Racial' no Brasil," *Revista USP* 28 (1995): 122–135; Peter Fry, "Why Brazil is Different," *Times Literary Supplement*, 1995, 6–7.

116   Peter Fry

[52]Yvonne Maggie has drawn attention to Florestan Fernandes's usage of a dichotomous taxonomy in consonance with his activist informants. Yvonne Maggie, "A Ilusão do Concreto: análise do sistema de classificação racial no Brasil," Professor Titular, Universidade Federal do Rio de Janeiro, 1991.

[53]Jessé Souza, "Multiculturalismo, Racismo e Democracia: por que comparar Brasil e Estados Unidos," in *Multiculturalismo e Rascismo: uma comparação Brasil–Estados Unidos*, ed. Alayde Sant'Anna and Jessé Souza (Brasília: Paralelo 15, 1997), 32; Souza, "Valores e Estratificação Social no Distrito Federal," in *Brasília: A Construção do Cotidiano*, ed. Brasilmar Nunes (Brasília: Paralelo 15, 1997), 141.

[54]Marisa Peirano, *Uma Antropologia no Plural: Três Experiências Contemporâneas* (Brasília, DF: Editora UnB, 1991).

[55]Peter Eccles, "Culpados até a prova em contrário: os negros, a lei e os direitos humanos no Brasil," *Estudos Afro-Asiáticos* (1991): 146.

[56]The law is so harsh that the police are reluctant to prosecute under it. Antonio Sérgio Guimarães shows that of 275 complaints of racial crimes brought to the São Paulo Police Station between 1993 and 1997, only 58, or 21.1 percent, were classified under the Caó Law. The majority were dealt with under the 'laws against personal offenses. Antonio Sérgio Guimarães, *Preconceito e discriminação. Queixas de ofenses e tratamento desigual dos negros no Brasil* (Salvador: Novos Toques, 1998).

[57]Article 68 of the 1988 Constitution states: "Definitive property rights of the descendants of maroon communities (*quilombos*) who continue to occupy their lands are recognized and the State is obliged to issue the respective titles."

[58]Yvonne Maggie drew my attention to this significant shift of emphasis, having herself observed the notable emphasis on culture and identity during the events surrounding the 1988 centenary of the abolition of slavery in Brazil. She observed that the vast majority of events were of a cultural nature, while few addressed the issues of inequality. Yvonne Maggie, "Cor, hierarquia e sistema de classificação: a diferença fora do lugar," *Estudos Históricos* (1994): 149–160.

[59]Fernando Henrique Cardoso and Octávio Ianni, *Côr e Mobilidade Social em Florianópolis: Aspectos das Relações Entre Negros e Brancos Numa Comunidade do Brasil Meridional* (São Paulo: Brasiliana, 1960).

[60]My emphasis.

[61]Fábio Wanderley Reis, "Mito e valor da democracia racial," in *Multiculturalismo e Racismo*, ed. Sant'Anna and Souza, 222.

[62]Ibid., 224.

[63]Roberto da Matta, "Notas sobre o Racismo à Brasileira," in ibid., 71.

[64]Ibid., 74.

[65]Antonio Sérgio Guimarães, "A Desigualdade que anula a desigualdade, notas sobre a ação afirmativa no Brasil," in ibid., 233.

[66]Ibid., 237.

[67]Ibid., 241.

[68]Ibid.

[69]Antonio Sérgio Guimarães, "Políticas Públicas para a ascenção dos negros no Brasil: argumentando pela ação afirmativa," *Afro-Ásia* 18 (1997): 179; Guimarães, *Racismo e Anti-Racismo no Brasil* (São Paulo: Editora 34, 1999).

[70]John Burdick has argued that one of the reasons the Brazilian black movement has remained so small is its insistence on imposing a dichotomous taxonomy, which is repelled by many ordinary Brazilians of all colors. John Burdick, *Blessed Anastacia: Women, Race and Popular Christianity in Brazil* (New York and London: Routledge, 1998).

[71]Hédio Silva, Jr., *Anti-Racismo: Coletânea de Leis Brasileiras (Federais, Estaduais, Municipais)* (São Paulo: Editora Oliveira Mendes, 1988).

[72]Sérgio Adorno's research cited above was conducted in conjunction with Geledês.

[73]Olívia Cunha and Marcia Silva drew my attention to the "positive" aspects of the failure of the judicial system to bring cases of racism to court.

[74]Joaze Bernadino, in a recent master's thesis, has argued cogently that the black movement's crusade in favor of affirmative action is in effect part of a wider strategy to develop a black identity in Brazil, substituting the complex taxonomy of colors with a binary one as in the United States. Joaze Bernadino, "Ação Afirmativa no Brasil: A Construção de Uma Identidade Negra?" Mestrado, Universidade de Brasília, 1999.

[75]Burdick, *Blessed Anastacia.*

[76]Peter Fry, "Feijoada e Soul Food: Notas sobre a Manipulação de Símbolos Étnicos e Nacionais," in *Para Inglês Ver: Identidade e Cultura na Sociedade Brasileira* (Rio de Janeiro: Zahar Editores, 1982), 47–53.

[77]Carlos Silva, "Da Terra das Primaveras à Ilha do Amor: Reggae, Lazer e Identidade em São Luís do Maranhão," Mestrado, Universidade Estadual de Campinas, 1992.

[78]Livio Sansone and Jocelio Telesdos Santos, *Ritmos em Trânsito: Sócio-Antropologia da Música Baiana* (Salvador: Dynamis Editorial/Programa Cor da Bahia/Projeto S.A.M.B.A., 1998).

[79]Bernadino, "Ação Afirmativa no Brasil."

[80]Burdick, *Blessed Anastacia*; Caetana Damasceno, "Cantando Para Subir: Orixá no Altar, Santo no PEJI," Mestrado, Museu Nacional, Universidade Federal do Rio de Janeiro, 1990.

[81]Olívia Gomes da Cunha, "Black Movements and the 'Politics of Identity' in Brazil," in *Culture of Politics/Politics of Culture: Re-visioning Latin American Social Movements*, ed. Sonia E. Alvarez, Evelina Dagnino, and Arturo Escobar (Boulder: Westview Press, 1998).

[82]Peter Fry, "Color and the Rule of Law in Brazil," in *The (Un)Rule of Law and the Underprivileged in Latin America,* ed. Juan E. Mendez, Guillermo

O'Donnell, and Paulo Sérgio Pinheiro (Notre Dame: University of Notre Dame Press, 1999).

[83]José Renato Perpétuo Ponte and Denise Ferreira da Silva, personal communication. See also Denise Ferreira da Silva, "Zumbi & Simpson, Farrakan & Pelé: as encruzilhadas do discurso racial," *Estuds Afro-Asiáticos* 33 (1999): 87–98.

[84]In a recent article in the Rio de Janeiro newspaper *O Globo*, the Archbishop of Rio de Janeiro, Cardinal Eugênio Sales, published an article entitled "Miscegenation" in which he extols the virtue of "mixture" while deploring the celebration of "racial" or "ethnic" identities. Eugênio de Araujo Sales, "O papel da miscegenação," *O Globo*, 1998, 7. This can only be a thinly veiled attack on the Black Pastoral, which he has never looked upon with favor. Damasceno, "Cantando Para Subir."

[85]Yvonne Maggie, "O Pré-Vestibular para Negros e Carentes: Universalismo, particularismo e a busca de novos caminhos para diminuir a exclusão e a desigualdade," *V Congresso Luso-Afro-Brasileiro, Maputo, Moçambique, 1998*.

[86]Pedro Sette Câmara, "The Black Night of Consciousness," *O Indivíduo*, November 1997.

[87]The "PT" is the Partido dos Trabalhadores (Worker's Party), which is to the left of the Brazilian party spectrum and enjoys much support among university students.

[88]Monica Grin, "Descompassos & Dilemas Morais: Percepções sobre a Questão Racial no Brasil," *Seminário Fronteiras e Interseções, Universidade Estadual de Campinas, 1998*.

[89]In an article in *O Globo*, journalist Hélio Gáspari argued along similar lines. Hélio Gáspari, "Dois abacaxis para a PUC," *O Globo*, Caderno Opinião, Quarta feira, 26 November 1997, 7.

[90]The concept of *jeitinho* refers to the ways in which rules can (and even should) be bent when they interfere with an individual's self-interest. Although often represented as a rather charming aspect of Brazilian irreverence, it is also at the root of inequality before the law and social inequality in general. Evidently the economically and politically powerful have greater recourse to *jeitinho* than the weak.

Culture as a Resource: Four Cases of Self-managed Indigenous Craft Production in Latin America*

Lynn Stephen
Northeastern University

I. Introduction

The production of indigenous crafts in Latin America for tourist and export markets depends on the commoditization of indigenous culture. While in many cases craft production for export has exacerbated increasing economic and political marginalization of the producers,[1] in some instances craft production has resulted in self-managed economic development that strengthens local cultural institutions. Four such cases include the Otaveleños of Ecuador, the Nahua and the Zapotec of Mexico, and the Kuna of Panama. In these cases, self-management and successful entrepreneurship are linked to an internal reinforcement of local cultural identity. While these cases of commercialized craft production also reflect increasing socioeconomic differentiation within producing communities indicative of incipient class formation, emerging class conflict in the relations of production is often mediated and redirected through kin-based relations of social reproduction built into local cultural institutions. The playing out of these relations of social reproduction can provide for a cohesive community identity when posed in relation to larger society and outside government and business agents seeking to gain control of indigenous craft production.

Outside appropriation of indigenous culture, whether for political or economic purposes, results in the "packaging" of indigenous identity, the content of which is largely determined by dominant external institutions and actors. Nevertheless, the creation of a marketable indigenous identity is not without consequences for the internal life of a community. In communities with a history of independent craft production for exchange (for sale) that maintain noncapitalist economic and social institutions (such as reciprocal labor exchanges and extended kin networks) as well as a relatively high level of ritual activity, the commoditization of an externally defined indigenous identity can result in a reinforcement of community institutions. Such cases of craft production are important examples for development planners seeking to foster productive projects that are consistent with a self-defined indigenous identity and economic self-management.

Four cases of indigenous communities with successful craft-production strategies are examined here. These cases are characterized by the fact that producers have maintained a high degree of control over marketing and distribution and have used a significant part of the income to reinvest in community institutions. The discussion begins with an outline of the conditions favoring self-management and integration of craft production with local cultural institutions. Specific communities and/or cooperatives are examined, though their specifics are not necessarily generalizable to all members of a particular ethnic group. This is followed by a brief discussion of the concept of ethnic identity and what these cases suggest about the way ethnic identity is formulated and maintained. Each case will then be discussed in terms of its specific economic history and its institutions of social reproduction, focusing on how these factors can contribute to the use of culture as a resource in economic production.

An examination of the common circumstances surrounding each of these successful artisan endeavors reveals both economic factors and continued maintenance of local institutions of social reproduction. Common economic circumstances include: (*a*) maintenance of a sufficient land base through the twentieth century; (*b*) production for exchange of craft products or agricultural production in the colonial period and into the twentieth century; and (*c*) commercial experience in local and regional market systems.

Introduction of the common factors of social reproduction requires a bit of preliminary discussion. Initial literature on the concepts of production and reproduction offered a definition of social reproduction that focused on replacement and maintenance of the labor force as well as biological reproduction of the family.[2] In reality, social reproduction refers not only to reproduction of the labor force but also to the maintenance and replication of institutions and events that define individuals as social actors, particularly those institutions that contribute to the formation of local ethnic identity.[3] Here the factors of social reproduction common to each of these cases include: (*a*) maintenance of reciprocal labor and goods exchanges; (*b*) reinvestment of labor and resources in community ritual and political institutions; and (*c*) integration of craft production with agricultural activities, other subsistence activities, and the ceremonial cycle.

II. Concepts of Ethnic Identity and the Commoditization of Culture

Anthropologists have yet to agree on a concise definition of ethnicity. While some have tried to bind ethnic groups to specific objective criteria such as language and territory, others have opted for a more dynamic definition that focuses on the interaction between ethnic groups, following F. Barth's discussion on the establishment of ethnic boundaries.[4] Recent studies of ethnicity have focused on self-identification, ethnic consciousness, and solidarity, drawing attention to the local construction of ethnic identity and social reproduction.[5]

This perspective draws us into the social and historical constitution of local ethnic identity and forces us to look at the conditions under which ethnic solidarity emerges. Ethnic solidarity may be a survival mechanism for legitimizing a group in the political arena, or internally constructed solidarity may be a way of redefining group identity from the inside in reaction to an outside appropriation of culture.

One of the key questions in contemporary anthropological studies of ethnicity concerns "the oppositional process" that E. Spicer refers to as the presence of a persistent ethnic identity.[6] Spicer and others maintain that persistent ethnic identities are the result of efforts to incorporate or assimilate groups into the larger whole, whether culturally, economically, socially, or religiously.[7] They argue that resistance to incorporation has varied from silence to violence, but that without the antagonism created by resistance to incorporation persistent identity systems would fail to develop.[8] This oppositional process produces intense collective consciousness and a high degree of internal solidarity. Spicer has used this analysis to explain the persistent ethnic identity of the Maya, Yaqui, and Navajo groups in Mexico and the U.S. southwest.

Other recent analyses of ethnic identity also focus on ethnicity as an oppositional process but seek to locate the conflict in both class and ethnic arenas, considering that the two systems of stratification are linked together, rather than declaring one subordinate to the other.[9] Using the comparative case of Kuna and Guaymi workers on a banana plantation, P. Bourgois is able to show how the two groups use their different political, economic, and institutional resources to utilize ethnicity as a tool for upward mobility. He emphasizes not only the position of each group in the relations of production but also the ideological relationship that each group has with wider society. He demonstrates how the Kuna manipulate a mestizo cultural ideology that promotes the Kuna as better, more desirable workers than the Guaymi. In the process, however, the Kuna rework this ideology from within. I will address this below in relation to a modification of Spicer's concept of the oppositional process involved in the construction of ethnic identities.

Taking a more political perspective, G. Sider examines the conditions that foster ethnic solidarity in the face of national racial and cultural oppression, distinguishing between what he calls cultural nationalism and political nationalism.[10] Drawing on the example of the Lumbee in the United States, Sider defines political nationalism as a call for autonomy and fundamental economic and political changes within a group, particularly with regard to material inequalities. Cultural nationalism is based on symbolic issues that internally colonized groups use to distinguish themselves from dominant ethnic groups that are the prime benefactors of state policy.[11] What is useful about Sider's formulation is his description of how a people who have been historically marginalized can simultaneously develop a collective identity based on their place outside of the state and a class structure dependent upon, but separate from, the class structure of the dominant state.[12]

In Latin America, dominant cultural attitudes about ethnicity, particularly "Indian" ethnicity, have been changing since the 1960s. Mexico's ruling political party sought to build a nationalist consciousness to support its continued domination of the political system. "Indian identity" became a part of a national identity, an identity to which all Mexicans can lay claim. Promoting "Indianness" as part of the Mexican national identity was a political strategy for incorporating indigenous communities into the political system and also provided a nationalist racial distinction to separate Mexico from its dominant northern neighbor. While general "Indianness" became acceptable, chic, and even desired in some social circles in urban capitals,[13] local ethnic identity was encouraged by the Mexican government as a marketing strategy for tourism. In many Latin countries indigenous ethnic groups have been encouraged to maintain and reproduce certain outwardly picturesque characteristics, in particular dress, ritual, and craft production, which make them identifiable as Indian to tourists.[14] The Guatemalan government currently has a contradictory policy. While the military discourages the use of dress as a form of ethnic distinction, the national tourist office continues to promote the indigenous costumes of Guatemala as a drawing card for tourists interested in visiting "real Indian villages."

Such government-defined "ethnic identity" stands in sharp contrast to the self-defined ethnic identity put forward by ethnic federations such as the Shuar of Ecuador and the Regional Indian Council of the Cauca (CRIC) in the southern Andean region of Colombia.[15] Ethnic federations that have become political groups lobbying national governments on land issues have not had their ethnic identity embraced and encouraged. Both the CRIC of Colombia and the Federación de Centros Shuar have had their leaders harassed and their property destroyed.[16]

The basic distinction between a self-chosen ethnic identity and that of an imposed "Indian" identity is discussed by R. C. Smith in his analysis of ethnic federations, peasant unions, and Indianist movements in the Andean republics. While speaking largely of foreign colonial powers, his characterization of Indian identity as a "political and racial label imposed on the indigenous population irrespective of tribal identity marking a hierarchical relationship" is a definition that could also be applied to outside appropriation and definition of specific ethnic identities.[17] State and private business marketing of "Indian culture," whether it is a specific culture or not, invokes the same relationship as the colonial designation of "indio" as an indication of the subordinate position of indigenous peoples.[18]

The phenomenon of both state and commercial appropriation of ethnic identity for the purposes of tourism and craft production for export makes it necessary to amend slightly Spicer's model of opposition and also consider E. Sapir's notion of genuine and spurious culture.[19] In a seminal essay, Sapir distinguishes between (1) the creation of an oppositional, internally generated culture that may exist within the confines of larger oppressive social relations and (2) an external or spurious culture that does not "build itself out of the central interests and desires of its bearers."[20] As pointed out by S. Diamond, genuine culture includes the creation of new cultural forms that combine the structure and content of older forms with new social and political reality.[21]

In the four cases considered here, local indigenous identity has been maintained and perhaps strengthened by indirect opposition to pressures of assimilation through the creation of a multidimensional ethnic identity. One dimension of that identity is produced for consumers of indigenous culture such as tourists, importers, and foreign visitors who purchase indigenous crafts; other dimensions are defined from within indigenous communities and are accessible only to those who are members of the community by virtue of their participation in networks and institutions that form the core of this identity.[22] Thus we might modify Spicer's model to accommodate situations of outside appropriation of ethnicity. Here the dynamic of opposition comes through a local redefinition of ethnicity as an alternative to the commoditized version of ethnic identity promoted by the state.

The four cases to be examined here provide important information about how the commoditization of a group's ethnicity can be used by that group to foster a successful cottage industry. What makes these cases unusual is that these communities have been able to direct their successful economic endeavors not only to promote individual gains but also to support community innovations and strengthen noncapitalist institutions, such as kin and ritual kin, *compadrazgo*, networks, reciprocal labor exchanges, and rituals. Strengthening local institutions and building ethnic solidarity bolsters not only community autonomy but also the persistence of institutions and networks that function with somewhat different principles than profit-oriented craft businesses.

III. Four Cases of Community-controlled Craft Production

Two and a half years of fieldwork in Teotitlán del Valle, Mexico, site of one of the most successful community-controlled craft production efforts in Mexico, demonstrated that production for export does not always result in a complete loss of autonomy for peasant communities. The Zapotec weavers of Teotitlán are active participants in shaping their own destiny through a strengthening of local ethnic identity rooted in household-level, kin-based economic production and ceremonial activity.[23] A preliminary review of the secondary literature reveals other Latin American examples that reflect conditions similar to those associated with Teotitlán del Valle. These include the *amate* bark painters of Ameytalteptec, Guererro, the Quechua weavers of Otavalo, and the Kuna *mola* makers in Panama. The Quechua weavers of Taquile in Lake Titicaca have also demonstrated an ability to maintain community control over a booming textile industry, but for lack of space they will not be discussed here.[24]

A. *Zapotec Weavers of Teotitlán de Valle, Oaxaca*

Teotitlán del Valle is the hub of four Zapotec communities that produce wool textiles for sale to the United States and Europe as well as to the Mexican elite. Since the 1960s, production and distribution networks have grown, making Teotitlán one of the most successful indigenous craft-producing communities in Mexico. Traditionally based on a subsistence economy with part-time weaving production as a source of supplementary income, weaving is now the primary source of income for a majority (90%) of the families in the community. Designs produced include traditional Zapotec motifs as well as Navajo designs and reproductions of modern artists such as Miró, Picasso, and Escher.

While there is not a long history of class distinctions based on differential access to capital and the means of production in the community, there are differences in income and in the positions people have in the relations of production that appear to be the basis of a more permanent class system based on occupational classes of merchants and weavers. In 1985, about 10% of the households in Teotitlán identified themselves as merchants and 80% as weavers, working either as independent laborers or as pieceworkers for merchants in the community. About 10% of the community of 5,000 continue to work as full-time farmers, supplementing their income with weaving. Merchants are so defined by their purchase of other people's labor, indirectly through the purchase of weavings.[25] Both merchants and weavers continue to farm part time, although about 50% of the community is now landless, with a greater proportion of the landless found among weaver households.

B. The Weavers of Otavalo, Ecuador

Located in the highlands of Ecuador, the *canton* (county) of Otavalo includes the mestizo town of Otavalo and 40,000 Quechua speakers scattered in over 75 communities.[26] Textile merchants from Otavalo travel as far as Argentina, Colombia, Panama, and Miami to sell wool ponchos, wall hangings, belts, and bags produced on treadle looms and backstrap looms. Like the weavers of Teotitlán del Valle, their work is known throughout the continental United States and is cited as an instance of a small-scale social and economic formation that can survive and even take advantage of an onerous succession of superimposed large-scale systems of domination.[27]

Like the Zapotec weavers of Oaxaca, Otavaleños continue to engage in farming as well as weaving. The household is the unit of production for both subsistence agriculture and weaving. While a significant number of Otavalan weavers continue to produce in family workshops, recent writers discuss the emergence of a group of indigenous merchants in the district capital of Otavalo who employ large numbers of indigenous Otavalans from outlying communities to work in medium- and large-scale commercial workshops.[28] Such workers may be evolving into a part-time weaving proletariat. Both L. Walters and G. Villavivencio mention the competition for the weaving market that has emerged between Otavalan Quechuas and local mestizos who have also begun to invest in large workshops. Both emphasize that the indigenous textile entrepreneurs maintain links to their communities of origin and continue their kinship and ceremonial kinship obligations, remaining strong defenders of Otavalan culture. They disagree, however, on the reasons for this cultural defense. The nature of their disagreement will be discussed below.

C. Nahuatl Amate Bark Painters of Guerrero, Mexico

In contrast to the consistency of the Zapotec and Otavalan weavers, the *amate* bark painters of Ameyaltepec, Guererro, have changed materials in their craft production for the tourist market. Engaged in pottery production for local consumption until the 1960s, the bark painters of Ameyaltepec took advantage of existing marketing networks to sell their pottery in initial tourist centers such as Acapulco and Taxco. Experimenting with various materials, they hit upon *amate* bark as a practical alternative to pottery for exhibiting their intricate designs. Because of better portability, *amate* bark paintings quickly became circulated for wider distribution, extending throughout Mexico and now for export to the United States.[29]

D. Kuna Mola Makers of San Blas, Panama

Current craft production among the Kuna involves the redefinition of the *mola* from clothing to art.[30] While not ancient, *molas* are defined as a traditional art form by the Kuna. They are believed to have come into their present form after the introduction of manufactured cloth, metal sewing needles, and scissors, perhaps as early as the 1860s.[31] A description of Kuna women's dress in 1816 mentions the use of cloth to cover the neck, head, and breasts.[32] *Molas* are either produced by women for their own wear or sold for export, rather than commercialized locally.[33] Most *molas* are sold directly by producers to tourists, through a cooperative network, or to Kuna and foreign middlemen who sell them abroad. Some *molas* are produced on a piecework basis as well, although this appears to be quite limited in scope.

The colorful *molas* sold to tourists either are a part of blouses that are no longer deemed suitable for wearing by Kuna women or are produced especially for a tourist market.[34] Large scale marketing of *molas* has made them one of the primary tourism symbols of Panama, now exported to many parts of the United States and Europe. *Mola* production now appears to be a major source of household income along with profits from coconut farming.[35]

IV. Ethnographic Data on Common Economic Circumstances

A. Maintaining a Community Land Base

In examining the historical trajectory of these cases of craft production, one of the most striking similarities is continued community control over significant amounts of land through most of the colonial period. In the Tlacolula valley of Oaxaca where Teotitlán del Valle is located, indigenous communities controlled large tracts of arable and grazing land with little competition from Spanish estates.[36]

Ethnohistorian C. Caillavet maintains that Otavalo, Ecuador, housed an overarching pre-Inca political unit that may have limited the impact of Inca rule in the area, resulting in less political atomization and land redistribution than in other areas.[37] During the colonial era, a significant number of Otavalo communities appear to have held status as "free" Indian communities, which retained ownership of their land, as opposed to "owned" Indians who had only use rights in return for their labor in an estate.[38] F. Salomon states that, like Oaxaca, Otavalo's *latifundia* (presence of large landed estates) appears "scarce and precarious when compared to those futher south in the Andes."[39] While *latifundia* existed in both Oaxaca, Mexico, and Otavalo, Ecuador, it was not the predominant model for farming. In the 1940s in Peguche, described by Elsie Clews Parsons, only a few families farmed *huasipangos,* small plots of hacienda land allotted in payment for heavy labor.[40] At the time of her fieldwork in 1940–41, Parsons reported that "economic independence is generally true of the Indians throughout the valley, who are more distinctively landowners than other mountain Indians in Ecuador."[41] Parsons as well as another ethnographer who worked in the Otavalo valley reported that the Indians had retained their old lands and were buying up local hacienda lands.[42] However, more recent ethnographic work suggests that land is in short supply in some Otavalo communities and landless peasants or those with pieces of land too small for a subsistence living are working in the larger weaving enterprises in the district capital.[43]

The Nahuatl *amate* bark painters described by C. Good Eshelman also appear to have maintained control over their communal land base through the colonial period. In the nineteenth century there were no ranches in the region and "apparently towns were able to plant the lands they wanted."[44] Good Eshelman speculates that the Nahua of Ameyaltepec did not suffer a loss of land like other indigenous groups did during the reign of Porfirio Díaz from 1876 to 1911.

According to Good Eshelman's current description of Ameyaltepec, every household has access to land for cultivation, either through communal lands or through *ejidal* lands given to the community through the agrarian reform.[45] Apparently the majority of land available falls into these two categories, which are characterized by a communal sense of ownership. While there is some private land in the community, even it is subject to collective control as manifested through the desires of traditional local authorities.[46] While Good Eshelman does not supply much historical information about land tenure throughout the colonial period, the current situation seems to indicate that the community successfully preserved a significant chunk of communal property. More important than the absolute quantity of land is the community's perception of all land as communal property.

The Kuna of Panama have made substantial changes in their land base and the basis of property ownership in this century. Unlike many Caribbean indigenous groups, the Kuna have historically retained political independence, which also resulted in the maintenance of communal lands.[47] Living for centuries under military threat from European colonials, roughly in the mid-nineteenth century the Kuna began the process of relocating their villages on the nearest inshore islands of the San Blas archipelago, completing the migration as late as the 1920s and 1930s.[48] Throughout the nineteenth century the Kuna traded with Spanish and English speakers and became increasingly specialized in coconut cropping.[49]

During the nineteenth century, the Kuna political economy underwent major changes. Over the course of the century mainland villages were abandoned for new villages in the inshore islands, private land tenure replaced communal property, women gave up their prominent role in agriculture, and a highly elaborate women's costume emerged including *molas*, trade-cloth skirts, headresses, and lavish gold jewelry.[50] Coconut cash cropping became the primary source of income. According to L. Hirschfeld, however, much of the sociopolitical organization remained unchanged. Thus like the Zapotec, Nahua, and Otavalo Quechua, the Kuna managed to retain significant amounts of land under their control through the colonial period. After the colonial period, land was alienated primarily as private property.

B. Production for Exchange and Commercial Experience
Another commonality in the economic history of the four cases examined here is craft or commercial production of another type from the colonial period into the current century. A history of production for exchange is tied to the ability of each of these groups to take advantage of existing marketing networks and skills when tourist and export markets opened up for their craft products. In each case, an established system of production for exchange also provides a basis for relations of production that are integrated with other community institutions such as reciprocal labor and reciprocal goods exchanges among the Nahua, Quechua, and Zapotec and large matrilocal households among the Kuna. Because of the continued importance of reciprocal labor exchange, particularly in the ceremonial realm, the large networks of kin and *compadres* (ritual kin) that can be mobilized to work in life cycle or saint's day celebrations may also be used in craft production and distribution. While this can be best documented in the case of the Zapotec weavers, it is also suggested in the literature for the Nahua, Otavaleños, and the Kuna. This will be discussed in detail in the next section. In these four cases, commercial production for a tourist market has not altered the basic unit of production or heavily disrupted its integration with other core cultural institutions.

Both the Zapotec and the Otavalo Quechua weavers have a long history of weaving production for exchange. That of the Otavaleños, however, has been commercially oriented for a longer period than that of the Zapotec. In both places the Spanish introduced stand-up treadle looms that changed earlier styles of weaving based on backstrap looms.[51] The woolen blanket industry that predated the production of rugs in Teotitlán and other Oaxaca Zapotec villages was well under way by the mid-seventeenth century. F. F. de Burgoa mentions the weaving of woolen blankets and serapes as an important economic activity in several communities.[52]

The Zapotec weavers of Teotitlán and other neighboring communities sold their wares in the cyclical market system of Oaxaca during the Colonial era.[53] The presence of Teotitlán merchants and traders is documented at the end of the 1800s with suggestions that merchants functioned throughout the colonial period in the southwest of Mexico.[54] Thus production of weaving for exchange throughout the regional market system was well-developed in Teotitlán and other weaving communities long before the establishment of a tourist market.

Otavalan weavers have a long history of producing for exchange, first through production for tribute payments and later as the producers of a large part of the colonial world's supply of textiles, particularly shirt cloth, woolen blankets, and ponchos. The primary form of production was the concentration of Indians in *obrajes* (primitive factories) that were under the auspices of the crown as part of former *encomiendas* (Spanish landgrants) or run as private enterprises.[55] While factory production and *mita* (conscripted labor) drained much of the Otavalo work force, there are reports that Otavalans were able to do independent business and adapt to domination of their resources by becoming suppliers to a supralocal open market.[56]

The *obraje* industry was dealt a death blow when newly independent Ecuador suddenly became an open market for imports from England. The flood of cheap factory-made cloth undercut the price of locally produced woolens.[57] The farming-weaving complex as reported by Salomon did not rise until the early 1900s when Quechua Otavaleños found that they could undersell machine-made luxury textiles by producing them on foot-powered treadle looms. While demand for Otavalo suit fabrics decreased after World War II, with the development of a national textile industry, textile production in Otavalo continued to undergo innovation.

According to Walters, during the 1950s the Ecuadorian government initiated programs to promote tourism and "among the attractions they promoted were the Otavaleños, their Saturday market and their ethnic textiles."[58] In conjunction with a series of projects sponsored by the government and development agencies, the Otavalo themselves began to expand their entrepreneurial activities. In 1951, a Centro Textil was established in Otavalo City, and later, in Quito, an institute with a manual arts section provided scholarships for Otavalans to come there to develop artistic designs and technical skills within the indigenous cultural tradition.[59] In the early 1960s, a weaving cooperative was established in Otavalo with the help of a Peace Corps volunteer.[60]

The market in the town of Otavalo has long been a center for distribution throughout the region and into other areas as far as Colombia and Peru.[61] Quechua-speaking Indians in the hamlets and villages surrounding the town have a history of funneling textile goods through this marketing system. More recently they have begun moving to Otavalo and opening their own stores as well as textile workshops. By 1980, there were at least 75 stores selling textiles in the town of Otavalo, most of them owned and operated by Quechua-speaking Indians.[62] Villavivencio reported in 1973 that there were 300–350 indigenous Otavalans who had stalls in the local Saturday textile market that serves primarily as a distribution point for both indigenous and mestizo entrepreneurs who sell outside of Otavalo and to tourists.[63] Thus historic experience with the Otavalo marketing system has translated into wider control of local and regional distribution networks by present-day Quechua Otavalans.

Since at least the eighteenth century the Kuna of Panama also have had a history of producing for exchange through production of ivory nut, chicle, and turtle shell.[64] They have engaged in commercial coconut cropping on a large scale since the mid-nineteenth century. J. Howe reports that at the turn of the century, Kuna in many parts of San Blas "planted every suitable uninhabited island with palms, along with great stretches of mainland shore."[65] The Kuna began selling their coconuts to both English and Spanish speakers from Panama, Colombia, and perhaps occasionally to Jamaica as well.[66] Later in the 1940s, they began to sell exclusively to traders from Colombia. Colombia continues to buy most of the coconuts the Kuna produce.[67] According to Howe, although the coconut trade has increasingly tied the Kuna to the outside world, the terms under which the recent coconut business developed have protected the Kuna's partial autonomy.[68]

Experience in the coconut trade in this century and the organization of a variety of public services and economic enterprises through voluntary societies, *sociedades,* has provided an important background for independence in the production of *molas* for export. R. Holloman distinguishes between two types of commercial enterprises in the Comarca of San Blas: the individual or family business and the *sociedad.* She notes that while the Kuna tend to label any type of voluntary or continuously operating community enterprise a *sociedad,* her definition refers to "nonkin groupings organized for commercial purposes or for the provision of services in the form of public utilities."[69] Holloman states that *sociedades* may be organizations of an entire community or one segment thereof. In describing the history of the *sociedades,* which probably began in the late 1920s, she states that they are an extension of the cooperative action and labor pooling that were a part of San Blas social organization at the time.[70] Membership in *sociedades* is voluntary and is acquired through a cash investment or labor contribution that entitles each member to a share of the enterprise's profits. *Sociedades* provide their members with an opportunity to participate in private enterprise without having to put up a large share of capital.[71] They also often provide people with a social group with which they may affiliate and which they can use as a source of political backing in local meetings.

The historical antecedents of *sociedades* include traditional organizational principles of cooperative labor as well as those of western market practices.[72] For example, coconut cooperatives (*sociedades*) operate on the basis of labor pooling. Each member is required to provide an equal share of labor, and failure to fulfill one's obligations results in a fine or, in cases of prolonged neglect, expulsion.[73] Absent cooperative members who may have temporarily migrated pay fines that often serve as a source of capital for cooperatives.

Membership in coconut and other types of cooperatives is inherited. Often cooperatives bring together people related by kinship and friendship. In such instances, this limits internal factionalism and facilitates consensus decision making.[74] The organizational structure of *sociedades* has also served to provide reciprocal labor for members in the construction of local dwellings and for farming, commercial enterprises, and savings associations.[75] As a setting to the establishment of the current *mola* cooperative, K. Tice states that *sociedades* and communal entrepreneurial activities expanded both men's and women's access to resources "while retaining egalitarian characteristics of Kuna social organization even as San Blas moved rapidly into the cash economy."[76]

With the commercialization of *molas* in the 1960s, sale of *molas* initially took place through already existing patterns of exchange. San Blas store owners and traders began to accept both *molas* and coconuts in exchange for merchandise.[77] Because selling *molas* became an easy way to raise cash, women of all ages sold their fine old *molas* and even felt pressured to sell blouses that they could still wear. According to Tice, at first many sold or traded their merchandise in stores and then, later, sold their *molas* for a higher price in Panama city. Kuna women felt a strong financial need to continue selling their *molas* but became unwilling to accept the low prices offered by intermediaries. In several Kuna communities the establishment of a *mola* cooperative proved to be a viable way for women to maintain control over production and receive a much higher price per *mola* than they would through an intermediary.

In describing the Kuna *mola* cooperative, N. Hatley states that the rationale of cooperation that provided the foundation for *sociedades* also worked in the formation of the *mola* cooperative. While the Kuna *mola* cooperative has its organizational roots in cooperative labor, it originated in a sewing school that was under the direction of a Peace Corps volunteer. Several Kuna women who worked with the volunteer were instrumental in starting the cooperative.[78] The cooperative was formally organized in 1968 and had its own store by 1969. After the Peace Corps was asked to leave Panama, the group of women who formed the cooperative struggled on. Awarded legal status in 1974, they had difficulty receiving credit or loans. In 1978, the group was awarded a grant from the Inter-American Foundation to purchase greater quantities of cloth in bulk and additional sewing machines. In 1981, three representatives from the *mola* cooperative attended the General Kuna Congress, the first women to do so officially.

According to Tice, by 1985 the *mola* cooperative had grown to include 17 local chapters and 1,496 members.[79] In addition to production and marketing, its chapters engaged in other activities, including bulk purchase and resale of staples and savings and loans programs. In the *mola* cooperative as in *sociedades*, each member of the co-op

owns an equal share of assets, has an equal right to profits, and shares
the risks. Each member is required to provide an equal share of labor
toward the production effort. Generally, the pattern of participation in
the *mola* cooperative was for one or two household producers (female)
to become official members. According to Tice, other members of the
household would then help them to sew *molas* for sale through the
cooperative.[80] Most of the chapters divided members into smaller
working groups that rotated use of the cooperative building. These
work groups could also be collectively involved in a wide range of
other income-producing activities, including selling rice, plantains, or
kerosene. In contrast with piecework producers who were operating
on a limited scale in one community, cooperative members were involved in all aspects of production.

When a cooperative member obtains cloth for a *mola* from one of
the cooperative's stores, the cost of the cloth is recorded. Women
produced *molas* for the cooperative, which sold in the cooperative
store for between $12 and $20. Each *mola* to be sold had an identification tag on it. Local chapters would stockpile a large quantity of *molas*
and then send them to Panama City. Cooperative members received
about 85%–90% of the selling price of the *molas,* a very high return
to primary producers. The remaining 10% included the cost of the
cloth, overhead costs, and personal savings that each member had
deducted from the amount returned from the sale of her *mola.* Overhead was used to pay the administrator of the co-op, for office supplies,
and for fuel for the cooperative's boat.[81]

While the cooperative does not dominate the marketing of all *mola*
products, its presence and the existence of many types of *sociedades*
and other entrepreneurial Kuna experiences such as commercial coconut production recently have been important in helping the Kuna to
gain control over the commoditization of *molas* as art objects. On
islands where the *mola* cooperative has a strong foothold, local intermediaries have gone out of business. On other islands, intermediaries
have begun to pay producers higher prices in order to compete with
the cooperative.[82] Tice concludes that equalizing access to the *mola*
market has been only partially realized by the cooperative, because in
some areas intermediaries, both Kuna and foreign, have continued to
control access to the market. Between Kuna intermediaries and the
cooperative, however, a major portion of the market is under Kuna
control. The most important function of the cooperative has been that
by representing a large number of Kuna women region-wide it has
promoted "not only women's interests, but also those concerning the
political, social, and economic autonomy of the Kuna people as an
indigenous group."[83]

Villages have also been an important locus of marketing control
through measures such as setting minimum prices for *molas,* coun-

tering the efforts of tourist guides who tell tourists that *molas* are available at bargain-basement prices. The standard price of *molas* has risen steadily since the 1970s not so much due to inflation but more to Kuna demand to get better returns for their labor. A similar situation has occurred among the Zapotec of Oaxaca, where weaving prices have steadily increased since the late 1970s, far outpacing inflated costs of primary materials. In both areas, indigenous producers have pushed the market to increase their returns as their products become better known and more widely desired.

While Good Eshelman's description of the Nahuatl *amate* bark painters does not contain much information about the colonial history of commercial exchange and local production, her discussion of the nineteenth-century salt-selling business conducted by the Nahuas of Ameyaltepec provides insight into the commercial tradition of the community. Stating that the sea salt business can be traced to the 1800s and probably colonially, Good Eshelman maintains that the Ameyaltepec Nahua have a long tradition of dealing with mestizos, having sold sea salt in many different rural markets and urban plazas until the bottom fell out of the business in the 1940s.[84] Sea salt was brought up on mules from the Costa Chica and sold along with local pottery. Like craft production, the sea salt business was conducted between agricultural seasons.

After a 20-year period of economic instability characterized by survival strategies combining wage labor, commercial agriculture, *bracería* (contract labor in the United States), and limited artisan and merchant activities, the Nahuas of Ameyaltepec entered the tourist market first with pottery and soon thereafter with the innovative *amate* bark paintings for which they are known. Their previous marketing experience was critical to their ability to move into the economic niche provided by the tourist market. At the same time, reciprocal goods and labor exchanges continued with the development of *amate* painting for tourists.[85]

V. Ethnographic Data on Maintenance of Institutions of Social Reproduction

A. *Reciprocal Labor and Reciprocal Goods Exchanges and Community Reinvestment in Ceremonial Activities and Public Works*

Perhaps the most tangible aspects of ethnic identity that are associated with the four cases of craft production discussed here are the maintenance of reciprocal labor and reciprocal goods exchanges and reinvestment in community ceremonial activities and public works. The maintenance and reproduction of community social and cultural institutions is the basis for ethnic identity in these communities.

What is most unique about these four cases is the degree to which traditional exchange, ritual, and political institutions have been maintained and enriched in conjunction with craft production for export. It is here where local reappropriation of a commercial indigenous identity is seen most clearly. The maintenance of institutions such as reciprocal goods and labor exchanges, local ritual cycles, and unique local political formations points to the continuity of social, economic, and political relations that are outside the direct influence of the state or private businesses—those who regulate the commercial version of indigenous ethnicity in craft-producing communities. Community maintenance of local ethnic institutions may be read as a statement of community resistance to outside control.

The Zapotecs of Teotitlán del Valle as well as other surrounding weaving communities have maintained a high level of participation in *guelaguetza* (which is defined below), reciprocal labor exchange on ceremonial occasions (also called *guelaguetza*) and for house construction, a high level of participation in the voluntary service of the local civil cargo system, and a complex system of ceremonies based on the individual life cycle and household saints.[86] *Mayordomías* (individual sponsorship of cult ceremonies for local saints) continue in a limited fashion in Teotitlán, but instead of abandoning many elements of these rituals, the community has transferred the ritual content of *mayordomías* to life-cycle ceremonies and it uses reciprocal networks to back up a ceremonial cycle that absorbs major portions of household labor and income.[87]

Reciprocal goods and labor exchange centers around the institution of *guelaguetza* in Teotitlán del Valle. *Guelaguetza* is a system of economic exchange in which interest-free loans of goods, cash, and labor are made from one household to another over long periods of time. Debts incurred in cash and in kind are recorded in notebooks, while labor debts are remembered through mental accounting. While labor *guelaguetza* can be used for farming, today it is primarily directed toward ceremonial activities. In Teotitlán, where male and female household heads may attend between 10 and 20 ceremonial events per year and may sponsor up to 20 in their lifetime, reciprocal goods and labor exchanges are critical to the on-going ceremonial life of the community.

In a random stratified sample of 150 households (approximately 15% of the total number in the community), more than 70% were found to have *guelaguetza* notebooks that recorded loans of in-kind goods made to other households and items received as loans. These notebooks are records of the preparations made largely by women as they get ready to feed crowds of up to 200 people for days at a time in association with the celebration of saints' days, marriages, engagement ceremonies, and other life-cycle events. While the average number of loans made and received under this system in the random sample was five, more than 20% of the households surveyed had 10 or more loans made and received, and 10% had more than 20 loans made and received. The highest number of entries recorded was 100 loans received. Each entry does not necessarily consist of only one item but includes the total number and weight of items received from a particular household. For example, "three turkeys weighing twenty kilos, six dozen eggs, and ten kilos of beans" is a typical entry.

Labor *guelaguetza* is not recorded in notebooks but is carefully remembered by everyone in the community. The large ceremonial events associated with *mayordomías* and life-cycle rituals bring to life the large networks of kin and *compadres* to which each household is connected. These kin and *compadrazgo* networks provide the labor for ceremonial events. An "invitation" to such an event is tantamount to a request to work for 3–5 days, at least 10 hours per day, particularly for women who now handle a bulk of the labor associated with putting on ritual events. Among the 150 households surveyed, the median number of ritual events attended during 1985 was 13.5, with each event lasting from 3–5 days. Twenty percent of those surveyed attended 25 events or more in 1 year, representing at least 75 days of time invested in ritual events. The amount of time and labor that will be invested in ritual events is not predictable or regular because it depends on the life cycles of a wide network of relatives and on individual choice in the sponsoring of saint's day rituals. During a given year household members may have only a few invitations to ritual events but the next year they may spend a majority of their labor time attending such events. In years where the latter is the case, ritual event attendance can detract significantly from weaving production. I have noted elsewhere the reluctance that merchants exhibit toward attending such ritual events, but they are often unsuccessful in completely evading such commitments.[88] Male merchants tend to try to escape their ritual labor duties while their wives remain behind to carry out their *guelaguetza* obligations.

As part of a labor allocation study, 12 households, both merchant and weaver, were monitored for 10 months to document the amount of labor they invested in ritual activity versus weaving, household activities and agriculture, and civil cargo duty and communal labor.[89] The average percentage of adult labor time spent by weavers in ritual activities (primarily labor *guelaguetza*) was 21%. The average percentage of adult labor time spent by merchants in ritual activities was 13%. The range of total adult labor time spent in ritual activities for the six weaver households monitored was between 12% and 29%. The range for merchant households was between 9% and 15%. While these data are limited in scope, they do suggest that for a majority of the households in the community that are weavers, one fifth of their labor time or more may be spent in ritual activities that involve a great deal of reciprocal labor exchange.

While profits from commercial textile production in Teotitlán have resulted in capital accumulation that is reinvested in business and individual household improvements, significant amounts of capital have been reinvested in community institutions such as public works, restoration of the church, and sponsorship of community-wide ceremonial activities.[90] Community authorities urge and push for reinvestment in community institutions as a strategy to alleviate dependence on the patronage system of the Partido Revolucionario Institucional (PRI), the ruling political party of Mexico, which has been in power over 60 years. Every improvement made with community funds prevents a political debt to officials in the state capital.[91]

The Nahua of Ameyaltepec have similarly been able to adapt what Good Eshelman calls "ethnic relations" to capitalist production. The economy of the Ameyaltepec Nahuas has a wide range of social and economic activity including reciprocal labor exchanges for agriculture, housebuilding and ritual events, an elaborate system of voluntary service in the local civil cargo system, and a high level of individual donations to community ceremonial occasions.[92] Good Eshelman provides a long list of reciprocal labor activities that includes many activities similar to the *guelaguetza* labor exchanges found in Teotitlán: agricultural work, use of animals for some types of agricultural labor, communal work for attaching roofs to houses, labor on communal land that is dedicated to the church, the work of women and men during life-cycle ceremonies and fiestas for saints, civil cargo labor, and the labor of ritual specialists and community elders.[93] While she does not provide statistical documentation of the percentage of labor time these activities take, her analysis indicates that as in Teotitlán, they may end up accounting for a significant amount of household members' available labor time, depending on the level of ritual activity among their network of kin and *compadres*. There are also special linguistic terms and vocabulary to refer to reciprocal labor and goods exchanges among the Nahua. Thus, as among the Zapotec of Teotitlán, these forms of reciprocal exchange and volunteer labor have continued to exist and have even flourished in the face of commercial craft production, suggesting in fact that the relations of what is labeled here "social reproduction" are necessary for an indigenous community to be successful in its production of crafts for a capitalist market.

Perhaps most impressive in both Ameyaltepec and Teotitlán del Valle is the degree of social mobilization and cooperation required to maintain the intense ceremonial cycle, both for events celebrated by the entire community and ceremonies centered on an individual's life cycle. Good Eshelman argues that while ceremonial obligations do not act to level wealth differences, those who participate in civil cargos and *mayordomías* and other ceremonial events do have a lower rate of profit,[94] but they are not sacrificing basic resources.[95] Instead, she maintains that the ceremonial cycle uses part of the commercial gains in a socially acceptable way as ceremonial life has expanded in quantity and quality, similar to the situation evidenced in Teotitlán over the past 20 years.[96]

The Otavalan weavers seem to exhibit a pattern similar to the Zapotec with regard to simultaneous presence of socioeconomic differentiation tied to entrepreneurial success and a continued reinforcement and participation in reciprocal goods and labor exchanges associated with the ceremonial cycle. Two ethnographers of the Otavaleños in the 1970s document the rise of an entrepreneurial class of indigenous textile producers who now run medium and, in some cases, large textile workshops in the district capital of Otavalo.[97] While Villavivencio and Walters disagree on the extent to which this entrepreneurial class has affected the subsistence economy based on reciprocal exchanges, both emphasize that Otavaleños continue to use their indigenous ethnic identity as a selling point for their textiles. Even young entrepreneurs continue to participate in the ceremonial life of their communities of origin, often making larger financial and in-kind contributions in community and family ceremonies because of their improved economic status.[98]

Like the Zapotec of Oaxaca, community ceremonial life in Otavalo *parcialidades* was organized around sponsorship of cult celebrations for local saints, which gave sponsors prestige and political authority.[99] In her description of the canton of Peguche in Otavalo in the 1940s, Elsie Clews Parsons found a thriving system of patronage to local saints in which locals serve as *priostes* (ceremonial hosts) in charge of sponsoring ceremonial activities. The system is almost identical to the *mayordomía* (cult sponsorship of local saints) system described in many parts of Mexico. Such activities were supported by extensive kin-*compadrazgo* networks. Walters, along with Bartlett, maintains that community religious fiestas are now on the decline, as is the case among the Zapotec.[100] However, both point out that people continue to uphold reciprocal obligations in relation to life-cycle ceremonies such as baptisms and funerals, suggesting that kin-*compadrazgo* networks remain vitally important in community ceremonial life. Walters further emphasizes how multistranded kin-*compadrazgo* relations also serve as a basis for labor recruitment in the weaving industry and as a way of maintaining indigenous control over weaving production and marketing.[101]

Like the other three cases discussed here, the Kuna of Panama also continue to engage in many forms of cooperative enterprise. Howe's recent monograph on the Kuna describes a wide range of labor cooperation for many purposes including women's puberty ceremonies, marriage, house and public building construction, cleaning and clearing of land surrounding communities, public works such as dock construction, and communal agricultural and fishing activities.[102] The Kuna are known for their village congresses characterized by chanting and village-wide puberty rituals for adolescent girls.[103]

The basis for cooperation may be either kinship or village membership, varying in different areas. According to Howe, the organizational model of communal labor emphasizes exchanges of labor and materials between individuals and the collectivity, although an ethos of mutual help among friends within the collectivity continues to inform and support the system.[104] Ties to the village are so strong that being a village member means making village needs a priority over all else. Howe writes: "Only by breaking all ties with his home and leaving forever can a man escape this pervasive interference in his life."[105] This strong sense of collectivity is the ethnic backdrop for *mola* production.

B. Integration of Craft Production with Subsistence Production, Ceremonial Activities, and Community Labor Obligations

The continued existence of reciprocal goods and labor exchanges, kin and *compadrazgo* networks, and high levels of participation in the community that govern institutions and local ceremonial cycles raises the question of how the organization of craft production is integrated with institutions of social reproduction—that is, "local ethnic institutions."

In the two Mexican cases and the case of the Quechua weavers of Otavalo, organizational networks that underlie local ethnic institutions also underlie the production and distribution of craft items. In all three areas, the household—which is a unit of consumption, partible inheritance, ritual participation, and participation in community government—is often the basis for a unit of production as well. Family labor is the basis of production and marketing, supplemented with apprentices or pieceworkers, as capital accumulation permits.[106]

While the household is important in craft production and distribution, the extended kin and *compadrazgo* networks that underlie the ceremonial systems in these indigenous cases are also important in relation to production. The links of *compadrazgo*, which place godchildren under heavy obligations to their sponsoring godparents as well as linking the ritual godparents with biological parents, often serve as a basis for labor recruitment in weaving. In Teotitlán, the mean number of godchildren per household in a random sample survey of 150 households was nine. Some households had none, while one, that of the largest merchant, had 246. In general, merchant households tend to have larger numbers of godchildren than weaver households. Many merchants have their godchildren working for them in a system where, as godparents, the merchants provide the materials for textile production and receive finished pieces from their godchildren or from the biological parents of their godchildren. Because of the reciprocal nature of the obligations and responsibilities associated with godparenthood, however, these merchants will also be invited to all of the ritual events held in the households of their godchildren and are expected to make significant in-kind and labor contributions. This arrangement works out more to the advantage of merchant godparents but by no means frees them of some reciprocal obligations.

What these relations mean in daily life is that a merchant may one day take on the role of invited guest (i.e., laborer) in the house of his or her godchild and the next week use that same relationship as a basis for pressuring a godchild to produce textiles on a piecework basis. A majority of merchants surveyed relied overwhelmingly on kin and godchildren and their godchildren's parents to provide them with finished goods in piecework arrangements, sometimes contracting up to 30 individuals this way. Weavers, when approached by government officials hoping to set up state-run cooperatives such as that managed by the National Fund for Folk Art (FONART) in Mexico, state that they far prefer to do business with their relatives and *compadres* than with state bureaucrats. Kin and *compadres* provide interest-free loans and other types of assistance that are not available from the state-sponsored programs for the promotion of craft production. The large kin networks that support extensive ceremonial activity in Teotitlán also appear to be a critical underlying structure in the production and distribution of weavings. They take labor relations out of the realm of strictly business by overlaying them with kinship and ritual interaction. Similar circumstances for Nahuatl *amate* painters and Quechua weavers are suggested by researchers. Extended kin and *compadrazgo* ties function simultaneously as family, ceremonial, and production relationships.

Walters describes the ceremonial, social, and economic life of an Otavaleño community as based on ties to kin and *compadres*. Similar to kin and *compadrazgo* ties in Teotitlán, she describes them as "manystranded," meaning that they structure many different types of social interactions and give to each the obligations and responsibilities implied by kinship. "Ahuangueños expect any manystranded tie, whether formalized by real or fictive kinship to include: (1) social interaction (visiting, attending family festivals, sharing food and drink on a regular and permanent basis), (2) reciprocal material support and labor assistance, (3) support for one another in conflicts with other households or outsiders, and (4) trust and respect."[107] Walters states that these many-stranded relationships are called "alliances" and the individuals in them "allies" by the people of Ahuango. Every household has a network of alliances, but the size of the network varies according to the extent to which a household is able to meet its obligations and is willing to exchange material resources for social prestige. She notes that the wealthier households in Ahuango are more sought after as allies and tend to retain more cash surplus from weaving, which enables them to participate in regular food and drink exchanges to reinforce their alliances with kin and *compadres.* Such allies are used to enhance political influence and prestige as well as to rally labor and support during religious fiesta sponsorship. Walters states that the wealthy continue to invest capital in the local prestige system, seeking security, influence, and prestige, rather than making investments in the larger economy.

While she does not provide exact data on the number of people who sponsor fiestas in Ahuango, Walters's research suggests that people who sponsor fiestas spend a significant portion of their household income in the process. In 1973, the average household earned 3,600 sucres from poncho production. The expenses for the most prestigious festival, which lasted 3 years, were approximately 10,000 sucres. One-time sponsorships could range from 100–500 sucres to pay for a mass for a patron saint to 6,000 sucres for a more elaborate fiesta.[108] For sponsoring households, the sponsorship is a major financial burden.

An analysis of reciprocal drinking ties among the Otavalo, carried out by Bartlett in another community, suggests some of the direct economic benefits of reciprocal ties. Ritual drinking ties can serve as a basis for providing or obtaining loans, can provide individuals with access to a wide network of people for political support (often used to pressure local officials), and can reduce risk as they provide sources of future loans and labor assistance for traders and others who have lost their businesses due to robbery, bad luck, or other circumstances.[109]

The community of Ahuango that Walters describes does not appear to have developed the entrepreneurial infrastructure that Teotitlán del Valle in Mexico and some other Otavalan towns have. While other Otavalan communities established textile factories and workshops as well as marketing and purchasing cooperatives, merchant activity did not have a high profile where Walters carried out her research. She notes that young men of wealthy families had yet to establish households and alliances within the community. Although they spoke of seeking opportunities outside of the community and did not regard themselves as future fiesta sponsors, they had yet to try to establish production systems as a basis for merchant activity.

In another Otavalo community, Bartlett argues that farmers and weavers, despite their importance as local officials or even as traders, will continue to participate in the ceremonial life of the community and engage in reciprocal ties because their financial security depends on their acceptance in the community as participating members. Among the Quechua Otavalans, participating in community ceremonial institutions is a way of laying to rest local suspicions that they are trying to separate themselves from the community. It also gives them a legitimate claim to the textiles that are the basis of their livelihood. While Walters remains pessimistic about the participation of aspiring young traders and merchants in the extensive alliance structure of the community, the reality may be that such alliances will also become the basis of labor relations as new merchants have to recruit laborers in an increasingly competitive situation. The case of Teotitlán suggests that, even with initial differentiation between merchants and weavers, kin and *compadrazgo* ties continue to be the basis for the relations of production, and the large amounts of labor and time invested in recip- rocal exchanges for ceremonial purposes do not disappear as easily as Walters proposes.

Among the Kuna, the organization of *mola* production is centered primarily in the matrilocal extended household, the basic unit of pro- duction and consumption. According to Howe, Kuna household auton- omy and self-regulation have diminished with the increasing presence of village control and the importance of village communal labor.[110] He further suggests that although most people reside in matrilocal households with the senior generation in charge, household heads now manage smaller domestic groups, have less influence over younger household members, have less to say, and work longer into old age.[111] According to Hirschfeld, however, the household does remain impor- tant in terms of learning to make *molas* and, to some extent, *mola* production.[112] Women from the same household will share designs and ideas, but *molas* are produced by individual women for their own use or for export. A woman learns to sew *molas* through instruction from her mother and other females in the household. Often production is supervised by the most senior female. As described by Hirschfeld, "*Mola* production is the concrete expression of female solidarity in the matrilocal, extended family household."[113] Work on *molas* is also carried out by women while sitting in the congress house as they listen to the chanting of local chiefs.[114]

The ideological and material role of the *mola* in Kuna culture appears to have varied locally, regionally, and historically. Hirschfeld suggests that in the 1970s, *mola* production and female puberty cere- monies in Tigre, San Blas, were wealth repositories that transformed economic surpluses from coconut production into nonproductive means. Descriptions of the *mola* cooperative suggest that at that same time in other areas commercial *mola* production was well under way.[115] Women in tourist areas were rapidly producing *molas* for sale. While women continue to wear *molas* as symbols of being Kuna, using them as local and national ethnic boundary markers, community- and

family-based forms of production (the matrilocal household) and distribution (village unity, the cooperative) have helped the Kuna to begin
to control a significant part of the *mola* market, although this control
is far from complete.

Because of the overlap between units of production, consumption,
ritual participation, and reciprocal exchange, the relations of craft production are multistranded and evoke many meanings each time they
are mobilized. Likewise, when kin-*compadrazgo* networks are acti-
vated for ceremonial activity, the fact of their mobilization indirectly
reinforces relations of craft production because they often involve the
same group of people. The constant interplay between community institutions of ethnic reproduction and institutions of production for exchange can underwrite the reclamation of "indigenous identity" by
craft producers.

VI. Conclusions

In this article I compare four cases of craft production for export,
where communities maintained significant levels of control over commercial enterprises that build on local cultural institutions. The comparison shows a historical similarity of economic circumstances that
accompanies the maintenance of ethnic identities in conjunction with
commercial craft production. While these circumstances might support
ethnic solidarity in general, the demand for handmade products implicit in the market for ethnic crafts provides a special niche for ethnicity as an economic resource. In all the cases, communities have
managed to preserve significant land bases, have engaged in commercial production for exchange (for sale) since the seventeenth or eighteenth century, and have a history of locally controlled marketing and
distribution through local and regional networks. Such a common history provided important economic and political resources and experience that contributed to success in tourist and export markets.

The second set of circumstances that unifies these four cases re-
volves around the maintenance and reproduction of noncapitalist institutions of exchange, such as reciprocal goods and labor exchanges,
high levels of participation in traditional community systems of government, the maintenance of intense ceremonial cycles, and reinvestment
in community public works and enterprises. These circumstances involve the maintenance of ethnic institutions responsible for social and
cultural reproduction.

The maintenance of such ethnic institutions provides the basis
for community self-management in cottage industries. While national
governments and foreign exporters have turned the ethnic identity of
the Kuna, the Zapotecs, the Otavalan Quechua, and the Nahuas into
a commodity, these groups appropriated in part the fruits of this commoditization and harnessed them to reinforce their own ethnic identities. In three of these cases, indigenous producers and entrepreneurs

have also built on the efforts of outside development agencies, such as the Peace Corps and the Inter-American Foundation, to either take over the management of projects or use the marketing networks set up by such projects to support private and community production efforts.

In each of the cases examined here there is an implicit tension between a tendency toward capital accumulation on the part of individuals and a community ideology of cooperation that is expressed through institutions of social reproduction. While craft production has certainly produced significant wealth differences between households in each of these cases, up to this point another dynamic has prevented these ethnic groups from being absorbed into the migrant farmworker or urban working populations. This dynamic is based on local reappropriation and self-definition of ethnic identity, an identity that is inaccessible and stands in contrast to the various Indian identities promoted by outsiders.

As suggested in the introduction, local indigenous identity has been maintained not only through a process of historical opposition but also through an indirect process of opposition where today communities consciously redefine their ethnicity as an alternative to the commoditized version of their ethnic identity. When communities have retained a significant land base, have experience in local and regional marketing, and maintain institutions of social reproduction, they can engage in reproduction for the world market. This can result in locally controlled capital accumulation and cultural self-defense. What is important for scholars and planners alike is to note that these unique conditions cannot be imposed, they can only be inherited.

Notes

* I would like to thank Jonathan Fox, James Howe, Jean Jackson, Frank Salomon, Christine Gailey, and D. Gale Johnson for their helpful criticism and suggestions on earlier drafts of this paper. Funding for research carried out among the Zapotec of Mexico was provided by the Inter-American Foundation, the Wenner-Gren Foundation for Anthropological Research, and the Damon Fellowship of Brandeis University.

1. See Lizabeth Berkeley and Charles Haddox, "Tarahumara Handicrafts and Economic Survival," *Cultural Survival Quarterly* 11, no. 1 (1987): 57–58. See also Victoria Novelo, "Para el estudio de las artesanías Méxicanas" (For the study of Mexican crafts), *American Indígena* 41 (1981): 195–210, and *Artesanias y capitalismo en México* (Crafts and capitalism in Mexico) (Mexico City: Secretaría de Educación Publica/Instituto Nacional de Antropología e Historia [SEP-INAH], 1976).

2. Felicity Edholm, Olivia Harris, and Kate Young, "Conceptualizing Women," *Critique of Anthropology* 3 (1977): 101–30. See also Lourdes Benería, "Reproduction, Production and the Sexual Division of Labor," *Cambridge Journal of Economics* 3 (1979): 203–25.

3. See Christine Gailey, "The State of the State in Anthropology," *Dialectical Anthropology* 9 (1985): 65–89; also, Timothy Parrish, "Class Structure and Social Reproduction in New Spain/Mexico," *Dialectical Anthropology* 7 (1982): 115–36.

4. On the connection to language, see Raoul Naroll, "On Ethnic Unit Classification," *Current Anthropology* 5 (1964): 283–312; and Harold E. Driver, "Geographical-historical versus Psycho-functional Explanations of Kin Avoidances," *Current Anthropology* 7 (1966): 131–82. For a more dynamic definition, see Frederick Barth's introduction to *Ethnic Groups and Boundaries*, ed. F. Barth (London: Allen & Unwin, 1969). Also Michael Moerman, "Ethnic Identification in a Complex Civilization: Who Are the Lue?" *American Anthropologist* 67 (1965): 1215–30; Dell Hymes, "Linguistic Problems in Defining the Concept of 'Tribe,' " in *Language in Use: Readings in Sociolinguistics*, ed. John Baugh and Joel Sherzer (Englewood Cliffs, N.J.: Prentice-Hall, 1984); and Alejandro Portes, "The Rise of Ethnicity," *American Sociological Review* 49, no. 3 (1984): 383–97.

5. Stefano Varese, "Multi-ethnicity and Hegemonic Construction: Indian Projects and the Global Future," in *Ethnicities and Nations: Processes of Interethnic Relations in Latin America, Southeast Asia, and the Pacific*, ed. Francesco Remo Guidieri (Austin: University of Texas Press, 1988).

6. Edward Spicer, "Persistent Cultural Systems: A Comparative Study of Identity Systems That Can Adapt to Contrasting Environments," *Science* 174 (1971): 795–800.

7. Ibid.; Anya Peterson-Royce, *Ethnic Identity: Strategies of Diversity* (Bloomington: Indiana University Press, 1982); George Castile, "Issues in the Analysis of Enduring Cultural Systems," in *Persistent Peoples: Cultural Enclaves in Perspective*, ed. George P. Castile and Gilbert Kushner (Tucson: University of Arizona Press, 1981).

8. Peterson-Royce, p. 46.

9. See Phillipe Bourgois, "Conjugated Oppression: Class and Ethnicity among Guaymi and Kuna Banana Workers," *American Ethnologist* 15, no. 2 (1988): 328–448; Pierre Van den Berghe, *The Ethnic Phenomenon* (New York: Elsevier, 1981).

10. Gerald Sider, "Lumbee Indian Cultural Nationalism and Ethnogenesis," *Dialectical Anthropology* 1, no. 2 (1976): 161–71, and *Culture and Class in Anthropology and History: A Newfoundland Illustration* (Cambridge: Cambridge University Press, 1986).

11. Sider, "Lumbee Indian Cultural Nationalism and Ethnogenesis," p. 163.

12. Ibid.

13. Judith Friedlander, *Being Indian in Hueyapan: A Study of Forced Identity in Contemporary Mexico* (New York: St. Martin's, 1975), pp. 165–88.

14. See Scott Cook, *Peasant Capitalist Industry* (New York: University Press of America, 1984); Nelson Graburn, *Ethnic and Tourist Arts* (Berkeley and Los Angeles: University of California Press, 1982); Nestor García Canclini, *Las culturas populares en el capitalismo* (Folk cultures and capitalism) (Mexico City: Editorial Nueva Imagen, 1982).

15. John H. Bodley, *Victims of Progress* (Palo Alto, Calif.: Mayfield, 1982).

16. On the CRIC of Colombia, see ibid., p. 177. And on the Federación de Centros Shuar, see Jaime Zallez and Olfonso Gotaire, *Organizarse o sucumbir: La Federación Shuar* (Organize yourself or succumb: the Shuar federation), Mundo Shuar Serie "B," no. 14 (Sucua, Educador: Centro de Documentación e Investigación Cultural Shuar, 1978).

17. Richard Chase Smith, "A Search for Unity within Diversity: Peasant Unions, Ethnic Federations, and Indianist Movements in the Andean Republics," in *Native Peoples and Economic Development*, ed. Theodore MacDonald, Jr. (Cambridge, Mass.: Cultural Survival, 1985).

18. Ibid.; Guillermo Bonfil Batalla, "Utopia y revolución: El pensamiento

político contemporaneo de los Indios en America Latina" (Utopia and revolution: contemporary political thought of the Indians in Latin America), in *Utopía y revolución*, ed. G. Bonfil Batalla (Mexico City: Editorial Nueva Imagen, 1981).

19. Edward Sapir, "Culture, Genuine and Spurious," in *Language, Culture and Personality*, ed. D. Mandelbaum (Berkeley: University of California Press, 1956).

20. Ibid., p. 93; also see Christine W. Gailey, "Culture Wars: Resistance to State Formation," in *Power Relations and State Formation*, ed. C. Gailey and T. Patterson (Washington, D.C.: American Anthropological Association, 1987), pp. 36–37.

21. Stanley Diamond, "Dahomey: A Proto-State in West Africa" (Ph.D. diss., Columbia University, 1951).

22. Lynn Stephen, *Zapotec Women* (Austin: University of Texas Press, 1991).

23. Lynn Stephen, "The Politics of Ritual: The Mexican State and Zapotec Autonomy, 1926–1989," in *Class, Politics, and Popular Religion in Mexico and Central America*, ed. Lynn Stephen and James Dow (Washington, D.C.: American Anthropological Association, 1990).

24. I have chosen to use the spelling "Quechua" as opposed to "Quichua" throughout this article. Kevin Healey and Elayne Zorn, "Turismo controlado por campesinos en el lago de Titicaca" (Tourism controlled by peasants in Lake Titicaca), *Desarollo de Base* 6, no. 2/7, no. 1 (1984): 3–10.

25. Lynn Stephen, "Weaving Changes: Economic Development and Gender Roles in Zapotec Ritual and Production" (Ph.D. diss., Brandeis University, 1987), pp. 20–21.

26. Lynn Meisch, "Archaic Residues in Traditional Dress in Otavalo and Saraguro, Ecuador" (paper presented at the symposium on Costume as Communication: Current Issues in Ethnographic Cloth and Costume from Middle America and the Central Andes of South America, Haffenreffer Museum of Anthropology, Brown University, March 6–7, 1987), p. 2.

27. Frank Salomon, "Weavers of Otavalo," in *Cultural Transformations and Ethnicity in Modern Ecuador*, ed. Norman E. Whitten, Jr. (Urbana: University of Illinois Press, 1981), pp. 420–21.

28. Lynn Walters, "Social Strategies and the Fiesta Complex in an Otavaleno Community," *American Ethnologist* (1981): 172–85, and "Otavaleno Development, Ethnicity, and National Integration," *America Indigena* 40, no. 2 (1981): 319–37; Gladys Villavivencio, *Relaciones interetnicas en Otavalo* (Mexico City: Instituto Indigenista Interamericano, 1973).

29. Catharine Good Eshelman, *Haciendo la lucha: Arte y comercio Nahua de Guerrero* (Trying to succeed: Nahuatl art and commerce of Guerrero) (Mexico City: Fondo de Cultura Economica, 1988).

30. *Molas* as clothing refers to applique panels that are sewn separately, then sewed together back to back along their sides, and added to a yoke with sleeves and a bottom extension to form a blouse. A polysemic word, *mola* refers to (1) clothing in general, (2) blouses and skirts in general, (3) women's *mola*-style blouses in particular, and (4) the front and back panels on the blouses (see Dina Sherzer and Joel Sherzer, "Mormaknamaloe: The Cuna *Mola*," in *Ritual and Symbol in Native Central America*, ed. Philip Young and James Howe, University of Oregon Anthropological Papers, no. 9 [Eugene: University of Oregon, 1976]).

31. James Howe, personal communication, March 1988.

32. Orlando Roberts, *Narrative on Voyages and Excursions on the East Coast and the Interior of Central America*, facsimile of the 1827 edition, introduction by H. Craggs (Gainesville: University of Florida Press, 1965), p. 44.

33. Larry Hirschfeld, "Art in Cunaland: Ideology and Cultural Adaptation," *Man* 12 (1977): 104–23; Karen Tice, "Gender, Capitalism and Egalitarian Forms of Social Organization in San Blas, Panama: Socioeconomic Differentiation of a Rural Region through Commercialization of *Mola* Handicrafts" (Ph.D. diss., Columbia University, 1989).

34. Mari Lyn Salvador, "The Clothing Arts of the Cuna of San Blas, Panama," in *Ethnic and Tourist Arts,* ed. Nelson H. Graburn (Berkeley: University of California Press, 1976); Margaret Byrne Swain, "Cuna Women and Ethnic Tourism: A Way to Persist and an Avenue to Change," in *Hosts and Guests,* ed. Valene L. Smith (Philadelphia: University of Pennsylvania Press, 1977).

35. See Nancy Brennan Hatley, "Cooperatism and Enculturation among the Cuna Indians of San Blas," in *Enculturation in Latin America,* ed. J. Wilbert (Los Angeles: UCLA Latin American Center Publications, 1976); Swain; Ann Hartfiel, "In Support of Women: Ten Years of Funding by the Inter-American Foundation," Monographs and Working Papers of the Inter-American Foundation (Rosslyn, Va.: Inter-American Foundation, 1982); Tice.

36. William Taylor, *Landlord and Peasant in Colonial Oaxaca* (Stanford, Calif.: Stanford University Press, 1972), p. 102; Stephen, "Weaving Changes" (n. 25 above), p. 52.

37. Chantal Caillavet, "La adaptación de la dominación incaica a las sociedades autoctonas de frontera septentrional del Imperio (Territorio Otavalo, Equador)" (The adaptation of Incaic domination to the autochthonous societies of the Imperial Frontier [Territory of Otavalo, Ecuador]), *Revista Andina* 3, no. 2 (1975): 417.

38. Walters, "Social Strategies and the Fiesta Complex in an Otavaleno Community" (n. 28 above), p. 184; Elsie Clews Parsons, *Peguche: Canton of Otavalo, Province of Imbabura, Ecuador* (Chicago: University of Chicago Press, 1945).

39. Salomon (n. 27 above), p. 425.

40. Parsons, p. 8.

41. Ibid.

42. Ibid.; Anibal Buitron and Barbara Salisbury Buitron, "Indios, Blancos, y Mestizos en Otavalo Ecuador" (Indians, Whites, and Mestizos in Otavalo, Ecuador), *Acta Americana* 3 (1945): 196.

43. Walters, "Social Strategies and the Fiesta Complex in an Otavaleno Community," and "Otavaleno Development, Ethnicity, and National Integration" (n. 28 above); Villavivencio (n. 28 above).

44. Good Eshelman, p. 129.

45. Ibid., p. 143.

46. Ibid., p. 129

47. Mac Chapin, "Curing among the San Blas Kuna of Panama" (Ph.D. diss., University of Arizona, 1983).

48. James Howe, *The Kuna Gathering: Contemporary Village Politics in Panama* (Austin: University of Texas Press, 1986); James Howe, personal communication, March 1988.

49. Howe, *The Kuna Gathering,* p. 10.

50. Ibid., pp. 10–11; Hirschfeld, "Art in Cunaland" (n. 33 above), p. 11.

51. Stephen, "Weaving Changes" (n. 25 above); Salomon (n. 27 above).

52. Fray Fransisco de Burgoa, *Geográfica descripción* (1674), 2 vols. (Mexico City: Archivo General de la Nación, 1934) as cited in John Chance, *Race and Class in Colonial Oaxaca* (Stanford, Calif.: Stanford University Press, 1978), p. 110.

53. Ibid.; Jill Appel, "A Summary of the Ethnohistoric Information Relevant to the Interpretation of Late Postclassic Settlement Patterns Data, the

Central and Valle Grande Survey Zone," in *Monte Albán's Hinterland*, pt. 1: *The Prehispanic Settlement Patterns of the Central and Southern Parts of the Valley of Oaxaca, Mexico*, ed. R. Blanton, S. Kowalewski, G. Feinman, and J. Appel, Memoirs of the Museum of Anthropology, no. 15 (Ann Arbor: University of Michigan, 1982), p. 147.

54. Stephen, "Weaving Changes," pp. 56–57.

55. Salomon, pp. 439–40.

56. Jorge Juan and Antonio de Ulloa, *A Voyage to South America: Describing at Large the Spanish Cities, Towns, Provinces, etc., on that Extensive Continent* (London, 1806): 1:301–2.

57. John Leddy Phelan, *The Kingdom of Quito in the Seventeenth Century: Bureaucratic Politics in the Spanish Empire* (Madison: University of Wisconsin Press, 1967), p. 68; Salomon, p. 440.

58. Walters, "Otavaleno Development, Ethnicity, and National Integration" (n. 28 above), p. 323.

59. Ibid., p. 324.

60. Johanna Mayhew Lessinger, "Weaving in an Ecuadorian Indian Village" (B.A. thesis, Harvard University, 1965); Walters, "Otavaleno Development, Ethnicity, and National Integration," p. 325.

61. Salomon (n. 27 above), p. 437.

62. Lynn Meisch, "The Weavers of Otavalo," *Pacific Discovery* 33, no. 6 (1980): 21–29, esp. 26.

63. Villavivencio (n. 28 above), pp. 108–9.

64. David Stout, *San Blas Acculturation: An Introduction*, Viking Foundation Publication no. 9 (New York: Wenner-Gren Foundation, 1947).

65. Howe, *The Kuna Gathering* (n. 48 above), p. 14.

66. James Howe, personal communication, March 1988.

67. Chapin (n. 47 above), pp. 462–65.

68. Howe, *The Kuna Gathering*, p. 14.

69. Regina Evans Holloman, "Developmental Change in San Blas" (Ph.D. diss., Northwestern University, 1969), p. 200.

70. Ibid., p. 173. James Howe notes that there is some discrepancy over when the *sociedad* became a formal institution ("Village Political Organization among the San Blas Cuna" [Ph.D. diss., University of Pennsylvania, 1974], p. 37, n. 11). Holloman and others describe it as a post-1925 phenomenon, while Howe notes that some of his informants suggested that subsistence cropping by groups of friends or whole villages occurred before 1925. These forms of organization seem clearly related to the formation of *sociedades*.

71. Richard William Costello, "Political Economy and Private Interests in Rio Azucar: An Analysis of Economic Change in a San Blas Community" (Ph.D. diss., University of California, Davis, 1975), pp. 168–202.

72. Ibid., p. 170.

73. Ibid., p. 171.

74. Ibid., p. 178.

75. Ibid.

76. Tice (n. 33 above), p. 48.

77. Ibid., p. 56.

78. Hatley (n. 35 above), p. 80.

79. Tice, p. 60.

80. Ibid., pp. 978–98.

81. Ibid., pp. 96–102.

82. Ibid., p. 233.

83. Ibid., p. 235.

84. Good Eshelman, pp. 177–81.

85. Ibid., pp. 187–88.

86. Stephen, "Weaving Changes" (n. 25 above).

87. Ibid.

88. Stephen, *Zapotec Women* (n. 22 above).

89. For total number of 12-hour days and percentages by household, see ibid.

90. Stephen, "Weaving Changes."

91. Stephen, "The Politics of Ritual" (n. 23 above).

92. Good Eshelman, pp. 162–72.

93. Ibid., p. 162.

94. Good Eshelman's discussion reflects issues related to the economics of cargo systems, a topic amply discussed in Mesoamerican anthropology. See Frank Cancian, *Economics and Prestige in a Mayan Community* (Stanford, Calif.: Stanford University Press, 1965); James Greenberg, *Santiago's Sword* (Berkeley and Los Angeles: University of California Press, 1981), and *Blood Ties: Life and Violence in Rural Mexico* (Tucson: University of Arizona Press, 1989).

95. Good Eshelman, p. 114.

96. Stephen, "Weaving Changes" (n. 25 above), pp. 88–110.

97. Walters, "Social Strategies and the Fiesta Complex in an Otavaleno Community" (n. 28 above), and "Otavaleno Development, Ethnicity, and National Integration" (n. 28 above); Villavivencio (n. 28 above), p. 90.

98. Walters, "Social Strategies and the Fiesta Complex in an Otavaleno Community," p. 174; Villavivencio, p. 102.

99. Villavivencio, pp. 101–14.

100. Walters, "Social Strategies and the Fiesta Complex in an Otavaleno Community," and "Otavaleno Development, Ethnicity, and National Integration"; Peggy F. Bartlett, "Reciprocity and the San Juan Fiesta," *Journal of Anthropological Research* 36, no. 1 (1980): 116–30.

101. Walters, "Social Strategies and the Fiesta Complex in an Otavaleno Community," and "Otavaleno Development, Ethnicity, and National Integration."

102. Howe, *The Kuna Gathering* (n. 48 above), pp. 130–36.

103. Ibid.; also see Lawrence Hirschfeld, "Art in Cunaland" (n. 33 above), and "A Structural Analysis of the Cuna Arts," in Young and Howe, eds. (n. 30 above).

104. Howe, *The Kuna Gathering*, pp. 143–44.

105. Ibid., p. 144.

106. See Cook (n. 14 above), pp. 199–200; Stephen, "Weaving Changes" (n. 25 above), pp. 172–75.

107. Walters, "Social Strategies and the Fiesta Complex in an Otavaleno Community" (n. 28 above), p. 176.

108. Ibid., p. 179.

109. Bartlett (n. 100 above), p. 122.

110. Howe, *The Kuna Gathering*, pp. 15–16, and "Marriage and Domestic Organization among the San Blas Kuna," in *The Botany and Natural History of Panama*, ed. W. D'Arcy and M. Correra A. (St. Louis: Missouri Botanical Garden, 1985).

111. Howe, *The Kuna Gathering*, p. 324.

112. Hirschfeld, "Art in Cunaland" (n. 33 above).

113. Hirschfeld, "A Structural Analysis of the Cuna Arts" (n. 103 above), p. 48.

114. Sherzer and Sherzer (n. 30 above), p. 29.

115. Hatley (n. 35 above).

Indigenous Language Skills and the Labor Market in a Developing Economy: Bolivia*

Barry R. Chiswick
University of Illinois at Chicago

Harry Anthony Patrinos
World Bank

Michael E. Hurst
University of Illinois at Chicago

I. Introduction

A little understood but widespread feature of many developing countries is the existence of population groups whose members do not speak the dominant language (or languages) of the country, that is, the language that predominates in the modern or formal sector of the economy. This characteristic exists in each of the major regions of developing economies.[1] In Latin America, for example. indigenous or native languages are spoken by segments of the population in nearly all of the countries, although the languages brought over by the European conquest, in particular Spanish and Portuguese, dominate political and economic life.[2] In Africa, the designation of country boundaries by the European colonial powers, with little or no regard for ethnic or language groups, combined with the migration of indigenous ethnic groups, has resulted in linguistic heterogeneity within individual countries. In Asia as well, linguistic heterogeneity in large countries (e.g., India and Indonesia), as well as in small ones (e.g., Laos, Papua New Guinea), has emerged as a frequently perplexing issue.

This linguistic heterogeneity has often been hidden. Government authorities frequently focused on promoting linguistic homogeneity, or pretending that it exists, as a way of creating a sense of national unity. Outside observers generally do not venture from the modern sector in developing countries' major cities, thereby missing exposure to the degree of linguistic heterogeneity. In the past, linguistic minorities have not forcefully expressed their linguistic and cultural uniqueness, although recent events suggest that this is changing.

In recent years there has been a growing interest in the role of indigenous peoples and linguistic heterogeneity, as the new nation states feel more secure, democratic principles and institutions are more firmly established, and the development process is spread from selected centers to the broader population. The research in this area, however, remains quite thin in large part because of the scarcity of data on language use. The purpose of this article is to expand the research base on linguistic minorities in developing countries through an analysis of data from a 1993 household survey conducted in Bolivia.

Section II provides a brief review of the literature on the labor-market implications of limited dominant language proficiency in developing economies, focusing on the research in Latin America. The data set analyzed for this study is described in Section III. Section IV presents the analyses of the determinants of dominant language skills, and the determinants of labor-force participation and labor-market earnings among men and women, with an emphasis on the effects of language skills on these labor-market outcomes. The article closes with a summary and conclusion.

II. Review of the Literature

There has been remarkably little systematic research on the skills and economic attainment of indigenous peoples, that is, the modern-day descendants of the original populations of an area that has also been settled by later arrivals. For example, in spite of the extensive economics research conducted in the United States on African Americans, Hispanic Americans, and immigrants, and in spite of the extensive studies of immigrants in other countries of overseas settlement, such as Canada, Australia, and New Zealand, the descendants of the original populations of these countries have received slight attention. Whether called Native Americans, First Nation, Aboriginals, or Maoris, these groups now constitute numerically very small segments of the population (except in New Zealand) and suffer disadvantages of geographic isolation, low levels of education, linguistic difficulties, and low earnings compared to the majority, primarily white, population.[3]

While a few studies have examined these issues in North America and Oceania, even less research has been carried out for indigenous and nonindigenous differences in Latin America. One exception is an analysis by Jonathan Kelley of the "cost of being Indian" in rural Bolivia.[4] Using a 1966 survey of about 1,000 male household heads in rural Bolivia, Kelley decomposed the earnings differential between indigenous and nonindigenous men into components based on education, occupation, and income. With background data on the respondents' education and occupations, and the respondents' fathers' education and occupations, Kelley concluded that nearly all (between 95% and 100%) of the overall differentials were due to class components (family background, education, and occupation) rather than ethnic differences per se. In other words, equalizing human capital and family backgrounds of individuals would result in the virtual elimination of ethnic inequalities. Kelly suggests that the main reason for the change from ethnic to class inequality in Bolivia was the 1952 revolution, which resulted in a considerable increase in the power and opportunities available to Bolivia's indigenous population.

The indigenous and nonindigenous education and earnings differences in Bolivia during the late 1980s were analyzed by George Psacharopoulos, using the 1989 national (urban) household survey that included about 10,000 employed individuals.[5] Indigenous workers were found to receive much lower rewards for schooling and labor-market experience, although data on family background were not available. Younger cohorts were found to be more educated and earned more in the labor market. We did not decompose the overall earnings differential into individual characteristics components.

Much of the overall differential in earnings between monolingual Spanish speakers and monolingual Guarani speakers in Paraguay is explained by human capital differences.[6] Thus, in Paraguay, narrowing differences in educational attainment would go a long way toward equalizing labor-market outcomes. In Peru, however, a large portion of the indigenous-nonindigenous wage gap is unexplained by human capital and other observable differences.[7] A study of education and earnings in Guatemala finds that the earnings of Spanish speakers are higher than any of the indigenous language groups, both overall and when other variables are the same.[8]

III. The Survey Data
The data used in this study are from the Encuesta Integrada de Hogares (Integrated Household Survey), a 1993 household survey of Bolivia conducted by the Instituto Nacional de Estadistica (National Institute of Statistics). The survey was conducted in the capital cities of the nine "departments" (states) of Bolivia, including the national capital, La Paz. The respondents of particular interest are those age 15 and older.

The survey includes the question: "What languages do you usually speak?" in answer to which the respondent could report more than one language. The six language categories were Spanish, three indigenous languages (Quechua, Aymara, and Guarani), "other native languages," and "other non-native languages." For the purpose of this study, these were reclassified into three language groups: "Spanish only" (including those who spoke Spanish and a nonnative language), "indigenous only" (those who spoke only one or more native languages), and "bilingual" (those who spoke Spanish and one or more native languages). These language variables serve as the dependent variable in the language analysis and as explanatory variables in the analysis of labor-force participation and earnings.

There are no questions in the survey on the respondent's ethnicity, that is, on whether the respondent is of indigenous origin. There is, however, a high degree of correspondence in Latin America between being of an indigenous origin and speaking an indigenous language. Usually few nonindigenous individuals speak an indigenous language, although there are individuals of indigenous origins who do not speak their ancestral language. Most household surveys use the language question to identify indigenous people.[9]

The other variables used in the analyses are straightforward. The variable "Age" is measured in years. The gender variable is "Male," which equals unity for males and is zero for females. Data were collected on the number of live births for women 13–49 years of age. The variable "Number of live births" is the number of live births for women age 15–49 years and is zero for men and for women over age 49. A dichotomous variable "Age greater than 49" is created that equals unity for individuals who were not asked the live births question, that is, women older than 49 and men. Controlling for sex and age, the number of live births variable reflects the effect of fertility of women ages 15–49 on the dependent variable.

Since this is a survey conducted only in department capital cities, and many of the respondents, in particular indigenous language speakers, are from rural areas, several geographic variables are created. "La Paz" is unity for those who live in the Bolivian capital city and is zero otherwise. "Rural birthplace" is unity for those born in a rural area, otherwise it is zero. In rural areas about 90% of the population is of indigenous origin. Three internal migration variables refer to the time when the respondent moved to the present city of residence: "Migrated—over 5 years ago" is unity for those who moved more than 5 years ago, "Migrated—1–5 years ago" is unity for those who moved more than 1 but less than 5 years ago, and "Migrated—less than 1 year ago" is unity for those who moved to their present city less than 1 year before the interview was conducted. The benchmark of these region variables is a person living in the department capital, other than La Paz, in which the person was born.

The analyses of earnings and labor supply include additional variables. Among the variables is years of schooling completed, obtained by converting the categorical schooling data into a continuous years measure. The variable for labor-market experience is the number of years since age 15 that the respondent has not been in school (i.e, experience = age − 15 or experience = age − schooling − 6, whichever is smaller). This measure of experience is based on the assumption that years of labor-market activity prior to age 15 are not relevant for skill formation in the adult labor market. "Second job" is unity if the respondent has one or more jobs in addition to his or her primary employment. This also serves as a proxy for working more hours in a week. "Self-employed" is unity if the person is self-employed.

The earnings variable is monthly earnings from the primary job, second jobs, and self-employment, if any. Since the dependent variable in the earnings analysis is in logarithmic form, only individuals with positive earnings are included in the analysis. A measure of the total income of all household members other than the earnings of the respondent is also included in the analysis of labor supply.

The means and standard deviations of the variables are reported in table 1.

IV. Analysis of Language Skills and Labor-Market Activities
A. Language Skills

The model adopted for the analysis of dominant language skills among Bolivia's population has been developed and tested for immigrant linguistic minorities in several developed countries.[10] The model is based on three conceptual variables—exposure to the dominant language, efficiency in the acquisition of dominant language skills, and economic incentives to acquire these skills. It is hypothesized that in Bolivia Spanish language proficiency would be less among those who have less exposure to Spanish, who are less efficient in learning language skills, and who have less of an economic incentive to acquire Spanish-language proficiency.

Exposure would be less among those born in rural areas that are populated almost exclusively by people who speak the indigenous languages. It would also be less among those who have more recently migrated to a department capital city.

Women have lower labor-force participation rates than do men, and participation for women is more episodic than it is for men. In addition, women in the labor market are less likely to be in the modern, formal sector. It is therefore expected that women would have less of an economic incentive to learn Spanish, the language in the dominant, modern labor-market economy. Other things being equal among women, those with more children are expected to have lower labor-force participation rates and hence a weaker incentive to learn Spanish.

Those who were older are less likely to have attended school and are less likely to be literate in any language. Moreover, for the same duration in the city older migrants would have come at an older age, and the efficiency in new language skill acquisition declines with age.[11] Thus, age would be associated with a lesser use of Spanish.

The data on language skills in the survey refer only to the languages usually spoken. The questionnaire provides for six language categories, but respondents may indicate using more than one language. There are

TABLE 1

MEANS AND STANDARD DEVIATIONS OF VARIABLES, OVERALL AND BY SEX, URBAN BOLIVIA, 1993

VARIABLE	POOLED		MALES		FEMALES	
	Mean	SD	Mean	SD	Mean	SD
Age	35.0	16.0	35.1	15.8	34.9	16.2
Age squared	1,482.6	1,373.2	1,480.7	1,336.9	1,484.3	1,403.8
Migrated—more than 5 years ago	.454	.498	.457	.498	.451	.498
Migrated—1–5 years ago	.069	.253	.067	.251	.070	.255
Migrated—less than 1 year ago	.018	.132	.017	.128	.019	.136
Number of live births	1.09	2.05	N.A.	N.A.	3.40	2.29
Older than 49	.188	.390	.186	.389	.189	.391
La Paz	.234	.424	.227	.419	.241	.428
Rural birth place	.258	.437	.261	.439	.255	.436
Labor force participation rate	.529	.499	.659	.474	.417	.493
Schooling	9.68	4.70	10.17	4.44	9.22	4.89
Experience	17.87	16.37	17.69	16.01	18.03	16.67
Experience squared	587.39	888.19	569.15	845.91	603.14	922.89
Single	.361	.480	.375	.484	.349	.477
Widowed, divorced, separated	.094	.292	.043	.203	.138	.345
Married	.545	.498	.582	.493	.513	.500
Monolingual Spanish	.536	.499	.542	.498	.531	.499
Monolingual indigenous	.016	.126	.005	.069	.026	.159
Bilingual	.448	.497	.453	.498	.443	.497
Yearly earnings	382.12	791.21	576.93	971.11	213.96	539.80
Yearly earnings, with positive earnings	722.23	968.30	875.31	1,081.52	513.28	738.56
Ln yearly earnings, with positive earnings	6.14	.91	6.38	.84	5.81	.88
Second job	.032	.176	.041	.199	.024	.154
Self-employed	.171	.377	.159	.366	.182	.385
Household income (nonearner)	1,116.97	1,687.10	896.78	1,279.72	1,307.04	1,952.45
Sample size	12,480		5,782		6,698	

SOURCE.—Encuesta Integrada de Hogares (La Paz: Instituto Nacional de Estadistica, 1993).

NOTE.—Variables are defined in the text; adults are age 15 and older. Means in table 1 are from the sample used to compute the language estimates in tables 2 and 3. Numbers of live births in the "pooled" column is for all observations. The number of live births in the female column is for women who are younger than 49 years. N.A. = Not applicable.

120

no data on levels of proficiency in the languages identified or on proficiency in other languages that are not usually spoken. The data are, therefore, qualitative (categorical). Proficiency in Spanish presumably increases with the level of schooling since this is the language of instruction in schools.[12]

To make the analysis more manageable, we divided the information on languages usually spoken into three mutually exclusive categories: Spanish only (including those who speak a non-native language), indigenous language(s) only, and bilingual (Spanish and at least one indigenous language). Multinomial logit analysis is the preferred statistical technique.

Table 2 reports the multinomial logit analysis coefficients and t-ratios. Because of the difficulty of interpreting multinomial logit coefficients, table 3 reports separately by gender the effects of changes in the values of the explanatory variables on the probability of being in each of the three language categories. The reference person used for the base group is an individual with the mean age (35 years) and for a female with the mean number of live births (3.4 live births), residing in the place of birth which is a department capital other than La Paz. For this reference group, 70% of the men speak Spanish only, 30% are bilingual, and 0.1% are monolingual native language speakers; for women the proportions are 64%, 36%, and 0.3%, respectively.

In the pooled analyses, as well as in the analyses done separately by gender, age is associated with language usage. Older persons are less likely to be monolingual Spanish speakers and more likely to speak an indigenous language. Among indigenous language speakers, older women are associated with speaking only the indigenous language. Among men there is no statistically significant effect of age on speaking Spanish.

Compared to the base or reference person, an additional 10 years of age lowers the probability of being a monolingual Spanish speaker from 70% to 61% for men, and from 64% to 61% for women. Those 10 years increase for men the probability of being bilingual from 30% to 39%, and from being solely an indigenous language speaker from 0.1% to 0.2%. For women the respective proportions increase from 36% to 38%.

Among women, the larger the number of live births, the less likely women are to speak Spanish, relative to being bilingual or relative to speaking only an indigenous language. For the reference woman an additional live birth beyond the mean level lowers the probability of speaking only Spanish from 64% to 60% and raises the proportion of women who are bilingual from 36% to 40%.

Place of birth and years since moving to the current department capital city also matter, partly because the rural population is largely indigenous. Those born in rural areas are less likely to be monolingual Spanish

121

TABLE 2

MULTINOMIAL LOGIT ESTIMATES OF LANGUAGE USAGE, OVERALL AND BY SEX, URBAN BOLIVIA, 1993

Variables	Pooled — Spanish Only vs. Indigenous	Pooled — Spanish Only vs. Bilingual	Pooled — Bilingual vs. Indigenous	Female — Spanish Only vs. Indigenous	Female — Spanish Only vs. Bilingual	Female — Bilingual vs. Indigenous	Male — Spanish Only vs. Indigenous	Male — Spanish Only vs. Bilingual	Male — Bilingual vs. Indigenous
Age	−.1917 (−4.50)	−.0952 (−13.64)	−.0965 (−2.27)	−.1713 (−3.47)	−.0290 (−2.30)	−.1422 (−2.91)	−.1570 (−2.34)	−.1150 (−12.81)	−.0420 (−.63)
Age squared	.0010 (3.06)	.0008 (9.17)	.0002 (.76)	.0009 (2.31)	.0002 (1.89)	.0006 (1.71)	.0006 (1.00)	.0009 (8.97)	−.0004 (−.66)
Male	1.5970 (7.06)	−.1835 (−3.11)	1.7804 (8.01)	*	*	*	*	*	*
Migrated—more than 5 years ago	−.0527 (−.18)	−.2854 (−5.42)	.2327 (.80)	−.0763 (−.24)	−.1897 (−2.49)	.1134 (.36)	.3334 (.43)	−.3479 (−4.76)	.6814 (.88)
Migrated—1–5 years ago	−1.0726 (−2.82)	−.5495 (−5.79)	−.5232 (−1.39)	−1.2524 (−3.03)	−.4059 (−2.80)	−.8465 (−2.10)	.5191 (.41)	−.6133 (−4.87)	1.1324 (.90)
Migrated—Less than 1 year ago	−1.6350 (−3.18)	−.4139 (−2.29)	−1.2211 (−2.44)	−1.0833 (−1.70)	.1150 (.40)	−1.1983 (−1.92)	−1.9147 (−1.86)	−.7353 (*)	−1.1794 (*)
Number of live births	−.2091 (−4.23)	−.0915 (−5.75)	−.1176 (−2.46)	−.2652 (−4.59)	−.1637 (−8.06)	−.1016 (−1.82)	*	*	*
Older than 49	−.8068 (−1.83)	−.1145 (−1.12)	−.6924 (−1.59)	−1.4014 (−2.63)	−.8730 (−5.16)	−.5284 (−1.01)	*	*	*
La Paz	.4939 (2.16)	−.4854 (−9.25)	.9794 (4.35)	.3941 (1.56)	−.6136 (−7.86)	1.0077 (4.10)	.7086 (1.19)	−.4063 (−5.66)	1.1149 (1.88)
Rural birth place	−2.8264 (−12.68)	−1.2020 (−20.37)	−1.6244 (−7.40)	−2.7215 (−11.27)	−1.1004 (−12.68)	−1.6211 (−6.89)	−2.9259 (−4.64)	−1.2564 (−15.57)	−1.6694 (−2.66)
Constant	11.3371 (9.71)	3.2180 (21.83)	8.1190 (6.96)	11.1207 (8.29)	1.7907 (6.77)	9.3300 (7.00)	11.5353 (5.85)	3.4828 (19.98)	8.0525 (4.09)

SOURCE.—Encuesta Integrada de Hogares (La Paz: Instituto Nacional de Estadística, 1993).
NOTE.—Asymptotic t-ratios in parentheses; adults ages 15 and older.
* Variable not entered.

122

TABLE 3

ESTIMATED PROBABILITIES OF LANGUAGE USAGE, BY SEX, URBAN BOLIVIA, 1993

VARIABLE	MALE			FEMALE		
	Spanish	Bilingual	Indigenous	Spanish	Bilingual	Indigenous
Reference person	.699	.300	.0007	.638	.359	.0026
Age = 25	.807	.193	.0002	.672	.327	.0008
Age = 45	.608	.391	.0019	.613	.380	.0068
Migrated—more than 5 years ago	.621	.378	.0005	.594	.404	.0026
Migrated—1–5 years ago	.557	.442	.0003	.538	.454	.0075
Migrated—less than 1 year ago	.525	.471	.0037	.661	.331	.0078
Number of live births + 1	*	*	*	.599	.331	.0031
Age older than 49	*	*	*	.397	.570	.0069
La Paz	.608	.392	.0003	.490	.509	.0013
Rural birth place	.395	.597	.0076	.363	.615	.0221

SOURCE.—Means from table 1, coefficients from table 2.

NOTE.—The reference person is a 35-year-old adult who was born in the current department capital city of residence and who did not live in La Paz in 1993. The reference woman also had 3.4 live births, which is the average for women younger than age 49.

* Variable not entered.

123

speakers, and among those who can speak an indigenous language a larger proportion speaks only an indigenous language. While for the reference person (as defined in table 3) born in the place of current residence 70% of the men speak only Spanish, and only 40% of those who were born in rural areas and who now live in the department capitals speak only Spanish. Among men born in rural areas, 60% are bilingual and 0.8% speak only an indigenous language. Among women born in rural areas, 36% speak only Spanish, 62% are bilingual, and 2% speak only an indigenous language.

There is a lower level of Spanish usage and a higher rate of bilingualism among those who migrate from urban areas to the department capital cities than among those who were born there. The use of Spanish tends to increase the longer the duration of residence in the department capital. An exception are women who migrated less than 1 year prior to the survey. They are more likely to be monolingual Spanish speakers and less likely to be bilingual than men or women born in the city of residence.

In the Bolivian capital, La Paz, Spanish monolingualism is less common. In La Paz, only 61% of the men are monolingual Spanish speakers, compared with 70% of the men in other department capital cities. Among women, 49% in La Paz are monolingual Spanish speakers, compared with 64% in other department capital cities. Spanish–indigenous language bilingualism is more common in La Paz for both men and women.

Thus, Spanish language usage appears to be greater among younger persons, those living in the department capital city in which they were born (other than La Paz), males, and females with fewer children. Those born in rural areas have very low levels of Spanish language skills.

B. Labor-Force Participation

In this section, we examine the labor-force participation behavior of men and women age 15 and older. Those with earnings are defined as being labor-force participants, and those without earnings (zero earnings) are defined as nonparticipants. With the dichotomous dependent variable, logit analysis is the statistical technique employed. The explanatory variables are as defined above.

Labor-market participation is expected to increase the higher the potential labor-market earnings are and is expected to decrease with greater home-sector productivity. Hence, labor-market participation is expected to increase with schooling level and with years of potential labor-market experience, until labor-market participation declines with the reduction in productivity associated with aging. Because of the income effect, it is expected that participation would be lower the greater the income is of other members of the household.

Because of a division of labor in the household associated with marriage, married women are expected to be less likely to work for earnings than never married (single) women and those who are widowed, divorced, or separated. Married men, on the other hand, are expected to be more likely to work than men in other marital statuses.

Table 4 reports separately for men and women the logit equations

TABLE 4

ANALYSIS OF LABOR FORCE PARTICIPATION, BY SEX, URBAN BOLIVIA, 1993

VARIABLE	MALES		FEMALES	
	Coefficients (t-Ratios)	Marginal Effects	Coefficients (t-Ratios)	Marginal Effects
Schooling	−.0325 (−3.556)	−.0066	.0598 (7.438)	.0149
Experience	.1591 (16.368)	.0324	.099 (9.612)	.0247
Experience squared	−.00354 (−20.114)	−.0007	−.00201 (−10.361)	−.0005
Single	−1.5221 (−13.713)	−.3102	1.2661 (9.463)	.3164
Widowed, divorced, separated	−.9638 (−5.623)	−.1964	.9549 (9.307)	.2386
Migrated—more than 5 years ago	−.0281 (−.310)	−.0057	.0178 (.217)	.0044
Migrated—1–5 years ago	.053 (.353)	.0108	−.0657 (−.442)	−.0164
Migrated—Less than 1 year ago	−.1602 (−.589)	−.0327	−.6375 (−2.026)	−.1593
La Paz	.1229 (1.453)	.0250	.2581 (3.084)	.0645
Monolingual Spanish	−.0396 (−.498)	−.0081	−.264 (−3.525)	−.0660
Monolingual indigenous	1.2425 (2.023)	.2532	.4379 (2.191)	.1094
Older than 49	*	*	−.3168 (−1.648)	−.0792
Number of live births	*	*	.0306 (1.385)	.0076
Rural birth place	.0421 (.407)	.0086	.0769 (.814)	.0192
Household income	−.00019 (−6.552)	−.00004	−.00005 (−2.174)	−.00001
Constant	1.2217 (6.772)	.2490	−1.6626 (−10.213)	−.4155
Chi square	1,942.2		457.2	
Sample size	5,574		3,941	

SOURCE.—Encuesta Integrada de Hogares (La Paz: Instituto Nacional de Estadistica, 1993).

NOTE.—Dependent variable: unity for persons with positive earnings, zero otherwise. Asymptotic t-ratios are in parentheses; adults are ages 15 and older. The marginal effect for an independent (regressor) variable is the percentage point change in the labor-force participation rate attributed to a 1-unit change in the value of the variable, or to a change from 0 to 1 for binary variables.

* Variable not entered.

for whether the respondent had positive earnings. Among women the likelihood of working increases with the schooling level. Among men, however, schooling has a significant negative effect ($t = -3.5$), although the marginal effect for men is very small (less than 1% per year of schooling). For men, the negative effect of higher levels of schooling on working does not appear to be strongly related to current school enrollment. If a school enrollment variable is included in the equation (not shown here) the magnitude of the negative effect of schooling diminishes but remains negative and significant ($t = -2.2$). When the analysis is computed for men not currently enrolled in school, the magnitude of the negative schooling effect is similar to the effect when enrollment is not held constant.

The marital status effects are in accord with expectations. That is, married women are less likely and married men are more likely to work for earnings than are men and women in other marital statuses.

The income effect is shown in the equations for both men and women. The higher the household income from sources other than the respondent's earnings, the less likely is the respondent to participate in the labor market.

The effect of geography on participation rates varies by gender. Among men, geography does not matter. The participation rate does not vary significantly by whether the man was born in a rural area, when he moved to the current department capital of residence, or whether he lives in La Paz.

Among women, however, geography does matter. Labor-market participation is about 6 percentage points higher in La Paz than in the other cities ($t = 3.1$), perhaps reflecting the higher earnings women receive in La Paz and the greater employment opportunities for women in government service occupations in the capital city. Women who are relative newcomers to the department capital are less likely to work. The participation rates are about 16% lower among women who migrated to the city less than 1 year before the survey. This may arise from their being "tied movers." That is, they moved to accompany a husband or father rather than on behalf of their own employment opportunities. Studies in developed countries have found that female tied movers have more difficulty finding employment than women who did not move or were unattached movers.[13]

The effect of language skills on working also varies by gender. Among men, those who speak only an indigenous language are more likely to be working than are bilingual or Spanish-only speakers. This may reflect unmeasured dimensions of low family income and large family size among indigenous language speakers. While among women Spanish-only speakers work about 7 percentage points less ($t = -3.5$) than bilingual speakers, and monolingual indigenous language speakers work about 11 percentage points more ($t = 2.2$) than bilingual speakers.

C. Earnings

Analysis of the earnings of the adult respondents in the department capitals in Bolivia is based on the human capital earnings function, now a standard statistical technique.[14] In this procedure, the natural logarithm of earnings is regressed as a linear function of years of schooling, years of potential labor-market experience and its square, and a set of variables describing other relevant demographic and human capital characteristics of the individual. For this study, these characteristics include dichotomous variables for marital status (single, widowed, divorced, separated), a second job, self-employed, rural birthplace, time of moving to the current city of residence (migrated more than 5 years ago, within 1–5 years, less than 1 year ago), and current residence in La Paz. The language variables indicate whether the respondent is a monolingual Spanish speaker or speaks only indigenous languages, with bilingual speakers as the benchmark.

For women, two additional variables are included in the analysis to reflect the interruption in work experience that would accompany raising children. These variables are the number of live births for women ages 15–49 (zero for those over age 49), and a dichotomous variable for a woman over age 49 for whom data on the number of live births are not available.

In table 5 the regression analysis of the natural logarithm of earnings is reported separately for men and women who show positive earnings. Earnings increase significantly with both schooling and years of potential labor-market experience for both men and women. The increase is 6.5% per year of schooling for men and 6.7% for women, but the difference between the genders is not statistically significant.

Men have a somewhat steeper experience-earnings profile. When evaluated at 10 years of potential labor-market experience, earnings increase by 3.3% per year for men and by 2.8% per year for women. This difference by gender may reflect greater investments in on-the-job training by men or greater measurement error for women because of the weaker correspondence between the proxy measure of potential labor market experience and women's actual experience arising from labor force withdrawal because of children and other home production activities.

Marital status has a different effect for men and women. Among men, those who never married earn about 25% less (coefficient -0.28) than those currently married, while widowed, divorced, and separated men earn about 13% less (coefficient −0.12) than their married counterparts. Among women, ceteris paribus, those who never married earn about 19% (coefficient −0.21) less than married women with earnings, but widowed, divorced, and separated women earn about 10% more (coefficient 0.10) than married women.

Among women 15–49 years old, earnings are lower by 2.6% per

TABLE 5

REGRESSION ANALYSIS OF EARNINGS, BY SEX, URBAN BOLIVIA,
1993

Variable	Males	Females
Schooling	.0633	.0650
	(23.302)	(15.500)
Experience	.0488	.0403
	(14.685)	(7.431)
Experience squared	−.0008	−.0006
	(−12.611)	(−5.371)
Single	−.2835	−.2098
	(−7.847)	(−3.455)
Widowed, divorced, separated	−.1249	.0976
	(−1.987)	(2.071)
Migrated—more than 5 years ago	.1005	.1080
	(3.476)	(2.513)
Migrated—1–5 years ago	.0102	.1434
	(.208)	(1.774)
Migrated—less than 1 year ago	.0862	−.0929
	(.934)	(−.495)
La Paz	.0431	.1516
	(1.550)	(3.559)
Second job	.4807	.2935
	(10.207)	(4.109)
Self-employed	.4777	.3338
	(17.413)	(7.772)
Monolingual Spanish	.2067	.2487
	(8.314)	(6.265)
Monolingual indigenous	.0504	−.2951
	(.296)	(−2.693)
Older than 49	*	−.1892
		(−1.936)
Number of live births	*	−.0257
		(−2.326)
Rural birth place	−.2150	−.2320
	(−7.006)	(−4.617)
Constant	5.0491	4.6074
	(86.508)	(48.276)
Adjusted *R*-square	.351	.246
Sample size	3,674	1,800

SOURCE.—Encuesta Integrada de Hogares (La Paz: Instituto
Nacional de Estadistica, 1993).

NOTE.—Dependent variable: natural log of earnings for persons
with positive earnings. *t*-ratios are in parentheses; adults are ages 15
and older.

* Variables not entered.

live birth. In Bolivia, for the average number of live births per woman
(about 3.4), earnings are lower by about 9% compared to childless married women. The negative effect of children on earnings may reflect less
time currently in the labor market the larger the number of children
women have had in the past. Among older women for whom data on the

number of live births are not available, earnings are lower by about 17% compared to younger women (ages 15–49 years) without children for whom live birth data are available.

Geographic origins and mobility matter. Among both men and women, those born in rural areas earn about 20% less than their urban-born counterparts. This may be a reflection of discrimination against those from rural origins or an indication of lower human capital because of the lower quality of schooling in rural areas and job training that is less relevant for the urban sector.

The longer an individual has lived in the department capital, the higher are the earnings. Among both men and women, there is no significant earnings difference between those born in urban areas who have lived in the current city of residence less than 1 year and those born in the city of residence. Among those who migrated 1–5 years ago there is no significant effect for men and a marginally significant positive effect for women. However, those who migrated more than 5 years ago earn about 10% more than those born and raised in the city, and the difference is highly statistically significant. This is consistent with the hypothesis that migrants tend to be favorably self-selected and that the full effects of this selectivity are muted in the first few years because they have less knowledge of the labor market in the destination and less firm-specific and city-specific job training. Once these handicaps have been overcome, the favorable selectivity of migrants tends to show higher earnings. This is similar to the patterns observed for immigrants in the United States and elsewhere.[15]

For men, the earnings in La Paz do not differ significantly from those in the other department capitals, but they are significantly higher (coefficient 0.15 or about 16% higher earnings) for women. Probably this reflects the greater employment opportunities in the female-intensive government sector in the nation's capital and the higher pay schedule for these jobs.

Earnings differ significantly by language skills. Among men, other variables being equal, Spanish speakers earn about 23% (coefficient 0.21) more than bilingual speakers. There is no significant difference in earnings between bilingual speakers and those who speak only an indigenous language, perhaps because so few men speak only an indigenous language.

The differences in earnings by language skills are greater for women. Monolingual Spanish speakers earn about 28% (coefficient 0.25) more than bilingual speakers, who earn about 25% (coefficient −.030) more than women who speak only an indigenous language.

These differences in earnings by language skills reflect the value of speaking Spanish in the department capitals' labor markets. The lower earnings of the bilingual speakers also reflect their poor Spanish language skills, the lower quality of schooling received by indigenous peoples, or discrimination against indigenous language speakers in the modern (as distinct from traditional) labor market.

V. Summary and Conclusions

In this article, we use the Encuesta Integrada de Hogares (Integrated Household Survey) that was conducted in 1993 in the department capital cities in Bolivia to analyze the determinants of Spanish and indigenous language usage in Bolivia, and the effects of language usage on labor-force participation and earnings. Three language groups are considered: those who speak Spanish but not an indigenous language, those who speak an indigenous language but do not speak Spanish, and bilingual Spanish–indigenous language speakers. The analysis is conducted for men and women age 15 and older.

Language patterns in Bolivia are found to be consistent with the model of language proficiency based on exposure, efficiency, and economic incentives. Spanish is more likely to be the only language used by those who are more active in the labor market (men and women with fewer children), those with more exposure to Spanish as distinct from indigenous languages (born in an urban area or having resided in the city for a longer duration), and those more efficient in acquiring language skills (moved to the city at a younger age). Surprisingly, Spanish monolingualism is less common in La Paz than in the other department capital cities, ceteris paribus. Indigenous language monolingualism is most common among older women, those born in rural areas, those with several children, and those who have recently arrived in the department capital city, especially if it is La Paz.

The determinants of the propensity to work for wages differ between men and women. As expected, women not currently married are more likely to work than currently married women, but there is no significant effect of the number of children on work propensity. Among men, however, marriage is associated with greater labor-force participation. Schooling has a positive effect on labor-market participation for women, but a surprising negative effect partly related to school attendance for men, although the magnitude of the latter effect is small. Women who have lived in the city less than a year are less likely to work, perhaps because they are recent tied movers. Among both men and women, greater household income from sources other than their own labor supply has a negative effect on labor-market participation.

Labor-force participation varies by language usage. Among men the relatively few who speak only an indigenous language have a higher participation rate. Among women, monolingual indigenous language speakers have a higher participation rate than the bilingual speakers, but monolingual Spanish speakers have a lower propensity to work, other variables being the same.

The analysis indicates that earnings increase with human capital among both men and women. Earnings rise with years of schooling (implying about a 6.5% rate of return for both genders), potential labor-market experience, being born in an urban area, and among migrants with a longer duration in the city. Migrants who have resided 5 or more years in the city have about 10% higher earnings than nonmigrants born there, other variables being the same, suggesting favorable selectivity in migration.

Earnings in La Paz are about 16% higher for women than they are in the other department capital cities, but there is no similar effect among men. The greater earnings and labor force participation of women in La Paz may be due to the greater female intensity of employment in the central government sector of the economy.

Language skills are important. Monolingual Spanish speakers earn about 25% more than those who speak both Spanish and an indigenous language, while women who speak only an indigenous language earn about 25% less than the bilingual speakers. Bilingual speakers may be penalized in the labor market because of a poorer proficiency in Spanish.

The analysis indicates that indigenous and modern-sector language skills can be modeled successfully for a developing economy and that these language skills have an impact on labor market participation and on earnings. It also suggests that there may be large benefits from programs designed to improve Spanish language proficiency, for example, through bilingual education, among people of indigenous origins.

Notes

* This article is an outgrowth of Barry Chiswick's Visiting Scholar appointment in the Human Development Network at the World Bank and was completed while he was John M. Olin Visiting Professor. Center for the Study of the Economy and the State, Graduate School of Business, University of Chicago. The support of these institutions is appreciated. The views expressed in this article are solely ours and do not necessarily express the views of our sponsoring organizations.

1. See, e.g., the detailed statistics on language usage around the world in Joseph E. Grimes and Barbara F. Grimes, *Ethnologue: Languages of the World*, 13th ed. (Dallas: Summer Institute of Linguistics, 1993).

2. See, e.g., George Psacharopoulos and Harry Anthony Patrinos, eds., *Indigenous People and Poverty in Latin America: An Empirical Analysis* (Washington, D.C.: World Bank, 1994).

3. See, e.g., for the United States a series of studies by Gary D. Sandefur and his colleagues: Gary D. Sandefur, "American Indian Migration and Economic Opportunities," *International Migration Review* 20 (1986): 55–68; Gary D. Sandefur and A. Sakamoto, "American Indian Household Structure and Income" *Demography* 25 (1988): 71–80; Gary D. Sandefur and A. Pahari, "Racial and Ethnic Inequality in Earnings and Educational Attainment," *Social Service Review* 63 (1989): 199–221; Gary D. Sandefur and Wilbur J. Scott, "Minority Group Status and the Wages of Indian and Black Males," *Social Service Research* 12 (1983): 44–68; Gary D. Sandefur, S. McLanahan, and R. A.

Wojtkiewicz, "Race and Ethnicity, Family Structure, and High School Graduation," Discussion Paper no. 893-89 (University of Wisconsin—Madison, Institute for Research on Poverty, 1989); and C. M. Snipp and Gary D. Sandefur, "Earnings of American Indians and Alaskan Natives: The Effects of Residence and Migration," *Social Forces* 66 (1988): 994–1008. See also Barry R. Chiswick, "Differences in Education and Earnings across Racial and Ethnic Groups: Tastes, Discrimination, and Investments in Child Quality," *Quarterly Journal of Economics* 103, no. 3 (August 1988): 571–97. Robert G. Gregory, Annie C. Abello, and Jamie Johnson, "The Individual Economic Well Being of Native American Men and Women during the 1980's: A Decade of Moving Backwards," *Population Research and Development Review* 16, nos. 1–2 (April 1997): 115–45; James D. Gwartney and James E. Long. "The Relative Earnings of Blacks and Other Minorities," *Industrial and Labor Relations Review* 31, no. 3 (1978): 336–46; and Michael E. Hurst, "The Determinants of Earnings Differentials for Indigenous Americans: Human Capital, Location or Discrimination?" *Quarterly Review of Economics and Finance* 37, no. 4 (Fall 1997): 787–807. For Canada, see, e.g.. C. Y. Kuo, "The Effect of Education on the Earnings of Indian, Eskimo, Metis, and White Workers in the Mackenzie District of Northern Canada," *Economic Development and Cultural Change* 24, no. 2 (1976): 387–98; E. H. Lautard, "Occupational Segregation and Inequality between Native and Non-native Canadians, 1971," *Canadian Journal of Native Studies* 2 (1982): 303–20; Harry A. Patrinos and Chris N. Sakellariou. "North American Indians in the Canadian Labour Market: A Decomposition of Wage Differentials," *Economics of Education Review* 11, no. 3 (1992): 257–66; and Jack C. Stabler, "Dualism and Development in the Northwest Territories," *Economic Development and Cultural Change* 3 (1989): 805–39. For Australia and New Zealand, see, e.g., Peter Brosnan, "Age, Education and Maori-Pakeha Income Differences," *New Zealand Economic Papers* 18 (1984): 49–61; and Paul W. Miller, "The Structure of Aboriginal and Non-Aboriginal Youth Unemployment," *Australian Economic Papers* 28 (1989): 39–56.

4. Jonathan Kelley, "Class Conflict or Ethnic Oppression? The Cost of Being Indian in Rural Bolivia," *Rural Sociology* 53, no. 4 (1988): 399–420.

5. George Psacharopoulos, "Ethnicity, Education, and Earnings in Bolivia and Guatemala," *Comparative Education Review* 37, no. 1 (1993): 9–20.

6. Harry A. Patrinos, Eduardo Velez, and George Psacharopoulos, "Language, Education and Earnings in Asuncion, Paraguay," *Journal of Developing Areas* 29, no. 1 (1994): 57–68.

7. Donna J. MacIsaac and Harry Anthony Patrinos, "Labor Market Discrimination against Indigenous People in Peru," *Journal of Development Studies* 32, no. 2 (1995): 218–33.

8. Harry Anthony Patrinos, "Difference in Education and Earnings across Ethnic Groups in Guatemala," *Quarterly Review of Economics and Finance* 37, no. 4 (Fall 1997): 809–22.

9. See, e.g., MacIsaac and Patrinos; Psacharopoulos and Patrinos; Patrinos; Martonez Plaza, "Towards Standardization of Language Teaching in the Andean Countries," *Prospects* 20, no. 3 (1990): 377–84; and Juan Chackiel and Alexia Peyser, "Indigenous Population from Latin American National Censuses" (photocopy. Latin American Demographic Centre, CELADE, August 1993).

10. See Barry R. Chiswick and Paul W. Miller, "The Endogeneity between Language and Earnings: International Analyses," *Journal of Labor Economics* 13, no. 2 (April 1995): 245–87, and "English Language Fluency among Immigrants in the United States," *Research in Labor Economics* 17 (1998): 151–200.

11. Michael H. Long. "Maturational Constraints on Language Development," *Studies in Second Language Acquisition* 12, no. 3 (1990): 251–85.

12. The language of instruction in the schools is Spanish even in the lowest grades in the rural areas in which most people speak an indigenous language and do not know Spanish. There have been only a few small experiments with Spanish–native language instruction in schools with indigenous-speaking children. See Lambros Comitas, "Education and Social Stratification in Contemporary Bolivia," in *Education and Development: Latin America and the Caribbean,* ed. Thomas J. LaBelle (Los Angeles: University of California Press, 1972), pp. 363–78; and Xavier Albo and Lucia d'Emilio, "Indigenous Languages and Intercultural Bilingual Education in Bolivia," *Prospect* 20, no. 3 (1990): 321–29.

13. For an analysis of this issue, see Jacob Mincer, "Family Migration Decisions," *Journal of Political Economy* 85, no. 5 (October 1978): 749–74.

14. Jacob Mincer, *Schooling, Experience and Earnings* (New York: National Bureau of Economic Research, 1974).

15. Barry R. Chiswick, "The Effect of Americanization on the Earnings of Foreign-Born Men," *Journal of Political Economy* 86, no. 5 (October 1978): 897–922.

Labour Market Discrimination Against Indigenous People in Peru

DONNA J. MacISAAC and
HARRY ANTHONY PATRINOS

In this article, the component of the gross wage differential that can be explained by productivity-enhancing attributes and that which is due to unexplained factors and labour market discrimination are empirically determined. Individual data from the 1991 Living Standards Measurements Survey of Peru are used to analyse labour market earnings and to decompose the gross earnings differential. A large portion of the indigenous/non-indigenous wage gap is unexplained by human capital and other observable differences.

INTRODUCTION

In recent years, the connection between ethnicity and economic inequality in developing economies has gained considerable attention. Yet while researchers have examined the experiences of ethnic groups, especially in developed economies, very little investigation has been made of the different economic circumstances of the indigenous population within a society – developed or developing. This is in spite of the fact that in many countries there exist diverse ethnic groups with very different levels of economic and social opportunities.

In recent years sociologists and economists have been exploring the socioeconomic status of indigenous people in the United States and Canada [*Gwartney and Long, 1978; Sandefur and Scott, 1983; Snipp and Sandefur, 1988; Chiswick, 1988; Snipp, 1988; Sandefur and Pahari, 1989; Kuo, 1976; Stabler, 1989; 1990; Patrinos and Sakellariou, 1992; 1993*]. These studies suggest that both labour market discrimination and lower levels of

Donna J. MacIsaac and Harry Anthony Patrinos, World Bank, Washington, DC. This is a revised version of a paper that was presented at the Meeting on the Demography of Indigenous People, IUSSP Conference, Montréal, Canada, 31 August 1993. The authors thank Juan Chackiel, George Psacharopoulos, Christopher Colclough and an anonymous referee for helpful comments. The views expressed here are those of the authors and should not be attributed to the World Bank.

134

human capital endowments are responsible for observed earnings differentials.

In the United States, Sandefur and Scott [1983] find that indigenous workers receive more favorable returns to human capital variables than do whites. However, as a group, indigenous people have less education, which suggests that discrimination occurs at an earlier point in their lives. Still, according to the authors, much of the earnings differential between indigenous and non-indigenous people would disappear if indigenous people had the same human capital, regional and job characteristics as do whites. More recent United States-based studies by Sandefur and Pahari [1989] find that improvements in educational attainment have a significant impact on the reduction of indigenous workers' earnings disadvantage. In Canada, however, the discrimination component is much higher and appears to be increasing over time [Patrinos and Sakellariou, 1993].

Studies of ethnicity and the education-earnings connection in Guatemala and Bolivia find that the indigenous populations have much lower levels of schooling, receive lower earnings and experience lower rates of return to schooling than does the non-indigenous population [Psacharopoulos, 1993; Patrinos and Psacharopoulos, 1993a; Kelley, 1988]. A recent study for Bolivia finds that most of the indigenous/ non-indigenous earnings differential is due to productivity (income-generating) differences between indigenous and non-indigenous workers [Patrinos and Psacharopoulos, 1993a]. However, that study was limited to urban Bolivia and included both monolingual and bilingual (Spanish and indigenous language) individuals.

While Peru has a large indigenous population which, according to various accounts, comprises between 25 and 40 per cent of the total population, there has been very little econometric work on the determinants of earnings for indigenous people. The effect of being indigenous was controlled for, however, in a study of education and earnings in Peru using census data for 1961 and 1972. While the percentage of Quechua/Aymara speakers in the labour force declined, their income relative to the non-indigenous population increased substantially (Toledo, as cited in Carnoy [1979]). Results of log earnings functions for the two periods reveals a considerable decrease over time in the penalty associated with speaking a native language.

In this article a model is developed for individual earnings based on economic and other factors. The primary purpose of the model is to examine the existence, and causes of, an earnings differential between indigenous and non-indigenous workers.

DATA AND METHODS

Data

Data from the *Encuesta Nacional De Niveles De Vida*, conducted in October and November 1991 by the *Instituto Cuanto*, are used. As one of the World Bank's Living Standards Measurement Studies, this survey is based on a common methodology and is usually referred to as the 1991 Peru Living Standards Survey (PLSS). The survey covers 11,491 individuals and provides household, demographic and individual level information. Unfortunately, due to security considerations, certain regions of Peru were not surveyed. The survey covers households in four regions: Lima, the Urban Coast, and the Rural and Urban Sierra. The Rural Coast, the entire Selva and the more remote areas of the Rural Sierra were inaccessible.

Individuals are identified as indigenous if they speak Quechua, Aymara or another indigenous language, indicated by their responses to the questions: *¿Cuál es la lengua materna?* (What is your maternal language?) and *¿Qué idioma habla?* (What language do you speak?). The resulting estimate of the Peruvian indigenous population is 11.3 per cent of the total population. Other estimates, using in some cases different definitions from that used in the PLSS, place the indigenous population at 31 per cent of the total Peruvian population in 1972 and 25 per cent in 1981 [*CELADE, 1992*]. From the PLSS it is found that Quechua-speakers account for the majority, or 63 per cent of the indigenous population, while Aymara-speakers account for the remaining 37 per cent. Since individuals are self-identifying with a particular language, it could be the case that some indigenous people are classified as non-indigenous, either through concealment of their indigenous origins or because they do not speak a non-Spanish language. It is also conceivable that the relatively low population estimate provided by the PLSS is due to its limited coverage. None the less, the indigenous sample population is sufficient to undertake the earnings analysis.

Language is an important factor in Peru, and despite the fact that both Quechua and Aymara are officially recognised languages and are widely spoken, indigenous languages have low status. Many indigenous people are forced to reject their own language and culture in order to improve their socioeconomic position. The Peruvian social pyramid is such that the Spanish-speaking European descendants are at the top, followed in turn by the *mestizos* (who mostly speak only Spanish) and the *cholos* (roughly, Spanish-speaking indigenous people, and a negative term not used in the presence of the person to whom it is applied [*Bourricaud, 1976*]), while the monolingual indigenous language speakers are found at the bottom. A 1963 study of the distribution of income by social groups documents that whites, which represent 0.1 per cent of the population, receive 20 per cent of the national income; *mestizos*, representing 20 per cent of the population, receive 53 per cent of the income; *cholos* represent 23 per cent of the population and receive 14 per cent of the income; and while the indigenous population receives only 13 per cent of the total national income it represents 57 per cent of the total population [*Paulston, 1971: 402*].

Methods

The standard procedure for analyzing the determinants of earnings differentials between two groups is used. The following two equations, or earnings functions, are fitted for employed members of the economically dominant group and employed members of the marginal group:

$$LnY_n = b_n X_n + u_n \tag{1}$$

$$LnY_i = b_i X_i + u_i \tag{2}$$

where subscripts n and i represent non-indigenous and indigenous workers; Y symbolizes labour market earnings; X represents measured productivity-determining characteristics of the workers, such as education, experience and other control variables. The regression coefficient, b, reflects the returns that the market yields to a unit change in characteristics such as education and experience. The error term, u, reflects measurement error, as well as the effect of factors unmeasured or unobserved by the researcher.

It is known that the regression lines pass through the mean values of the variables so that

$$Ln\overline{Y}_n = \hat{b}_n \overline{X}_n \tag{3}$$

$$Ln\overline{Y}_i = \hat{b}_i \overline{X}_i \tag{4}$$

where hats (^) denote estimated values and bars (⁻) represent mean values.

If indigenous workers receive the same returns for their endowments of wage-determining characteristics as do non-indigenous workers, then their average earnings would be:

$$Ln\overline{Y}_i * = \hat{b}_n \overline{X}_i \tag{5}$$

Subtracting equation (5) from (3) gives the difference between average non-indigenous earnings and the average hypothetical indigenous earnings that are assumed to prevail if indigenous workers were paid according to the pay structure faced by non-indigenous workers. This difference reflects their unequal endowments of income-generating characteristics, so that:

$$\mathrm{Ln}\overline{Y}_n - \mathrm{Ln}\overline{Y}_i * = \hat{b}_n \,\overline{X}_n - \hat{b}_n\overline{X}_i = \hat{b}_n \,(\overline{X}_n - \overline{X}_i) \tag{6}$$

Subtracting equation (4) from (5) yields the difference between the hypothetical non-discriminatory earnings of indigenous workers and their actual earnings. This difference reflects the different returns to the same income-generating characteristics:

$$\mathrm{Ln}\overline{Y}_i* - \mathrm{Ln}\overline{Y}_i = \hat{b}_n\overline{X}_i - \hat{b}_i\overline{X}_i = \overline{X}_i(\hat{b}_n - \hat{b}_i) \tag{7}$$

Adding equations (6) and (7) yields:

$$\mathrm{Ln}\overline{Y}_n - \mathrm{Ln}\overline{Y}_i = \hat{b}_n \,(\overline{X}_n - \overline{X}_i) + \overline{X}_i \,(\hat{b}_n - \hat{b}_i) \tag{8}$$

This could be written as:

$$\mathrm{Ln}\overline{Y}_n - \mathrm{Ln}\overline{Y}_i = \hat{b}_i \,(\overline{X}_n - \overline{X}_i) + \overline{X}_n \,(\hat{b}_n - \hat{b}_i) \tag{9}$$

Thus, according to equation (8), the overall earnings gap can be decomposed into two components: one is the portion attributable to differences in the endowments of income generating characteristics $(\overline{X}_n - \overline{X}_i)$ evaluated with the non-indigenous worker pay structure $(\hat{b}_n)$; the other portion is attributable to differences in the returns $(\hat{b}_n - \hat{b}_i)$ that non-indigenous and indigenous workers receive for the same endowment of income-generating characteristics $(\overline{X}i)$. This latter component is often taken as reflecting wage discrimination. This is known as the Oaxaca [1973] (see also Blinder [1973]) decomposition, which allows for estimation of discrimination from earnings functions estimated at the indigenous means (or non-indigenous wage structure). According to equation (9), the components are attributable to differences in the endowments of income generating characteristics $(\overline{X}_n - \overline{X}_i)$ evaluated with the indigenous worker pay structure $(\hat{b}_i)$, and to differences in the returns $(\hat{b}_n - \hat{b}_i)$ that non-indigenous and indigenous workers receive for the same endowment of income-generating characteristics $(\overline{X}_n)$. Similar to equation (8), this latter component is often taken as reflecting wage discrimination. Equation (9) is known as the Oaxaca decomposition, but evaluated at non-indigenous means (or indigenous wage structure).

However, the wage structure that would prevail in the absence of discrimination is not known. This is referred to as the 'index number problem' (see, for example, Cotton [1988]; Gunderson [1989]; Neumark [1988]). One solution to this problem is to obtain estimates from both formulations and thus report a range.

Also, one does not know the wage that would prevail in the absence of discrimination. In other words, the level of the 'non-discriminatory wage' is unknown. Nevertheless, it is fairly certain that the non-discriminatory wage is not the current minority wage structure, since this would mean that this group would have no particular economic reason for desiring an end to discrimination since their wages would be unaffected by the change. Similarly, if it is assumed that the majority wage structure is the equilibrium level, then one would be faced with the situation whereby the majority group would not object to ending discrimination since their own wages would not be affected. But as Cotton [1988] argues, neither the majority nor the minority wage structure would prevail in the absence of discrimination. The reason being that both wage structures are a function of discrimination. The non-discriminatory wage lies somewhere between the wage structure of the majority and that of the minority group (see also Reimers [1983]). Cotton [1988], therefore, proposes the following formulation for decomposing the differential:

$$Ln\overline{Y}_n - Ln\overline{Y}_i = b^* (\overline{X}_n - \overline{X}_i) + \overline{X}_n (\hat{b}_n - b^*) + \overline{X}_i (b^* - \hat{b}_i) \qquad (9)$$

The decomposition component is made up of two elements, one representing the amount by which the majority productivity characteristics are overvalued $(\overline{X}_n(\hat{b}_n - b^*))$, and the other the amount by which minority productivity characteristics are undervalued $(\overline{X}_i(b^* - \hat{b}_i))$. The coefficient b^* is the non-discriminatory wage structure. This method will give estimates that lie between those that can be derived from equations (8) and (9); in other words, the Oaxaca method either overestimates productivity differences and underestimates discrimination (equation (8)), or it underestimates productivity differences and overestimates discrimination (equation (9)).

The non-discriminatory wage structure, b^*, however, is unobserved and its estimate is based on a number of assumptions about its nature: (1) in the absence of discrimination, the majority group would receive a lower wage than they currently receive and the minority group would receive a higher wage; (2) b^* is a linear combination of $\hat{b}_n$ and $\hat{b}_i$; and (3) the nondiscriminatory wage structure will be closer to the majority wage structure than to the minority wage structure. The non-discriminatory wage structure, then, is operationalised in the following manner:

$$b^* = f_n\hat{b}_n + f_i\hat{b}_i \qquad (11)$$

where f_n and f_i are the proportions of the employed population from the majority and minority groups.

Oaxaca and Ransom [1989; 1994] also examine the index number problem and the caveats surrounding the determinants of gender wage rates in the absence of discrimination and propose a decomposition method similar to Cotton [*1988*], but with one very important difference. The nondiscriminatory wage structure in Oaxaca-Ransom is a blend of the current wage structures for males and females, and the corresponding coefficient, b^*, is an estimate of the common wage structure derived from a wage equation (estimated by OLS) using a pooled sample of males and females.

In this article all four decomposition methods will be used and the corresponding estimates of discrimination will be reported and commented upon. But it should be noted that in economic terms, discrimination refers to differences in economic outcomes between groups that cannot be accounted for by the skills and productive characteristics of these groups [*Schultz, 1991*]. While this method allows one to determine the extent of discrimination in the labour market, it does not allow one to determine the origins of discrimination. Discrimination in the labour market can directly affect earnings, occupational attainment and training access; or it can be indirect, through discrimination in the acquisition of skills, prior to entering the labour market [*Chiswick, 1987*].

The use of earnings functions to estimate discrimination is not exclusive of the problem of omitted variables. This type of data problem means that the unexplained component is not only a measure of discrimination, but also of our ignorance [*Filer, 1983*]. Therefore, due to omitted and unobserved factors the 'unexplained' component is taken as an 'upper bound' estimate of wage discrimination in the labour market. Included among the omitted variables that are expected to account for some of the unexplained component are: labour quality, labour force attachment, lack of specific training, work career interruptions and tastes and personality [*Hill, 1979; Goldin and Polachek, 1987; Polachek, 1975; Mincer and Polachek, 1974; 1978; Filer, 1983*]. There is also evidence to suggest that much of the discrimination against the minority group is due to occupational segregation; that is, the 'crowding' of the minority group into certain occupations where rates of pay and chances for promotion are low. This, of course, suggests that some degree of prior discrimination has taken place. The results of a number of studies have shown that the greater the number of variables used to control for differences in productivity related factors, the smaller the productivity-adjusted earnings gap (unexplained component) relative to the unadjusted gap. In fact, when the gap is close to zero, this usually results from the inclusion of control variables whose values themselves may reflect prior discrimination [*Gunderson, 1989*]. However, even when an extensive list of control variables is used, most studies find some residual gap that they attribute to discrimination.

One important aspect of human capital is 'language capital' – speaking, reading and writing skills in one or more languages. Language skills are an important form of human capital. For most minority groups, however, their mother tongue is not the majority or dominant language spoken in the country. An ethnic minority group member who does not know the dominant language might find a language-minority enclave within which mother-tongue skills can be fruitfully used. A language-minority enclave may, however, limit training opportunities and job mobility, and thereby limit earnings opportunities. Furthermore, greater dominant-language skills would enhance productivity in the enclave and the non-enclave labour market by increasing efficiency in job search and through greater productivity on the job. There is, therefore, a labour market incentive to acquire dominant-language skills [*Chiswick, 1991; Chiswick and Miller, 1995*]. In this analysis, language proficiency is not known, but schooling is strongly correlated with Spanish language skills since other than a few areas that offer initial education in the mother tongue, all schooling is conducted in Spanish in Peru. And given the construction of the identifying variable, being indigenous does not imply not knowing Spanish.

LABOUR MARKET DESCRIPTION

In general, the potential labour force is composed of work-aged individuals who are eligible for work. Given the high labour force participation rate for young Peruvians [*Patrinos and Psacharopoulos, 1993b*], the potential labour force sample used here contains individuals age 12 to 65 years, and excludes those who work less than 30 hours per week while attending school.

Labour earnings are higher for non-indigenous workers than for indigenous workers. The average earnings of Spanish-speaking workers are more than double the average earnings of indigenous workers. Spanish-speaking workers predominate in the private sector (23 per cent versus ten per cent), the public sector (11 versus seven per cent) and among the self-employed (23 versus 13 per cent). In stark contrast, the farming sector contains 54 per cent of the indigenous labour force and only 7 per cent of the Spanish-speaking labour force.

Within the public sector, the earnings differential is dependent on employment as either a worker or a professional. Indigenous public sector workers receive only 46 per cent of the wages of non-indigenous workers. Given the positive association between education and job placement in the public sector, it appears that indigenous public sector workers are restricted to lower level or menial jobs. In contrast, public sector indigenous professionals have virtual wage parity with Spanish-speaking public sector professionals and their educational difference is minimal. Within the private sector, indigenous workers and professionals receive 58 and 61 per cent of non-indigenous labour earnings.

DECOMPOSITION OF EARNINGS DIFFERENTIALS

In order to fully understand the position of indigenous people in the labour market it is necessary to examine the respective roles of ethnicity and personal endowments such as schooling and experience in determining the level of labour market earnings. The analysis is restricted to males. This limitation avoids compounding the results by including the discrimination to which women as a group are subjected. Unfortunately, the sample of indigenous women who report employment earnings is insufficient to generate confident estimates of female earnings equations. The sample contains 2,174 males who report labour earnings within the past year. In order to gain an understanding of the factors which contribute to the earnings differential between groups, 'upper bound' estimates of discrimination due to ethnicity are obtained using the four decomposition techniques outlined above.

The mean characteristics of indigenous and non-indigenous males are presented in Table 1. Average earnings in the sample are 152.3 million new *soles* per month. Indigenous workers earn less than half the income of non-indigenous workers. The level of educational attainment of the two groups differs substantially. Indigenous men have only 6.7 mean years of schooling relative to 10.0 mean years of schooling for Spanish-speaking men. In terms of levels attained, nearly 60 per cent of the indigenous group have not exceeded primary school education, whereas only 23 per cent of the non-indigenous group belong to this category. Only five per cent of indigenous workers have post secondary education as compared to 25 per cent of non-indigenous workers.

The PLSS contains information on actual labour market experience. The average years of labour market experience reported in the survey is dramatically greater for indigenous people. On average, indigenous workers have almost twice the experience of non-indigenous workers, at 17 years for indigenous male workers versus almost ten years for non-indigenous male workers.

The most prevalent occupation for indigenous people is farming, which contains 50 per cent of indigenous males. This sector contains only eight per cent of non-indigenous males. In contrast, at 41 per cent, the private sector employs the largest proportion of non-indigenous males, while it contains only 21 per cent of indigenous males. Indigenous workers are also half as likely to be self-employed and less likely to work in the public sector than are non-indigenous workers. At 68 per cent, the majority of indigenous

TABLE 1

MEAN CHARACTERISTICS BY ETHNICITY

Characteristic	Indigenous	Non-indigenous	All
Earnings (millions new *soles*)	70.6	64.7	152.3
Schooling (years)	6.7	10.0	9.6
Highest Educational Attainment (per cent)			
Incomplete Primary/None	27.9	8.2	10.7
Complete Primary	28.8	15.0	16.8
Secondary	38.0	51.9	50.2
Non-University Higher	2.0	8.2	7.4
University	3.3	16.6	14.9
Actual Experience (years)	17.3	9.8	10.8
Hours Worked/Month	222.3	204.0	206.4
Economic Sector (percent)			
Farming	50.1	7.7	13.3
Public	12.9	18.4	17.7
Private	21.9	43.1	40.3
Self-employed	15.1	30.8	28.7
Age	39.3	37.6	37.8
Married (percent)	64.0	55.7	56.8
Region (percent)			
Lima	8.9	51.5	45.9
Rural	67.8	11.1	18.5
N	315	1,858	2,174

Source: PLSS1991.

workers are located in rural areas, whereas the majority, 52 per cent, of non-indigenous workers are located in Lima. Average age and hours worked as well as per cent married are marginally higher among indigenous workers.

Earnings Equations

The determinants of earnings are estimated using an earnings function (Table 2). Indigenous workers earn 44 per cent less than non-indigenous workers. In other words, even if indigenous people had the same amount of education and experience or, more importantly, the same proportion of workers in farming and rural locations as non-indigenous people, they would still earn about one-half that of non-indigenous people.

Non-indigenous men receive positive yet diminishing returns to labour

TABLE 2

EARNINGS FUNCTIONS, POOLED AND BY ETHNICITY

Variable	Pooled (with indigenous dummy)	Pooled	Indigenous	Non-indigenous
Schooling (*residual=less than primary complete*)				
Completed Primary	0.0425 (0.7)	0.0714 (1.1)	-0.1546 (1.2)	0.1152 (1.5)
Some Secondary School	0.1041** (1.7)	0.1416* (2.3)	-0.0700 (0.5)	0.1744* (2.5)
Non-University Higher	0.3199* (3.8)	0.3798* (4.5)	0.3640 (1.0)	0.3924* (4.3)
Some University	0.6206* (8.4)	0.6766* (9.1)	0.5245** (1.7)	0.6929* (8.9)
Experience	0.0274* (6.1)	0.0258* (5.6)	-0.0006 (0.1)	0.0297* (6.0)
Experience^2	-0.0005* (4.7)	-0.0005* (4.3)	-0.0001 (0.4)	-0.0005* (4.0)
Hours Worked (log)	0.3597* (9.1)	0.3409* (8.5)	0.2215* (2.0)	0.3828* (9.1)
Indigenous	-0.4415* (7.5)			
Married	0.2872* (7.9)	0.2819* (7.7)	0.0670 (0.6)	0.3072* (8.0)
Economic Sector (residual=private)				
Farm Employment	-0.4119* (5.2)	-0.4647* (5.9)	-0.4142* (2.6)	-0.2726* (2.8)
Public Sector Employment	0.0763 (1.5)	0.0672 (1.3)	0.4533* (2.5)	0.0292 (0.6)
Self Employment	0.2327* (5.6)	0.2295* (5.5)	0.3654* (2.1)	0.2167* (5.2)
Lima	0.1224* (3.3)	0.1434* (3.8)	0.4164* (2.2)	0.1139* (3.0)
Rural	-0.3907* (5.6)	-0.5224* (7.7)	-0.2032 (1.3)	-0.4721* (5.9)
Constant	2.2669	2.3070*	2.8624	2.0641
N	2174	2174	315	1,858
Adjusted R^2	0.337	0.320	0.262	0.268

Source: Computed from PLSS 1991.
Notes: Dependent variable is the natural logarithm of earnings. Numbers in parentheses are t-ratios. *signifies statistical significance at the 5 per cent level or better; **signifies statistical significance at the 10 per cent level or better.

market experience; indigenous men are not rewarded for labour market experience. This suggests that the experience reported by indigenous men may represent time 'trapped' in low-paying sectors.

The factors which are significant in predicting the earnings of indigenous men are location- and job-specific. Employment in the public sector, self-employment and living in Lima increase the earnings of the indigenous population, while employment in the farming sector negatively affects earnings. Public sector employment has a particularly large earnings impact on the earnings of indigenous men; for non-indigenous men public sector employment has no effect on earnings. The relative proportions of indigenous to non-indigenous people in the areas above support the distinct earnings advantage found for non-indigenous workers. It is also interesting to note the differential effect of marriage on the earnings of indigenous and non-indigenous populations. Marriage increases the earnings of non-indigenous men by 3.3 per cent while marriage has no effect on the earnings of indigenous men. Hours worked has a significant and positive impact on earnings, but more so for non-indigenous workers. Living in the capital, Lima, raises indigenous earnings considerably (more than 40 per cent), much more than for non-indigenous workers (11 per cent).

A series of dummy variables for school levels are used to measure the impact of education on earnings. For indigenous workers, obtaining some university schooling is the only significant educational factor to increase earnings. Relative to those with less than a primary education, some university increases indigenous earnings by more than 50 per cent. But as with the other factors associated with significant and large impacts on indigenous earnings, not many indigenous people have acquired any university education. Indigenous workers lack precisely those factors that raise their earnings the most. For example, university schooling is the only level of education that is associated with large, positive and significant effects on indigenous workers' earnings; but only three per cent of the indigenous workforce has some university education. Also, public sector employment has a very large, positive impact on indigenous workers' earnings; but only 13 per cent of the indigenous workforce is in the public sector (*vis-à-vis* 18 per cent of the non-indigenous workforce). And while residence in Lima is associated with a large earnings impact, only nine per cent of indigenous workers reside in the capital (more than half of the non-indigenous sample resides in Lima).

Decomposition Results

Estimation of four decomposition equations – the two Oaxaca equations (with indigenous means and with non-indigenous means), the Cotton equation and the Oaxaca–Ransom equation – reveals that the proportion of the overall indigenous/non-indigenous earnings differential that is due to the productive characteristics of individuals is equivalent to between 50 and 70 per cent of the differential in log of earnings between indigenous and non-indigenous men (Table 3). This range represents the extremes. Attempts to estimate the discrimination components using the non-discriminatory wage produce rather different results. The Cotton method, which estimates the non-discriminatory wage somewhere between the wage structure of the majority and that of the minority group, gives an estimate close to the Oaxaca decomposition evaluated at indigenous means (or non-indigenous wage structure), at 53 per cent. The Oaxaca–Ransom, or pooled method, which bases its estimate of the non-discriminatory wage on observation, assesses the proportion of the over-all indigenous/non-indigenous earnings differential that is due to the productive characteristics of individuals to be close to the Oaxaca decomposition evaluated at non-indigenous means (or indigenous wage structure), at 66 per cent. Since the pooled method bases its estimate of the non-discriminatory wage structure on empirical observation, it may be 'a more natural method' for decomposing earnings differentials [*Oaxaca and Ransom, 1994: 18*].

TABLE 3

DECOMPOSITION RESULTS

Specification	Portion of Overall Earnings Differential due to Differences in:	
	Endowment	Wage Characteristics
Evaluated at Indigenous Means	49.8	50.2
Evaluated at Non-indigenous Means	69.8	30.2
Cotton	52.8	47.2
Pooled	65.6	34.4

Source: Calculated from the results presented in Table 2.

DISCUSSION

Overall, the earnings of indigenous workers are less than half those of non-indigenous workers. Better paying occupations are dominated by non-indigenous workers. While sections of the indigenous population have moved to new occupations as wage labourers, teachers and in trade, the majority of the population remains involved in agricultural work. Estimation of earnings functions by ethnic group show that the returns to schooling for Spanish-speaking workers are higher than those for indigenous workers. Indigenous men are not rewarded for labour market experience. This suggests that the experience reported by indigenous men may represent time 'trapped' in low paying sectors. And although higher levels of education provide higher earnings, university education is the only significant educational factor to increase earnings for indigenous men in Peru.

In Peru, the proportion of the overall earnings differential that is due to the productive characteristics of individuals is equivalent to between 50 and 70 per cent. The remaining difference in wages is unexplained, and may include any unmeasured factors which contribute to the earnings differential such as ability, health, the quality of education, labour force attachment and culture. However, wage discrimination against the indigenous population may account for as little as 30 per cent and as much as 50 per cent of the overall earnings differential.

While the returns to schooling for non-indigenous workers are high, only university education is profitable for indigenous male workers. Rural location is a major disadvantage to the economic well being of indigenous people. Yet, rural location does not affect non-indigenous workers as negatively as it does indigenous workers, with the result that indigenous people are unduly penalised for their location. For the same amounts of work and labour market experience, indigenous people are paid less than non-indigenous people.

As previous studies of ethnicity in Latin America show indigenous people have much lower levels of schooling, receive lower earnings and experience lower rates of return to schooling than does the non-indigenous population [*Psacharopoulos, 1993; Patrinos and Psacharopoulos, 1993a; Kelley, 1988*]. Depending on the decomposition technique used, discrimination and unexplained components account for less than half of the portion of the overall earnings differential. In other words, equalising the human capital characteristics of indigenous workers would reduce the earnings differentials between indigenous and non-indigenous workers in Peru by as much as 66 per cent. This is very similar to the results obtained for Bolivia [*Patrinos and Psacharopoulos, 1993*]. But the factors that raise indigenous earnings the most are those factors that indigenous people desperately lack. While a university education is the only profitable schooling level for indigenous people, only three per cent of the indigenous workforce has some university education. Although public sector employment has a very large impact on indigenous workers' earnings, only 13 per cent of the indigenous workforce is in the public sector. And while residence in Lima is associated with a large positive effect on indigenous workers' earnings, only nine per cent of indigenous workers reside in the capital.

The limitation of this analysis should be borne in mind when interpreting the evidence. The indigenous population is defined according to language.

Missing are those who chose not to identify as indigenous and indigenous people who conceal their identity or who do not speak their language. And the fact that university schooling affects indigenous workers' earnings so much suggests that schooling does have a significant effect. Perhaps at the higher levels school quality is more equal, while at lower levels indigenous people suffer as a result of low quality and irrelevant schooling. Given that so few indigenous people report having a university education, it could be that their returns signify scarcity and that more indigenous workers with a university education would suppress earnings differentials and lower the returns. Clearly, further research on indigenous and non-indigenous earnings differentials and the ethnic factor of labour force dynamics in Peru is warranted.

final version received April 1995

REFERENCES

Blinder, A.S., 1973, 'Wage discrimination: Reduced form and Structural Estimates.' *Journal of Human Resources* 8, pp.436–65.
Bourricaud, F., 1976, 'Indian, Mestizo, and Cholo as Symbols in the Peruvian System of Stratification', in N. Glazer and D.P. Moynihan (eds.), *Ethnicity: Theory and Experience.* Cambridge, MA: Harvard University Press.
Carnoy, M., 1979, *Can Educational Policy Equalise Income Distribution in Latin America?*, Westmead: Saxon House for the International Labour Office.
CELADE (Latin American Demographic Center), 1992, *Demographic Bulletin*, 25, Santiago, Chile.
Chiswick, B.R. 1991, 'Speaking, Reading and Earnings among Low-Skilled Immigrants', *Journal of Labour Economics*, 9, pp.149–70.
Chiswick, B.R. and P.W. Miller, 1995, 'The Endogeneity between Language and Earnings: International Analyses', *Journal of Labour Economics* (forthcoming).
Chiswick, B.R., 1987, 'Race Earnings Differentials', In G. Psacharopoulos (ed.), *Economics of Education: Research and Studies*, Oxford: Pergamon Press.
Chiswick, B.R., 1988, 'Differences in Education and Earnings Across Racial and Ethnic Groups: Tastes, Discrimination, and Investments in Child Quality', *Quarterly Journal of Economic*, 103, pp.571–97.
Cotton, J., 1988, 'On the Decomposition of Wage Differentials', *Review of Economics and Statistics*, 70, pp.236–43.
Filer, R.K., 1983, 'Sexual Difference in Earnings: The Role of Individual Personalities and Tastes', *Journal of Human Resources*, 18, pp.82–99.
Goldin, C. and S. Polachek, 1987, 'Residual Differences by Sex: Perspectives on the Gender Gap in Earnings', *American Economic Review*, 77, pp.143–51.
Gunderson, M., 1989, 'Male–Female Wage Differentials and Policy Responses', *Journal of Economic Literature*, 27, pp.46–72.
Gwartney, J.D. and J.E. Long, 1978, 'The Relative Earnings of Blacks and Other Minorities', *Industrial and Labour Relations Review*, 31, pp.336–46.
Hill, M.S., 1979, 'The Wage Effects of Marital Status and Children', *Journal of Human Resources*, 14, pp.579–94.
Kelley, J. 1988, 'Class Conflict or Ethnic Oppression? The Cost of Being Indian in Rural Bolivia', *Rural Sociology*, 53, pp.399–420.

Kuo, C.-Y., 1976, 'The Effect of Education on the Earnings of Indian, Eskimo, Metis, and White Workers in the Mackenzie District of Northern Canada', *Economic Development and Cultural Change*, 24, pp.387–98.

Mincer, J. and S. Polachek, 1974, 'Family Investments in Human Capital: Earnings of Women', *Journal of Political Economy*, 82, pp.S76–S108.

Mincer, J. and S. Polachek, 1978, 'Women's Earnings Reexamined', *Journal of Human Resources*, 8, pp.118–34.

Neumark, D., 1988, '"Employers" Discriminatory Behavior and the Estimation of Wage Discrimination', *Journal of Human Resources*, 23, pp.279–95.

Oaxaca, R., 1973, 'Male–female Wage Differences in Urban Labour Markets', *International Economic Review*, 14, pp.693–701.

Oaxaca, R. and M.R. Ransom, 1989, 'Overpaid Men· and Underpaid Women: A Tale of the Gender Specific Wage Effects of Labour Market Discrimination', Paper presented at the International Economics Association World Congress, Athens, 28 August to 1 September 1989.

Oaxaca, R. and M.R. Ransom, 1994, 'On Discrimination and the Decomposition of Wage Differentials', *Journal of Econometrics*, 61, pp.5–21.

Patrinos, H.A. and G. Psacharopoulos, 1993a, 'The Cost of Being Indigenous in Bolivia: an Empirical Analysis of Educational Attainments and Outcomes', *Bulletin of Latin American Research*, 12, pp.293–309.

Patrinos, H.A. and G. Psacharopoulos, 1993b, 'Schooling and non-Schooling Activities of Peruvian Youth', (mimeo).

Patrinos, H.A. and C.N. Sakellariou, 1992, 'North American Indians in the Canadian Labour Market: A Decomposition of Wage Differentials', *Economics of Education Review*, 11, pp.257–66.

Patrinos, H.A. and C.N. Sakellariou, 1993, 'Decomposing Aboriginal/non-Aboriginal Earnings Differentials in Canada: Culture versus Discrimination', (mimeo).

Paulston, R.G., 1971, 'Sociocultural Constraints on Educational Development in Peru', *Journal of Developing Areas*, 5, pp.401–16.

Polachek, S.W., 1975, 'Potential Biases in Measuring Male-Female Discrimination', *Journal of Human Resources*, 10, pp.205–229.

Psacharopoulos, G., 1993, 'Ethnicity, Education, and Earnings in Bolivia and Guatemala', *Comparative Education Review*, 37, pp.9–20.

Reimers, C.W., 1983, 'Labour Market Discrimination against Hispanic and Black Men', *Review of Economics and Statistics*, 65, pp.570–9.

Sandefur, G.D. and A. Pahari, 1989, 'Racial and Ethnic Inequality in Earnings and Educational Attainment', *Social Service Review*, 63, pp.199–221.

Sandefur, G.D. and W.J. Scott, 1983, 'Minority Group Status and the Wages of Indian and Black Males', *Social Science Research*, 12, pp.44–68.

Schultz, T.P. 1991, 'Labour Market Discrimination: Measurement and Interpretation', in N. Birdsall and R. Sabot (eds.), *Unfair Advantage: Labour Market Discrimination in Developing Countries*, Washington, DC: The World Bank.

Snipp, M., 1988, 'On the Costs of Being an American Indian: Ethnic Identity and Economic Opportunity.', in J.H. Johnson, Jr. and M.L. Oliver (eds.), *Proceedings of the Conference on Comparative Ethnicity: Ethnic Dilemmas in Comparative Perspective*, University of California, Los Angeles, 1–3 June 1988.

Snipp, M. and G.D. Sandefur, 1988, 'Earnings of American Indians and Alaskan Natives: The Effects of Residence and Migration', *Social Forces*, 66, pp.994–1008.

Stabler, J.C., 1989, 'Dualism and Development in the Northwest Territories', *Economic Development and Cultural Change*, 37, pp.805–39.

Stabler, J.C., 1990, 'A Utility Analysis of Activity Patterns of Native Males in the Northwest Territories', *Economic Development and Cultural Change*, 39, pp.47–60.

Racial Representation and Brazilian Politics: Black Members of the National Congress, 1983-1999

Ollie A. Johnson III

> There is a stereotype of who can be intelligent
> and competent, who can have power. In Brazil it is
> rich, white men who represent the face of power.
> —*Benedita da Silva, Afro-Brazilian Senator*

In examining politics, legislatures, and elected officials, scholars often make a distinction between descriptive and substantive representation. In the former, representatives share the social or demographic characteristics of the represented (Pitkin 1967, 60–91; Mansbridge 1996). In the latter, representatives pursue policies favorable to the interests of the represented (Swain 1993, 5; Lublin 1997, 12). From the perspective of these scholars, substantive representation may be achieved without descriptive representation. At the same time, these two types of representation are not mutually exclusive.

In the 1980s and 1990s, several events highlighted the overrepresentation of whites and the underrepresentation of blacks in Brazilian politics. During this period, Abdias do Nascimento became the first black federal deputy, and later black senator, to wage a consistent and explicit defense of the Afro-Brazilian population from within the National Congress. Benedita da Silva became the first black woman to serve as a federal deputy and then a senator. Deputy Paulo Paim introduced legislation calling for reparations for the descendants of slaves. Celso Pitta became the first black mayor of São Paulo, Brazil's largest city and one of the world's most populous. African Brazilian politicians Alceu Collares, João Alves, and Albuino Azeredo all served as state governors at the same time. Through their electoral victories, political activities, or support of race-specific public policies, these national black politicians have highlighted the question of racial representation.

This study uses the terms *black, African Brazilian*, and *Afro-Brazilian* interchangeably to refer to Brazilians of African ancestry, including people whom popular discourse might call "morenos," "mulattos," or other terms indicating mixed racial and ethnic background. The official Brazilian census has five main color (or racial) categories: white, black, yellow, brown, and indigenous. The Instituto Brasileiro de Geografia e Estatística (IBGE) also counts those individuals who do not declare a color or race. Following Nascimento (1978) and Andrews (1991), this study combines the black and brown categories for analytical purposes.

This essay is the first scholarly attempt to investigate the racial composition of the Brazilian Congress, to analyze black underrepresentation, and to examine the behavior of black members. The central thesis consists of two propositions: that Afro-Brazilians are dramatically underrepresented in Congress in relation to their proportion of the general population, and that racial underrepresentation and related political and cultural factors greatly reduce Afro-Brazilian effectiveness in Congress.

The black members of Congress have attempted nevertheless to change Brazilian politics in important and consequential ways. Black politicians have encouraged white political actors and the general public to address racism and racial inequality. These Afro-Brazilian leaders have organized formally and informally within political parties and government institutions to pursue race-conscious public policies. They have also advocated a new and more prominent role for blacks in Brazilian society and 'politics.

Most studies of Brazilian politics usually ignore or minimize the question of race.[1] Experts on Brazilian political institutions avoid race for two primary reasons. First, it is argued that Brazilian society is allegedly not organized in a rigid racial manner and therefore race is not a relevant cleavage that might provoke conflict, violence, or some type of disruption to the polity (that is, mass movement or riot). Second, some commentators suggest that Brazilians do not have a strong racial consciousness and therefore do not behave racially in politically relevant ways (that is, voting along racial lines, organizing influential racial organizations and movements, or engaging in clear and persistent racial discrimination). One of Brazil's top political scientists, Bolívar Lamounier, observes,

> while differences and eventual tensions in the relationship between ethnic and religious groups may exist in Brazil, there has not been to the present an explosive projection of cleavages of this type in the political arena warranting special or privileged treatment. The basic divisions of Brazilian society are essentially socioeconomic and, to a lesser degree, regional and ideological. (1993, 120)[2]

In addition, the numerous studies on political parties, presidentialism, and democratization in Brazil and Latin America have paid minimal attention to racial issues in general and the role of blacks in particular (O'Donnell and Schmitter 1986; Reis and O'Donnell 1988; Stepan 1989; Mainwaring and Scully 1995; Mainwaring and Shugart 1997).

Race has been relevant to Brazilian politics nevertheless. While Brazilians have not always spoken of or struggled over politics in explicitly racial terms, racial politics has played a strong historical and contemporary role in society. Racial slavery existed in Brazil for approximately 350 years (from the 1530s to 1888), even though it was intertwined with socioeconomic inequality, regional diversity, and ideological differences. Racial representation is significant because at a general level, the vast majority of Brazil's rulers in the twentieth century have been white or relatively light-skinned while the majority of the poor and marginalized have been black or of a darker complexion (Toledo 1989; Nascimento 1978). This political reality, especially following more than three centuries of black enslavement, warrants empirical investigation and theoretical reflection.

The remainder of this essay is divided into four sections. A brief overview of Brazilian politics shows that the racial question, especially the elite concern with the role of blacks in the country, has been present throughout the twentieth century. Second, an analysis of political and racial representation highlights the strong underrepresentation of African Brazilians in Congress. A third section examines black political activity in Congress, drawing on personal interviews with several black representatives. The conclusion discusses the need for additional research on the question of race, representation, and politics in Brazil and throughout Latin America.

Racial Views, Regime Change, and Party Politics

After the abolition of slavery, Brazilian national politics can be divided into five basic periods: the early republican period of constitutional oligarchy, 1889–1930; the Brazilian Revolution and first regime of Getúlio Vargas, 1930–45; the period of competitive politics, 1945–64; the period of military authoritarianism, 1964–85; and finally the period of (re)democratization, 1985 to the present. One of the remarkable consistencies over this more than one-hundred-year history is the elitist nature of Brazilian politics. As Senator Benedita da Silva notes in the epigraph (Silva et al. 1997, 61) and throughout her autobiography, most Brazilian leaders have come from white, wealthy, male, privileged sectors of the society (see also Lamounier 1989; Conniff and McCann 1989; Roett 1992) while many poor and black Brazilians have been prevented from participating in politics through literacy requirements for the franchise and other elite control mechanisms (Leal 1986; Love 1970).

Political elites over the years have held racially explicit views. In the first period, the dominant elite view can be described as overtly racist (Skidmore 1993b; Schwarcz 1993). There was even widespread concern that Brazil's population was too black or too dark. This view contributed to a malign neglect of the recently "freed" population and a motivation to import "lighter" and "better" immigrant workers. Thus *embranquecimento*, or whitening, became unofficial policy for those who believed in white superiority and black inferiority. This policy was explicit in the state of São Paulo, which received most of the country's European immigrants during that period (Andrews 1991, 54–89). Blacks were seen as physically and intellectually inferior to whites (Nascimento 1978).

By the 1930s, the country's racial and ethnic composition had changed dramatically. The proportion of blacks had decreased and the percentage of whites had increased. The European (especially Portuguese, Italian, and German) influence was strongest in the southeastern and southern regions. During this period, whitening as an ideology was formally challenged by part of the Brazilian elite. Many politicians and intellectuals were repulsed by one of the ultimate expressions of white supremacy, Hitler's Nazi Germany. In dramatic fashion, the elite reversed itself: Gilberto Freyre and other intellectuals began to argue that Brazilians were a people of mixed blood and that this was the key to their allegedly harmonious race relations.

Freyre's major book, *Casa grande e senzala* (The Masters and the Slaves), exploring slavery and miscegenation, appeared in 1933; in 1934 Freyre organized an Afro-Brazilian congress to examine the contributions of blacks to Brazilian society. The elite began to take pride in comparing the Brazilian racial situation and the racial segregation in the United States. Brazil, however, soon entered one of its most repressive periods, the *Estado Novo* (New State), which lasted from 1937 to 1945. Ironically, while Brazilian white elites were celebrating harmonious race relations, the most prominent black political group of the postslavery period, the Black Brazilian Front (Frente Negra Brasileira), was banned, as were all other political parties. The banning serves as a strong example of how a formally nonracial policy (that is, elimination of political opposition) can have explicit racial consequences (the disorganization of a black political movement) (Fernandes 1969, 1978; Leite and Cuti 1992).

The third political period (1945–64) was characterized by competitive politics and the notion of racial democracy. For the first time in its history, Brazil had national parties with mass participation (Santos 1986, 1987). It was an optimistic time politically and racially. Freyre and others continued to promote the notion that Brazil was unique in its solution of the racial problem with racial mixing, fluidity of racial identity, and no explicit racial division or segregation. To confirm that racial discrimination was intolerable in Brazil, the Congress passed the Afonso Arinos Law in 1951. This law punished overt acts of racial discrimination, such as denying someone a hotel room because of race. The government continued to argue that all Brazilians had equal access to channels of social advancement (Skidmore 1993b, 212–13).

At the same time, black intellectuals and politicians were having great difficulty getting their concerns heard and black candidates elected to office. The most notable achievement may have been the work of the Teatro Experimental do Negro (Black Experimental Theater), a forum for black cultural and political expression (Nascimento and Nascimento 1994,

24–33).[3] In an important but neglected article, Souza (1971) has argued that in the early 1960s there was a racial polarization of party preferences in the state of Guanabara. Blacks favored the populist Brazilian Labor Party (PTB) while whites supported the conservative National Democratic Union (UDN).

In the fourth period, from 1964 to 1985, the military governed harshly and tolerated only moderate civilian participation (Sorj and Almeida 1984; Skidmore 1988). Most radicals and progressives were exiled or banned; such opponents of the military dictatorship were often tortured and killed. The military did allow two political parties to exist, a promilitary party, ARENA (National Renovating Alliance), and a moderate opposition party, the MDB (Brazilian Democratic Movement). The Brazilian economic miracle of 1968–73 was a period of high growth rates that brought some economic relief, especially to the middle and upper classes.

The first half of this period represented a challenge to Brazil's racial elites. In the United States, the civil rights movement had triumphed; blacks gained the right to vote in the South and defeated so-called Jim Crow laws mandating segregation. In Brazil, explicit black political activity was considered subversive. Brazilian intellectuals began to call the concept of racial democracy a myth that, to a certain degree, perpetuated racial inequality and discrimination by diverting attention from racial oppression and black subordination (Fernandes 1969, 1978; Hasenbalg 1979; Hanchard 1994).

The second half of this period further challenged that myth. Blacks in the major urban areas, especially São Paulo and Rio de Janeiro, organized a movement against racial discrimination and for black pride, political democracy, and improved black social and economic conditions. In the context of political liberalization of the late 1970s and early 1980s, blacks participated in all the social movements challenging the status quo, including the labor movement, the student movement, and the women's movement.

During this same period, black activists began to struggle for recognition within the various political parties. The military government had allowed multiple parties to organize as a way to divide the opposition and prolong authoritarian rule. The opposition did divide, but the military did not anticipate that some elite opposition leaders would embrace the racial question and attempt to mobilize and incorporate blacks. Leonel Brizola, a veteran leftist politician who spent 15 years in exile, was the first major white politician to address the race issue as an important national problem. He also advocated *socialismo moreno* (brown socialism) as a way of linking race, class, and the need to redistribute wealth and power (Nascimento and Nascimento 1994, 68–69; Soares and Silva 1987). Brizola's political party, the PDT (Democratic Labor Party), identified blacks as the fourth-priority group in its program, after children, workers, and women (Monteiro and Oliveira 1989, 122).

The military withdrew from government in 1985. Since then, Brazil has experienced its most profound experiment in democracy. The Constitution of 1988 guaranteed practically all Brazilian adults (including illiterates) the right to vote. This context has given black politicians the opportunity to voice their concerns. Although blacks are underrepresented in the Congress compared to their percentage in the national population, they are visible in elective office as never before. This presence has already had identifiable consequences for Brazilian politics and society.

BLACK MEMBERS OF CONGRESS IN THE 1980S AND 1990S

Before the 1980s, very few blacks were leaders in national parties or had been elected to the Congress. Adalberto Camargo from São Paulo and Alceu Collares from Rio Grande do Sul are two rare examples of black federal deputies from the 1970s. The emergence of the black movement in the 1970s contributed directly to the rise of the current group of black politicians. During this time, African Brazilian political activists, scholars, students, and workers actively fought for space in Brazilian politics. This activity occurred at the same time that new political parties were organizing, political exiles were returning to the country, and some traditionally minded white leaders were beginning to pay more attention to blacks as voters, interest groups, and competitors (Gonzalez 1985; Mitchell 1985; Fontaine 1985a, 1985b).

Before examining black representation in the Congress, an overview of the Brazilian political system is required. Since the 1982 elections, Brazil has once again had a competitive, multiparty political system. Since 1985, when José Sarney became the first civilian president in 21 years, the country has maintained a civilian presidential system of government. The 1988 Constitution outlines Brazil's current formal institutional structure.

Members of the Chamber of Deputies are elected from each state to four-year terms using an open-list system of proportional representation. The entire state serves as the electoral district; Brazil does not have a system of intrastate legislative districts, which, in the United States, have been so important to the election of blacks to the House of Representatives (Swain 1993; Lublin 1997). The total number of deputies (currently 513) should be proportional to the population, with no state having fewer than 8 or more than 70 deputies. Each state also elects, by plurality vote, 3 federal senators, who serve eight-year terms. Brazil has 27 states (including the federal district) and therefore 81 senators.

Most analyses of political representation in Brazil focus on the historical and contemporary overrepresentation of small states and the underrepresentation of large states, especially São Paulo, in the Chamber of Deputies (Nicolau 1993, 86–91; Lima and Santos 1991). This problem is manifest in the contradiction between two constitutional clauses: Article 14, which supports universal suffrage and equal voting rights; and Article 45, which sets forth the minimum and maximum state delegations of 8 to 70 deputies. The ratio of 8 to 70 is much greater than the population (or electorate) ratio between the least and most populous states. For example, if the Chamber had proportional representation with a single seat as minimum state representation, the state of São Paulo would have approximately 115 deputies and Roraima, Amapá, and Acre each would have one deputy.

Aside from other problems with Brazil's electoral system, this disproportionality by state has drawn attention not only because it is obvious and correctable, but also because scholars believe that it has had substantive consequences in important votes in the Chamber of Deputies (Soares 1984, 106–8). This highly disproportional system of proportional representation persists because elected officials from the small states have managed to create and maintain majority coalitions in the Congress to resist any serious reform efforts (Aragão and Fleischer 1991, 10–11).

Since 1983, an estimated 29 black representatives have served in the Congress. Seventeen have been elected to two or more terms. Table 1 lists these representatives by state, party affiliation, and terms in office. In the Chamber of Deputies, blacks were 4 of 479 members (0.84 percent) between 1983 and 1987, 10 of 487 members (2.05 percent) between 1987 and 1991, 16 of 503 members (3.18 percent) between 1991 and 1995, and 15 of 513 members (2.92 percent) between 1995 and 1999. Afro-Brazilians clearly represented a very small percentage of the total number of deputies.

In the Senate, the number of blacks remains small, but their overall percentage is greater than that of black deputies. One politician of African ancestry, Nelson Carneiro, served in Congress as a deputy and senator for more than 30 years. Although he was a distinguished and respected statesman, Carneiro apparently rarely addressed the racial question in his legislative initiatives and activities. One black senator, Abdias do Nascimento, served briefly in the early 1990s and returned in the late 1990s. Two black women, Benedita da Silva and Marina Silva, were elected to the Senate in 1994. Thus, there are now three black senators in the Federal Senate.

At the level of descriptive representation, the percentage of Afro-Brazilians in the general population is much greater than their percentage in the Congress. The concept of underrepresentation refers to the difference between the percentage of blacks in the general population and the percentage of blacks in the Congress. This is shown in the last column of table 2. By this measure, blacks are underrepresented from each state in the Brazilian federation. On the other hand, whites are overrepresented in Congress because they are the overwhelming congressional majority but

Table 1. Black Members of Congress by State, Party,
and Legislature, 1983–1999

Senator	State	Party	Status
50th Legislature (1995–1999)			
1. Benedita da Silva	Rio de Janeiro	PT	
2. Marina Silva	Acre	PT	
3. Abdias do Nascimento	Rio de Janeiro	PDT	Suplente
49th Legislature (1991–1995)			
1. Abdias do Nascimento	Rio de Janeiro	PDT	Suplente
47th–49th (1983–1995)			
1. Nelson Carneiro	Rio de Janeiro	PMDB	

Federal Deputy	State	Party	Status
50th Legislature (1995–1999)			
1. Eraldo Trindade	Amapá	PPB	
2. Chico Vigilante	Distrito Federal	PT	
3. Salatiel Carvalho	Pernambuco	PPB	
4. Agnaldo Timoteio	Rio de Janeiro	PPB	Suplente
5. Carlos Santana	Rio de Janeiro	PT	
6. Paulo Paim	Rio Grande do Sul	PT	
7. Luiz Alberto	Bahia	PT	Suplente
8. Paulo Rocha	Pará	PT	
9. Wagner Nascimento	Minas Gerais	PPB	Suplente
10. Haroldo Lima	Bahia	PC do B	
11. Benedito Domingos	Distrito Federal	PPB	
12. Telma de Souza	São Paulo	PT	
13. Inacio Arruda	Ceará	PC do B	
14. Domingos Dutra	Maranhão	PT	
15. Chicão Brigido da Costa	Acre	PMDB	
49th Legislature (1991–1995)			
1. Eraldo Trindade	Amapá	PFL	
2. Lourival Freitas	Amapá	PT	
3. Chico Vigilante	Distrito Federal	PT	
4. Benedito Domingos	Distrito Federal	PP	
5. Aloízo Santos	Espirito Santo	PMDB	

6. Wagner do Nascimento	Minas Gerais	PTB	
7. Salatiel Carvalho	Pernambuco	PP	
8. Benedita da Silva	Rio de Janeiro	PT	
9. Carlos Santana	Rio de Janeiro	PT	
10. Ruben Bento	Roraima	PFL	
11. Paulo Paim	Rio Grande do Sul	PT	
12. Antonio de Jesus	Goiás	PMDB	
13. Ricardo Moraes	Amazonas	PT	
14. Edmundo Galdino	Tocantins	PSDB	
15. Paulo Rocha	Pará	PT	
16. Haroldo Lima	Bahia	PC do B	

48th Legislature (1987–1991)

1. Eraldo Trindade	Amapá	PFL	
2. Milton Barbosa	Bahia	PMDB	
3. Miraldo Gomes	Bahia	PMDB	Suplente
4. Antonio de Jesus	Goiás	PMDB	
5. Benedita da Silva	Rio de Janeiro	PT	
6. Carlos Alberto Caó	Rio de Janeiro	PDT	
7. Edmilson Valentim	Rio de Janeiro	PC do B	
8. Paulo Paim	Rio Grande do Sul	PT	
9. Edmundo Galdino	Tocatins	PSDB	
10. Haroldo Lima	Bahia	PC do B	

47th Legislature (1983–1987)

1. Agnaldo Timoteo	Rio de Janeiro	PDT	
2. Abdias do Nascimento	Rio de Janeiro	PDT	Suplente
3. Carlos Alberto Caó	Rio de Janeiro	PDT	Suplente
4. Haroldo Lima	Bahia	PMDB	

Note: The term *suplente* refers to an elected official who was not originally voted high enough on the party's list to take office but who eventually assumes office because of the resignation, removal, or death of the party representative.

Sources: *Deputados brasileiros: repertorio biográfico 1984–1995.* This official document, published by the Chamber of Deputies for every legislature, contains basic biographical information and a photo of each deputy. For 1991–95: list of black deputies from Deputy Benedita da Silva's congressional office; Aragão and Fleischer 1991. For 1995–99: list of black members of Congress from Deputy Paulo Paim's congressional office; *Folha de São Paulo* 1996. Generally: Numerous social scientists, staff members of the Congress, and black political activists were consulted. This was not a formal survey.

Table 2. Black Underrepresentation in the Chamber of Deputies,
50th Legislature

Region and state	Total population	Percent black population	Percent black deputies	Difference
North				
Acre	417,102	76.00	12.50	63.50
Amapá	289,035	77.20	12.50	64.70
Amazonas	2,102,766	78.66	0.00	78.66
Pará	4,949,222	77.98	5.88	72.10
Roraima	217,583	66.33	0.00	66.33
Rondônia	1,133,265	59.57	0.00	59.57
Northeast				
Alagoas	2,512,658	71.75	0.00	71.57
Bahia	11,867,336	79.13	5.13	74.00
Ceará	6,366,132	70.35	4.55	65.80
Maranhão	4,929,676	78.69	5.56	73.13
Paraíba	3,201,324	63.17	0.00	63.17
Pernambuco	7,127,956	66.64	4.00	62.64
Piauí	2,582,075	77.98	0.00	77.98
Rio Grande do Norte	2,415,077	64.39	0.00	64.39
Sergipe	1,491,878	73.23	0.00	73.23
Center-West				
Dístrito Federal	1,601,093	52.37	25.00	27.37
Goiás	4,017,506	52.21	0.00	52.21
Mato Grosso	2,026,069	58.33	0.00	58.33
Mato Grosso do Sul	1,780,385	44.36	0.00	44.36
Tocantins	918,400	74.83	0.00	74.83
South				
Paraná	8,448,620	23.03	0.00	23.03
Santa Catarina	4,542,048	9.89	0.00	9.89
Rio Grande do Sul	9,138,463	12.70	3.23	9.47
Southeast				
Espirito Santo	2,600,619	51.78	0.00	51.78
Minas Gerais	15,743,536	48.30	1.89	46.41
Rio de Janeiro	12,807,197	44.33	4.35	39.98
São Paulo	31,588,794	25.40	1.43	23.97

Note: Total number of deputies in the 50th Legislature: 513.
Sources: IBGE 1991; Table 1; Nicolau 1996, 34; Mainwaring 1995, 366.

only 52 percent of the population. There are also a few members of Congress of Asian, Arab, and indigenous ancestry.

Fifteen states have no black representation in the Chamber of Deputies. They are located in each of the five major regions. The largest gap between the Afro-Brazilian population and Afro-Brazilian representation occurs in the Northeast and the North, precisely those regions with the largest percentages of Afro-Brazilians in the population. In both regions, the average gap is nearly 70 percent. The Central-West and Southeast have gaps of approximately 50 and 40 percent, respectively, between Afro-Brazilian population and representation. The South has the smallest Afro-Brazilian population and the smallest average percentage of Afro-Brazilian underrepresentation, at 14 percent. If blacks were represented in the Chamber of Deputies in numbers equal to their percentage of the general population, there would be 236 black deputies. The current official national percentage of African Brazilians in the population (blacks, 5 percent, and browns, 42 percent) is 47 percent. The country has 69,651,215 African Brazilians (IBGE 1991).

A socialist political party, the PT (Workers' Party), has sent by far the largest number of black representatives to Congress. Twelve of the 29 black members of Congress since 1983 have come from the PT. Six have come from the centrist PMDB (Party of the Brazilian Democratic Movement) and three from the progressive PDT (Democratic Labor Party) and PC do B (Communist Party of Brazil). This is significant because some of the PT's national leaders are still uneasy about the racial question (Santana 1994). These leaders argue that the class question is fundamental and the racial aspect derivative or a distraction. The PT did advocate greater worker representation in Congress. Some black political activists have supported descriptive representation in racial terms analogous to the PT's call for a greater working-class presence.

The state of Rio de Janeiro has sent more black politicians to Congress than any other state. Seven black politicians have represented Rio de Janeiro and four, Bahia. Still, the small number of black elected officials from Bahia deserves mention. Bahia is universally recognized as the state with the strongest black cultural and social presence. Its population of 12 million is approximately 80 percent Afro-Brazilian. The number of black Bahian politicians elected to Congress, however, historically has been very low. São Paulo, Brazil's largest state in population, also has a large black population and one of the country's best-organized and most effective black political movements (Hanchard 1994). Nevertheless, this state has had minimal black representation in Congress over the past 15 years.

A final notable characteristic of black members of Congress is that they are generally male. Only three black women have been elected to Congress since 1983. Benedita da Silva is the most prominent and has been elected regularly since 1986. The underrepresentation of black women is similar to the general underrepresentation of women in the Congress and in Brazilian politics generally. This picture confirms that Brazil's political leaders have been white and male (Silva et al. 1997, 60–67).

Why are blacks so greatly underrepresented throughout the country? Have sufficient black candidates been qualified to run for office? Have these candidates had adequate resources to run competitive campaigns? Very few studies have addressed these questions (for an exception, see Valente 1986). There seems to have been no lack of black candidates for Congress. There probably were, however, many underfinanced and ineffective campaigns by blacks, because Brazilian campaigns can be among the most expensive in the world (Fleischer 1993; Mainwaring 1995, 381). Some scholars and politicians have suggested that white supremacy and racism may produce an electorate less likely to vote for blacks (Twine 1998, 62–63; Silva et al. 1997, 61–62). Only additional research will help explain black underrepresentation in Congress.

THE BLACK EXPERIENCE IN CONGRESS

The activities of blacks in the Brazilian Congress were constrained by the transition to political democracy in the 1980s and 1990s. In the 1982 elections, the military regime allowed multiparty elections for the first time since 1965. Despite authoritarian manipulation of the electoral process, the opposition gained control of the Chamber of Deputies under the leadership of Ulysses Guimarães (PMDB-São Paulo). But a military officer, General João Figueiredo, was still president, and the new promilitary party, the PDS, controlled the Senate. Thereafter, the dilemma for opposition leaders in Congress was how to continue and deepen the democratization process without provoking the military into abandoning the transition and reverting to brutal authoritarianism (Fleischer 1988). The situation of blacks in Congress was even worse during this period because they tended to belong to political parties (that is, the PT and PDT) that were in radical, not moderate, opposition to conservative military rule. Therefore they had to be careful in their speechmaking, presentation of legislation, and investigation of problems.

The nature of racial representation in Congress has inhibited the passage of legislation targeted to the black population and the creation of a united black front among their representatives. Black representatives are small in number not only in relation to the total congressional membership but also in their own parties. This has been the case in every legislative session since the early 1980s. Moreover, the heavy representation of blacks in the PT has isolated them from the congressional leadership. In Brazilian terms, the PT is a radical leftist opposition party (Mainwaring 1995, 379–82; Keck 1992).

As a leading black political activist for more than 50 years, Senator Abdias do Nascimento (PDT-Rio de Janeiro) has used his service in Congress to document the subordinate position of blacks in Brazil and to offer legislation penalizing racial discrimination, promoting affirmative action programs, and establishing a black national holiday, among other initiatives. Although his legislative projects rarely passed, Nascimento used the Congress to educate his congressional colleagues, black Brazilians, and all Brazilians on behalf of the black population.

> I say always that I was the first black deputy in Congress . . . in the sense of consciousness. I was defending that [black] cause as my priority, that's what I was doing there. (Nascimento 1994)

As a federal deputy in the 47th Legislature, Nascimento denounced Brazilian racism against blacks, the myth of racial democracy, and widespread poverty among blacks. He then had the Chamber publish his speeches and proposals as an eventual six-volume series, *Combate ao racismo* (Fight Against Racism). By his emphasis on racism, Nascimento was able to focus his activities and provoke his colleagues. On March 21, 1985, to the frustration of one of his fellow deputies, Nascimento argued that racism was so pervasive in Brazilian society that Afro-Brazilians lived in more oppressive conditions than blacks in the United States or South Africa. Conservative deputy Gerson Peres (PDS-Pará) interrupted Nascimento's speech to argue that no racial discrimination existed in Brazil, although he admitted that there was social prejudice. A heated exchange followed between Nascimento and Peres (Nascimento 1985, 15–21). This type of exchange did not deter Nascimento, however, who generally used his post as a federal deputy to articulate key policy positions of black movement groups.

Blacks were, and are, rarely congressional or party leaders. Like the U.S. Congress, the Brazilian Congress is organized along party lines, despite its members' great degree of individual autonomy (Baaklini 1992, 39–55; Mainwaring 1995; Zirker 1995; Desposato 1997). Seniority and party service are two key factors for selecting congressional leaders. Almost all black members of Congress were only elected for the first time in the 1980s or 1990s, whereas most white congressional leaders had many years of experience; for example, Ulysses Guimarães, who became opposition president in 1982, was first elected to the Chamber in the 1950s. Thus, black politicians lacked political experience at the national level. They had not yet achieved leadership positions within their parties. Therefore they wielded less influence in setting their parties' political and legislative agendas, and they generally followed the agendas set by others (Silva et al. 1997, 53–81).

The 48th Congress had the responsibility to write a new constitution. Although the number of blacks elected had more than doubled, they still accounted for only 3 percent of this Congress. While Nascimento was not reelected, several new black deputies, including Carlos Alberto Caó, Benedita da Silva, and Paulo Paim, continued and expanded his legislative work through their committment to fighting racism and assisting poor blacks. Deputy Caó focused on passing legislation to outlaw racial discrimination. He and most black activists believed that the Afonso Arinos Law of 1951 was worthless because it was unenforceable; racist intent had to be proved, and even then, the penalty or fines were negligible. Deputy Silva used her energy to describe the difficult lives of poor, black women and to sponsor legislation to enhance their condition (Silva 1988). Deputy Paim, one of the black union leaders in the Chamber, worked to improve the employment and living conditions of blacks and other workers (Paim 1997). These and other representatives succeeded in passing a new constitution that directly outlawed racism (Article 5, section 42) and outlined various socioeconomic rights and guarantees (Title 8, Da Ordem Social).

The Constituent Assembly, however, illustrated that as the number of black representatives grew, so did the diversity of their opinions on key socioeconomic issues. This shows in the scores that the Intersindical Department of Parlimentary Support (DIAP), a labor union research and lobbying organization, gave to deputies based on their votes on ten issues important to workers (see table 3). A score of ten indicates a perfect score in favor of workers' interests, and zero indicates a perfect score against workers.

The black representatives' ratings partly parallel the overall division within the Constituent Assembly between conservative and progressive coalitions. The former was represented by the *Centrão* (or Big Center) and the latter by the more leftist and nationalist forces (Fleischer 1990).

In the 49th Legislature, some black members articulated the need for unity and coordinated action in addressing the impoverished and unequal situation of blacks in Brazil (Hasenbalg 1979; Silva 1985; Lovell 1994). Benedita da Silva was the leader of this effort during her second term as a federal deputy (1991–95). She organized formal and informal gatherings at her home and initiated personal conversations with black members of Congress to promote the idea of creating a black congressional caucus. She did not succeed in formalizing the group, partly because of the great partisan and ideological diversity of blacks in Congress. The 16 black members of the Chamber of Deputies held conservative, liberal, centrist, social-democratic, socialist, and communist political orientations and represented seven political parties. In addition, some of these deputies had ambivalent feelings about racial identity (Vigilante 1994).

The socialist PT contained Marxist-Leninists, such as Deputy Carlos Santana, who believed that capitalism was a fundamentally unjust economic system; while the moderate PFL (Party of the Liberal Front) had neoliberals like Ruben Bento, who supported capitalism with minimal

Table 3. DIAP Rating of Black Deputies Voting on Key Issues in the
1987–88 Constituent Assembly

Deputy	State	Party	DIAP rating
1. Milton Barbosa	Bahia	PMDB	3.75
2. Carlos Alberto Caó	Rio de Janeiro	PDT	10.00
3. Miraldo Gomes	Bahia	PMDB	5.75
4. Antonio de Jesus	Goiás	PMDB	3.25
5. Haroldo Lima	Bahia	PC do B	10.00
6. Paulo Paim	Rio Grande do Sul	PT	10.00
7. Benedita da Silva	Rio de Janeiro	PT	10.00
8. Eraldo Trindade	Amapá	PFL	7.75
9. Edmilson Valentim	Rio de Janeiro	PC do B	10.00

Source: DIAP 1988.

state intervention in the economy. Despite identifying themselves as Brazilians of African ancestry, these politicians had radically different political visions of the changes necessary to help the country and its black population. Santana believed that class was more important than race in terms of political organization and public policy. He did acknowledge, however, an important link between race and class in terms of the life chances of Afro-Brazilians (Santana 1994). Bento, by contrast, rejected race as a legitimate basis for political organization or an important political issue. He did not see the need for the type of racial caucus advocated by Benedita da Silva (Bento 1994). Consequently, the combination of socialist and race-conscious views of some PT members, such as Silva, has ultimately been incompatible with the moderate, nonracial political perspectives of PFL members such as Bento.

Afro-Brazilian deputy Chico Vigilante confirmed the difficulties involved in creating a black caucus.

> You can approach the question at the level of representation that we have here. Take the high command of the armed forces. I don't know if there is any black general in a command position in the armed forces. In a country where the majority is black, more than 50 percent of the country is black, and the high command does not have [any blacks]. You take the presidential elections. You do not see a black candidate disputing the presidential elections. You take the level right here in the Parliament. The black delegation here is very small. And above all it's not united. I believe that the racial question is above ideology, independent of party. . . . Benedita [da Silva] tried in every way. . . . But things didn't go forward because people don't accept [their blackness]. (Vigilante 1994)

Despite those past difficulties of racial organization in Congress, the current, 50th legislature contains some of the country's most prominen black political leaders, including Abdias do Nascimento and Benedita da Silva (both now senators) and Deputies Paulo Paim and Luiz Alberto. These leaders have renewed efforts at creating a black caucus. Meetings have been held in Congress, but no formal organizational structure has been created.

At the same time, a national debate on race and public policy is beginning, in which the leading black members of Congress are active participants. On November 20, 1995, black activists from around the country mobilized thousands in the national capital to mark the three hundredth anniversary of the death of Afro-Brazilian hero Zumbi dos Palmares (Cardoso 1996).[4] At this time, Deputy Paim also presented his proposal (Projeto de Lei n. 1,239) for reparations of 102,000 reals for each descendant of slaves in Brazil (Paim 1997, 44–45). In a related development, President Fernando Henrique Cardoso has created an interministerial working group to develop public policies to improve the situation of blacks.

Finally, some black activists and intellectuals who are not members of Congress are working in and around Congress to assist black representatives and inform the black community about various developments. For example, longtime black movement leaders Carlos Medeiros from Rio de Janeiro and Edson Cardoso from Bahia are now working with Senator Nascimento and Deputy Paim, respectively (Medeiros 1997; Cardoso 1997). In 1996, Edson Cardoso and other black activist colleagues created a newsletter, *Irohin*, specifically designed to inform the black community about relevant legislation, document and publicize the activities of black members of Congress, and promote interest in institutional politics and public policy among black movement organizations (*Irohin* 1996, 1). In 1997, Nascimento created the journal *Thoth* as a way to communicate with his constituents and give additional coverage to various historical, political, cultural, and economic developments related to the Afro-Brazilian community.

CONCLUSIONS

This article argues that black members of Congress are engaged in significant political activity. They have proposed legislation to outlaw and severely penalize acts of racism and racial discrimination, to introduce African and African Brazilian history into the public schools, to institute affirmative action programs, and to give reparations to descendants of slaves, among many other race-specific projects. These leaders have also used the National Congress to educate the public on the Afro-Brazilian condition. For example, some speeches by Abdias do Nascimento have been essentially lectures on black history and the relationship between that history and blacks' contemporary predicament.

Several factors, however, have made these efforts more difficult. First, African Brazilians are dramatically underrepresented in Congress in relation to their proportion of the Brazilian population. In a sense, they have much work to do, but few workers. Second, the most active black leaders are members of the PT and PDT, small, leftist political parties. They therefore are not generally part of the congressional leadership and have great difficulty gaining majority support for their proposals. Third, efforts to unite and form a black caucus have been inconclusive because of ideological and partisan diversity. Deputy Chico Vigilante argues that there is also a hesitancy among some black representatives to accept their blackness; that is, their racial identity as blacks and their political responsibility as privileged blacks to work to improve the situation of the black masses.

Scholars, especially political scientists, should address these issues. Because of their descriptive underrepresentation in the legislative branch, blacks are clearly at a great disadvantage in the distribution of political power and economic resources in Brazil. The ongoing research of Oliveira (1991), Guimarães (1995), Prandi (1996), Reichmann (1995), and many Afro-Brazilian intellectuals and activists linked to universities, think tanks, and political movements will expand the understanding of basic questions related to race, representation, and politics in Brazil.

In this regard, the following research questions require investigation. Are blacks also underrepresented in elective office at the state and local levels? Why have Rio de Janeiro and the PT sent more black politicians to Congress than other states and political parties, respectively? Do Rio de Janeiro and the PT have a similar record of electing black politicians at the state and local levels? Why have the black members of Congress almost always been men rather than women?

The role of blacks in politics also needs to be examined from a cross-national perspective. Winant (1994) and Skidmore (1993a) have asked whether or not the United States and Brazil are more similar than different in their race relations. Skidmore notes that scholars have traditionally emphasized the biracial, black-white dimension of U.S. race relations. At the same time, social scientists have historically highlighted the multiracial, black-white-mulatto aspects of Brazilian race relations. Skidmore concludes that the United States may be growing increasingly multiracial while Brazil shows signs of increasing biracialism. Skidmore calls for additional research on racial inequality, discrimination, and identity.

Scholars should also study and compare racial politics in these two countries; for example, the role blacks have played in congressional, presidential, and judical politics in the twentieth century. While three recent works (Minority Rights Group 1995; Moore et al. 1995; Walters 1993) have provided important new information on black political activity, more comparative analyses are needed of the black political situation in Latin

America, especially the countries where blacks form a visible and substantial proportion of the population: Brazil, Colombia, Cuba, the Dominican Republic, Ecuador, the United States, and Venezuela (see Hasenbalg 1996; Wade 1997). Focusing on blacks and politics will help place race and the Brazilian political process in the proper national and international context.

NOTES

For early discussions and research on this topic, I thank Professor Gil Shidlo. For comments on earlier versions of this article, I thank Professors Luiza Bairros, Kim Butler, Ken Conca, Rosana Heringer, Bolívar Lamounier, Rebecca Reichmann, Eric Uslaner, Ernest Wilson, and colleagues from the Brazilian Studies Association. The University of Maryland at College Park provided critical support for research in Brazil through its Committee on Africa and Africa in the Americas and General Research Board. Special thanks to Pam Burke and Wen-Heng Chao for research assistance.

1. Wade notes, "To talk about 'blacks,' 'indians,' and 'race' in Latin America, or indeed anywhere else, is in itself problematic. It is generally accepted that 'races' are social constructions, categorical definitions based on a discourse about physical appearance or ancestry. This is not a universalizing definition good for all places and times because what is to count as relevant 'physical difference' or relevant 'ancestry' is far from self-evident" (1993, 3).

2. It should be noted that Lamounier has written on race, class, and politics in Brazil (1968). He has also engaged in comparative research on Brazilian and South African politics (personal communication, November 22, 1997).

3. Founded in October 1944, TEN became the country's most important black theater group in the postwar period. Its performances challenged Brazilian racial stereotypes and gave working-class and poor blacks in Rio de Janeiro a positive self-image. In addition, TEN's founder, Abdias do Nascimento, regularly battled Brazil's white elites in the media.

4. Zumbi was the last African-Brazilian leader of Palmares, the major *quilombo* (maroon society) during the Portuguese colonial era. Palmares was situated in the Serra da Barriga in Northeastern Brazil from 1595 to 1696; Zumbi died defending it (Nascimento and Nascimento 1994, 178).

REFERENCES

Andrews, George Reid. 1991. *Blacks and Whites in São Paulo, Brazil, 1888–1988.* Madison: University of Wisconsin Press.

Aragão, Murillo de, and David Fleischer. 1991. *Perfil parlamentar brasileiro.* São Paulo: Editora Três.

Baaklini, Abdo I. 1992. *The Brazilian Legislature and Political System.* Westport: Greenwood Press.

Bento, Ruben. 1994. Member, Chamber of Deputies. Author interview. Brasília, 21 July.

Brazil. Câmara dos Deputados. *Deputados brasileiros: repertório biográfico 1984–1995*. Brasília: Câmara dos Deputados, Centro de Documentação e Informação, Coordenação de Publicações.

Cardoso, Edson Lopes. 1997. Author, activist. Brasília. Author telephone interview. 24 August.

Cardoso, Edson Lopes, ed. 1996. *Por uma política nacional de combate ao racismo e à desigualdade racial: marcha Zumbi contra o racismo, pela cidadania e a vida*. Brasília: Cultural Gráfica e Editora.

Conniff, Michael L., and Frank D. McCann, eds. 1989. *Modern Brazil: Elites and Masses in Historical Perspective*. Lincoln: University of Nebraska Press.

Desposato, Scott. 1997. Party Switching in Brazil's 49th Chamber of Deputies. Paper presented at the Annual Meeting of the American Political Science Association, Washington, DC, 27–31 August.

Departamento Intersindical de Assessoria Parlamentar (DIAP). 1988. *Quem foi quem na constituinte—nas questões de interesse dos trabalhadores*. São Paulo: Obore.

Fernandes, Florestan. 1969. *The Negro in Brazilian Society*. New York: Columbia University Press.

———. 1978. *Integração do negro na sociedade de classes*. São Paulo: Atica.

Fleischer, David. 1990. The Constituent Assembly and the Transformation Strategy: Attempts to Shift Political Power in Brazil from the Presidency to Congress. In *The Political Economy of Brazil: Public Policies in an Era of Transition*, ed. Lawrence S. Graham and Robert H. Wilson. Austin: University of Texas Press. 210–58.

———. 1993. Financiamento de campanhas políticas no Brasil. In *Sistemas eleitorais e processos políticos comparados: a promessa de democracia na América Latina e Caribe*, ed. Luiz Pedone. Brasília: UnB/OAS/CNPq. 243–59.

Fleischer, David, ed. 1988. *Da distensão à abertura: as eleições de 1982*. Brasília: Editora Universidade de Brasília.

Folha de São Paulo. 1996. Olho no congresso. Special supplement. January 14.

Fontaine, Pierre Michel. 1985a. Blacks and the Search for Power in Brazil. In Fontaine 1985b. 56–72.

Fontaine, Pierre Michel, ed. 1985b. *Race, Class, and Power in Brazil*. Los Angeles: Center for Afro-American Studies, University of California.

Gonzalez, Lélia. 1985. The Unified Black Movement: A New Stage in Black Political Mobilization. In Fontaine 1985b. 120–34.

Guimarães, Antonio Sérgio Alfredo. 1995. Raça, racismo e grupos de cor no Brasil. *Estudos Afro-Asiáticos* 27 (April): 45–63.

Hanchard, Michael George. 1994. *Orpheus and Power: The Movimento Negro of Rio de Janeiro and São Paulo, Brazil, 1945–1988*. Princeton: Princeton University Press.

Hasenbalg, Carlos. 1979. *Discriminação e desigualdades raciais no Brasil*. Rio de Janeiro: Graal.

———. 1996. Racial Inequalities in Brazil and Throughout Latin America: Timid Responses to Disguised Racism. In *Constructing Democracy: Human Rights, Citizenship, and Society in Latin America*, ed. Elizabeth Jelin and Eric Hershberg. Boulder: Westview Press. 161–75.

Instituto Brasileiro de Geografia e Estatística (IBGE). 1991. Censo Demográfico. http://www.ibge.gov.br/população residente (Accessed 15 May 1997) *Irohin* (Brasília). 1996. No. 1 (May–June): 1.

Keck, Margaret. 1992. *The Workers' Party and Democratization in Brazil.* New Haven: Yale University Press.

Lamounier, Bolívar. 1968. Raça e classe na política brasileira. *Cadernos Brasileiros* 47: 39–50.

———. 1989. Brazil: Inequality Against Democracy. In *Democracy in Developing Countries: Latin America*, ed. Larry Diamond, Juan J. Linz, and Seymour Martin Lipset. Boulder: Lynne Rienner. 111–57.

———. 1993. Institutional Structure and Governability in the 1990s. In *Brazil: The Challenges of the 1990s*, ed. Maria D'Alva G. Kinzo. London: Institute of Latin American Studies, University of London/British Academic Press. 117–37.

Leal, Victor Nunes. 1986. *Coronelismo, enxada e voto (O município e o regime representativo no Brasil).* São Paulo: Alfa-Omega.

Leite, José Correia, and Cuti [Luiz Silva]. 1992. *E disse o velho militante José Correia Leite.* São Paulo: Secretaria Municipal de Cultura.

Lima, Olavo Brasil de, Jr., and Fabiano Guilherme dos Santos. 1991. O sistema proportional no Brasil: lições de vida. In *Sistema eleitoral brasileiro: teoria e prática*, ed. Olavo Brasil de Lima, Jr. Rio de Janeiro: IUPERJ. 133–52.

Love, Joseph L. 1970. Political Participation in Brazil, 1881–1969. *Luso-Brazilian Review* 7, 2: 3–24.

Lovell, Peggy A. 1994. Race, Gender, and Development in Brazil. *Latin American Research Review* 29, 3: 7–35.

Lublin, David. 1997. *The Paradox of Representation: Racial Gerrymandering and Minority Interests in Congress.* Princeton: Princeton University Press.

Mainwaring, Scott. 1995. Brazil: Weak Parties, Feckless Democracy. In Mainwaring and Scully 1995. 334–98.

Mainwaring, Scott, and Timothy R. Scully, eds. 1995. *Building Democratic Institutions: Party Systems in Latin America.* Stanford: Stanford University Press.

Mainwaring, Scott, and Matthew Soberg Shugart, eds. 1997. *Presidentialism and Democracy in Latin America.* Cambridge: Cambridge University Press.

Mansbridge, Jane. 1996. In Defense of "Descriptive" Representation. Paper presented at the Annual Meeting of the American Political Science Association, San Francisco, 28–31 August.

Medeiros, Carlos. Author, activist. 1997. Author interview, Bowie, MD, 15 September.

Minority Rights Group, eds. 1995. *No Longer Invisible: Afro-Latin Americans Today.* London: Minority Rights Publications.

Mitchell, Michael. 1985. Blacks and the Abertura Democrática. In Fontaine 1985b. 95–119.

Monteiro, Brandão, and Carlos Alberto P. de Oliveira. 1989. *Os partidos políticos.* São Paulo: Global.

Moore, Carlos, Tanya R. Sanders, and Shawna Moore, eds. 1995. *African Presence in the Americas.* Trenton, NJ: Africa World Press.

Nascimento, Abdias do. 1978. *O genocídio do negro brasileiro: processo de um racismo mascarado.* São Paulo: Paz e Terra.

Nascimento, Abdias do. 1994. Brazilian Senator. Author interview. Rio de Janeiro, 21 June.

Nascimento, Abdias do, ed. 1985. *Povo negro: a successão e a "Nova República."* Rio de Janeiro: IPEAFRO.

Nascimento, Abdias do, and Elisa Nascimento. 1994. *Africans in Brazil.* Trenton: African World Press.

Nicolau, Jairo Marconi. 1993. *Sistema eleitoral e reforma política.* Rio de Janeiro: Foglio Editora.

———. 1996. *Multipartidarismo e democracia.* Rio de Janeiro: Fundação Getúlio Vargas.

O'Donnell, Guillermo, and Philippe C. Schmitter. 1986. *Transitions from Authoritarian Rule: Tentative Conclusions About Uncertain Democracies.* Baltimore: Johns Hopkins University Press.

Oliveira, Clóves Luiz Pereira. 1991. O negro e o poder—os negros candidatos a vereador em Salvador, em 1988. *Caderno CRH* (Salvador), Supplemento. 94–116.

Paim, Paulo. 1997. *Em defesa da cidadania dos afro-brasileiros.* Brasília: Centro de Documentação e Informação, Coordenação de Publicações, Câmara dos Deputados.

Pitkin, Hanna Fenichel. 1967. *The Concept of Representation.* Berkeley: University of California Press.

Prandi, Reginaldo. 1996. Raça e voto na eleição de 1994. *Estudos Afro-Asiáticos* 30 (December): 61–78.

Reichmann, Rebecca. 1995. Brazil's Denial of Race. *NACLA Report on the Americas* 28, 6 (May–June): 35–45.

Reis, Fabio Wanderley, and Guillermo O'Donnell, eds. 1988. *A democracia no Brasil: dilemas e perspectivas.* São Paulo: Vértice.

Roett, Riordan. 1992. *Brazil: Politics in a Patrimonial Society.* Westport: Praeger.

Santana, Carlos. 1994. Member, Chamber of Deputies. Author interview. Brasília, 20 July.

Santos, Wanderley Guilherme dos. 1986. *Sessenta e quatro: anatomia da crise.* São Paulo: Vertice.

———. 1987. *Crise e castigo: partidos e generais na política brasileira.* São Paulo: Vertice.

Schwarcz, Lilia Moritz. 1993. *O espetáculo das raças: cientistas, instituições e questão racial no Brasil, 1870–1930.* São Paulo: Companhia das Letras.

Silva, Benedita da. 1988. *Mulher negra.* Brasília: Centro de Documentação e Informação, Coordenação de Publicações, Câmara dos Deputados.

Silva, Benedita da, Medea Benjamin, and Maísa Mendonça. 1997. *Benedita da Silva: An Afro-Brazilian Woman's Story of Politics and Love.* Oakland: Institute for Food and Development Policy.

Silva, Nelson do Valle. 1985. Updating the Cost of Not Being White in Brazil. In Fontaine 1985b. 42–55.

Skidmore, Thomas E. 1988. *The Politics of Military Rule in Brazil, 1964–1985.* New York: Oxford University Press.

———. 1993a. Biracial U.S.A. vs. Multiracial Brazil: Is the Contrast Still Valid? *Journal of Latin American Studies* 25, 2: 373–86.

————. 1993b. *Black into White: Race and Nationality in Brazilian Thought.* Durham: Duke University Press.

Soares, Glaucio Ary Dillon. 1984. *Colégio eleitoral, convenções partidárias e eleições diretas.* Petrópolis: Vozes.

Soares, Glaucio Ary Dillon, and Nelson do Valle Silva. 1987. Urbanization, Race, and Class in Brazilian Politics. *Latin American Research Review* 22, 2: 155–76.

Sorj, Bernardo, and Maria Hermínia Tavares de Almeida, eds. 1984. *Sociedade e política no Brasil pós-64.* São Paulo: Brasiliense.

Souza, Amaury de. 1971. Raça e política no Brasil urbano. *Revista de Administração de Empresas* 11, 4 (Oct.–Dec.): 61–70.

Stepan, Alfred, ed. 1989. *Democratizing Brazil: Problems of Transition and Consolidation.* New York: Oxford University Press.

Swain, Carol M. 1993. *Black Faces, Black Interests: The Representatives of African Americans in Congress.* Cambridge: Harvard University Press.

Toledo, Roberto Pompeu de, ed. 1989. *O álbum dos presidentes: a história vista pelo JB* [Jornal do Brasil]. Rio de Janeiro: Jornal do Brasil.

Twine, France Winddance. 1998. *Racism in a Racial Democracy: The Maintenance of White Supremacy in Brazil.* New Brunswick: Rutgers University Press.

Valente, Ana Lúcia E. F. 1986. *Política e relações raciais: os negros e as eleições paulistas de 1982.* São Paulo: FFLCH/Universidade de São Paulo.

Vigilante, Chico. 1994. Member, Chamber of Deputies. Author interview. Brasília, 21 July.

Wade, Peter. 1993. *Blackness and Race Mixture: The Dynamics of Racial Identity in Colombia.* Baltimore: Johns Hopkins University Press.

————. 1997. *Race and Ethnicity in Latin America.* London: Pluto Press.

Walters, Ronald W. 1993. *Pan-Africanism in the African Diaspora: An Analysis of Modern Afrocentric Political Movements.* Detroit: Wayne State University Press.

Winant, Howard. 1994. *Racial Conditions: Politics, Theory, Comparisons.* Minneapolis: University of Minnesota Press.

Zirker, Daniel. 1995. The Legislature and Democratic Transition in Brazil. In *Legislatures and the New Democracies in Latin America,* ed. David Close. Boulder: Lynne Rienner. 89–112.

J. Lat. Amer. Stud. 32, 207–234 Printed in the United Kingdom © 2000 Cambridge University Press 207

A Political Analysis of Legal Pluralism in Bolivia and Colombia*

DONNA LEE VAN COTT

Abstract. In this article the author compares recent efforts in Bolivia and Colombia to implement constitutionally mandated regimes of legal pluralism, and identifies the most important factors affecting the practical realisation of legal pluralism: the capacity of the political system, the legal tradition and society to tolerate normative diversity; the geographic isolation and cultural alienation of indigenous communities; the degree of internal division within indigenous communities and movements regarding legal pluralism in general, and in specific cases, that have arisen, and the availability of effective legal mechanisms to indigenous communities seeking to protect this right.

Among the greatest challenges facing democratic societies today is that of incorporating populations claiming distinct group identities and cultural norms into a single polity governed by a constitution that reflects and affirms the identities and norms of all citizens. During the last decade ethnic minorities have mobilised as never before to demand recognition of their distinct identities and to claim special constitutional rights. Many new constitutions reflect their success.

Some of the most dramatic and unexpected achievements in the constitutional recognition of cultural differences have occurred in Latin America. The region's independent states have long wrestled uncomfortably with the persistence of partially unassimilated, ethnically distinct populations. Approximately 10 per cent of Latin Americans are considered indigenous, with proportions ranging from less than one per cent in Brazil, to more than 50 per cent in Bolivia and Guatemala. For most of their history, states pursued nation-building policies that sought to eliminate or make invisible ethnic distinctions. Over the past decade, however, seven – Bolivia, Colombia, Ecuador, Mexico, Nicaragua, Paraguay and Peru – adopted or modified constitutions to recognise the multiethnic, multicultural nature of their societies. Securing such recognition was the result of local and national-level political mobilisation

Donna Lee Van Cott is Assistant Professor in the Department of Political Science at the University of Tennessee.

* Research for this article was supported by a Fulbright dissertation scholarship and a grant from the Cordell Hull Fund of the University of Tennessee, Knoxville. The author would like to thank José Antonio Lucero, Rachel Sieder and the anonymous reviewers of this journal for helpful comments on a previous draft.

by indigenous peoples organisations that originated in the late 1960s[1] and
and peaked in the early 1990s, when Indians throughout the Western
hemisphere organised to present an alternative reading of the 500th
anniversary of the arrival of Europeans in the Americas.[2] But this
recognition is not attributable solely to the canny mobilisation of
indigenous organisations. Improving the representation and participation
of excluded groups and codifying fundamental rights is a strategy
employed by Latin American states in the 1990s for consolidating the
fragile legitimacy and legality of democratic institutions.[3]

Having secured a foothold in national psyches and constitutions,
indigenous and African–American organisations are now attempting to
put the principle of respect for diversity into practice. One barometer of
their success is the status of efforts constitutionally to incorporate the
practice of customary law – the mostly unwritten forms of dispute
resolution and social control practiced by ethnic communities or language
groups among their members. This article analyses efforts in Bolivia and
Colombia to put into practice new constitutional provisions that recognise
the jurisdiction of indigenous authorities over the administration of

[1] The United Nations Sub-commission on the Prevention of Discrimination and
Protection of Minorities defines indigenous peoples as follows: "Indigenous
communities, peoples and nations are those which, having a historical continuity with
pre-invasion and pre-colonial societies that developed on their territories, considered
themselves distinct from other sectors of the societies now prevailing in those
territories, or parts of them. They form at present non-dominant sectors of society and
are determined to preserve, develop and transmit to future generations their ancestral
territories, and their ethnic identity, as the basis of their continued existence as peoples,
in accordance with their own cultural patterns, social institutions and legal systems."
UN, *Study of the Problem of Discrimination Against Indigenous Populations* (New York,
1986), para. 379.

[2] On these movements, see H. D. Polanco, *Autonomía regional. La autodeterminación de los
pueblos indios* (México, 1991), pp. 111–49; R. Stavenhagen, 'Challenging the Nation-
State in Latin America', *Journal of International Affairs*, vol. 34, no. 2 (1992); D. L. Van
Cott (ed.), *Indigenous Peoples and Democracy in Latin America* (New York, 1994); P.
Wade, *Race and Ethnicity in Latin America* (London, 1997); and D. Yashar, 'Indigenous
Protest and Democracy in Latin America', in J. I. Domínguez and A. F. Lowenthal
(eds.), *Constructing Democratic Governance. Latin America and the Caribbean in the 1990s*
(Baltimore, 1996).

[3] On recent reforms of the state affecting indigenous peoples see, Willem Assies,
'Pueblos indígenas y reforma del estado en América Latina', paper prepared for the
workshop on Indigenous Peoples and Reform of the State, Amsterdam, October
29–30, 1998; J. Dandler, 'Indigenous Peoples and the Rule of Law in Latin America:
Do They Have a Chance?' paper prepared for the Academic Workshop on the Rule of
Law and the Underprivileged in Latin America, Kellogg Institute for International
Studies, University of Notre Dame, 1996; D. Iturralde, 'Demandas indígenas y
reforma legal: retos y paradojas', *Alteridades*, vol. 7 (1997), pp. 81–98; E. Sánchez,
(comp.) *Derechos de los pueblos indígenas en las constituciones de América Latina* (Bogotá,
1996); and D. L. Van Cott, *The Friendly Liquidation of the Past: The Politics of Diversity
in Latin America* (Pittsburgh, 2000).

justice within specified territorial units. The theoretical debate over the compatibility of liberalism and group rights is left to others.[4] The article's approach is empirical and comparative. It identifies variables that account for the 'success' of legal pluralism, which are defined along two qualitative continua: the extent to which multiple legal systems are able to operate without interference, and the extent to which conflicts among legal systems are managed institutionally. It concludes that the success of legal pluralism is determined by the outcome of repeated strategic interactions among indigenous peoples' organisations, the professional judiciary, and state institutions. These interactions are affected by the capacity of the political system, the legal tradition and society to tolerate normative diversity; the geographic isolation and cultural alienation of indigenous communities; the degree of internal divisions within indigenous communities, movements on legal pluralism, in general, and in specific cases that have arisen; and the availability of effective legal mechanisms to indigenous communities seeking to protect legal rights.

Although legal pluralism has long been a concern of anthropologists and legal scholars, it is fundamentally a political issue. But it is one that most political scientists have ignored.[5] The goal of this article is to provide a more explicitly political analysis of legal pluralism by focusing both on interactions among political actors and on the broader political context in which the recognition of legal pluralism takes place. The term 'legal pluralism' connotes the simultaneous existence of distinct normative systems within a single territory, a condition usually associated with colonial rule.[6] Under colonial rule, the exercise of sub-state legal systems was commonly restricted to cultural or personal matters in which the state was not concerned, and was tempered by the invocation of a 'repugnancy clause' in the event that customary practices offended the sensibilities of European judges.[7] Since the 1970s, jurists have recognised that practically all societies exhibit some aspects of legal pluralism. Many multiethnic states in Asia, Africa and Latin America that succeeded the colonial powers and adopted European-style legal systems continue to recognise

[4] For an introduction to the literature on this topic, see S. Benhabib (ed.), *Democracy and Difference: Contesting the Boundaries of the Political* (Princeton, 1996); A. Gutmann (ed.), *Multiculturalism: Examining the Politics of Recognition* (Princeton, 1994); W. Kymlicka, *Multicultural Citizenship* (Oxford, 1995); and J. Tully, *Strange Multiplicity: Constitutionalism in an Age of Diversity* (Cambridge, 1995).

[5] D. Iturralde, 'Movimiento indio, costumbre jurídica y usos de la ley', in R. Stavenhagen and D. Iturralde (eds.), *Entre la ley y la costumbre. El derecho consuetudinario indígena en América Latina* (México, 1990), p. 59.

[6] B. da Sousa Santos, *Estado, derecho y luchas sociales* (Bogotá, 1991), p. 69.

[7] M. B. Hooker, *Legal Pluralism: An Introduction to Colonial and Neo-colonial Laws* (Oxford, 1975).

some scope for customary law, particularly for religious minorities and geographically isolated and culturally alienated indigenous peoples. Most contemporary cases reflect the efforts of post-colonial or multiethnic states to accommodate the claims of sub-state groups in order to reduce inter-ethnic conflict, as well as to serve other state aims, such as extending the rule of law and state authority into peripheral areas. Horowitz observes that another frequent impetus for legal change is the need to make the legal system more 'authentic', that is to create a better fit between society and its norms.[8] In many cases, achieving such authenticity involves re-cuperating and revaluing traditional practices that enjoy greater popular legitimacy than the edicts of the state, and that have persisted, in part, due to the geographic vacuum of state authority in peripheral regions. All these goals motivated legal reform in the cases discussed below.

Until the 1980s most national legislation in Latin America did not recognise indigenous customary law (an exception is Peru's 1977 recognition of *rondas campesinas* [peasant patrols]). Today, in response to claims by indigenous groups, in addition to Bolivia and Colombia, the constitutions and/or laws of Brazil, Chile, Ecuador, Nicaragua, Paraguay and Peru recognise some scope for indigenous customary law. Constitutional recognition of this right affirms protections under International Labor Organisation (ILO) Convention 169 (1989) on the rights of indigenous and tribal populations in independent states, which nine Latin American countries have ratified, including Bolivia and Colombia.[9] Draft international declarations on the rights of indigenous peoples are being prepared by the United Nations and Organization of American States and also protect the right to exercise customary law.

Comparing Colombia and Bolivia provides an opportunity to examine constitutional language recognising how strikingly similar legal pluralism is implemented in two distinct political contexts. The similarity in language is due to the use of the earlier Colombian example as a model by Bolivian government personnel. The recognition of legal pluralism in both countries was part of comprehensive reforms undertaken in 1991 and 1994, respectively, in which the legitimacy of state institutions, particularly the judicial system, was a priority. The two cases also enable us to explore whether legal pluralism has different implications depending on the proportion of the population that is indigenous. At the legal and philosophical level, there is no difference. In both countries constitution-

---

[8]   D. Horowitz, 'The Qur'an and the Common Law: Islamic Law Reform and the Theory of Legal Change', *American Journal of Comparative Law*, vol. XLII, nos. 2 & 3 (1994), pp. 233–93, 543–80.

[9]   They are Costa Rica, Ecuador, Guatemala, Honduras, Mexico, Paraguay and Peru. Argentina signed ILO 169 in 1992 but the deposit of its ratification has been delayed. Denmark, Fiji, Holland and Norway also have ratified ILO 169.

makers sought to construct a new basis of legitimation for the state by making the legal and political systems more inclusive and participatory. Recognising and empowering oppressed ethnic groups suited this purpose equally well in both cases. However, at a practical level, the positive and negative implications of legal pluralism are magnified in the Bolivian case, where the indigenous population constitutes a majority and the territory where indigenous jurisdiction is recognised covers a substantial portion of the country. Another striking difference between the two cases is the process through which both reforms were achieved. In Colombia, two Indians representing the country's major indigenous organisations were elected to the national constituent assembly in 1991. During this cathartic public process both played a highly visible and symbolic role by personifying the inclusion of society's most marginalised groups. In Bolivia, President Sánchez de Lozada managed a closed process confined to a handpicked team personally loyal to the president, which produced legislation passed by a legislature lacking representatives of the organised indigenous movement. The president's team included the Aymara vice president and anthropologists with close ties to the country's indigenous organisations.[10] Nevertheless, the new constitutions are strikingly similar with respect to legal pluralism.

The achievement of a genuinely pluralistic legal regime is crucial to the realisation of the new multicultural conception of the nation enshrined in the new Bolivian and Colombian constitutions. As Colombia's Interior Minister observed in 1997, the articulation of indigenous legal systems with Colombian law is one way in which the plural nation is constructed 'with regard to themes like the public and the private, the scope of state autonomy and that of indigenous peoples and territories, and the rights and duties of citizens and of national public and indigenous authorities'.[11] For Latin America's indigenous peoples the recuperation of customary law is part of a long struggle to reject a 'neo-colonial' Latin American state and to adjust the Latin American elites' mythical homogenous nation to the reality of heterogeneous populations. The indigenous demand for recognition of legal pluralism is part of a larger project to assert a collective right to self-determination: it is one aspect of the autonomous, collective citizenship that they seek within the state.[12]

Indigenous organisations struggling on behalf of this project engage in a variety of strategic interactions. Their struggle has occurred mainly in

[10] For a thorough discussion of the reform process in both countries, see D. L. Van Cott, *The Friendly Liquidation of the Past: The Politics of Diversity in Latin America* (Pittsburgh, 2000).

[11] H. Serpa 'Introducción: Justicia, diversidad y jurisdicción especial indígena', in '*Del olvido surgimos para traer nuevas esperanzas.' La Jurisdicción especial indígena* (Bogotá, 1997), p. 22. Translation by the author.   [12] See note 3.

spheres dominated by national and international legal discourses, which shape the way indigenous organisations articulate their identities and aspirations. As Sieder and Witchell argue, the necessity to assert claims in ways compatible with legal discourse has resulted in the essentialisation, reification and idealisation of indigenous customary law practices. Indigenous leaders paint a picture of coherent, widely understood and uncontested norms and procedures that have been passed down for generations, systems that have operated autonomously from the state, maintaining a cultural purity that must now be protected from any intrusion. These legal systems are portrayed as promoting and protecting a harmonious way of life particular to indigenous peoples.[13] But in fact this idealised vision obscures the reality of most indigenous customary law systems in at least three ways.

First, many practices indigenous communities claim are traditional were adopted quite recently. Clear examples included the *rondas campesina* adopted by many indigenous communities in highland Peru in the 1990s, and the new normative structures adopted by Guatemalan Maya internally displaced by the civil war.[14] Indigenous communities continually adopt new practices as new needs arise. Although the antiquity of customary law is often invoked to legitimise it, the authenticity of these new structures and norms comes not from their age but, rather, from their autonomous adoption in the absence of effective access to state justice. Secondly, indigenous communities are not immune from the internal contestation of culture and norms common to all human groups. Even the smallest, most isolated indigenous communities contain power differentials and conflicting interests, the most obvious being those between women and men.[15] Internal dissensus within indigenous communities has increased in recent years due to patterns of urbanisation, displacement due to violence and migration that bring Indians into closer contact with one another and with Indians from different geographic areas and linguistic backgrounds, as well as the growth of Protestant faiths in once-hegemonically Catholic communities. The assertion that indigenous cultures are uniquely characterised by harmony and consensus is a typical counter-hegemonic

---

[13]   R. Sieder and J. Witchell, 'Advancing Indigenous Claims Through the Law: Reflections on the Guatemalan Peace Process', in J. Cowan and R. Wilson (eds.), *Culture and Rights* (forthcoming); D. Iturralde, 'Usos de la Ley y usos de la costumbre: La reivindicación del derecho indígena y la modernización del Estado', Alberto Wray et al., *Derecho, pueblos indígenas y reforma del Estado* (Quito, 1993), p. 132.

[14]   On the former, see W. Ardito, 'The Right to Self-Regulation. Legal Pluralism and Human Rights in Peru', *Journal of Legal Pluralism*, vol. 39 (1997), pp. 1–42; on the latter see R. Sieder, *Customary Law and Democratic Transition in Guatemala* (London, 1997).

[15]   Ardito, 'The Right to Self-Regulation', p. 25; R. Sieder, 'Customary Law and Local Power in Guatemala', in R. Sieder (ed.), *Guatemala after the Peace Accords* (London, 1998), p. 114.

strategy of dominated groups, and should be examined critically in each case. As Sieder argues, perpetuating the myth that customary law is characterised by tradition and consensus runs the risk of 'freezing' methods and customs particular to certain historical circumstances and of reifying traditions which may no longer be applied in practice, or which may not be shared by the entire group.[16] Third, very few extant indigenous legal systems are autonomous, self-contained or 'culturally pure'. The vast majority developed in opposition to state law in a 'dynamic, asymmetrical relationship'.[17] This is even more the case in Latin America, as compared to other colonised regions, because the Spanish were more disposed to modify the internal structure of indigenous communities and to promote the eventual disappearance of Indians as a distinct group, rather than to sign treaties with them or to treat them as external to the nation. Thus, the challenge of articulating indigenous customary law to state systems, required by the new constitutional recognitions of customary law, is posed incorrectly, since this articulation has been negotiated and renegotiated in practice since colonial times in response to changing political conditions. The challenge now is to codify this relationship formally to represent the transformation in indigenous-state relations implied by the new constitutions.

Colombia

An estimated 2.7 per cent of Colombia's population of almost 35 million is indigenous; 84 per cent live on indigenous *resguardos* covering about one-quarter of the national territory.[18] The widely dispersed indigenous population is comprised of 81 distinct ethnic groups speaking 64 languages. Contemporary indigenous organisations formed in the 1970s, mainly to struggle for the recuperation of ancestral lands. Nevertheless, a set of cultural rights including language, educational and customary law has long been part of the indigenous agenda.

The administration of César Gaviria, which presided over the constituent assembly in 1991, accorded implementation of the judicial reform its highest priority. Judicial reform was viewed as its ultimate guarantee.[19] Among the first measures implemented was the *acción de tutela* (writ of protection), the citizen's primary defence against the violation of fundamental constitutional rights. The most important new judicial

---

[16] Sieder, *Customary Law and Democratic Transition*, pp. 17–19.   [17] *Ibid.*, p. 16.
[18] Paraphrasing from Decree 2001 (1988), an indigenous *resguardo* is a legal and socio-political institution that corresponds to an indigenous community and a specific territory. Under Colombian law, the internal affairs of the *resguardo* are governed by the community according to its customs and traditions.
[19] Interview, Fernando Carrillo, Washington, 18 Sept. 1997.

institution established was the Constitutional Court which, already in its first year, gained public prestige by defending the rights of the common citizen with respect to virtually all of the constitution's fundamental rights. Among the Court's most innovative rulings are those concerning indigenous rights, including three rulings with respect to customary law, pursuant to Article 246 of the 1991 Constitution on Special Indigenous Jurisdiction, which reads:

The authorities among the native peoples may exercise judicial functions within their territorial areas in accordance with their own rules and procedures, which must not be contrary to the Constitution and laws of the Republic. The law shall establish the forms of coordination of this special jurisdiction with the national judicial system (translation by the author).

Other constitutional provisions establishing anomalous indigenous territories and recognising the official status of indigenous traditional authorities as public authorities with territorial jurisdiction (Articles 329–330) provide the political and territorial context for the exercise of this right.

In order to prepare Colombian courts for the challenge of adjudicating cases involving indigenous customary law, the Gaviria government commissioned studies of the legal systems of 20 indigenous language groups. Anthropologists criticised the project for imposing Western, positivist categories and concepts onto more flexible, oral traditions that defy such categorisation, and for separating the practice of customary law from the fabric of indigenous society.[20] Positive and customary law, they argued, do not even share the same purpose: while positive law seeks to punish the guilty, customary law generally seeks if possible to reconcile parties in order to conserve the harmony of the group. The overriding value of group harmony often reaches the extreme of expelling or executing community members whose behaviour is deemed sufficiently disruptive of group harmony, usually where prior efforts to negotiate a solution or enforce conformity to group norms have failed. In such cases customary law may trample on principles common to a Western, liberal tradition of positive law with respect to minority rights and may even sanction behaviour that is not deemed unlawful by the state. This controversy underscores a fundamental debate within juridical anthropology over whether it is possible or desirable to attempt to analyse other societies in terms of the concepts of the social scientists doing the analysis. Western jurists tend both to distort indigenous law and to deny the legal character of indigenous culture and practices to the extent that these do not exhibit Western-style legal artifacts – such as courts, written texts and

[20] Interview, Esther Sánchez, Bogotá, 3 Feb. 1997.

professional judges. Some anthropologists err in the other direction by incorporating under the category of 'law' all behaviours, structures and norms connected to practices of social control which are not properly assimilable to a western definition of law.[21] The Colombian project directors defended their methodology as the most effective means of presenting information about indigenous administration of justice to the judges that must rely on them in making important judicial decisions and, thereby, facilitating coordination of the indigenous and positive systems.[22]

In his introduction to one of the studies, Carlos César Perafán identified difficulties in the coordination of indigenous and national law. First, whereas the national system is highly segmented and specialised, indigenous systems lack these distinctions and even lack separation between forms of social control, self-government and the administration of justice. Secondly, national law is applied to individuals, whereas indigenous communities generally apply sanctions to the unit of society of which the offender is a member. Entire families may feel the weight of fines or even be expelled from the community. Thirdly, in indigenous communities punishments are not necessarily pre-existing for each crime, as in the national system. An appropriate punishment is designed for each case, and is often negotiated with the social group of the victim. Fourthly, in indigenous communities, corporal punishment, forced labour and loss of community rights are common, while imprisonment is rare. Most seriously, many indigenous communities punish homicide and witchcraft with the death penalty, which is illegal in Colombia.[23] These normative and procedural disparities posed difficult problems for the creation of implementing legislation with broad-based support.

In fact, the implementing legislation required by Article 246 was never passed because a consensus could not be reached on the meaning of 'coordination'. The subordination of indigenous special jurisdiction to the Colombian constitution and legislation would appear to imply that

[21] R. Stavenhagen, 'Derecho consuetudinario indígena en América Latina', in R. Stavenhagen and D. Iturralde (eds.), *Entre la ley y la costumbre. El derecho consuetudinario indígena en América Latina* (México, 1990), p. 42; Santos, *Estado, derecho y luchas sociales* (Bogotá, 1991), pp. 65–7.

[22] C. Perafán et al., *Sistemas jurídicos indígenas: Pueblos Awa, Cocama, Maku, Uioto, U'wa y Yukpa* (Bogotá, 1996), p. 7.

[23] C. Perafán, *Sistemas Jurídicos Páez, Kogi, Wayúu y Tule* (Bogotá, 1995), pp. 33–41, 112; Perafán, et al., *Sistemas Jurídicos Tukano, Embera, Sikuani y Guambiano* (Bogotá, 1997), p. 6; M. Vásquez, 'Antecedentes sobre la aplicación de la jurisdicción Especial Indígena', in '*Del olvido surgimos para traer nuevas esperanzas*', pp. 259–60. In comparison to national sentences for comparable offenses, indigenous sentences appear to be shorter. For example, Perafán gives the example of the different penalties for murder: 16 years of prison, under Colombian law, compared to six years of hard labour in other *resguardos* under Páez law, although in the most aggravated cases the death penalty may be applied.

conflicting elements in customary law are to be superseded. As Dander observes, this limitation on customary law is typical of language in most Latin American constitutions, which 'tends to downgrade the role of traditional norms or relegate them to further study, special legislation or other "future" measures which are not easily forthcoming'.[24] Yet, no less an authority than the former chief magistrate of the Colombia Constitutional Court, Carlos Gaviria Díaz, argued that to subject indigenous jurisdiction to this limit would be absurd, since it would nullify the meaning of autonomy under Article 246 by implying that Indians must conform to all the procedures of the Colombian penal code, including the creation of pre-existing written laws.[25]

The Organización Nacional Indígena de Colombia (ONIC) presented its own legislative proposal to coordinate indigenous and national justice administration shortly after the close of the constituent assembly in 1991. The ONIC plan failed to address the question of coordination between the two systems, stipulating that this would be worked out later in consultation with indigenous communities.[26] The proposal envisaged indigenous jurisdiction as mandatory within the territorial jurisdiction of indigenous authorities, unless the authorities elect to 'delegate' their authority. Jurisdiction over Indians committing crimes outside their community falls to the national justice system, which would be required to take the culture of the defendant into account in determining guilt and sentencing.[27] ONIC also called on the government formally to recognise zonal and regional indigenous organisations as the courts of second instance in cases where indigenous community justice is appealed, recognising what had already become the practice in many communities.[28] This practice exacerbates the conflict when there are intra- or inter-ethnic antagonisms within the organisations, (as occurred in the case of the murder of the mayor of Jambaló, discussed below).

In early 1992, the Justice Ministry offered its own draft legislation. In response to harsh criticism from anthropologists and legal experts, the

[24] J. Dandler, 'Indigenous Peoples and the Rule of Law in Latin America', pp. 14–15.

[25] C. Gaviria Diaz, 'Alcances, contenidos y limitaciones de la Jurisdicción Especial Indígena', in '*Del olvido surgimos para traer nuevas esperanzas*', p. 165.

[26] In Perafán's opinion, the project confused territorial and personal jurisdiction while referring substantive and procedural questions with respect to the development of indigenous jurisidiction to written legislation, notwithstanding the fact that the constitution had not called for legislation developing indigenous jurisdiction, apart from the problem of coordination with the national judicial system. Perafán, *Sistemas Jurídicos Páez, Kogi, Wayúu y Tule*, p. 20.

[27] Jurisdicción Indígena, Código de Procedimiento Penal, Régimen Transitorio, Propuesta presentada por la ONIC a la Comisión Legislativa (Congresito), 1991.

[28] This is also the case in some provinces of Peru, where *rondas campesinas* have formed federations that act as appellate bodies. Ardito, 'The Right to Self-Regulation', p. 9.

Ministry declined to present the proposal to congress.[29] No subsequent attempt has been made to legislate Article 246. According to Perafán, a consensus exists between the government and indigenous organisations that there should be more study of indigenous justice systems and more reflection on the possible ways to coordinate with the ordinary justice system.[30]

In the absence of implementing legislation, the Constitutional Court has ruled on the constitutional limitations on indigenous jurisdiction. This was in response to three *tutelas* presented by indigenous defendants claiming that their fundamental constitutional rights had been violated by indigenous justice. (It is actually more often the victim's family that tries to move jurisdiction to Colombian courts because indigenous sentences usually are deemed more lenient than those of the national system.)[31] In so doing the Court relied on the 1991 Constitution as well as ILO Convention 169. In decision T-254 (1994), the Court began developing a standard for implementing Article 246. First, it ruled that cultural traditions are to be respected, depending on the court's judgment with respect to the extent that those traditions have been preserved. That is, the more contact an indigenous community has had with Western culture, the less weight may be given to its cultural traditions. The Peruvian Criminal Code includes the principle, exempting Indians from criminal liability in proportion to the extent that the norms violated are culturally alien to them.[32] Secondly, the decisions and sanctions imposed by indigenous tribunals must not violate fundamental constitutional or international human rights. Finally, the Court established the supremacy of indigenous customary law over ordinary civil laws that conflict with cultural norms, and over legislation that does not protect a constitutional right of the same rank as the right to cultural and ethnic diversity.[33]

---

[29] In a memorandum to the Interior Minister, Indigenous Affairs Office director Luis José Azcárate identified problems with the proposal. First, the proposal's stipulation of causes for which indigenous legal authorities may be removed by a new state institution that polices the legal profession interfere with indigenous communities' constitutional right to autonomy in choosing their own authorities. Some authorities exercising judicial functions hold permanent or hereditary office and are not removable. Secondly, the project includes Western legal concepts that are not applicable to indigenous justice system, including the idea that an authority's ruling might be revocable by some outside higher authority. Finally, the project allows Colombian judges to determine who is indigenous, a violation of ILO Convention 169. Memorandum from Luis José Azcárate to Humberto de la Calle, 'Comentarios al Proyecto Preliminar de Ley Sobre Organización de la Jurisdicción Especial Indígena, Elaborado por el Ministerio de Justicia', 3 February 1992.

[30] Perafán, *Sistemas Jurídicos Páez, Kogi, Wayúu y Tule*, p. 20.   [31] *Ibid.*, p. 117.

[32] Ardito, 'The Right to Self-Regulation', p. 28.

[33] Cepeda, 'Democracy, State and Society in the Colombian Constitution: The Role of the Constitutional Court', unpublished manuscript (1995), p. 37, n. 126.

The Court further defined the scope of indigenous special jurisdiction in a 1996 ruling on a claim brought by an Embera-Chamí Indian that his *cabildo* (a form of community government imposed on Colombian Indians by the Spanish crown and later adopted and 'indigenised' by indigenous cultures) had violated his right to due process,[34] ruling that the standard for interpreting indigenous jurisdiction must be 'the maximum autonomy for the indigenous community and the minimisation of restrictions to those which are necessary to safeguard interests of superior constitutional rank'.[35] Restrictions on the right to autonomy must protect a more important interest than that of cultural diversity (i.e. national security, the right to life, prohibition of slavery and torture) and must represent the manner of protecting that right that is least destructive to indigenous autonomy. As the minimum basis for 'intercultural dialogue' the Court offered the limitation of indigenous autonomy by the right to life and freedom from torture and slavery, arguing that indigenous cultures in Colombia do not practice torture or slavery, but *do* sanction murder. According to these criteria, the defendant did not have a right to 'due process', as that term is understood in Western law, but only to the legitimate procedures used by his community in similar cases. However, the Court did take issue with the decision of the *cabildo* to condemn the claimant to a Colombian jail, since this is not a traditional sanction of this community. While acknowledging that cultures are dynamic and that sanctions might change over time, the Court admonished indigenous authorities not to act arbitrarily but, rather, to follow custom and tradition. The Court offered the *cabildo* the alternative of either retrying the case and imposing a more traditional sanction, or of remanding the case to the Colombian courts.

The decision is also noteworthy for its defense of the *cepo*, a form of corporal punishment common to indigenous communities that was imported from Spanish colonial law. A number of the punishments used today by indigenous communities are derived from Spanish colonial rule, but indigenous authorities insist that these have become part of their own 'authentic' culture, as most cultures continuously borrow and adapt practices from cultures with which they have contact. As Horowitz argues

---

[34] The *cabildo* found the defendant, who had escaped from captivity during the investigation, guilty of murder. *Cabildo* authorities had initially condemned the defendant to eight years in prison, but subsequently lengthened the term to 20 years in response to the defendant's flight and his refusal to submit to their authority. A municipal court granted the *tutela*, arguing that the defendant was not allowed to defend himself, since the *cabildo* decided the case while he was in the municipal jail; that there had been no precedent of the *cabildo* ruling on a case of homicide; and that the judges in the case were biased because they were relatives of the murder victim.
[35] Tutela-349/1996, p. 10.

based on his study of contemporary Malaysian legal reform, authenticity need not be derived from practices or norms considered 'indigenous'.[36] The Court argued that the *cepo*, although painful, does no permanent damage to the offender, and is used for a brief duration. As such, it does not constitute cruel or inhumane treatment. Finally, the Court exempted indigenous customary law from the Western expectation that pre-established sanctions would be meted out in similar cases. Nevertheless, as Magistrate Carlos Gaviria ruled, this does not imply:

an opening for absolute arbitrariness, in that authorities are necessarily obligated to act in conformance with what has been done in the past, with a basis in the traditions that serve to sustain social cohesion. On the other hand, this requirement may not be extended to the point of holding traditional norms completely static, inasmuch as all cultures are essentially dynamic, even though the weight of tradition may be strong.

A 1996 decision (T-496) extended the territorial scope of indigenous jurisdiction beyond indigenous territories to a 'personal jurisdiction' in cases where a judge deems the cultural alienation of an indigenous defendant to warrant it, although in the specific case brought by a Páez Indian, the Court ruled that ordinary jurisdiction was appropriate.

The issue of special indigenous jurisdiction gained national attention in 1997, when a third indigenous defendant, Francisco Gembuel, a Guambiano Indian living in a Páez community, filed a *tutela* against the *cabildo* of Jambaló, Cauca. The Páez are the largest (approximately 120,000 individuals) and politically most dominant indigenous group in the southwestern department of Cauca, the area of greatest indigenous concentration in the country and the origin of the national indigenous movement. It is an area of intense rural land conflict where several guerrilla organisations maintain active fronts and vie with drug traffickers, paramilitary organisations, and public authorities for control over the legitimate means of force. In this case a conflict had erupted between the *cabildo* and seven indigenous defendants banished from the community, stripped of their political rights as Indians, and sentenced to varying amounts of lashes with a leather whip (*fuete*). The sentence, announced by *cabildo* authorities on 24 December 1996, followed the defendants' conviction as 'intellectual authors' of the assassination of the town's indigenous mayor, Marden Betancur. Local guerrillas actually claimed responsibility for the murder; the indigenous defendants were convicted of publicly linking Betancur to the paramilitaries and, thus, inspiring an indigenous sector of the Ejército de Liberación Nacional (ELN) guerrillas to kill him. Gembuel's supporters argue that the *cabildo*'s ruling violated Páez norms of procedure – a claim sustained by a confidential mem-

[36] Horowitz, 'The Qur'an and the Common Law', p. 570.

185

orandum from indigenous law expert Perafán, in which he argued that there is no evidence of intellectual authorship, but only of '*tardecer*' – a concept in Páez law that attributes guilt to a prior act that may have inspired a later outcome, although no causal link can be proven.[37] Moreover, in Páez law the expulsion of a community member is never applied as a punishment for the first offence, as it was applied against Gembuel and his associates. A lower court ruled that the *cabildo* had denied the defendants the opportunity to defend themselves, that the judges in the case were biased, that the whipping constituted torture and, thus, was illegal under international law, which has constitutional rank in Colombia. A new investigation and trial were ordered. Following an appeal by the Páez Cabildo Association of the North, a higher court affirmed the ruling, observing that corporal punishment, even if it did no permanent physical harm, violated the defendants' fundamental constitutional rights.

The case generated international controversy when Amnesty International accused the *cabildo* of condoning torture. It became controversial within the indigenous movement as well, particularly in the Cauca, since the murdered mayor and Gembuel belonged to rival political factions of the Consejo Regional Indígena del Cauca (CRIC) and had recently been engaged in a close electoral battle for the mayorship of Jambaló. The then-president of the CRIC, Páez leader Jesús Piñacué, publicly took the side of his political constituency in the *cabildo* against that of his rivals, disobeying the decision taken by the executive board of the CRIC (and the traditional practice of the organisation) to remain neutral and seek reconciliation in such cases. Gembuel and his followers claimed they were being persecuted because they are political rivals of the *cabildo* leadership and that Piñacué exceeded his authority by becoming involved in the capture and judgment of the accused. They accused Piñacué, a former candidate for vice president and senator, of using the issue to gain national media attention. In fact, Piñacué was elected to the national senate in 1998 with a level of electoral support that exceeded that of any prior indigenous candidate for national office. Ironically, in the summer of 1998 Piñacué found himself fighting a *cabildo* sentence of more than 100 lashes with the *fuete* as punishment for having announced his support for Liberal Party candidate Horacio Serpa in the 1998 presidential run-off without the approval of his political organisation or the Páez leadership. After negotiating with the *cabildo*, the sentence was converted to a ceremonial dunking in a pond in Tierradentro.

On 15 October 1997, the Constitutional Court upheld the *cabildo*'s

[37] Memorandum from Carlos César Perafán to Jesús E. Piñacué, dated 12 March 1997, subject: 'Concepto Sentencia 001 Cabildo de Jambaló'.

determination of guilt and sentencing (T-523/1997). In his decision, Magistrate Carlos Gaviria Díaz concurred with the Páez Cabildo Association of the North that the intention of the whipping is not to cause excessive suffering but, rather, to represent the ritual purification of the offender and the restoration of harmony to the community. The extent of physical suffering was ruled insufficient to constitute torture (which would be to violate international human rights law) – an affirmation of the Court's defense of corporal punishment in Tutela-349/1996. Gaviria Díaz concluded with the observation that only a high degree of autonomy would ensure cultural survival.

The Jambaló decision strengthened the autonomy of indigenous jurisdiction beyond the Court's 1994 standard. Not only were corporal punishment and expulsion ruled constitutional, the Court in the Jambaló case applied its decision to a community whose level of cultural assimilation is high relative to more isolated, less educated communities. This would appear to lower the burden of proving cultural 'purity' on the part of indigenous authorities. The decision also contributes to the inconsistencies demonstrated by the Constitutional Court in developing and applying the constitution's ethnic rights regime – inconsistencies and contradictions that the magistrates themselves admit, and which reflect their lack of experience with the issues and categories presented by the constitution with respect to ethnic rights, the internal normative contradictions of the constitution itself, as well as the differing philosophical tendencies within the Court.[38] The Court has fluctuated between a vision that seeks a consensus on minimal universal norms and the restriction of the exercise of indigenous jurisdiction to a sphere of universally accepted rights, and a vision that recognises an intangible sphere of ethnic diversity whose integral nature precludes restriction. According to ex-Magistrate Ciro Angarita, this reflects a division within the Court between those who:

absolutely reject the possibility that indigenous '*usos y costumbres*' can be considered sources of law…[and] another, which accepts, on the contrary, that respect for this alternative source of law – to the extent that it is not contrary to the Constitution and the law – constitutes an expression of the ethnic and cultural diversity of the Colombian Nation and, as such, has a firm but conditional pretext in our [normative] system.[39]

[38] C. Angarita, 'Constitución política, jurisdicción especial indígena y autonomía territorial', in '*Del Olvido surgimos para traer nuevas esperanzas*', pp. 176–7; Gaviria Díaz, 'Alcances, contenidos y limitaciones', p. 162; L. S. Mosquera de Meneses, 'Conflicto entre la JEI y la jurisdicción ordinaria', in '*Del olvido surgimos para traer nuevas esperanzas*', p. 282; Santos, 'Pluralismo jurídico y Jurisdicción Especial Indígena', in '*Del olvido surgimos para traer nuevas esperanzas*', p. 203.

[39] Translation by the author. C. Angarita, 'Constitución política, jurisdicción especial indígena y autonomía territorial', in '*Del olvido Surgimos para traer nuevas esperanzas*',

The larger impact of the Jambaló dispute is the alarm it generated within the indigenous community over the intrusion of the state in what were considered to be internal indigenous affairs, and the negative image of Indians, who were portrayed in the press as violators of human rights who may not be capable of managing the jurisdictional powers recognised by the 1991 Constitution. At a March 1997 conference on indigenous special jurisdiction, among the most controversial issues was whether any Colombian court has jurisdiction to review the decisions of autonomous indigenous *cabildos*, and whether indigenous jurisdiction should be restricted by some universal conception of human rights, as manifest in international law. The latter, 'total-autonomy' position puts indigenous organisations in the ambiguous position of rejecting the control of a constitution on which their own elected representatives left such an indelible mark, a constitution that recognises indigenous authorities as legitimate public authorities and, therefore, part of the Colombian state. It also puts indigenous organisations in the position of rejecting international human rights law, while at the same time using international human rights conventions to argue for expanding indigenous rights in national law. The human rights limitation is a serious concern for states throughout the region, since some indigenous cultures are known to have practices that offend Western sensibilities. The most common of these is the use of physical punishment or death as a sanction, but there are also cases where the community practice is to kill or abandon infant twins or babies born handicapped, female or to large families, as well as old or very sick people, because they are considered to be a burden on the community. Another community conflict concerns the practice of older indigenous men taking wives at the age of first menstruation, which countries such as Peru prosecute as statutory rape.[40]

A 1998 decision (SU-510) further developed Article 246. It required the Court to balance two fundamental rights of equal rank: cultural diversity and religious freedom. In this case, traditional Ika authorities had imposed physical punishments on evangelical protestant Indians for rejecting traditional beliefs and proselytising within the community. In this theocratic community, spiritual deviation violates community law.

---

p. 111. See also Angarita, 'Colombia: Indígenas y Constitución de 1991,' in *Seminario Internacional de Administración de Justicia y Pueblos Indígenas* (La Paz, 176–7); E. Sánchez. 'Conflicto entre la JEI y jurisdicción ordinaria', in '*Del olvido surgimos para traer nuevas esperanzas*', pp. 291–2.

[40] Ardito, 'The Right to Self-Regulation', p. 10; J. Aroca, 'El papel de la justicia en la resolución de conflictos multiétnicos: El caso peruano', unpublished manuscript. 1999, p. 5.

The Court ruled that Ika authorities must respect the right of community members to hold different religious beliefs, but it required the dissenters to restrict religious activities such as proselytisation, and to locate the Pentacostal church outside the borders of the community.

Despite the problems discussed above, the Colombian case provides the most ambitious attempt of any Latin American state to implement legal pluralism. The singularity of the Colombian effort may be attributed both to the fact that its constitutional model of indigenous rights is among the most comprehensive and progressive to date, as well as to the fact that its indigenous population is among the smallest in proportion to its total population, presenting a more modest threat to traditional views of national identity and the interests of rural power brokers. Perhaps this explains why Costa Rica, whose indigenous population is less than one percent of the total, is second to Colombia in jurisprudence favouring indigenous peoples' rights. Costa Rica's Supreme Court has decided more than five cases concerning indigenous constitutional rights since 1992, mostly in favor of indigenous organisations.[41]

Other factors also may be important. Colombian Indians developed a tradition in the nineteenth century of using the legal system to defend rights and of taking legal petitions to every possible channel of redress of grievances within the state. They have enjoyed numerous successes, blocking or modifying laws detrimental to their interests and defending colonial-era privileges.[42] They enjoy the support of numerous human rights organisations with experience in arguing rights cases before national and international fora. Many Colombian Indians choose law as a profession or field of study – such as Senator Francisco Rojas Birry, who served in the 1991 constituent assembly. Indians have taken advantage of a culture that is particularly litigious and in which judges have traditionally played an important role in conflict resolution.[43]

Colombia's constitutional tradition is also unusual. Unlike most Latin American countries, Colombia retained colonial-era institutions with respect to collective rights for Indians and other corporate actors in its constitution and laws into the 1990s. Colombian jurisprudence has a tradition of recognising the source of indigenous collective rights –

[41] Although Costa Rica's constitution is silent on indigenous rights, the country has signed ILO Convention 169, which has the rank of constitutional law. Organización Internacional del Trabajo, 'Pueblos Indígenas, Sentencias, Fallos y Opiniones consultivas, Costa Rica, Cinco sentencias de la sala constitucional relacionadas con los derechos de los pueblos indígenas'.

[42] R. Roldán, 'Los convenios de la OIT y los derechos territoriales indígenas, en las políticas de gobierno y en la administración de justicia en Colombia', in *Seminario Internacional de Administración de Justicia y Pueblos Indígenas* (La Paz, 1998), pp. 53–4.

[43] Interview, Manuel José Cepeda, Fribourg, Switzerland, 30 April 1999.

particularly territorial rights – in the existence of indigenous peoples prior to the formation of the state, a tradition based in colonial Indian law. Colombian jurists have a longstanding tradition of recognising the duty of the state to protect indigenous communities. There is no other country in the region with such a long history of jurisprudence reflecting this commitment. The work of jurists is supported by a strong tradition of scholarly work on indigenous peoples among Colombian social scientists, which has generated a place of respect for indigenous cultures within Colombian society, despite their small proportion of the population.[44] Colombia also traditionally has supported international human rights conventions, particularly with respect to the rights of minorities. It was among the most active participants in the debate on ILO Convention 169, in which it pushed for a broad recognition of autonomy for indigenous peoples.

Additional explanations for the singularity of the Colombian case are the exceptionality of the country's professional judiciary and its unusual tradition of judicial activism. Colombian Supreme Court magistrates exercised judicial review in the nineteenth century, a practice that increased after 1910. Colombians became habituated to the judiciary's involvement in important political issues. The Constitutional Court has drawn its magistrates from the ranks of the country's most prestigious law professors and most experienced Supreme Court magistrates. Like other Colombian judges they are paid good salaries: Constitutional Court magistrates have among the highest salaries in the public sector, earning the same as the president and cabinet ministers.[45]

Bolivia

Bolivia's indigenous population comprises 66 per cent of the total population of about eight million, the largest proportion in South America. The largest indigenous group is Quechua (about 35 per cent of Bolivians), followed by the Aymara (about 25 per cent). Highland indigenous organisations are descendants of peasant unions formed by the Movimiento Nacional Revolucionario (MNR) party after the 19?? revolution to control the indigenous population. These organisations began to assert their independence in the 1970s when the Banzer military government imposed economic policies less favorable to their interests. In

---

[44] F. Correa, 'El indígena ante el Estado Colombiano', in E. Sánchez (ed.), *Antropología Jurídica. Normas formales—costumbres legales* (Bogotá, 1992), pp. 93–4; Roldán, 'La Convenios de la OIT', pp. 54–63.

[45] Interview, Manuel José Cepeda, 30 April 1999. Cepeda estimates that Constitutional Court magistrates earn approximately US$7,500 per month.

1979 peasant organisations formed an independent confederation (CSUTCB) to unite the *campesino* contingent within Bolivia's militant labour movement. In the late 1980s and early 1990s, as the coherence and power of the labour movement declined rapidly, traditional *ayllu* organisations,[46] which had been overshadowed politically by the *campesino* federations, reasserted their authority and established large federations that now vie for the allegiance of the highland indigenous population. Organising among the lowland population began to gain momentum after 1985, reaching national attention with a massive march from the lowlands to La Paz in 1990. As in Colombia, decades of grassroots mobilisation enabled indigenous organisations to assert constitutional claims during the 1993–6 reforms.

Unlike the Colombian constitution, replaced *in toto* via a constituent assembly, the 1967 Bolivian Constitution was altered through a process of piecemeal reforms, beginning in the administration of Jaime Paz Zamora in 1993, and extending through the administration of Gonzalo Sánchez de Lozada (1993–7). The bulk of Bolivia's new constitutional regime for indigenous rights is contained in Article 171, which was adapted from the 1991 Colombian Constitution. The relevant language from Article 171 reads:

The natural authorities of the indigenous and campesino communities may exercise functions of administration and application of their own norms as an alternative solution in conflicts, in conformity with their customs and procedures, always providing that they are not contrary to the Constitution and the laws. The law will establish the coordination of this special jurisdiction with the judicial power (translation by the author).

In Colombia, President Gaviria had prioritised the implementation of judicial reform. In Bolivia, President Sánchez de Lozada's Justice Ministry prepared a comprehensive set of laws to modernise the judicial system, but few of the laws were sent to congress, owing to the greater priority placed by Sánchez de Lozada on other aspects of the constitutional reform and his efforts to diminish the growing prestige and popularity of his able Justice Minister, whom he may have perceived as a political rival. The implementation of Bolivia's 1994 constitutional reforms with respect to the judiciary also fell victim to a counter-reform drive by traditional politicians within the governing MNR party, who resisted relinquishing

[46] An *ayllu* is an Andean form of community organization of pre-colombian origin. It is territorially discontinuous in order to take advantage of the diverse ecological zones in the Andes, enabling a community to produce a variety of agricultural crops while raising animals suited to higher elevations. There are approximately 140 *ayllus* in Bolivia's central highlands. X. Izko, 'Etnopolítica y costumbre en los andes bolivianos', in A. Wray et al., *Derecho, pueblos indigenas reforma del estado* (Quito, 1993), p. 193.

control over the political quotas available to the ruling party under the existing system.[47] Implementing legislation for the judicial reform was not prepared until the end of the Sánchez de Lozada administration, and it was never introduced in the National Congress. Only the new Penal Code was approved during his term. Fulfilling a longstanding public commitment, President Hugo Banzer, who took office in July 1997, passed legislation establishing the new judicial institutions created by the 1994 reform, including the Constitutional Tribunal. That tribunal began operating only in 1999. Implementing the judicial reform is part of the Banzer government's strategy to recover from the ignominious experience of being named the world's second-most corrupt country by Transparency International.[48]

For the Sánchez de Lozada government, the indigenous customary law issue was part of a larger effort to accommodate Bolivia's formal legal system to the reality of a country where justice is administered mainly in informal, oral, local settings and to create a more humane system, closer to the people, that promotes reconciliation and human rights. As in Colombia, a main goal was the recuperation of legitimacy for the state by incorporating community justice systems with high levels of legitimacy.[49] As Justice Ministry officials argued:

the recognition of community justice is the most effective alternative for satisfying the demands for justice of the national majority, without imposing a legal order and formal justice, which are alien and ultimately ineffective for resolving conflicts.[50]

They contend this, because community members actively take part in the proceedings, interact with familiar community authorities, and because the decision rendered is negotiated among the parties to the conflict. In contrast, ordinary justice is handed down unilaterally by a non-community member in a formal procedure in which the parties are passive subjects.[51]

Due to the delay in implementing the judicial reform, legislation to implement the right of indigenous peoples to exercise their customary legal systems was unfinished at the end of the Sánchez de Lozada

---

[47] Confidential interviews in La Paz with former justice administration officials; interviews in La Paz, Luis Vásquez, 17 June 1997; Gustavo Fernández, 9 June 1997; Ramiro Molina R., 6 May 1997; *La Razón*, 11 Oct. 1996, p. 2A.

[48] Interview, Jorge Quiroga, La Paz, 14 Dec. 1998.

[49] The greater legitimacy of indigenous community authorities relative to state courts is confirmed by a 1998 poll on public support for public and private institutions, in which indigenous authorities placed second after the Catholic Church, while courts placed 13th out of 15 institutions listed. See M. Seligson, 'La cultura política de la democracia en Bolivia: 1998', unpublished study prepared for USAID, 1998.

[50] Translation by the author. 'Justicia Comunitaria y Jueces de Paz', Documento de Trabajo, Ministerio de Justicia, 1997, p. 9.

[51] Interview, Silvina Ramírez, La Paz, 7 May 1997.

administration. Preparation of this legislation has been assigned to a team of Justice Ministry anthropologists, headed by Ramiro Molina. During the last eight months of the Sánchez de Lozada administration, Molina supervised a World Bank-funded project to prepare case studies of the customary legal systems of the three largest ethnic groups, as well as two urban cases, and to draft implementing legislation to accommodate oral traditions to positive law. Due to heavy urban migration in the last decade, indigenous community justice is not confined to rural areas. Migrants typically bring their legal systems with them to urban areas, a practice facilitated by the custom of settling with fellow migrants.[52] The project was completed during the Banzer administration and was published in 1999. The studies are intended to serve as guidelines for judges in interpreting the constitutional right to customary law and in determining the guilt and sentencing of indigenous defendants, although in practice they barely cover the great diversity of Bolivian customary legal systems, since even within language groups there may be variations in procedures and norms.[53]

As in Colombia, indigenous organisations offered legislative proposals for the implementation of the right to exercise customary law. The confederation uniting most of the lowland organisations, the Confederación de los Pueblos Indígenas de Bolivia (CIDOB), proposed the establishment of an indigenous justice administration hierarchy parallel and similar to that for non-indigenous law. Justice ministry officials rejected the proposal because it imposes a system of authority on a diversity of systems that may not have the judicial figures contemplated in the CIDOB proposal – that is, the authority to administer justice may be rotated, or may lie in a group of people or an assembly rather than in a single person, as in ordinary law. In addition, the CIDOB proposal called for the codification of customs into positive law, which would strip them of their flexible, dynamic character. Thus ironically, as in Colombia, proposals prepared by the major indigenous organisations were rejected by government officials as being too restrictive of indigenous communities' constitutional rights.

It is not surprising that Bolivians faced similar problems in creating a law coordinating indigenous and national jurisdictions, since the ambiguous and vague language contained in Article 171 is almost identical to that of the Colombian Constitution's Article 246. Bolivian Justice Ministry staff observed that this language may recognise an indigenous jurisdiction that is entirely separate from the national system, or one that is subordinate to it. As in Colombia, it is unclear whether

[52] Interview, Esteban Ticona, La Paz, 16 Dec. 1998.
[53] Interviews in La Paz, Lorena Ossio, 18 Dec. 1998; Ramiro Molina, 6 May 1997.

Indians have the right to choose indigenous jurisdiction over that of the state, or whether indigenous jurisdiction is mandatory. This issue was resolved in the 1999 revised Code of Penal Procedure, which gives defendants the option of choosing *either* state *or* community jurisdiction. Penal action is extinguished in cases where the community has resolved the issue. It remains unclear whether indigenous customary law has broad territorial or functional scope, or whether it is restricted to internal, cultural matters not regulated by the state.[54] It is possible to interpret the limits of indigenous jurisdiction as either 'fundamental rights' or as the constitution and other laws. The scope of indigenous autonomy in the administration of justice is restricted in Bolivia by the absence of constitutional recognition of the territorial autonomy of indigenous peoples. Whereas the Colombian Constitution clearly extends jurisdictional, politico-territorial authority to indigenous communities, in Bolivia indigenous organisations and their advocates had to settle for collective property rights. The greater resistance of Bolivian elites to recognising a territoriality for indigenous authority is understandable, given the implications of extending this recognition to more than 60 per cent of the population.

The most difficult conceptual question the Justice Ministry team is struggling with is that of limits to customary jurisdiction. Anthropologist Ivan Arias, a consultant on the customary law project, argues that, although there are many positive aspects of *campesino* justice – such as the use of strong moral sanctions, the prominence of orality and dialogue in the development of consensus among the accused and the community, and the ultimate aim of achieving harmony within the community – there are a number of problems in the treatment of women and children that violate constitutional, statutory and international law that the state and non-indigenous Bolivians should not be expected to tolerate. The difficulty will be excising these practices and norms from traditional legal systems without doing violence to the culture.[55] The team is leaning toward identifying the constitution as the only limit, since international conventions are not well integrated into Bolivian law, as they are, for example, in Colombia and Costa Rica. With a view toward promoting a dialogue on this key point, the team devised a strategy to engage the public, lawyers, judges and indigenous communities, and undertook a training project with the Judicial Counsel.[56]

To fend off resistance from the older legal establishment, the Justice Ministry team studied historical texts revered by the legal establishment

[54] Interview, Silvina Ramírez, La Paz, 7 May 1997.
[55] Interview, Ivan Arias, La Paz, 16 Dec. 1998.
[56] Interview, Lorena Ossio, La Paz, 18 Dec. 1998.

for language that would support an interpretation of customary law as potentially public, formal, and positive in nature.[57] They also looked at the experience of constitutional courts in other countries as interpreters of this law, with particular interest in the Colombian case, since Bolivian politicians and elites are accustomed to adopting norms and practices that have international prestige. Some politicians and congressional deputies have questioned the very concept that indigenous and *campesino* communities practice anything that could be called justice, pointing to practices such as physical punishment to demonstrate their 'savageness' and 'barbarity'. Nevertheless, the Banzer government's indigenous affairs office has encountered enthusiasm for the project among the younger generation of judges and law clerks, who have participated in government-sponsored training programmes.[58]

These educational programmes are important because Bolivia's legal education tradition is fundamentally positivist, and has denied the existence of legal pluralism. It offers no training in indigenous legal systems and has produced no lawyers or judges who understand the topic. During the Sánchez de Lozada administration, the government sponsored a variety of fora to educate the country's senior judges about the issues involved in recognising indigenous justice systems, including an international conference on the administration of justice in indigenous communities. Through the participation of Colombian constitutional magistrates and juridical anthropologists, the Bolivian government became familiar with the Colombian experience.[59] It was the first time that indigenous justice systems were discussed at such a high level of judicial power. Despite the existence of numerous laws on these matters, the Bolivian Supreme Court has never issued a ruling on indigenous rights or on the issues of diversity or multiculturalism.[60]

The Bolivian government and courts have continued the pre-reform policy of staying out of indigenous community justice administration. For example, the government responded only weakly to a 1991 case of reported witch-burning in the Guaraní-Izozog community of Alto y Bajo Izozog, in the lowland department of Santa Cruz, where it is the custom for authorities to expel community members judged to be witches and, if they return, to execute and burn them. When the aunt of Capitán Grande Bonifacio Barrientos and her husband – both declared to be witches and expelled from the community of Cuarirenda – were shot upon returning to the community and their bodies burned, the municipal authorities of

[57] Interview, Lorena Ossio, La Paz, 18 Dec. 1998.
[58] Interviews in La Paz, Esteban Ticona, Ernesto Muñoz, 16 Dec. 1998.
[59] Interview, Rene Orellana Halkyer, Santa Cruz, 18 July 1997.
[60] Interview, Jorge Luis Vacaflor, La Paz, 13 May 1997.

Charagua sent the police to arrest the perpetrators. However, the police left without making an arrest after the entire community claimed responsibility for the murders. A nearby army post also attempted to intervene, but was rebuffed. The matter is currently not being pursued by the state.[61] The prosecution of witches by indigenous communities is perhaps the archetypal case of indigenous customary law, severely punishing behaviour that is not considered unlawful under positive law. Normative conflicts between the two justice systems are likely to emerge on this issue throughout the region, where numerous indigenous communities sanction witchcraft, often with execution.

Beginning in 1994, in an effort to protect their new constitutional rights to customary law against possible state intervention, the Guaraní–Izozog worked with anthropologists to write down their statutes and regulations. They are the only indigenous people in Bolivia with written norms of administration of justice. To avoid conflicts with constitutional and international law, these written statutes formally prohibit execution. The most severe penalty that may be applied is expulsion from the community. Anthropologists working with the group believe that communities may continue the practices of expulsion and witch-burning clandestinely to avoid the intervention of human rights organisations, since the state is disposed to intervene in cases where the right to life is considered to be violated.[62]

There are four possible explanations for the Bolivian state's lesser intervention in indigenous community justice issues. First, unlike Colombia, expelled witches have not sought legal action to protect their constitutional rights, despite the existence of a significant community of expelled witches in the city of Santa Cruz. Indigenous communities – including the families of the executed witches – have maintained solidarity on the issue of customary law in the few cases in which authorities have been challenged. As Orellana explains,

The authorities are not obeyed out of fear of their power; rather, there exists a broad participation and acceptance on the part of the communal society, such that a great degree of legitimacy and validity is bestowed on the administration of justice.[63]

Perhaps there is greater community solidarity behind the administration of justice by indigenous authorities because the factionalism that comes with electoral participation has not yet generated community divisions –

[61] Interviews in Santa Cruz, René Orellana Halkyer, 18 July 1997; Isabelle Combes, 18 July 1997.

[62] Interviews, Silvina Ramírez, La Paz, 7 May 1997; René Orellana, Santa Cruz, 18 July 1997; Isabelle Combes, Santa Cruz, 18 July 1997.

[63] Translation by author. Orellana, 'Un derecho sobre muchos derechos', p. 27.

as occurred in the Páez community of Jambaló. Partisan politics did not enter indigenous communities in a major way until the 1995 municipal elections. Greater community-level solidarity may also explain the absence of a key role for zonal and regional indigenous organisations in resolving intra-community disputes over the administration of justice. As opposed to the situation obtaining in Colombia and Peru, there does not appear to be a tradition of referring intractable community disputes to zonal or regional organisations, even though such organisations do exist in Bolivia.[84]

Secondly, according to Ramiro Molina, Bolivian indigenous law has been consistently and autonomously practiced and is well known and understood within the communities. Over the centuries, ethnic and Western norms adapted to each other and to changing political conjunctures. This may be more the case in Bolivia due to the more centralised and rural nature of the country, and the greater dispersion of its population. Although the Colombian and Bolivian territories are approximately the same size, the Bolivian population is hardly larger than the population of Colombia's capital city (seven million), and 36 per cent of the population lives in communities of 250 people or fewer. Bolivian courts have been a largely urban phenomenon. As a result, in much of the country there has been little challenge to indigenous law from the state, not to mention the guerrillas, military units and paramilitaries that compete for norm-making authority with indigenous authorities throughout Colombia. In addition, according to Molina, in Bolivia judicial authority is exercised democratically and rotated, ensuring that punishments are fair and widely accepted. Thus, occasions do not emerge, as in the Jambaló case, where one sector of elites within the community challenges another's interpretation of indigenous law.[65]

Thirdly, the tradition in Bolivia is to negotiate rather than adjudicate conflicts, a preference that arose out of necessity. Courts are inaccessible to most of the population due to their concentration in urban areas, which limits access for the 42 per cent living in rural areas, who must invest considerable time and expense to visit the local provincial capital. Bolivian courts commonly impose user fees – 25 per cent of the judicial budget – which are beyond the reach of the 70 per cent living in poverty. Other barriers are the predominant use of Spanish and written procedures in a country where many are illiterate and do not understand Spanish, the insufficient supply of legal advisors for the indigent, and the slowness of the judicial process, due in part to the scarcity of judges. A decade ago a total of 424 judges served a population of about seven million, a ratio of approximately one to every 16,000 inhabitants – a low rate of judges/

[84] Orellana, p. 25.   [65] Interview, Ramiro Molina R., 6 May 1997.

population even for Latin America.[66] Courts are distrusted more than any other Bolivian institution with the exception of political parties and the police, due to the permeation of judicial appointments by partisan politics and corruption.[67] In contrast to the situation in Colombia, judges lack professionalism, enjoy low public prestige and are poorly paid. Where conflicts between indigenous rights and the state have occurred, lawyers negotiate these with the appropriate authority, rather than filing suit. Thus, no tradition ever emerged of defending indigenous rights in the courts.[68] And, again in contrast to Colombia, no non-governmental organisations emerged devoted to defending rights in courts. Bolivia's lively NGO sector and social science professionals have traditionally worked on economic development and cultural issues rather than on the issue of rights *per se*.[69] Due to the far lower incidence of political violence and human rights violations in Bolivia, there is no battery of attorneys' organised to defend human rights comparable to that existing in Colombia.[70]

Conclusion

Political elites in both countries understand the urgency to provide a cheaper, more accessible, more face-to-face form of justice administration, particularly in rural areas, in order to legitimise the authority of the state and extend the presence of the rule of law throughout the territory. This goal was the principal reason that they were willing to recognise indigenous customary law. The fact that neither country was able to codify the coordination of the two systems does not imply that this is impossible. Other states have imposed an interpretation of this term. The jurisdiction of tribal courts in the United States, for example, is well settled. In our cases, however, both states' democratic legitimacy is fragile and both have made public commitments to recognise diversity. Neither seems willing to impose its vision of legal pluralism on authorities that enjoy greater popular support and legitimacy than the state. It is better to muddle through without a statutory law than to risk impugning the regime of rights and the legality that the recent constitutional reforms were intended

---

[66] For example, according to Gamarra, Colombia has one judge for every 8,000 inhabitants. Eduardo Gamarra, *The System of Justice in Bolivia: An Institutional Analysis*. Monograph 4 (Miami, 1991), p. 92.

[67] Seligson, 'La Cultura Política de la Democracia'.

[68] Interviews, Jorge Luis Vacaflor, 13 May 1997; Silvina Ramírez, 7 May 1997.

[69] The exception to this rule, the Santa Cruz-based CEJIS, operates primarily through negotiations with the executive rather than the courts.

[70] On the observations made here about the Bolivian justice system, see D. L. Van Cott. 'The Role of Justice in Conflict Resolution in Multiethnic Countries: The Bolivian Case', paper presented at the Workshop on Multiethnic Nations in Developing Countries: Colombia as a Latin American Case, Fribourg, Switzerland, April 30, 1999.

to construct. In practice, the formal demarcation of jurisdictions has not been a major source of conflict, since in both countries informal coordinating mechanisms have been created and adapted as state and indigenous legal systems have developed over time. As Iturralde observes with respect to Latin America in general, in virtually all cases customary law is practised in interrelation with positive law, depending on the problem the community is addressing. Many communities, particularly in the Andes, often choose to refer disputes to the state rather than to handle them internally.[71] Although indigenous organisations in Latin America claim a broad scope for the exercise of autonomous judicial authority as part of a larger effort to assert political autonomy, in practice the bulk of the scope of indigenous customary law has to do with disputes over the use of community lands, family law (abandonment of minors, relations between married people, inheritance), and a number of minor crimes such as petty theft and assault. Normally customary law is applied only to those persons identified by community authorities, and who identify themselves as community members.[72]

In Colombia, more conflicts over the jurisdiction of customary law have erupted than in Bolivia because of factionalism within indigenous communities; the greater level of urbanisation in Colombia and, thus, the lesser geographic isolation and privacy for community practices; the more pronounced tradition of claiming rights before Colombian courts, particularly within the indigenous movement; and the failure of the Colombian congress to pass legislation establishing the Indigenous Territorial Entities that were to provide the politico-territorial basis of indigenous jurisdiction. These problems are balanced by the unusual propensity of a sector of Colombia's professional judiciary to permit a wide scope of autonomy for indigenous special jurisdiction and by the persistent efforts of regional and national indigenous organisations to gain public support for their interpretation of indigenous autonomy. The indigenous movement has been able to maintain public interest in, and government attention to, cultural diversity through high-profile mobilisations, and by steadily increasing its representation in government office.[73] In Bolivia, indigenous autonomy is facilitated in the absence of sustained governmental support and of a judiciary interested in or

[71] D. Iturralde, 'Movimiento indio, costumbre jurídica y usos de la ley' in R. Stavenhagen and D. Iturralde (eds.), *Entre la ley la costumbre. El derecho consuetudinario indígena en América Latina* (México, 1990), pp. 43, 58; Iturralde, 'Usos de la Ley y usos de la costumbre', pp. 136–7; A. Wray, 'El problema indígena y la reforma del Estado', in Alberto Wray et. al, *Derecho, pueblos indígenas y reforma del Estado* (Quito, 1993), p. 33.

[72] Ministerio de Justicia, 'Justicia Comunitaria y Jueces de Paz', p. 23.

[73] Indigenous political parties hold three senate seats, two seats in the lower chamber, one governship, 12 mayorships, and more than 100 municipal council seats.

knowledgeable about legal pluralism or multiculturalism, largely through the geographic cultural isolation of indigenous communities, the lack of interest on the part of the state and the historical weakness of justice administration.

In both countries, the multicultural zeitgeist of the 1990s has sensitised the general public to the status of indigenous peoples and has created a public mood at least passively hospitable to indigenous rights claims. The disposition to tolerate indigenous customary law despite the existence of practices that offend Western sensibilities is reinforced by the international discourse on multiculturalism and the growing acceptance of legal pluralism in constitutions and international human rights law.[74] The most important challenge today is that of allocating sufficient resources to educate judges and attorneys about indigenous legal practices and the new national and international norms on indigenous rights, and to train Indians from all language groups as judges, advocates and translators.

[74] See the literature cited in note 4.

Weak Weapons, Strong Weapons?
Hidden Resistance and Political Protest
in Rural Ecuador

TANYA KOROVKIN

The article critically applies the theory of everyday forms of peasant resistance (EFPR) to an analysis of land struggles in the Ecuadorean Andes. It explores the effectiveness of 'weapons of the weak' used by indigenous peasants in conflicts with the haciendas. The relationship between hidden resistance and the rise of political organisation is also examined. Special attention is paid to the structural context and cultural underpinning of both covert and overt peasant action.

Few social theories have produced as much controversy as that of everyday forms of peasant resistance (EFPR), developed by Scott, Kerkvliet, and Adas on the basis of rural experiences in Asia.[1] Its focus on peasant resistance to the expansion of the market economy and hidden or, to use Scott'ss expression, 'Brechtian' forms of struggle [*Scott*, 1986: 7] earned many foes among students of peasant movements, even though few of them took the trouble to support their theoretical critiques with careful historical or empirical data. Moreover, the critics also seem to ignore the body of literature on the Andean, largely Peruvian, peasantry that supports some of the everyday resistance tenets.

Below, I will examine the EFPR approach in the light of Andean

Tanya Korovkin, Department of Political Science, University of Waterloo, 200 University Ave.E, Waterloo, Ontario, N2L 3G1, Canada; tkorovki@watarts.uwaterloo.ca. Field research for this article was conducted between 1993 and 1995, in collaboration with Imbabura's Indigenous and Peasant Federarion (FICI) and Imbabura's Provincial Board of Bilingual and Inter-Cultural Education. The analysis draws on information gathered in six Otavalo communities: Carabuela, Peguche, Chuchuqui, Pijal, San Francisco de Cajas and San Agustin de Cajas. The author would like to thank people who live in these communities and work with indigenous organisations for their generous support for the study. Her special thanks to Vidal Sánchez, Carmen Imbaquingo, José Isama and Francisca de la Cruz. Funding for the project was provided by Social Sciences and Humanities Council of Canada (SSHRCC).

The Journal of Peasant Studies, Vol.27, No.3, April 2000, pp.1–29
PUBLISHED BY FRANK CASS, LONDON

peasants' hidden and open struggles for land. The focus will be on the relations between indigenous peasant communities and haciendas (owned by whites and mestizos) in the canton of Otavalo, Imbabura province, Northern Ecuador. Section I examines the theory of everyday forms of resistance in relation to the literature on the Andean (mostly Peruvian) peasantry in general. Special attention is paid to the cultural underpinnings of hidden peasant resistance and its social and political implications. Section II explores the relations between Otavalo's indigenous peasant communities and hacienda owners prior to Ecuador's land reform, which accelerated the process of capitalist agricultural modernisation. It is argued that hidden peasant resistance, largely of ethnic origin, was an important factor behind the sale of large portions of hacienda land to indigenous peasant families. Section III is focused on the factors behind the transformation of hidden peasant resistance into open political struggle and the linkages between the two. In conclusion, it is argued that a careful and historically specific application of the EFPR theory, with its focus on contending cultural values and unorganised spontaneous action, is indispensable to our understanding of the dynamics of rural political change.

I. EVERYDAY FORMS OF PEASANT RESISTANCE IN
   COMPARATIVE PERSPECTIVE

One of the main strengths of the EFPR approach lies in the attention it pays to long periods of apparent political calm, which are largely ignored by students of peasant movements. Nevertheless, it is precisely these uneventful years and decades that provide a key to our understanding of the roots of peasant political mobilisation, for this is when peasants' grievances are vented and their objectives are sometimes achieved in an unheroic and inconspicuous way. Unable or unwilling to resort to open political protest, they often become involved in everyday forms of resistance: small covert acts of defiance against local elites. EFPR theorists argue that these acts reflect peasant refusal to accept the legitimacy of the existing structure of domination even in the absence of organised protest movements [Scott, 1986: 6; 1990: 79–82]. In the literature on the Andean peasantry, these views are echoed by Stern [1987: 10] who also calls for greater attention to peasant resistance and self defence during the apparently tranquil periods.

Some common forms of hidden peasant resistance include trespassing, unauthorised utilisation of privately owned land, and, generally speaking, a refusal to recognise large landowners' property rights. These forms of behaviour have also been documented widely in the literature on Andean haciendas and indigenous peasant communities. Back in the 1960s, Baraona (cited in Martinez-Alier [1977: 45]) coined the phrases 'internal siege' and 'external siege' to describe a systematic encroachment by hacienda service tenants upon hacienda land. Building on Baraona's work, Martinez-Alier [1977] pointed to the persistent incapacity of many hacienda owners in the Peruvian Andes to curb the growth in the numbers of peasant livestock illicitly grazing on hacienda pastures. More recently, Smith [1989], Sylva [1986] and Thurner [1993] discussed similar practices on service-tenure commercial haciendas in Southern Peru and Ecuador.

One of the most contentious issues, of course, is whether such forms of action should be considered as resistance at all. Thus Joseph [1990: 34] warns of the danger of indiscriminately equating poorly documented self-interested acts with resistance, which in his opinion blurs the distinction between delinquency and protest to the point where both lose their analytical value. Joseph is certainly right here. While most acts of resistance among subordinate classes or groups include an element of self-interest, not all self-interested acts directed against privileged members of local society can be described as resistance. EFPR theorists seem to agree, however, that to qualify as such, acts must be backed by a consensus among a significant sector of the local population – admittedly difficult to measure – on the moral legitimacy of certain social practices. Kerkvliet [1993: 486–7] argues that in the case of the land take-overs in the Philippines, for example, there was a consensus on the existence of entitlement norms, according to which 'land should be farmed in a manner that benefits local people who desperately need livelihood', and not merely for profit. In a similar vein, Martinez-Alier [1977: 159] points out that Andean peasants justified their encroachment on hacienda land in terms of their customary systems of rights and obligations, which were often violated by modernising landlords.

To be sure, if a consensus behind small acts of peasant defiance develops at all, its content and manifestations are likely to vary depending on historical and cultural conditions. Nevertheless, it seems that in many instances it is related to peasants' resistance to proletarianisation in the context of the capitalist transformation of agriculture. Combined with agricultural mechanisation and high rates of urban unemployment and underemployment, it is increasingly associated with economic marginalisation, the prospect of which spurs peasant struggles for land, overt or covert. These struggles, as well the preceding processes of capitalist expansion, have been extensively documented not only in the EFPR literature but also in Wolf's seminal study of peasant movements and numerous analyses of Andean agrarian politics [*Wolf*, 1969; *Scott*, 1985; *Smith*, 1989; *Mallon*, 1983; *Handelman*, 1975].

The notion of peasant resistance has been extensively criticised by Marxist scholars, relying on Lenin's analysis of the rise of agrarian capitalism in Russia. Thus, Brass [1991: 174; 1996–97] describes Scott as a

Chayanov-style neo-populist who, along with Wolf, became infatuated with the idea of the land-bound and backward-looking middle peasant, the middle peasant who had long disappeared as a result of peasant socio-economic differentiation. However, even though Scott and Kerkvliet actually write about peasant resistance, it is not the middle peasant, as in Wolf's writings, who is its protagonist, but rather impoverished and semi-proletarianised peasants largely dispossessed of land.[2] Moreover, not all students of peasant resistance see peasants as 'backward-looking'. While Scott [1976, 1977] emphasises the importance of 'traditional' elements in the cultural underpinnings of peasant resistance (such as norms of reciprocity, the right to subsistence and millenarian beliefs), Kerkvliet [1990] is more inclined to see consensual EFPR as a product of modern cultural influences, associated with notions of citisenship and nation-state.

While acknowledging that peasants may draw upon cultural values and norms rooted in the past, Kerkvliet argues that peasant struggles in the Philippines were informed by the notion of basic rights: rights to human dignity and a decent standard of living, as distinct from the subsistence rights of any 'traditional' moral economy. The situation is even more complex in the Andes with its largely indigenous peasantry, formed as a result of the forced homogenisation of a culturally diverse and socially stratified pre-columbian population. In Andean societies, where representations of a pre-colonial past exert a powerful cultural influence, peasant resistance is intrinsically intertwined with the ethnic question.[3] Thus, Flores Galindo [1988] points to the persistence of what he calls the Andean utopia: an idealised vision of Inca rule, intertwined with modern political values, including the marxist ones embraced by the Shining Path.[4] Clearly, we need a better understanding of the complex cultural universe of the impoverished and semi-proletarianised peasantry, as well as of the origins and political implications of this complexity. Moreover, it is plausible that under certain conditions the process of socio-economic differentiation may give rise to local political leadership rather than undermine peasant solidarity. This is especially the case of indigenous peasants, bound by ethnic loyalties and sharing the experience of ethnic discrimination. Thus, in many areas of the Ecuadorian Andes migratory work and access to formal education contributed to the emergence of a new generation of indigenous leaders who played a crucial role in the land struggles of the 1970s and 1980s [Korovkin, 1997a].

This brings us to the second set of criticisms with regard to the EFPR theory: its alleged neglect of political organisations and social change. Brass observes [1991: 176] that Scott concentrates on EFPR instead of revolutionary struggles. Similarly, Gutmann [1993: 87] suggests that Scott's theory is a 'conservative one. It does not expect or explain change.'

Nevertheless, whether it is collective political struggles only that generate structural change is an open question. While it is doubtful that hidden resistance is likely to generate economic and social change on its own, it can certainly do so in combination with other factors. Scott [1986: 8] argues that 'individual acts of foot dragging and evasion, often reinforced by a venerable popular culture of resistance, and multiplied many-thousand fold, may, in the end, make an utter shambles of the policies dreamed up by their would be superiors in the capital', a statement that strikes a responsive chord among many students of Latin American land reforms, who have documented peasants' amazing ability to deflect, manipulate and in some cases defeat government policies [*Colburn*, 1986; *Montoya*, 1982; *Korovkin*, 1990]. Scott [1987] documents peasants' success in reducing or nullifying the clergy's material claims, while Orlove [1991] points to similar success in relation to the state bureaucracy.

As for any relation between hidden defiance and open forms of struggle, we remain almost completely in the dark. Existing studies seem to point in different directions. In his analysis of colonial experiences in Asia, Adas [1986: 82] suggests that the 'denial protests' (foot dragging, feigned incompetence, fleeing to remote areas) serve as a safety valve for social discontent, leaving the peasantry even more fragmented and vulnerable to repression. Protests of 'retribution' (destruction of crops, arson, etc.) are more likely, in his opinion, to lead to open political struggles. But also in this case, argues Adas, the limited organisational skills and ideological sophistication of the participants generally work against them. For a political protest to happen, external political leadership is necessary.

A similar view was generally adopted in older studies of peasant politics in Latin America, which saw urban-based political leadership as a prerequisite for the transformation of peasant unrest into a political – nationalist or left-wing – movement [*Hobsbawm*, 1973; *Landsberger*, 1974]. This may be the case, but more recent studies of guerrilla movements in Latin America in general, and Peru in particular, also point to numerous and sometimes tragic misunderstandings between left-wing political leaders and their would-be peasant supporters [*Brown and Fernandez*, 1991; *Wickham-Crowley*, 1991; *Berg*, 1992; *Isbell*, 1992]. Similarly, Burdick [1992] describes the internal weaknesses of many Christian base communities in Brazil which, although headed by progressive clergy, fail to express the needs and sentiments of the less progressive and less sophisticated local residents. At the same time, Smith [1989] attributes the success of the political struggle of Huasicancha peasants in the Peruvian Andes to a local culture of resistance and community-based leadership. In his view, everyday forms of peasant resistance – including trespassing, pilfering and the covert use of hacienda pastures – were intrinsically linked to peasant political mobilisation. This view is congenial with Kerkvliet's study of land invasions in the Philippines. Indeed, Kerkvliet [1993: 481] argues that small acts of defiance can prepare the ground for organised land takeovers, and also emphasises that these were led not by external organisers but by local leaders.

If the presence of urban political activists is not a crucial factor behind the transformation of hidden into open resistance, what is? Kerkvliet [1993: 471] believes that, in the Philippines, the single most important reason for this transformation was the end of Marcos's rule. This started a process of national political democratisation which offered minimum physical safety to peasant leaders and provided them with interlocutors in the local and national government. Greater political openness has also been seen as a catalyst of peasant political struggles in Latin America, while Scott argues that fear of political repression, along with social fragmentation and the availability of economic alternatives, such as migration, is one of the major considerations that force peasants to opt for hidden rather than open forms of resistance [*Eckstein*, 1989; *Scott*, 1986]. So what are the relationships between processes of political democratisation, the collapse of customary rights and obligations, and the tactics of peasants in defence of their rights? And what kind of rights are we talking about here? In the following sections, I discuss the nature and effectiveness of indigenous peasant hidden resistance in Otavalo at different historical stages and in different structural contexts. I also analyse the relationship between hidden and open forms of indigenous peasant struggles, as well as their cultural underpinnings.

II. OTAVALO: FROM DEFEAT TO HIDDEN RESISTANCE

Peasant resistance in Otavalo has unmistakable ethnic roots. It can be traced back to the defeat of the 1777 ethnic uprisings and forced peasantisation of the Quichua-speaking population of Otavalo and Cayambe ethnic origins. The uprising, along with subsequent attempts on the part of some hereditary chiefs (*curacas*) to protect indigenous lands continues to form part of the present-day community lore, eagerly told to newcomers and incorporated in the local system of bilingual education.[5] By the first half of the twentieth century, however, ethnic leadership had virtually disappeared while most of the indigenous population had been transformed into bonded labourers on private landed estates (haciendas), often combining agricultural and textile production. To escape labour tribute and/or avoid prison for debt, an increasing number of impoverished indigenous people looked for the 'protection' of powerful hacienda owners with whom they also incurred heavy debts.

The legal abolition of imprisonment for debt (put into practice in 1918) ended this system of debt peonage, while the growth of plantation agriculture and urban manufacturing created an increasing demand for wage labour. Still, many peasants preferred to stay on the haciendas, in effect opting for a new system of bonded labour. Working six days a week for the owners, they would receive a subsistence plot of land (*huasipungo*) within the hacienda boundaries along with access to the hacienda pastures, water and firewood.[6] The unwillingness of hacienda peasants to join proletarian ranks caused dismay among Ecuadorean liberals and socialists who were quick to attribute this to the inherent backwardness of the indigenous peasantry.

> One of the most important reasons [why the majority of *huasipungueros* refused to leave the haciendas] is the exaggerated sense of nostalgia that the Indian has for his own plot of land, even though it may only be a *huasipungo*. This is why he would put up with injustice [on the hacienda] and forsake the higher wages that he could have received as a free labourer [*Oberem*, 1977: 28].

Thus the myth of the passive Indian among politicians and academics, who often portrayed indigenous people as mistrustful and melancholic, burdened by an inferiority complex, and unable to join 'progressive' urban and rural struggles for socialism [*Aguiló*, 1992; *Zamosc*, 1989; *Velasco*, 1979]. A closer look at relations between the hacienda and the indigenous peasantry, however, promptly dispels this myth. In Otavalo, at least, these relations were much more complex and conflict-ridden than the supporters of the passive Indian thesis seem to be willing to admit. Refusing to leave the hacienda areas, which they considered as their ancestral lands, Otavalo's indigenous people were not eager to engage in *huasipungo* relations either.

Generally speaking, the importance of the *huasipungo* in Andean labour relations seems to be grossly overemphasised. Clearly, Ecuadorean haciendas were more effective in controlling land than they were in controlling indigenous labour. According to the 1954 agricultural census (the first in Ecuador), landed estates over 100 hectares contained the bulk of national farmland. In Imbabura they constituted only 1.07 per cent of the total number of holdings but controlled 64.26 per cent of the land. While the hacienda sector's dominance over land relations is beyond any doubt, this was not the case of labour relations. Despite all the attention that *huasipungo* relations have received in the academic literature and political debates of the day, only a small proportion of the total rural labour force – eight per cent in Imbabura, or the same as the average of Ecuador's ten Andean provinces taken together – worked on haciendas as *huasipungueros* [*INEC*, 1954, Table 4]. Moreover, the proportion of *huasipungueros* was higher in rural areas with relatively high levels of capitalist development and acculturation. Thus in Pichincha province, the administrative and economic heartland of the Andean region, *huasipungueros* constituted 23 percent of the total number of landholders, as compared to only 12 per cent in Chimborazo and eight per cent in Imbabura, the two Andean provinces with the largest proportion of Quichua-speaking population [*INEC*, 1954: Table 4; *Zamosc*, 1995].

The relatively low incidence of *huasipungo* labour in Imbabura does not have a simple explanation. It is associated with the predominance of extensive cattle-raising in contrast to more labour-intensive food crop production in Pichincha, with its proximity to Quito's markets. But market constraints alone cannot explain the preference of Imbabura's landowners for extensive livestock production. Other and probably equally decisive factors were the inability of hacienda owners to completely displace indigenous communities from their land and the continuous refusal by the local indigenous population to recognise the legitimacy of hacienda claims, a sign of stand-off rather than of a clear-cut hacienda victory.

While growing demographic pressure on land in communities pushed their members towards economic relations with haciendas, the result was not *huasipungo* but *yanapa* ('help' in Quichua). Under *yanapa* arrangements, families worked for two days a week for hacienda owners in exchange for access to hacienda pastures. In other words, they continued to live in their communities, conducting their usual activities and obeying their communal authorities – rather than hacienda managers – for most of the time.[7] While *yanaperos* enjoyed much more decisional and cultural autonomy than *huasipungueros*, the relations of both categories of labourers with hacienda owners were fraught with hidden conflicts which resulted variously in the demise of haciendas or further tightening of hacienda labour discipline. The contrasting experiences of Quillcapamba, Pinsaqui, and Cajas illustrate the point.

Hacienda Qillcapamba was founded at least a century ago on the slopes of Imbabura mountain, then covered by trees and bush, while the fertile lowlands around San Pablo Lake remained under the control of local indigenous communities, now known as Huaycopungo and Chaquiopamba. The name of the hacienda presumably came form its first owner's habit of pulling a feather (*quillca*, in Quichua) from any nearby chicken in order to write down the names of indigenous families offering their services as *huasipungueros*. These were notoriously few. Local families were not eager to work for the '*mishu*' (mestizo, in Quichua). The first *huasipungueros* seemed to be social outcasts who had fled their communities after breaking their marriages and choosing a new partner. The frontier-style, quasi-egalitarian atmosphere in Quillcapamba, where nobody had proper marriage arrangements and the owner rose at three o'sclock in the morning to join his workers in the field, represents a striking contrast to conventional images of the hacienda. Apparently, Quillcapamba was self-sufficient in everything except alcohol. This was brought from the city which also provided a market for cattle. Hacienda cattle were apparently sold in relatively large numbers (even though nobody at the hacienda had proper arithmetic skills; the owner himself, according to the lore, could count to 40, using a *taptana* – a pre-columbian counting board – for larger numbers; others could not count at all).

The hacienda workforce grew as a result of demographic pressure on land within the neighbouring communities. This turned out to be a mixed blessing for the hacienda owner. On one hand, he himself did not have to work in the fields any more. On the other, he had to confront his workers' mounting requests for land within the hacienda boundaries. These requests were announced in an especially uninhibited way during the annual hacienda celebration: Catholic *corpus cristi* for the hacienda owner; pre-columbian *abagos* (the meaning of which has been largely forgotten) for his Quichua-speaking workers. During this celebration the owner would set aside status considerations (that had increased in importance along with the growth of the hacienda labour force) and drink and dance with his workers in their ritual dances. At one of these celebrations, dancers apparently staged such a belligerent performance that the owner's son, visiting the hacienda, privately begged his father to put a ban on hacienda celebrations for the sake of his physical safety. This was not easy though: annual celebrations – when ritual drinking and dancing eroded the established hacienda hierarchy at least temporarily – became part of the established arrangements along with *huasipungo* and grazing rights.

After the years of 'siege', the owner sold most of the hacienda for what was described to me as a symbolic price. After his death, his heirs finished off the job, selling the rest of the hacienda to hacienda workers and their relatives. By the 1950s, Quillcapamba had disappeared, engrossing family holdings in the older indigenous settlements and giving rise to a new community known as Chuchuqui. At approximately the same time, a similar fate befell two other hillside haciendas, Pilchibuela and San Javier.

To protect their newly acquired domains from the competing claims of urban dwellers, an increasing number of indigenous communities availed themselves of the 1937 Law of Communes, electing community councils (*cabildos*) and obtaining legal recognition. The result was a significant transfer of Otavalo's hillside hacienda land to community control. It is worth noting that this happened without any overt collective action or government intervention, which points, among other things, to the amazing ability of these peasants to achieve their goals by using hidden pressures in the overall context of white-mestizo domination.

In the cases of Quillcapamba, Pilchibuela and San Javier, peasant pressures conspired with low land fertility to provoke the demise of haciendas.[8] On the fertile lowlands, this demise had to wait for land reform legislation passed in 1964 and 1973 by progressive military regimes. Due to various factors, it was implemented in a curtailed and diluted fashion, adding fuel to the lingering conflict between haciendas and communities and forcing some of the former to sell their lands to the latter.[9] This was the outcome, for example, for Hacienda Pinsaqui, located on the lowlands in a densely populated indigenous area. For decades prior to land reform, Pinsaqui had been the site of a tug-of-war between the owners and the neighbouring indigenous communities whose members worked on the hacienda mostly as *yanaperos*. As was often the case in this area, Pinsaqui *yanaperos* clearly took pride in challenging the hacienda order. Some ingeniously avoided their labour service while others grazed their cattle on the owner's pastures or used hacienda woods and springs without the mayordomo's permission. Hacienda managers retaliated, using whips and dogs or confiscating peasant livestock and personal belongings. An additional instrument to ensure compliance was the excessive use of cheap alcohol, known locally as *guarapo*. As in the case of Quillcapamba, this could easily turn into a double-edged sword during annual celebrations. In Pinsaqui, however, drinking seemed to become part of the labour process and its control:

> He [the hacienda owner] always had a lot of booze for us [a former hacienda worker recalls as he laughs]. When we had to do the weeding, there was *guarapo*; cutting barley, *guarapo*; harvesting maise, *guarapo*; planting, *guarapo*; making ditches, *guarapo* again! [field interview]

As such, it was mostly devoid of any ritual or political significance, blunting workers' capacities rather than pushing them into action.

This situation changed during the hacienda festival, known in Pinsaqui as *uyanzas*. Historically, *uyanzas* had been celebrated in indigenous peasant communities at the end of the harvest, with more prosperous families sharing their crops with those who helped them work in the fields. The hacienda celebrations imitated community and family festivals, at the same time reaffirming the dominant position of the hacienda. As in Quillcapamba, however, Pinsaqui workers took advantage of this opportunity to test and question – under a festive guise – the hacienda's dominance. Among other things, they 'took over' a corn field assigned for this purpose by the owner (and against the will of the mayordomo who saw this as disrespectful and potentially dangerous). After collecting the corn, women workers, with corn cobs wrapped in their shawls, 'broke' into the hacienda house which they normally entered only as servants. Having 'chased' and 'captured' the owner, they tied a shawl with cobs around his waist and took him triumphantly to the porch, where he had to distribute the cobs to his jubilant and jeering workers. It is hardly surprising that many local landowners tried to avoid organising hacienda celebrations, as they also tried to avoid providing all their workers with access to land. In addition to putting the owners into an awkward and ambiguous position, these celebrations interfered with production by encroaching upon the limited time and space available for the haciendas' agricultural activities.[10]

While the Quillcapamba and Pinsaqui cases illustrate hidden conflicts between haciendas and adjacent communities, and the final victory of the latter, they differ considerably in terms of their historical and structural context. Contrary to Quillcapamba, Pinsaqui survived well into the 1960s when land reform legislation tilted the local balance of power, albeit only slightly, in favour of the indigenous communities. Furthermore, Pinsaqui's *yanaperos*, especially those living in the community of Carabuela, combined family agriculture with artisan production. As a result, they benefited from the commercial expansion of Otavalo's indigenous textile crafts that took place in connection with the post-war economic boom and growth of tourism. Spinning, weaving ponchos, and knitting sweaters for sale left Carabuela's *yanaperos* with little time for, or interest in, continuing labour service on the hacienda. Moreover, as their monetary income increased considerably, so did their interest in purchasing land. Caught between the continuing animosity of their workers, the threat of government intervention in the process of land reform, growing labour shortages, and escalating indigenous offers to buy their land, the owners of Pinsaqui opted to subdivide and sell the hacienda. By the 1970s, its land was absorbed by Carabuela and other local communities.

Both Qillcapamba and Pinsaqui were located in densely populated indigenous areas with an ancient ethnic culture and exceptionally strong communal traditions, characteristics absent in Cajas, a mountainous area on the border with Pichincha province. Unpopulated prior to the arrival of the Spaniards, it was colonised by indigenous migrants from Pichincha, probably in the late seventeenth and early eighteenth centuries.[11] Hacienda expansion took place at approximately the same time, largely through the extension into Imbabura of the famous Pichincha haciendas, owned by powerful families firmly integrated in national economic and political circuits. Contrary to the situation in Quillcapamba or Pinsaqui, the Cajas haciendas relied on *huasipungo* relations, with most *huasipungueros* brought, unsurprisingly, from Pichincha province. Hacienda owners in Cajas had almost absolute power over their *huasipungueros* who could be uprooted and moved by their patron from one hacienda to another, according to production needs, or even 'lost' and 'won' (along with the land on which they lived) in gambling. While enjoying access to relatively large subsistence plots (by community standards), they had to work on the hacienda for six or seven days a week, experiencing daily humiliation and abuse. To select the chiefs of work gangs, for instance, mayordomos were known to organise mock fights among the workers. The winners were promoted and losers whipped. Drinking competitions were also encouraged, with the losers also whipped. Drinking and fighting generally reached its peak at San Juan, a local festival in Cajas tightly controlled by Catholic priests and hacienda owners.

> All the *huasipungueros* and *yanaperos* had to '*pasar el gallo*' [sponsor the San Juan celebrations, which among other things involved a symbolic offering of roosters – *gallos*, in Spanish – to hacienda owners]. People agreed to do it because the priest convinced them that if they did so, ... in the other life, after death, the rooster would flap its wings to put out the flames in which they would burn ... The patrons would also encourage the mayordomos, and for no good reason at all, they would say to workers who had grudges against other workers: 'Damn it, San Juan is coming. If you are men, beat the shit out of them! Kill one at least!' That's how they manipulated the people [field interview].

To be sure, there were signs of hidden resistance on the Cajas haciendas too: stories were circulated about unscrupulous priests who, long ago, had stolen the fertile lowlands from the indigenous people; the church statues of saints had to 'compete' with peasant ones, dressed in ponchos and jealously guarded in Pijal houses, etc. However, this resistance failed to develop into a hidden counter-offensive that ended in the sale of hacienda land, as in Quillcapamba and Pinsaqui. While the land reform ended *huasipungo* relations in Cajas – as it did in other areas of Otavalo – it was not accompanied by significant sales of hacienda land to peasant communities. Lacking an artisan tradition, Cajas peasants did not benefit from the commercial boom of the 1960s. Their participation in the commodity economy was reduced to work for minimum or below minimum wages, which generally precluded saving [*Korovkin*, 1997b]. Moreover, firmly grounded in the aristocratic tradition, Cajas hacienda owners refused to sell land to their indigenous workers even when they had enough money to buy it.

The only exception in Cajas was Hacienda San Agustin, owned initially by the Catholic Church. After the 1909 liberal revolution, San Agustin, along with many other Church-owned haciendas, was brought under state control [*Bustamante and Prieto*, 1985]. These exceptional circumstances account for the greater scope of the land reform in San Agustin. After transferring *huasipungo* plots to hacienda workers in the early 1960s, the Ministry of Agriculture proposed to transform the centrally-managed area into an agricultural production co-operative, named Mojanda Cooperative. To the dismay of public officials, few if any of San Agustin's former workers showed interest in joining the co-operative, which they perceived as an alien and hierarchically structured body. As one of them pointed out later, '[m]ore than anything else, there seemed to be no need for a cooperative. Perhaps what people thought was: how much longer are we going to live under the patrons's law? ...That's why nobody was really interested in joining the coop [field interview].' A co-operative was eventually formed by a small group of workers who accepted the Ministry's initiative in order to obtain access to additional land, even though they disliked and resented the co-operative organisation. Since the co-operative incurred sizeable debts with the Ministry as a result of the land transfer, all important production decisions were controlled by government officials, which, in the eyes of San Agustin peasants, amounted to continuation of 'the patrons' law'.

Even worse was the fact that the co-operative's statutes did not allow the creation of new family holdings for members's children out of the 'scientifically' managed co-operative property. New family plots were carved out in the co-operative area anyway, with its administrative council turning a blind eye to this practice. Even though council members agreed that this practice eroded co-operative profits, the need to ensure subsistence for all members of local families was seen as paramount.[12] Thus, like private haciendas, the co-operative also found itself under siege, though this time a siege mounted by its own members. As soon as Mojanda Cooperative cleared its debts with the Ministry of Agriculture and obtained formal property rights, most co-operative land was subdivided into small holdings to accommodate young families.

Along with older co-operative members, the new generation of San Agustin residents organised a new indigenous peasant community, San Agustin de Cajas. Among the advantages of community organisation, they generally mentioned the distribution of land holdings to young families and a more democratic and inclusive form of government with the community assembly attended by all residents rather than by heads of household only, as in the co-operative. No less importantly, they also pointed to the versatility and political strength of communal organisation. Contrary to the co-operative, which dedicated itself almost exclusively to production matters, the community leadership was able to obtain governmental and, most importantly, non-governmental funds for infrastructural projects such as roads, electricity, schools, and a medical post. In the post-reform neo-liberal period – with the Ministry of Agriculture on the defensive and community organisation on the rise nationally – the idea of state-sponsored co-operative agriculture had clearly lost its clout. Once again, the old and the new – indigenous pressure and a new economic and political climate — combined to complete the transfer of former hacienda land to indigenous communities.

III. OTAVALO: FROM HIDDEN RESISTANCE TO ORGANISED POLITICAL ACTION

Hidden resistance to hacienda dominance in Otavalo evolved into open political protest in the 1970s and 1980s, as indigenous peasant and non-peasant communities developed local and provincial inter-communal organisations, represented at the national level by Ecuador's Confederation of Indigenous Nationalities (CONAIE) [*Chiriboga*, 1986; *Ibarra*, 1992; *Selverston*, 1994]. The role of national political leadership in indigenous struggle should not be overestimated though. One of CONAIE's major political asset was its unprecedented ability to build on local cultural practices and long-standing covert struggles, which distinguished it from two other national organisations that had claimed indigenous peasant support, FEI and FENOC. FEI (Ecuador's Indian Federation) was organised in 1944 by the Communist Party with the objective of incorporating indigenous peasants into the struggle for socialism. FEI leaders focused their organisational efforts on the *huasipungueros*, whom they identified as the incipient agricultural proletariat. Prior to the land reform, FEI-sponsored rural unions and associations gained considerable influence in Pichincha and Chimborazo, that they later lost to indigenous federations affiliated with CONAIE. FEI never had a significant presence in Imbabura, not even in Cajas which was structurally and culturally similar to Pichincha. The main reason is probably the relatively low incidence of *huasipungo* combined with strong ethnic tradition in the core Otavalo area. In other words, what was interpreted by many observers as Indians' political backwardness was more likely a sign of indigenous cultural and political autonomy.

In the 1960s, FEI was joined by the National Federation of Peasant Organisations (FENOC). Linked to the urban trade union movement of socialist and progressive Catholic persuasion, FENOC's leadership shared FEI's assumptions about the class nature of indigenous peasant struggles. Over time, however, FENOC incorporated ethnic elements into its political ideology and gave rise to a sister organisation, FENOC-I ('I', for indigenous, National Federation of Peasant and Indigenous Organisations). In Imbabura, both FENOC and FENOC-I had strongholds in the indigenous peasant communities of Cotacachi Canton, neighbouring on Otavalo Canton. In Otavalo, however, FENOC was able to gain influence only among the *yanaperos* of Hacienda Quinchuqui in the vicinity of Pinsaqui. In the 1960s, Quinchuqui's association of *yanaperos* demanded wage payment in accordance with existing labour legislation. It is probable, however, that, as in the case of Chimobrazo's *huasipunguero* political mobilisation, what was actually at stake was land [*Sylva*, 1986]. In the 1970s, the association took over the hacienda which, after several years of struggle, was transformed by the Ministry of Agriculture into the Quinchuqui Agricultural Production Cooperative, similar to Mojanda in Cajas. And, like its Cajas counterpart, Quinchuqui was eventually subdivided, under pressure from its members, into family holdings which were absorbed by neighbouring communities.

FENOC's influence in Otavalo, limited as it was, was soon challenged by a new generation of indigenous political leaders. Unpersuaded by the mystique of proletarian revolution, they turned to indigenous land and cultural rights as the centrepiece of their new ideology. In the 1970s a group of indigenous intellectuals from the core Otavalo area and community leaders from Cajas created the Indigenous and Peasant Federation of Imbabura (FICI). Along with provincial indigenous federations from Chimborazo and Pastaza Provinces, FICI played a crucial role in the organisation of CONAIE. As in Imbabura, some CONAIE leaders came from relatively well-off indigenous families and had many years of schooling. Others were of peasant background, skilled in peasant arts of resistance. Despite their obvious social differences, both groups of leaders had – or were remembered as earlier having – kin in peasant communities. Despite reservations inspired by their relative prosperity, education, and/or political skills, they became seen by many of Otavalo's indigenous people as 'their' political leadership, probably for the first time since the disappearance of the *curacas* (see note 7).

The growth of indigenous leadership in Otavalo coincided with, and to some extent was a product of, nation-wide economic and political changes. The 1964 and 1973 land reforms, in combination with the oil boom of the 1970s, shattered service–tenure relations in the countryside and triggered a series of covert and overt confrontations between indigenous peasant communities and a new class of capitalist farmers in dairy production and the cut-flower industry. These confrontations were especially intense in Cajas where the hacienda system had successfully survived earlier periods of hidden counter-offensive and land reform. The owners of three Cajas haciendas – Clemencia, San Francisco and Cruz de Cajas – opted for selling parts of the hacienda land to outsiders, ignoring the offers of their workers who, in many cases, were ready to pay only a 'symbolic' price for what they considered their land. The owners of Clemencia, for example, sold part of their land to middle-class families from the neighbouring town of San

Pablo. Historically, these urban families had been involved in administration and trade but in the 1960s, in a climate of state-sponsored market expansion, they were willing to try their fortunes in dairy agribusiness.[13] In 1967, under the auspices of the Ministry of Agriculture, they formed the Social Justice Agricultural Cooperative on former Clemencia land. Even though this sector of the hacienda had been used mostly as pasture for the hacienda cattle, *yanaperos* from local communities had also used it to obtain drinking water, cut grass for their domestic animals, and collect herbs for their own meals. The former owner did not mind any of these activities, as he did not seem to mind *yanapero*-owned cattle sometimes grazing on his premises either.

What appeared to the new owners as administrative laxity was in fact a tacit agreement between the former owner and *yanaperos* who in a sense agreed to disagree about property rights. Legally, it was the hacienda's land; by custom it also belonged to the *yanaperos*. Such subtleties were not part of the cultural repertoire of the new co-operative members who insisted on enforcing their legal property rights and confiscated peasant livestock grazing on their property along with their owners's much valued personal belongings against fines in the form of labour service. Clemencia *yanaperos*, most of them from the community of Huaycopungo, fought back, forming the Huaycopungo Agricultural Association. Assisted by FICI and CONAIE, the Association filed a land claim with the Ministry of Agriculture. When this legal action failed, Association members took over the disputed land with the support of Huaycopungo and other local communities. They also organised several protest marches. Accompanied by musicians and dancers, the protesters carried San Juan roosters, not as a traditional sign of respect for the hacienda and church authorities, but as a new symbol of their own strength.

The Clemencia conflict developed over the 1970s and played an important role in helping FICI to define its political identity as both an ethnic and a class-based organisation. In the 1980s similar conflicts were reported in San Francisco and Cruz de Cajas. Tired out by the tug-of-war with *yanaperos* and lured by skyrocketing land prices, San Francisco's owner subdivided the hacienda and put it on sale. The *yanaperos*, organised in the San Francisco Agricultural Association, offered to buy part of it, but the owner asked for the market price, far beyond the Association's ability to pay. This appeared an outrage to Association members. Virtually all of them formed part of San Francisco Community, created from the former *huasipunguero* settlement after the abolition of *huasipungo*. Even though most of their ancestors came from the hacienda owner's properties in Pichincha, they claimed the hacienda as their ancestral land:

> It was our fathers and grandfathers who worked the hacienda, for more than one hundred years. And now they want to sell it, some people say, to a foreign company. ... [If the company wants to buy it,] it can pay whatever it feels like paying. But as for us, we have the right to a discount price, because this land is ours, and we have worked on it for a long time [field interview].

San Francisco's owner ignored his workers's protestations and sold the disputed land to a local capitalist farmer who intended to use it for dairy farming. As a first step, the new owner fenced the land and banned the livestock of former *yanaperos* from the hacienda, claiming, as one of the respondents later recalled indignantly, that their animals 'were sick, that they had parasites, that they had worms!'. Deprived of customary access to land, the Association took over the disputed pastures, filing a lawsuit in the Ministry of Agriculture (as in the case of Clemencia).

A third open confrontation took place in Cruz de Cajas, whose owner also put a portion of his land up for sale. The *yanaperos*, mostly from Pijal Community, organised an association (named after an indigenous hero, Ruminahui) and, as in the other two cases, offered to purchase the land collectively. The owner, however, sold it to a Colombian cut-flower company, apparently for a price considerably below the market rate. According to former *yanaperos*, he sold it so cheap to somebody else 'because he was mad' at them. What first appeared to the management of the Colombian company as a bargain, quickly turned into a nightmare. When Association members saw company workers bringing construction materials for green houses, they decided it was time to act.

> We saw them coming, with their engineers, topographers, security guards: all of them, coming here, to our land. So we got the community together and said: what shall we do? The people said: well, let's evict them! There were three hundred of us, more or less, all in favour of kicking them out. We left [for the construction sight] at 11 p.m. ... The security guards were there, asleep. We tied their hands while they were still sleeping. They had their firearms with them, but we took them all away. Then we carried tools, bricks, everything, to the community store, with the security guards stumbling along with us. And then we dug a ditch across the road. Don't you ever step on our land here! Don't you ever step on our land again! Don't you even try to step on our land again! [field interview].

After several rounds of negotiations, the company decided to pull out of the area, reselling the land to the Association for the same price they had paid. The story, however, did not end here. Emboldened by their success, Association members took over another sector of the hacienda in retaliation against the landowner who, in their opinion, had violated the customary rights and obligations they continued to respect:

> We told them [the hacienda owners]: our commitment was to you. And you, why did you do this to us? Why did you trust those people [the Colombian company] more than us? [field interview].

The moralistic overtone of this statement, as well as the indignation of the *yanaperos* of Clemencia y San Francisco with what they considered unethical behaviour by the hacienda owners, recalls peasant responses to the capitalist modernisation of large-scale agriculture in other parts of the Ecuadorean and Peruvian Andes [*Crain*, 1989; *Handelman*, 1975; *Smith*, 1989] and seems to provide support to Scott's moral economy argument. Still, the notion of moral economy does not adequately describe Andean cultural and structural realities. As the previous discussion makes clear, in Otavalo, at least, relations between communities and haciendas reflected profound ethnic and class antagonisms. In the 1940s and 1950s, this antagonism failed to develop into open confrontations partly because of the repressive political environment and partly because of customary rights and obligations that provided indigenous peasants with minimum economic security, no matter how much they might despise and resent their oppressors.

Over the 1960s, 1970s and 1980s, this customary system was increasingly dismantled by modernising landowners. The local and national political climate also changed. In the countryside traditional hacienda owners who ruled their domains, whip in hand, were replaced by relatively polite and infinitely more distant capitalist farmers. Moreover, in 1979 the military regime gave way to a political democracy. None of this precluded the periodic use of repression against organised peasant action, of course. The land conflicts in San Francisco and Clemencia, for example, involved the use of force by hacienda owners.[14] Nevertheless, the land reform and transition to democracy created a favourable climate for organised rural political action. In effect, Otavalo's land take-overs became part of a nation-wide wave of land seizures, which culminated in 1990 in a week long national indigenous uprising, coordinated by CONAIE. In many cases, land seizures were triggered by the collapse of customary arrangements in processes of capitalist restructuring of the hacienda. Indigenous organisations, however, did not seek to restore such arrangements but (in addition to cultural demands, advanced mostly by new indigenous intellectuals) they sought legal access to hacienda land and support for small agricultural producers in the context of communal organisation [Rosero, 1990; *Almeida et al.*, 1993].

The evolution of the three agricultural associations that emerged from of the land conflicts in Clemencia, San Francisco, and Cruz de Cajas illustrates this point. In the 1980s and 1990s, with the Ministry of Agriculture trimmed and restructured along neo-liberal economic lines, much of the funding for collective land purchases in Otavalo came from a fund created as the result of a debt-for -development swap between Holland and Ecuador. The fund was managed by FEPP (Ecuador's *Populorum Progressio* Fund), a Catholic-based non-governmental organisation which also provided technical assistance to indigenous peasant communities and associations. FEPP's institutional commitment to the idea of sustainable grassroots development contrasted with the Ministry of Agriculture's state-centred and market-oriented developmentalist ideology. FEPP was also much more sensitive to the peasants's cultural and political concerns. Thus, the three associations, supported by FEPP, formed part of local communities and worked in coordination with FICI and CONAIE.

In tiny San Francisco, there was no difference between the association and the community, with one member of the community council in charge of the association management. In Pijal, with several thousand residents, Ruminahui Association included only a small segment of families. The Association leaders, however, explicitly recognised the superior authority of the communal council and assembly. As one of them put it, using a characteristic kinship metaphor:

> [w]e respect the community. We take care of both, the association and the community. To us the community is like a father. That is, we feel like we're its sons. When something has to be done in the community, we put on hold what we are doing in the association and give a hand ... with the roads, or schools, or community houses. It's us [the association] who start all these things in the community. That's the way it is: we start things here [field interview].

The acceptance of communal authorities was rooted not only in a common culture and shared experiences but was also a product of practical necessity. Since Pijal community leaders were active in the organisation of FICI and CONAIE, community councils were also able to provide the Association with legal and political support. Moreover, due to their dual membership, Ruminahui families enjoyed access to the community-controlled social and physical infrastructure: schools, roads, electricity, and running water. On the other hand, involved in collective agriculture providing a relatively steady source of cash income, Ruminahui could cover some of the communal expenses, notably those of the San Juan festival. In the 1990s, the Association took part in a province-wide event, organised by FICI and known by its pre-hispanic name, Inti-Raimi, to symbolise the end of the era of Catholic priests and hacienda owners. Attending the San Juan mass in church became a question of personal preference. The centre of celebrations moved to Pijal's community plaza, and the symbolic offering of roosters now circulated between the new centres of local power: community council, community schools, and agricultural associations.

IV. CONCLUSION: SOME REFLECTIONS

Turton [1986: 41] is right to note the importance of the specific social contexts of hidden struggles.[15] Outside such contexts, the concept of EFPR is little more than an umbrella for phenomena that are superficially similar yet substantially different. Combined with adequate historical and structural analysis, however, EFPR provides a useful tool for the study of rural politics in general and rural political protest in particular.

One of the historical specificities of peasant resistance in Otavalo, as probably in many other Andean areas, is that it was (and remains) peasant and ethnic at the same time. This was often overlooked in Ecuador's academic and political circles, enamoured with a narrow version of class analysis, until the rise of ethnic-based indigenous organisations in the late 1970s and 1980s demonstrated the limits of their approach. The new indigenous movements also suggested the role of hidden resistance as a basis of (subsequent) organised political action. Prior to land reform, resistance was directed largely, although not exclusively, at the precapitalist commercial hacienda as the dominant rural institution introduced by colonialism. Rather than becoming permanent bonded labourers on the hacienda (*huasipungueros*, often compared to slaves but with access to land) Otavalo's indigenous peasants opted for what Orlove [1991: 30], in his study of relations between Peruvian peasants and the state, described as 'desistance'. Unable to overturn the hacienda system, they tried to distance themselves from it, eking out their living on their tiny plots of land and limiting their interaction with the hacienda, if possible, to two days a week service (*yanapa*). In the context of white-mestizo domination, this appeared as the lesser evil: *yanapa* gave access to hacienda pastures, while permitting a relative cultural and political autonomy. Indeed, it seems that much, if not most, *huasipunguero* labour in Otavalo was provided by the descendants of semi-acculturated Pichincha *huasipungueros* rather than by local residents.

This should not surprise anybody suspicious of the 'passive Indian' myth of the 1960s, that associated *huasipungo* with the Indian and both with political apathy. Not only did Otavalo's indigenous peasants preserve their relative autonomy through 'desistance' tactics, they also used it to start the internal siege of the hacienda, with *yanapa* or *huasipungo* as a Trojan horse for claims to hacienda land.[16] This hidden counter-offensive to the overt triumph of the hacienda system often led to the partition and sale of hacienda land to labourers from local communities, who promptly incorporated it into their communal domains. To be sure, there were also other factors at work. Market competition contributed to the collapse of haciendas in remote and/or low-productivity areas, while land reform legislation could tilt the local balance of power in favour of the hacienda workers, albeit slightly. Market competition and land reform, however, took place in the context of a hidden war between communities and haciendas, helping or hindering peasant efforts to (re)gain control over hacienda land.

The term 'war' may appear exaggerated in this context. There were no armed confrontations in Otavalo, at least not on a regular basis, but there was a multitude of covert acts of defiance reminiscent of guerrilla warfare. There were also punitive operations led by haciendas: corporal punishment and confiscation of peasant property. These continuous confrontations hardly fit Scott's notion of a moral economy predicated on a shared culture of reciprocity and subsistence ethics.[17] The concept of patron-clientelism, used by Paige [1975] to describe hacienda relations, is not quite appropriate either. Patron-client relations presuppose economic individualism and political passivity among members of the lower classes. This clearly was not the case in Otavalo where hacienda labourers, and especially *yanaperos*, maintained a strong sense of communal solidarity and engaged in numerous covert acts of resistance.

While the notion of everyday forms of resistance, or a hidden ethnic and class war, probably best describes relations between Otavalo's communities and haciendas, this war remained hidden, and not only because of the highly skewed distribution of power and the threat of repression. The warring parties were also bound together by a grudging recognition of a mutual, albeit asymmetrical, dependence: hacienda owners depended on indigenous people for labour, while the latter depended on hacienda owners for access to additional land. Landowners could not rely on coercion alone to ensure an uninterrupted supply of labour during peak agricultural seasons but also had to make concessions to indigenous peasants. Most importantly, they had to bow to their demand for land and accommodate, albeit superficially, some elements of their culture. The result was an elaborate and negotiated nexus of customary rights and obligations, above all land rights and labour obligations. Given the underlying antagonisms, both parties sought their own advantage: peasants surreptitiously expanded their use of hacienda resources; landowners abused and terrorised their workers. And yet both probably recognised that without implicit compromise, the hidden war would escalate into an open one, an outcome that both parties tried to avoid. In the context of the 1940s and 1950s and its balance of forces, any open war would probably have ended in massacre of the peasants, also incurring high costs in the form of labour shortages and material damage for the hacienda owners.

Circumstances changed with the acceleration of the transition to capitalist agriculture in Andean haciendas following land reform. Significantly, peasants' hidden counter-offensive contributed to and, to some extent, shaped this transition. Low-productivity haciendas were subdivided and sold relatively cheaply to peasant families. Better endowed haciendas were transformed into capitalist farms, and unruly peasants – with their families, crops, and animals – expelled and replaced with more obedient wage workers disciplined by the labour market. Indeed, in the Andean context, the figure of the proletarian with nothing to lose but his or her chains was certainly more attractive to modernising hacienda owners than the communal peasant with his or her ancient and rebellious culture. Thus, the most important cumulative effect of hidden peasant resistance in Otavalo was socio-economic differentiation of the haciendas (parallel to socio-economic differentiation of the peasantry) in the capitalist transformation of agriculture.[18] In short, 'weak' haciendas were swallowed by surrounding communities while 'strong' ones developed into capitalist production units, severing customary ties with the surrounding peasantry.

Scott [1986] describes a similar process in the more homogeneous social context of a Malaysian village. In his analysis, the breakdown of what he called human dependencies in the process of the green revolution resulted in a hidden war between impoverished and marginalised peasants and well-off capitalist-minded villagers. Similar decline in relations of reciprocity following land reform and capitalist agricultural modernisation in Peru is identified by Berg [1992] as an important factor in the growth of organised political violence in the 1970s and 1980s. In his study of Brazil's Contestado rebellion, Diacon [1990] also points to social crisis generated by capitalist transformation of rural economy, in that case leading to a millennial movement. The decline of customary land and labour relations in Otavalo produced different, though equally significant, results. The hidden war between communities and haciendas, together with the emergence of a new ethnic leadership in Otavalo, was conducive to the development of indigenous political organisations which combined direct political action, such as land take-overs, with legal action and political negotiation.

This outcome can be understood only in the context of national political processes, and especially democratisation, singled out by Kerkvliet [1993] as the most important factor in the transition from hidden resistance to open political struggles. The concept of democratisation, however, must be used with caution. In rural Ecuador community-based organisational activities were spurred not so much by the transition to liberal democracy as by land reforms implemented under military regimes. By undermining the oppressive power of large landowners, these reforms made an important contribution to democratisation in rural Ecuador. The subsequent transition to liberal democracy, however, enabled the relatively uninhibited operation of indigenous political organisations that originated with the land reforms. It also facilitated the development of a political alliance between indigenous and non-indigenous popular organisations, characteristic of the 1990 uprising.

As in the Philippines, local leadership, skilful in the arts of hidden resistance, played an important role in organised political action. But so did urban political leadership, whose importance is downplayed by Kerkvliet in his analysis of land conflicts. What is remarkable though in Ecuador and especially Otavalo, is that this was an indigenous political leadership without any explicit party or trade union affiliation. In contrast to left-wing, largely white-mestizo organisers associated with FEI and FENOC, Otavalo's indigenous leaders of urban background had relatively little difficulty in relating to the peasantry or positioning themselves in the long history of hidden struggles between community and hacienda. In effect, many of them came from relatively prosperous families of peasants and artisans who had been investing in trade and education for their children. Not peasants any more, these new leaders developed an ideology that emphasised ethnic grievances dating back to the conquest and colonisation. Curiously, this ideology appealed to indigenous peasants who found themselves increasingly involved in migratory labour as a result of the demographic pressure on land. It is no exaggeration to note that for the first time since the demise of the ethnic aristocracy, Otavalo's peasantry embraced a leadership that they identified as their own, however much they might also criticise it. Thus, peasant differentiation contributed to the resurgence of ethnic values which in the 1980s and 1990s provided a powerful glue for the progressively proletarianised indigenous communities [*Korovkin*, 1997b, 1998].

The rise of indigenous organisations in the context of capitalist expansion and political democratisation reduced the importance, and changed the nature, of everyday forms of resistance in Otavalo's countryside, but did not eliminate them altogether. Their continuing prominence was suggested in the case of state-controlled co-operatives, such as San Agustin de Cajas. Even though the Ministry of Agriculture played a benign role during the land reform period, it prevented peasants from adopting patterns of production structured around household and community, which would probably have been their first choice if given a chance to participate in drafting the land reform legislation. Given how land reform was implemented, however, San Agustin workers confronted an alien form of organisation which they opposed by deploying their usual hidden weapons. The *de facto* and later *de jure* subdivision of co-operative land into family parcels and the formation of San Agustin community parallels the fate of 'weak' haciendas in Otavalo. It also reminds us of the successes of peasant hidden resistance to collective forms of agriculture in other parts of the world.

While opposing capitalist modernisation led by private landowners or by the Ministry of Agriculture, Otavalo's peasants have absorbed many elements characteristic of modern capitalist economy and society. Elements of historical continuity, often emphasised by indigenous political leaders and non-indigenous students of ethnohistory, should not obfuscate profound changes in both the content and context of indigenous peasant struggles. Stern [1987] correctly points to a dialectical unity of resistance and adaptation in the Andean world, while Starn [1992: 94] insists that indigenous peasant values and protest should be seen 'as being formulated from particular positions *within* the global village'. No matter how much amusement the latter term might give Otavalo's peasants, they would probably agree with both statements. While claiming hacienda land, they availed themselves, when possible, of white-mestizo arrangements, customary and/or formal (legal). They also intertwined their social practices with those of white-mestizo cultural baggage, starting from the use of *guarapo* and ending with the election of community councils.

The full scope and implications of this amalgamation in Otavalo became visible only after the disappearance of the pre-capitalist commercial hacienda and the rise of indigenous organisations. Far from advocating a return to the (pre-capitalist or pre-colonial) *status quo ante*, Otavalo's indigenous communities linked their aspirations to governmental and non-governmental organisations that supply them with credit and technical assistance. Having subdivided most of the cooperative land, San Agustin community members maintained their close ties with commodity economy. Under pressure from non-governmental organisations, Otavalo's agricultural associations also adopted a collective form of agriculture expected to facilitate the generation of a commercial surplus. Contrary to state-sponsored co-operatives, however, such agricultural associations situated themselves from the very start within the jurisdiction of communal authorities and developed a symbiotic relation with the surrounding peasant community, with its strong interest in roads and schools.

This evidence goes against the concept of moral economy as the main driving force of either everyday peasant defiance or organised political protest in the context of capitalist expansion and increasing political openness. Undoubtedly, moral outrage at the violation by modernising hacienda-owners of customary arrangements, provided a strong impulse for peasant covert and overt action. However, there were also other values involved, those that Kerkvliet [1993], Foley [1990], and León [1994] identify as basic universal rights, such as the rights to education and a decent, not simply subsistence, standard of living, inseparable from the idea of full citisenship in a modern nation-state. There is a certain irony in this endorsement of modern social and political values by Otavalo's indigenous peasantry, for it came at a moment when notions of basic rights and their national political conditions were subverted by the proponents of economic liberalisation and globalisation. At the turn of the millennium, Otavalo's indigenous peasant communities emerged fortified, if not exactly victorious, after decades if not centuries of hidden and open struggles with the hacienda, only to confront new and formidable political challenges.

NOTES

1. See Scott [1985, 1986, 1987, 1990]. Kerkvliet [1986m 1990m 1993]. Adas [1981; 1986]. For a critical analysis, conceptual extension, and/or application of the EFPR approach in the Latin American context, see Joseph [1990]. Joseph and Nugent [1994]. Colburn [1986]. Edelman [1990]. Gutmann [1993]. Orlove [1991] and Vandergeest [1993].
2. Scott [1985] provides a detailed analysis of peasant socio-economic differentiation as a result of the green revolution, while Kerkvliet [1993: 479] specifically points out that 'participants in the Philippine take-overs have been primarily villagers without land'.
3. Glave [1990] uses the concept of forced peasantisation to describe the origins of the Andean peasantry. Stern [1987] emphasised the limits of a narrow class approach to the study of peasant movements, pointing to the ethnic underpinnings of Andean peasant politics. In the Ecuadorean case, this approach is adopted by Ramón Valerza [1987, 1990] and Thurner [1993].
4. A similar cultural blend was described in the Ecuadorean case by Rosero under the name of the Andean Code [*Rosero*, 1990]. For a general discussion of the millennial underpinnings of peasant rebellions and guerrilla movements, see Desai [1990].
5. For a discussion of the colonial ethnic rebellions, see Moreno Yáñez [1976] and San Félix [1986]. *Nuestras comunidades* [1994] represents an attempt to incorporate indigenous oral history into the provincial system of bilingual education.
6. In many cases they also received small cash wages and help in the case of an emergency. *Huasipungo*, an Ecuadorean version of service tenure, is discussed by Guerrero [1977] and Oberem [1977].
7. In the 1950s and 1960s, communal authorities in Otavalo were represented by two sets of officials: *alcaldes y regidores*, appointed by local government officials and/or clergy, and *cabildos*, elected by community members in accordance with the 1937 Law of Communes. The difference between appointed and elected communal officials was less pronounced than might appear at first glance. In both cases communal officials came from the most influential indigenous families, often the descendants of hereditary chiefs (*curacas*), and had to mediate relations between their communities and what the latter saw as the white-mestizo system of government. For discussions of communal authorities, see Sánchez Parga [1986, 1993] and Lentz [1986].
8. A similar process of disintegration of haciendas in the Peruvian Andes is discussed by Caballero [1981].
9. For a brief overview of Ecuador's land reform, see Zevallos [1989]. Contrasting interpretations of the consequences of the land reform in Ecuador are offered by Velasco [1979], Barsky [1988] and Korovkin [1997a].
10. Crain [1989], in her analysis of *uyanzas* on Imbabura haciendas, suggests that exorbitant

costs involved in the organisation of traditional annual celebrations were one of the factors behind the capitalist modernisation of the hacienda.

11. Pijal, the largest and oldest of the Cajas communities, has a land title dated 1720.
12. A similar practice is discussed by Almeida Vinueza [1984]. Godoy [1991] argues that one of the most important functions of common fields in Andean communities was to serve as a land fund for successive generations.
13. For an analysis of state support for dairy production, see Cosse [1984] and Commander and Peek [1987].
14. The owners hired armed guards who terrorised the indigenous communities. At some point, the military and the police were called in. Several people were injured, killed, or jailed, and in San Francisco, houses were set on fire.
15. White [1986] makes a similar observation in her case study of Vietnam.
16. In a similar vein, de la Torre [1989] describes the ability of bonded labourers on Andean haciendas to manipulate debt peonage to their advantage.
17. Scott'ss concept of moral economy provoked a prolonged and heated academic debate; see Popkin [1979], Paige [1983], Skopol [1992], Hawes [1990], Pripstein Posusney [1993], Lichbach [1994], among others.
18. There exists a vast body of academic literature on peasant socio-economic differentiation in Latin America. For a brief review, see Kay [1995]; for a study of peasant differentiation in Otavalo, see Korovkin [1997b].

REFERENCES

Adas, Michael, 1981, 'From Avoidance to to Confrontation: Peasant Protest in Precolonial and Colonial Southeast Asia', *Comparative Studies in Society and History*, Vol.23, No.1, pp.217–47.
Adas, Michael, 1986, 'From Footdragging to Flight: The Evasive History of Peasant Avoidance Protest in South and Southeast Asia', *The Journal of Peasant Studies*, Vol.13, No.2, pp.64–86.
Aguiló, Federico, 1992, *El Hombre del Chimborazo*, Quito: Abya-Yala.
Almeida Vinueza, José, 1984, 'Cooperativas y comunidades: integración u oposición de dos formas de organisación campesina?', in Cristina Farga y José Almeida Vinueza, *Campesinos y haciendas de la Sierra Norte*, Otavalo: IOA.
Almeida Vinueza, José et al., 1993, *Sismo étnico en el Ecuador*, Quito: CEDIME, Abya Yala.
Bartlett, Peggy F., 1988, 'La reciprocidad y la fiesta de San Juan en Otavalo', *Allpanchis* (Cusco, Peru), Vol.20, No.32 pp.73–99.
Barsky, Osvaldo, 1988, *La reforma agraria ecuatoriana*, Quito: Corporacion Editora Nacional.
Berg, Ronald, 1992, 'Peasant Responses to Shining Path in Andahuaylas', in David Scott Palmer (ed.), *Shining Path of Peru*, London: Hurst.
Brass, Tom, 1991, 'Moral Economists, Subalterns, New Social Movements, and the (Re-) Emergence of (Post-)Modernised (Middle) Peasant'. *The Journal of Peasant Studies*, Vol.18, No.2, pp.173-205.
Brass, Tom, 1996-99, 'Popular Culture, Populist Fiction(s): The Agrarian Utopiates of A.V.Chayanov, Ignatius Donnelly and Frank Capra'. *The Journal of Peasant Studies*, Vol.24, Nos.1–2, pp.173–205.
Brown, Micael F. and Eduardo Fernandez, 1991, *War of Shadows: The Struggle for Utopia in the Peruvian Amazon*, Berkeley, CA: University of California Press.
Burdick, 1992, 'Rethinking the Study of Social Movements: The Case of Christian Base Communities in Urban Brazil', in Arturo Escobar and Sonia Alvarez (eds.), *The Making of Social Movements in Latin America: Identity, Strategy and Democracy*, Boulder, CO: Westview Press.
Bustamente, Teodoro and Mercedes Prieto, 1985, 'Formas de organisación y de acción campesina e indígena: experiencias en tres zonas de Ecuador', in Miguel Murmis (ed.), *Clase y región en el agro ecuatoriano*, Quito: Corporación Editora Nacional.
Butler, Barbara, 1992, 'Espiritualidad y uso de alcohol entre la gente otavaleña', in *Ecuador*

indígena: espiritualidad, música y artesanía. Quito: Abya Yala.

Caballero, José María. 1981. *Economía agraria en la sierra peruana*. Lima: IEP.

Chiriboga, Manuel. 1986. 'Crisis económica y movimiento campesino e indígena en Ecuador'. *Revista Andina* (Cusco, Perú), Vol.4, No.1, pp.7–30.

Colburn, Forrest D., 1986. 'Footdragging and Other Peasant Responses to the Nicaraguan Revolution'. *The Journal of Peasant Studies*, Vol.13, No.22, pp.77–96.

Commander, Simon, and Peter Peek, 1987. 'Oil Exports, Agrarian Change and the Rural Labour Process: The Ecuadorian Sierra in the 1970s'. *World Development*, Vol.14, No.1, pp.79–96.

Cosse, Gustavo, 1984. *El Estado y el agro en el Ecuador*. Quito: Corporación Editora Nacional.

Crain, Mary M., 1989. *Ritual, memoria popular y proceso político en la sierra ecuatoriana*. Quito: Corporación Editora Nacional.

de la Torre, Patricia, 1989. *Patronos y conciertos: la hacienda serrana*. Quito: Corporación Editora Nacional.

Desai, Raj and Harry Eckstein, 1990. 'Insurgency: The Transformation of Peasant Rebellion', *World Politics*, Vol.42, No.4, pp.441–65.

Diacon, Todd A., 1990. 'Peasants, Prophets, and the Power of a Millenarian Vision in Twentieth-Century Brazil', *Comparative Studies in Society and History*, Vol.32, No.3, pp.487–514.

Eckstein, Susan, 1989. 'Power and Popular Protest', in Susan Eckstein (ed.), *Power and Popular Protest: Latin American Social Movements*. Berkeley, CA: University of California Press.

Edelman, Marc, 1990. 'When They Took the "Muni": Political Culture and Anti-Austerity Protest in Rural Northwestern Costa Rica', *American Ethnologist*, No.17, pp.736–57.

Foley, Michael W., 1990. 'Organising, Ideology, and Moral Suasion: Political Discourse and Action in a Mexican Town', *Comparative Studies in Society and History*, Vol.32, No.2, pp.455–87.

Flores Galindo, Alberto, 1988. *Buscando un inca: identidad y utopía en los Andes*, Lima.

Glave, Luis Miguel, 1990. 'Conflict and Social Reproduction: An Andean Peasant Community', in Mats Lundahl and Thommy Svensson (eds.), *Agrarian Society and History*, London: Routledge.

Godoy, Ricardo, 1991. 'The Evolution of Common-Field Agriculture in the Andes: A Hypothesis', *Comparative Studies in Society and History*, Vol.33, No.2, pp.395–414.

Guerrero, Andrés, 1977. *Haciendas, capital y lucha de clases andina*. Quito: El Conejo.

Guerrero, Andrés, 1991. *La semántica de la dominación: el concertaje de los indios*, Quito: Ediciones Libri Mundi.

Gutmann, Matthew C., 1993. 'Rituals of Resistance: A Critique of the Theory of Everyday Forms of Resistance', *Latin American Perspectives*, Vol.20, No.2, pp.74–92.

Handelman, Howard, 1975. *Struggle in the Andes: Peasant Political Mobilisation in Peru*, Austin, TX: University of Texas Press.

Hawes, Gary, 1990. 'Theories of Peasant Revolution: A Critique and Contribution from the Philippines', *World Politics*, Vol.92, No.2, pp.261–96.

Hobsbawm, E.J., 1973. 'Peasant and Politics', *The Journal of Peasant Studies*, Vol.1, No.1, pp.3–22.

Ibarra, Alicia, 1992. *Los indígenas y el Estado en el Ecuador: la práctica neo-indigenista*, Quito: Abya Yala.

Isbell, Billie Jean, 1992. 'Shining Path and Peasant Responses in Rural Ayachucho', in David Scott Palmer (ed.), *Shining Path of Peru*, London: Hurst.

INEC (Instituto Nacional de Estadística y Censos). 1954. *Primer censo agropecuario*, Quito: INEC.

Joseph, Gilbert M., 1990. 'On the Trail of Latin American Bandits: A Reexamination of Peasant Resistance', *Latin American Research Review*, Vol.25, No.3, pp.7–53.

Joseph, Gilbert M. and Daniel Nugent, 1994. 'Popular Culture and State Formation in Revolutionary Mexico', in Gilbert M. Joseph and Daniel Nugent (eds.), *Everyday Forms of State Formation: Revolution and the Negotiation of Rule in Modern Mexico*, Durham, NC: Duke University Press.

Kay, Cristobal, 1995, 'Rural Development and Agrarian Issues in Contemporary Latin America', in John Weeks (ed.), *Structural Adjustment and the Agricultural Sector in Latin America and the Caribbean*, New York: St.Martin'ss Press.

Kerkvliet, Benedict J. Tria, 1986, 'Everyday Resistance to Injustice in a Philippine Village', *The Journal of Peasant Studies*, Vol.13, No.2, pp.107–23.

Kerkvliet, Benedict J. Tria, 1990, *Everyday Politics in the Philippines: Class and Status Relations in a Central Luzon Village*, Berkeley, CA: University of California Press.

Kerkvliet, Benedict J. Tria, 1993, 'Claiming the Land: Everyday Politics in the Philippines with Comparisons to Indonesia, Peru, Portugal, and Russia', *The Journal of Peasant Studies*, Vol.20, No.3, pp.459–91.

Korovkin, Tanya, 1990, *The Politics of Agricultural Co-operativism: Peru, 1969–1983*, Vancouver: University of British Columbia Press.

Korovkin, Tanya, 1997a, 'Indigenous Peasant Struggles and Capitalist Modernisation of Agriculture: Chimborazo, 1964–1991', *Latin American Perspectives*, Vol.24, No.3, pp.25–49.

Korovkin, Tanya, 1997b, 'Taming Capitalism: The Evolution of Peasant Economy in Northern Ecuador', *Latin American Research Review*, Vol.32, No.3, pp.89–110.

Korovkin, Tanya, 1998, 'Commodity Production and Ethnic Culture: Otavalo, Northern Ecuador', *Economic Development and Cultural Change*, Vol.47, No.1, pp.125–54.

Landsberger, Henry A., 1974, 'Peasant Unrest: Themes and Variations', Henry A. Landsberger (ed.), in *Rural Protest: Peasant Movements and Social Change*, London: Macmillan.

Lentz, Carola, 1986, 'De regidores y alcaldes a cabildos: cambios en la estructura socio-política de la comunidad indígena de Cajabamba, Chimborazo', *Ecuador Debate* (Quito, Ecuador), No.12, pp.189–212.

León, Jorge, 1994, *De campesinos a cuidadanos diferentes*, Quito: Abya Yala.

Lichbach, Mark I., 1994, 'What Makes Rational Peasants Revolutionary? Dilemma, Paradox, and Irony in Peasant Collective Action', *World Politics*, Vol.46, No.3, pp.383–418.

Mallon, Florencia E., 1983, *The Defence of Community in Peru's Central Highlands: Peasant Struggles and Capitalist Transition, 1869–1940*, Princeton, NJ: Princeton University Press.

Martinez-Alier, Juan, 1977, 'Relations of Production in Andean Haciendas: Peru', in Kenneth Duncan and Ian Rutledge (eds.), *Land and Labour in Latin America*, Cambridge: Cambridge University Press.

Montoya, Rodrigo, 1982, 'Class Relations in the Andean Countryside', *Latin American Perspectives*, Vol.9, No.3, pp.62-78.

Moreno Yáñez, Segundo, 1976, *Sublevaciones indígenas en la Audiencia de Quito desde comienzos del siglo XVIII hasta fines de la época colonial*, Bonn: Studios Americanistas de Bonn.

Nuestras comunidades ayer y hoy, 1994, Quito: Abya-Yala.

Oberem, Udo, 1977, *Contribución a la historia del trabajador rural de America Latina: 'conciertos' y Ahuasipungueros'en Ecuador*, Bielefeld: Universidad de Bielefeld.

Orlove, Benjamin S., 1991, 'Mapping Reeds and Reading Maps: The Politics of Representation in Lake Titicaca', *American Ethnologist*, No.18, pp.3-38.

Paige, Jeffrey, 1975, *Agrarian Revolution: Social Movements and Export Agriculture in the Underdeveloped World*, London: Free Press.

Paige, Jeffrey, 1983, 'Social Theory and Peasant Revolution in Vietnam and Guatemala', *Theory and Society*, pp.699–737.

Palmer, David Scott (ed.), 1988, *Shining Path of Peru*, London: Hurst.

Popkin, Samuel, 1979, *The Rational Peasant*, Berkeley, CA: University of California.

Pripstein Posusney, Marsha, 1993, 'Irrational Workers: The Moral Economy of Labour Protest in Egypt', *World Politics*, Vol.46, No.1, pp.83–120.

Ramón Valerza, Galo, 1987, *La resistencia andina: Cayambe 1500–1800*, Quito: CAAP.

Ramón Valerza, Galo, 1990, 'El Ecuador en el espacio andino: idea, proceso y utopía', *Allpanchis* (Cusco, Peru), Vol.22, Nos.35–36, pp.538–74.

Rosero, Fernando, 1990, *Levantamiento indígena: tierra y precios*, Quito: CEDIS.

San Félix, Elver, 1986, *Monografía de Otavalo*, Otavalo: IOA.

Sánchez Parga, José, 1986, *La trama del poder en la comunidad andina*, Quito: CAAP.

Sánchez Parga, José, 1993, *Campesinado indígena y el desafío de la modernidad*, Quito: CAAP.

Scott, James C., 1976, *The Moral Economy of the Peasant: Rebellion and Subsistence in Southeast Asia*, New Haven, CT: Yale University Press.

Scott, James, 1977, 'Hegemony and the Peasantry', *Politics and Society*, Vol.7, No.3, pp.267–96.

Scott, James C., 1985, *Weapons of the Weak: Everyday Forms of Peasant Resistance*, New Haven, CT: Yale University Press.

Scott, James C. 1986, 'Everyday Forms of Peasant Resistance', *The Journal of Peasant Studies*, Vol.13, No.2, pp.5–35.

Scott, James C., 1987, 'Resistance without Protest and without Organisation: Peasant Opposition to the Islamic *Zacat* and Christian Tithe', *Comparative Studies in Society and History*, Vol.29, No.3, pp.417–52.

Scott, James C.,1990, *Domination and the Art of Resistance: Hidden Transcripts*, New Haven, CT: Yale University Press.

Scott, James C. and Benedict J. Tria Kerkvliet (eds.), 1986, *Everyday Forms of Peasant Resistance in South-East Asia*, London: Frank Cass.

Selverston, Melina, 1994, 'The Politics of Culture: Indigenous People and the State in Ecuador', in Donna Lee van Ccott (ed.), *Indigenous People and Democracy in Latin America*, New York: St.Martins Press.

Skopol, Theda, 1992, 'What Makes Peasants Revolutionary?', in Robert P. Weller and Scott E. Guggenheim (eds.), *Power and Protest in the Countryside*, Durham, NC: Duke University Press.

Smith, Gavin, 1989, *Livelihood and Resistance: Peasants and the Politics of Land in Peru*, Berkeley, CA: University of California Press.

Starn, Orin, 1992, '"I Dreamed of Foxes and Hawks": Reflections on Peasant Protest, New Social Movements and the *Rondas Campesinas* of Northern Peru', in Arturo Escobar and Sonia Alvarez (eds.), *The Making of Social Movements in Latin America: Identity, Strategy, and Democracy*, Boulder, CO: Westview Press.

Stern, Steve J., 1987, 'New Approaches to the Study of Peasant Rebellion and Consciousness: Implications of the Andean Experience', in Steve J. Stern (ed.), *Resistance, Rebellion, and Consciousness in the Andean Peasant World: 18th to 20th Centuries*, Madison, WI: University of Wisconsin Press.

Sylva, Paola, 1986, *Gamonalismo y la lucha campesina: estudio de la sobrevivencia y disolución de un sector terrateniente: el caso de la provincia de Chimborazo*, Quito: Abya Yala.

Thurner, Mark, 1993, 'Peasant Politics and Andean Haciendas in the Transition to Capitalism: An Ethnographic History', *Latin American Research Review*, Vol.28, No. 3, pp.41–82.

Turton, Andrew, 1986, 'Patrolling the Middle-Ground: Methodological Perspectives on "Everyday Peasant Resistance"', in Scott and Kerkvliet [1986].

Vandergeest, Peter, 1993, 'Constructing Thailand: Regulation, Everyday Resistance, and Citisenship', *Comparative Studies in Society and History*, Vol.35, No.1, pp.133–57.

Velasco, Fernando, 1979, *Reforma agraria y movimiento campesino indígena en la sierra*, Quito: El Conejo.

Wolf, Eric, 1969, *Peasant Wars of the Twentieth Century*, New York: Harper & Row.

White, Christine Pelzer, 1986, 'Everyday Resistance, Socialist Revolution and Rural Development: The Vietnamese Case', in Scott and Kerkvliet [1986].

Wickham-Crowley, Timothy, 1991, *Exploring Revolution: Essays on Latin American Insurgency and Revolutionary Theory*, Armonk, NY: M.E. Sharpe.

Zamosc, Leon, 1989, *Peasant Struggle and Agrarian Reform: The Ecuadorian Sierra and the Colombian Atlantic Coast in Comparative Perspective*, Allegheny College and University of Akron, Latin American Issues, Monograph Series No.8.

Zamosc, Leon, 1995, *Estadística de las areas de predominio etnico en la sierra ecuatoriana*, Quito: Abya Yala.

Zevallos L., Jose Vicente, 1989, 'Agrarian Reform and Structural Change: Ecuador since 1964', in William C. Thiesenhusen (ed.), *Searching for Agrarian Reform in Latin America*, Boston, MA: Unwin Hyman.

RACIAL INEQUALITY IN BRAZIL AND
THE UNITED STATES: A STATISTICAL COMPARISON

By George Reid Andrews   University of Pittsburgh

Writing in the late 1970s, comparative historian George Fredrickson observed that the study of slavery and black/white race relations forms "the most highly developed subject of comparative historical study in the United States."[1] During the 1980s, such comparisons were most likely to focus on the United States and South Africa.[2] Over the twentieth century as a whole, however, the country with which United States race relations have been most frequently compared is Brazil.[3]

The Brazil/United States comparison has a compelling logic. The two countries are the largest multiracial societies in the Americas. They share a history of plantation slavery which extends into the second half of the 1800s.[4] And over the course of the 1900s both societies have confronted the legacy of slavery in the form of deeply entrenched racial inequality.

Early comparative treatments of that inequality contrasted Brazilian "racial democracy" with American segregation, arguing that Brazilian society offered much greater opportunities than the United States for black upward mobility and advancement.[5] Following World War II, however, such comparisons began to be revised. A series of UNESCO-sponsored research projects carried out in the early 1950s, and more recent research conducted during the 1970s and 1980s, documented high levels of racial inequality in Brazil and the existence of subtle, flexible forms of racial discrimination which effectively hinder black and brown people's access to social and economic advancement.[6] Noting the changes that have taken place in both countries since 1950, some observers have argued that American and Brazilian race relations may actually be converging and becoming more similar in character.[7] While racial tensions have intensified and emerged into the open in Brazil, the overturning of state-imposed segregation and the implementation of equal opportunity and affirmative action programs in the United States have broken the back of formal, institutional racism in this country. Such programs have not eliminated discrimination from American life, however. Rather, they have driven it underground and forced it to become more subtle, unpredictable, and "Brazilian" in character.[8]

The comparative discussion of race relations in Brazil and the United States is thus by now reasonably well developed and has undergone substantial evolution over time. A crucial element of that discussion, however, remains missing. Any comparative examination of race relations hinges on the question of racial inequality: in what ways are blacks disadvantaged in relation to whites in each society, and in which society are those disadvantages more severe? This is in large part a statistical question, answered by data on racial differentials in employment, education, earnings, health, and so on; and indeed, evaluations and criticisms of race relations in both Brazil and the United States are often based on material of this kind, furnished by the national census or other sources. The

231

resulting statistical indicators are readily comparable between the two countries; yet no one, to my knowledge. has ever attempted such a comparison.

This article undertakes that comparison, using statistical data to measure various forms of racial inequality in Brazil and the United States and how that inequality has changed over time. Doubtless one reason for the lack of such research until now has been the relative scarcity of racial data for Brazil. No national census was taken in that country in 1910 or 1930; the censuses of 1900, 1920, and 1970 contain no information on race; and most of the racial data from the census of 1960 were never published. Racial data are available, however, in the censuses of 1872, 1890, 1940, 1950, and 1980, and in the national household surveys of 1976, 1984, and 1987. My strategy will be to match whatever indicators are available for Brazil with similar indicators from the same year for the United States. Given the limitations of the Brazilian sources, this means that most of the comparisons presented will be drawn from the 1940–1987 period, with occasional additional data from 1872 and 1890.[9]

This comparison is based on published aggregate data. It is important to specify at the outset what these data permit us to measure, and what they do not. For the purposes of this essay, racial inequality is defined as differences between the statistical distributions of the black (or in the case of Brazil, the black and brown—see below) and white populations.[10] What is the difference in each country in the percentage of black and white students completing elementary school, high school, and college? What is the difference in the percentage of black and white workers holding manual, service, and white-collar jobs? What is the difference in black and white median incomes. Aggregate census data show these differences; but they do not permit us to measure, in any statistical sense, the *causes* of those differences, which consist of a complex mix of social, economic, demographic, political, and cultural factors. some documented in the census, and some not.

The tables and figures presented below therefore should not be read as comparative indicators of racial prejudice or discrimination in the two countries; they measure inequality of achievement, not inequality of opportunity. Nevertheless, the exercise of comparing how the published data have changed over time does suggest some general conclusions, presented in the essay's final section, concerning the causes of racial inequality in Brazil and the United States, and the role of discrimination in maintaining, increasing, or reducing such inequality.

Brazil and the United States: Economy and Population

Our analysis must take into account some salient structural differences between the two societies. The first is their respective levels of economic development. Throughout the 1900s the United States has been the world's largest industrial producer, and despite some signs of weakness in recent decades it remains a technologically advanced, highly developed economy. Brazil, by contrast, is a relative latecomer to industrialization and modernization. Not until the 1950s did its industrial output surpass its agricultural output, a point which the United States reached in the 1880s.[11] Since World War II Brazil has experienced impressive economic growth, which averaged 7.4 percent per year from 1950 through 1980, and which by the 1980s had made it the seventh-largest industrial economy in the capitalist world.[12] But by 1980 Brazilian per capita GNP was still only one-sixth (16.9 percent) of American per capita GNP. By 1988, after six years of economic turmoil set off by the international debt crisis of 1982, Brazilian per capita GNP was slightly lower in real terms than it had been in 1980, and was only one-eighth (12.4 percent) of its American counterpart.[13]

Not only is Brazil a much poorer country than the United States; it is also one in which such wealth as there is is badly maldistributed.[14] The roots of that maldistribution can be traced back to Brazil's colonial-period and nineteenth-century reliance on slave-based plantation agriculture. But in recent decades wealth and income have become even more concentrated as Brazil has experienced the effects of the Kuznets curve.[15] Economists and economic historians have noted a tendency for growth in less developed economies, and particularly those in the early-to-intermediate stages of industrialization, to increase income inequality; income data from 1960–1980 show this process taking place in Brazil (Figure 1). The United States, meanwhile, has experienced the benign effects of the other side of the curve: as societies attain higher levels of economic development, continued growth tends to reduce the concentration of income, as happened in the United States between 1930 and 1950. Distribution of income was relatively stable between 1950 and 1975 and then started to become more

Figure 1

Percentage of Aggregate Income Received by Each Fifth of the Population, Brazil and the United States, 1960–1988

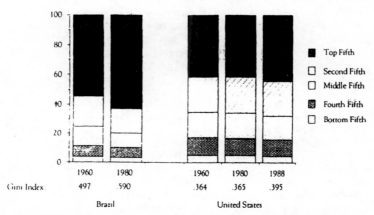

Gini Index	1960	1980		1960	1980	1988
	.497	.590		.364	.365	.395
	Brazil			United States		

Sources. Brazil: Charles H. Wood and José Alberto Magno de Carvalho, *The Demography of Inequality in Brazil* (Cambridge and New York, 1988), table 3.5, p. 76. United States: 1960, 1980, United States Bureau of the Census (hereafter USBC), *Current Population Reports*, Series P-60, No. 137, *Money Income of Households, Families and Persons in the United States: 1981* (Washington, 1983), table 17, p. 47; 1988, USBC, *Current Population Reports*, P-60, 166, *Money Income and Poverty Status in the United States: 1988* (Washington, 1989), table 5, p. 31.

unequal.[16] But even by 1988, income was distributed much more evenly in the United States than in Brazil.

The greater overall inequality of Brazilian society, and the worsening of that inequality since 1960, have struck particularly hard at the Afro-Brazilian population. Before examining the data on racial inequality in the two countries, however, it is important to note two important differences between the Afro-American and Afro-Brazilian racial groups. First, people of African ancestry have historically formed a much smaller proportion of the total population in the United States than in Brazil (Table 1). Whites were the overwhelming majority in the nineteenth-century United States, but were a minority in Brazil. Strong European migration between 1880 and 1930 resulted in the white population of both countries peaking, as a proportion of the total, in 1940, at which point whites comprised 90 percent of the US population, and 64 percent of Brazil's. The white representation in both countries then declined markedly between 1960 and 1980; but the rate of decline has been more rapid in Brazil, where whites now form a bare majority of the national population. [17]

A second difference between the two countries' nonwhite populations is that, while the North American model of race relations places the entire Afro-American population into a single "black" category, Brazilian society recognizes a division within the Afro-Brazilian population between "blacks" (pretos; people of predominantly African ancestry) and "browns" (pardos, or mulattoes; people of mixed racial ancestry). Ever since the first national census, in 1872, pardos have formed the majority of Afro-Brazilians. Their representation in the Afro-Brazilian population has undergone considerable variation over time, however, declining from 1872 to 1940 and then rebounding from 1940 to 1980, by which point pardos composed 39 percent of the national population, and 87 percent of the Afro-Brazilian population (Table 1, Figure 2). The distribution of blacks and browns among the Afro-American population has been precisely the opposite. Between 1850 and 1920 United States censuses distinguished between "Negroes" and "mulattoes." During that period people of pure African ancestry formed the overwhelming majority of the nonwhite population; and unlike Brazil, the mulatto population almost doubled its representation within the Afro-American population during the second half of the 1800s before declining sharply between 1910 and 1920.

In both countries, the accuracy of population data on mulattoes is open to question. In Brazil census takers are instructed to accept individuals' own assessments of their racial status, which has opened the door for many pretos to reclassify themselves as pardos. According to the censuses of 1940 and 1950, for example, the cohort of pardos born between 1910 and 1939 grew from 6.3 million in 1940 to 7.2 million in 1950. In the absence of significant nonwhite immigration into Brazil during that decade, or indeed at any point during the twentieth century, such an increase is theoretically impossible, and can only be explained by transfers from the preto to pardo racial category.[19] And recent research by demographer Charles Wood indicates that more than a third (38 percent) of the individuals born between 1920 and 1939 and classified as pretos in the census of 1950 reclassified themselves as pardos in the census of 1980.[20]

In the United States, by contrast, the direction of inaccuracy has been the reverse: while Brazilian censuses have tended to inflate the size of the mulatto

Table 1[18]
Percentage Distribution, Total Population by Race, Brazil and the United States, 1860–1980

	Brazil				
	White	Pardo	Preto	Other[a]	Total (in 000s)
1872	38.1	38.3	19.7	3.9	9,930
1890	44.0	32.4	14.6	9.0	14,334
1940	63.5	21.2	14.6	0.7	41,236
1950	61.7	26.5	11.0	0.8	51,944
1960	61.0	29.5	8.7	0.8	70,191
1980	54.2	38.9	5.9	1.0	119,011

[a]Other: 1872, 1890: caboclos (Indians); 1940–1980: amarelos (Asians) and unknown.

	United States			
	White	Black	Other	Total (in 000s)
1860	85.6	14.1	0.3	31,443
1890	87.5	11.9	0.6	62,948
1940	89.6	9.7	0.7	132,165
1950	89.3	9.9	0.8	151,326
1960	88.6	10.5	0.9	179,323
1980	83.1	11.7	5.2	226,546

Sources. Brazil: 1872, Directoria Geral de Estatística, Recenseamento da população do Império do Brasil a que se procedeu no dia 1 de agosto de 1872. Quadros geraes (Rio de Janeiro, 1873), table 1; 1890, Directoria Geral de Estatística, Synopse do recenseamento de 31 de dezembro de 1890 (Rio de Janeiro, 1898), pp. 2–3; 1940, Instituto Brasileiro de Geografia e Estatística (hereafter IBGE), Recenseamento geral de 1940. Censo demográfico: Estados Unidos do Brasil (Rio de Janeiro, 1950), table 4, pp. 6–7; 1950, IBGE, Recenseamento geral de 1950. Censo demográfico: Estados Unidos do Brasil (Rio de Janeiro, 1956), table 1, p. 1; 1960, IBGE, Recenseamento geral de 1960. Censo demográfico: Brasil (Rio de Janeiro, n.d.), table 5, p. 10; 1980, IBGE, Recenseamento geral do Brasil—1980. Censo demográfico—dados gerais, migração instrução, fecundidade, mortalidade—Brasil (Rio de Janeiro, 1983), table 1.4, pp. 10–11. United States: 1850–1890, USBC, Negro Population in the United States, 1790–1915 (Washington, 1918), table 2, p. 25; 1940–1980, USBC, 1980 Census of Population (Washington, 1983), Volume 1, Chapter B, Part 1, table 45, pp. 1-42-43.

Figure 2

Mulattoes as Percentage of Total Black Population, Brazil, 1872–1980, and the United States, 1850–1920

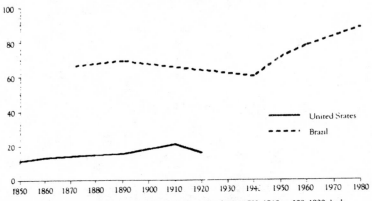

Sources. Brazil: see Table 1. United States: 1850–1910, *Negro Population, 1790–1915*, p. 208; 1920, Joel Williamson, *New People: Miscegenation and Mulattoes in the United States* (New York, 1980), p. 113.

population, US censuses tended to undercount them. In the United States, mulatto racial status was determined, not by the individuals being canvassed, but by the census takers, who for the most part failed to recognize or acknowledge color gradations within the "black" racial group. The Census Bureau itself questioned the accuracy of the figures yielded by this procedure, noting in 1918 that mulattoes might actually constitute as much as seventy-five percent of the Afro-American population, a proportion almost five times greater than that indicated in the census of 1920.[21] Apparently many, and perhaps most, American mulattoes were being counted as "Negro"; and after 1920 all American mulattoes were counted as black, following the elimination of the mulatto racial category from the census.

These divergences in the statistical treatment of the brown and black populations in Brazil and the United States underline the central importance for comparative analysis of the mulatto racial group in the two countries. Carl Degler states the case most forcefully. "The key that unlocks the puzzle of the differences in race relations in Brazil and the United States is the mulatto escape hatch": the ability of Brazilian nonwhites to achieve upward mobility by leaving the "black" racial category and acquiring an intermediate "brown" racial status which was "neither black nor white."[22] However, recent research using Brazilian income data from the 1960s, 70s, and 80s has questioned this formulation, showing that brown racial status is not "neither black nor white," but is in fact quite similar to that of blacks. *Pardo* earnings are only slightly higher than those of *pretos*, while both groups rank far below the white and "yellow" (Asian) racial groups. As one such study concludes, "the 'color line' [in Brazil] seems to be located between whites and nonwhites, and not between mulattoes and blacks, as it is sometimes believed to be."[23]

The earnings and education data presented in this article tend to confirm those findings. Other indicators show significant differences between the *pardo* and *preto* populations, but not always in the anticipated direction. On some the *preto* population approximates the white population more closely than do the *pardos*; and on yet others the relative relationship among *pardos*, *pretos*, and whites undergoes substantial variation over time.

In order to deal with these complexities, the remainder of this essay compares measures of black/white inequality in the United States to similar measures of brown/white and black/white inequality in Brazil. The topics examined include spatial distribution, demographic indicators, education, and employment and earnings.

Spatial Distribution

One of the major factors obstructing black upward mobility in both Brazil and the United States has been the black population's concentration in less economically dynamic geographic locales: in the former plantation zones of the American South and the Brazilian Northeast; in rural areas as opposed to cities; and within cities, in racially segregated neighborhoods. This section compares indices of black/white inequality for regional distribution, urban/rural distribution, and residential segregation within major Brazilian and American cities.

Table 2 provides information on white and nonwhite regional distribution in Brazil and the United States and uses that information to calculate indices of dissimilarity among the various racial groups.[24] Those data indicate that at the end of the nineteenth century the black and white populations of the United States were far more dissimilar in their regional distribution than the white and nonwhite populations of Brazil. The American black population was overwhelmingly concentrated in the South, and the white population in the North. In Brazil, by contrast, the *pardo* population was concentrated in the Northeast, but not nearly to the same degree as American blacks in the South; and the regional distribution of *pretos* actually approximated that of whites fairly closely.

By 1950 racial disparities in regional distribution had increased substantially in Brazil while declining in the United States. *Pardo*/white difference in Brazil was now slightly greater than black/white difference in the United States. And by 1980 racial dissimilarity in the United States had fallen to less than half the level of *pardo*/white dissimilarity in Brazil, and was at essentially the same levels as those separating *pretos* and Brazilian whites.

These data reflect very different patterns of internal migration in the two countries. Between 1890 and 1970 the United States experienced massive black migration out of the South, with most of those migrants heading north, and substantial white migration out of the North, with most of that migration heading west. The result of those migratory flows was to reduce racial imbalances in regional distribution, particularly in the North. In Brazil, by contrast, the dominant tendency has been migration out of the Northeast and into other regions, but migration in which whites apparently participated at a higher rate

Table 2

**Percentage Distribution, Regional Distribution by Race, Brazil and the
United States, 1890, 1950, 1980**

| | | Brazil | | | | United States | |
	White	Pardo	Preto			White	Black
1890							
Northeast	32.8	52.1	40.2	South		23.9	90.2
Southeast	46.5	37.4	51.7	Northeast		31.1	3.6
South	16.4	4.5	5.0	North Central		39.8	5.8
Rest of Brazil	4.3	5.9	3.1	West		5.2	0.4
Index of White/							
Nonwhite							
Dissimilarity	—	21.0	12.4			—	66.3
1950							
Northeast	23.4	58.3	42.0	South		27.3	65.7
Southeast	49.8	26.1	46.9	Northeast		27.7	13.2
South	21.9	2.9	6.4	North Central		31.2	14.9
Rest of Brazil	4.9	12.6	4.6	West		13.8	6.3
Index of Dissimilarity	—	42.7	18.7			—	38.4
1980							
Northeast	14.5	49.6	33.2	South		31.1	52.2
Southeast	53.2	28.3	51.5	Northeast		22.4	18.6
South	24.8	5.0	8.5	North Central		27.1	20.5
Rest of Brazil	7.5	17.1	6.7	West		19.4	8.6
Index of Dissimilarity	—	44.7	18.8			—	21.2

Sources. Brazil: 1890, *Synopse, 1890*, pp. 2–3; 1950, *Recenseamento, 1950*, table 39, p. 69; 1980, *Recenseamento, 1980*, table 1.11, pp. 34–35. United States: 1890, *Negro Population*, table 13, p. 44; 1950, USBC, *Census of Population: 1950* (Washington, 1953), Volume 2, Part 1, table 60, p. 1–107; 1980, USBC, *Current Population Reports*, P-20, 442, *The Black Population in the United States: March 1988* (Washington, 1989), table B, p. 3.

than browns and blacks. By 1980 the center of *pardo* settlement was still in the Northeast, while the center of white settlement had moved southward.

Because of the enormous regional disparities in levels of economic development in Brazil, those *pardos* who remained in the Northeast paid dearly for their decision to do so. As of 1987 they had on average less than a third of the education acquired by *pardos* in the more economically developed Southeastern states: 1.0 year of schooling versus 3.2 in the Southeast. (Whites obtained on average 2.7 years of schooling in the Northeast, and 4.0 in the Southeast.) The median earnings of *pardo* wage-earners in the Northeast were only half those of *pardo* workers in the Southeast: US $33 per month, versus US $67 per month in the Southeast. (White workers in the Northeast earned on average $47 per month, versus $107 for white workers in the Southeast.)[25] In the United States, by contrast, strong economic growth in the South since World War II has come close to eliminating regional disparities in income, education, and other indicators.[26] By

1988, black residents of the South received almost the same level of education as Afro-Americans in the North and West (11.3 years of schooling, versus 11.6; whites received 11.5 years of schooling in the South, 11.7 in the North and West) and earned median incomes that were 84 percent of their Northern and Western counterparts.[27] Thus *pardos* suffer much graver consequences from their continuing concentration in the Northeastern states than do Afro-Americans from their concentration in the American South.

Another obstacle to Afro-Brazilians' upward mobility is their concentration in rural areas, where incomes, educational opportunities, and material living conditions are much poorer than in the cities.[28] Historical data on urban and rural residence by race are unavailable for Brazil, but figures from 1980 show that *pardos* lag well behind whites in their tendency to live in urban areas. As in regional distribution, *pretos* occupy an intermediate position between *pardos* and whites (Table 3).

Like Afro-Brazilians, Afro-Americans have historically been more likely than American whites to live in the countryside. Over the course of the 1900s, however, black Americans have moved to urban areas at rates higher than the white population. By 1950 blacks and whites had achieved relative parity in urban/rural distribution, and by 1980, in a reversal of Brazilian patterns, the black population was considerably more urban than the white. This is all the more noteworthy given that the percentages of white people living in urban areas in 1980 were virtually the same in the two countries (74 percent in Brazil, 71 percent in the United States).

Table 3
Percentage Distribution, Urban and Rural Residence by Race, Brazil and the United States, 1890, 1950, 1980

| | Brazil | | | United States | |
	White	Pardo	Preto	White	Black
1890					
Urban	N.A.	N.A.	N.A.	38	20
Rural	N.A.	N.A.	N.A.	62	80
1950					
Urban	N.A.	N.A.	N.A.	64	62
Rural	N.A.	N.A.	N.A.	36	38
1980					
Urban	73.7	58.9	67.7	71.3	85.3
Rural	26.3	41.1	32.3	28.7	14.7

Sources. Brazil: *Recenseamento, 1980,* table 1.4, pp. 10–11. United States: 1890, 1950, USBC, Current Population Reports, Series P-23, No. 80, *The Social and Economic Status of the Black Population in the United States: An Historical Overview, 1790–1978,* (Washington, 1980), table 6, p. 14; 1980, *1980 Census,* 1, B, 1, table 38, p. 20.

When Afro-Americans moved to the cities, they encountered a much more excluding and segregated urban environment than was the case in Brazil. Historical data on residential segregation in Brazilian cities are not available; but research using the census of 1980 has generated indices of dissimilarity for a number of Brazilian cities. Table 4 compares measures of segregation (as in Table 2, indices of dissimilarity) for the ten largest American metropolitan areas with the ten largest Brazilian metropolitan areas. Those data indicate that residential separation of the races does exist in Brazilian cities, but is much less pronounced

Table 4
Indices of Racial Dissimilarity in Urban Residential Patterns, Ten Largest Metropolitan Areas, Brazil and the United States, 1980

City	Brazil Population (1987) (in 000,000s)	Pardo/White	Preto/White
São Paulo	16.2	39	41
Rio de Janeiro	10.8	38	43
Belo Horizonte	3.3	43	42
Recife	2.8	39	50
Porto Alegre	2.8	41	42
Salvador	2.3	49	53
Curitiba	2.0	42	48
Fortaleza	2.0	41	56
Brasília	1.7	41	42
Belem	1.0	35	50
Mean	—	41	47

City	United States Population (1980) (in 000,000s)	Black/White
New York	9.1	78
Los Angeles	7.5	79
Chicago	7.1	88
Philadelphia	4.7	78
Detroit	4.4	88
San Francisco	3.3	71
Washington	3.1	71
Dallas	3.0	78
Houston	2.9	74
Boston	2.8	77
Mean	—	78

Sources. Brazil: Edward E. Telles, "Contato racial no Brasil urbano: Análise da segregação residencial nas quarenta maiores áreas urbanas do Brasil em 1980," in Peggy A. Lovell, ed., Desigualdade racial no Brasil contemporâneo (Belo Horizonte, 1991), table 3, p. 355. United States: Gerald David Jaynes and Robin M. Williams, Jr., eds., A Common Destiny: Blacks and American Society (Washington. 1989), table 2-5, pp. 78–79.

than in the United States. *Pretos* are somewhat more segregated from whites than are *pardos*, particularly in the North and Northeast (Fortaleza, Belem, Recife); and the Northeastern city of Salvador, often referred to as the capital of Afro-Brazil, emerges as the most residentially segregated of Brazilian cities. But overall residential segregation is only about half as high for Brazilian *pardos* as for Afro-Americans, and 60 per cent as high for *pretos*.[29]

Demographic Indicators

Black life expectancy has consistently lagged behind white in both Brazil and the United States. As in regional distribution, however, the United States began from a position of greater inequality in the first half of the 1900s and moved to a position of lesser inequality by 1980. In 1950 the difference between white and black life expectancy in the United States was 8.3 years, while in Brazil it was 7.5 years. By 1980 life expectancy in both countries had increased, and black/white differentials had declined. However, the decline had been more rapid in the United States, where the difference between white and black life expectancy was now 6.3 years, than in Brazil, where it was 6.7.

A similar trend appears in fertility rates, where racial differentials were greater in the United States up until 1960, after which they were greater—much greater, in fact—in Brazil. In the United States, total fertility rates (total number of children born per woman) rose rapidly for both races during the baby boom years of the late 1940s and 1950s, and then declined sharply during the 1960s and 1970s. In Brazil, rates rose somewhat between 1940 and 1960 (remaining lower for *pretos* than for whites), and then began to decline after 1960. That decline was much more pronounced for the white population than for the *pardos* and *pretos*—reflecting, demographic theorists would argue, Afro-Brazilians' lower levels of education and urbanization. The result was that, by 1984, the differential between white and nonwhite fertility rates in Brazil (1.4 child per woman for *pardos*, 1.3 for *pretos*) was over three times greater than the black/white differential in the United States (.4 child per woman).

Higher fertility rates and lower life expectancies have meant that, in both countries, the black and brown populations tend to be younger than the white

Table 5
Average Life Expectancy, by Race, Brazil and the United States, 1950, 1980

	Brazil			United States		
	White	Black[a]	W-B	White	Black	W-B
1950	47.5	40.0	7.5	69.1	60.8	8.3
1980	66.1	59.4	6.7	74.4	68.1	6.3

[a]*Pardos* and *pretos* combined.

Sources. Brazil: Wood and Carvalho, *Demography of Inequality*, p. 145. United States: USBC, *Statistical Abstract of the United States, 1989* (Washington, 1989), table 106, p. 71.

Table 6

Total Fertility Rates, by Race, Brazil and the United States, 1940–1984

	White	Pardo	Brazil Preto	Pa-W	Pr-W
1940	6.0	6.3	5.5	0.3	−0.5
1950	6.1	6.9	5.8	0.8	−0.3
1960	6.2	6.9	5.8	0.7	−0.4
1980	3.6	5.6	5.1	2.0	1.5
1984	3.0	4.4	4.3	1.4	1.3

	United States White	Black	B-W
1940	2.2	2.9	0.7
1950	2.9	3.8	0.9
1960	3.5	4.5	1.0
1980	1.8	2.3	0.5
1988	1.7	2.1	0.4

Sources. Brazil: Alícia M. Bercovich, "Considerações sobre a fecundidade da população negra no Brasil," in Peggy A. Lovell, ed., *Desigualdade racial no Brasil contemporâneo* (Belo Horizonte, 1991), p. 312. United States: Reynolds Farley and Walter R. Allen, *The Color Line and the Quality of Life in America* (New York, 1987), pp. 58–62; Gerald David Jaynes and Robin M. Williams, eds., *A Common Destiny: Blacks and American Society* (Washington, 1989), pp. 513–514.

population. From 1940 to the present, racial differences in median age have been greater in the United States than in Brazil, but since 1960 those differences have declined in the former country while increasing in the latter. The difference between white and *preto* median ages remains small, but has changed in direction since 1960, from negative to positive; and by the late 1980s the *pardo*/white differential was pulling close to the American black/white differential. In percentage terms those differentials are already approximately equal: in 1987–1988 the *pardo* median age was 82 percent that of Brazilian whites, while the Afro-American median age was 83 percent that of American whites.

Fertility and median age are indicators in which racial disparities in the United States have declined in recent years while racial disparities in Brazil have tended to increase. The story is different with marriage, the only demographic indicator in which racial differentials have increased in the United States while narrowing in Brazil (Table 7). In 1890 the proportion of the US black population never married was larger than its white counterpart, but only by four percentage points among males, and less than that among females. By 1950 the differential had dropped to 2.7 percentage points, and less than one percentage point among females. Black marriage rates began to drop sharply after 1970, however, and by 1980 the proportion of black males and females never married was 13 percentage

Table 7

Median Age, by Race, Brazil and the United States, 1940-1988

	White	Pardo	Brazil Preto	W-Pa	W-Pr
1940	18.7	18.0	19.2	0.7	-0.5
1950	19.2	17.6	19.7	1.6	-0.5
1960	19.2	17.1	19.7	2.1	-0.5
1980	21.7	18.1	21.6	3.6	0.1
1987	23.7	19.4	23.3	4.3	0.4

	United States White	Black	W-B
1940	29.5	25.3	4.2
1950	30.7	26.1	4.6
1960	30.3	23.5	6.8
1980	31.3	24.9	6.4
1988	33.1	27.3	5.8

Sources. Brazil: 1940, *Recenseamento, 1940*, table 4, pp. 6–7; 1950, *Recenseamento, 1950*, table 5, p. 5; 1960, *Recenseamento, 1960*, table 5, p. 10; 1980, *Recenseamento, 1980*, table 1.4, pages 10–11; 1987, IBGE, *Pesquisa nacional por amostra de domicílios— 1987* (Rio de Janeiro, 1990), Volume 1, table 1, pp. 2–3. United States: 1940–1980, *1980 Census*, 1, B, 1, table 45, pp. 1-42-43; 1988, *Black Population, 1988*, table C, p. 5.

points greater than among their white counterparts.[30] In Brazil, by contrast, racial differentials in marriage had increased between 1890 and 1950 but then declined between 1950 and 1980 as *pardo* and *preto* rates of marriage rose. By 1980 the racial differential between the proportion of females never married was only 3 percentage points for *pardos* and whites, and 6 points for *pretos* and whites.

The decline in black marriage rates in the United States is visible in the differences in family structure in the two countries. Tabulating those living units which qualify as families under the US Census Bureau's definition,[31] we find that, as of the late 1980s, nonwhite families in Brazil were much more likely to be headed by couples than were nonwhite families in the United States (Figure 3). Female-headed households were slightly more numerous among the *pardo* population than among the whites, and almost twice as numerous among *preto* families. But in the United States female-headed households were almost three-and-a-half times more numerous in the black population than in the white.

The demographic indicators examined in this section yield a striking longitudinal comparison. In 1950 the United States was the more racially unequal of the two societies in every area except for marriage. By 1980, this comparative relationship had been reversed on every indicator except for median age. Racial differentials in life expectancy and fertility were now greater in Brazil than in

Table 8
Percentage Distribution, Marital Status by Race and Sex, Brazil and the United States, 1890, 1950, 1980

Brazil

	White Male	White Female	Pardo Male	Pardo Female	Preto Male	Preto Female
1890[a]						
Single	69.3	64.7	72.9	70.2	73.1	73.0
Married	28.1	29.2	24.5	24.1	24.2	22.0
Widowed or divorced	2.7	6.1	2.5	5.6	2.7	5.0
1950[b]						
Single	40.1	32.3	46.0	39.5	47.6	45.7
Married	56.9	58.0	50.6	50.2	48.2	42.4
Widowed or divorced	3.1	9.7	3.5	10.3	4.2	11.9
1980[b]						
Single	N.A.	30.3	N.A.	33.4	N.A.	36.6
Married	N.A.	58.0	N.A.	55.1	N.A.	48.1
Widowed or divorced	N.A.	11.6	N.A.	11.5	N.A.	15.3

United States

	White Male	White Female	Black Male	Black Female
1890[a]				
Single	61.7	55.8	65.7	59.3
Married	35.4	37.1	31.6	31.7
Widowed or divorced	2.8	7.0	2.6	8.9
1950[c]				
Single	26.0	20.0	28.7	20.8
Married	68.0	66.2	64.1	62.0
Widowed or divorced	6.0	13.8	7.2	17.2
1980[b]				
Single	28.2	21.2	41.1	34.4
Married	64.0	59.2	48.8	43.8
Widowed or divorced	7.8	19.6	10.2	21.8

[a]Percentage of total population
[b]Percentage of population aged 15 or over
[c]Percentage of population aged 14 or over

Sources. Brazil: 1890, *Synopse, 1890*, pp. 2–3; 1950, *Recenseamento, 1950*, table 7, pp. 6–7; 1980, Elza Berquó, "Demografia da desigualdade," *Novos Estudos CEBRAP* 21 (July, 1988), table 4, p. 78. United States: 1890, *Negro Population, 1790–1915*, table 4, p. 238; 1950, *Census, 1950*, 2, 1, table 46, p. 1–97; 1980, *1980 Census*, 1, B, 1, table 46, pp. 1-45-46.

Figure 3

Percentage Distribution of Family Heads, by Race,
Brazil, 1987, and the United States, 1988

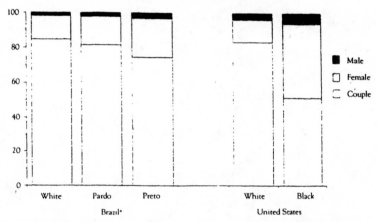

■ Male

□ Female

⊏ Couple

White   Pardo   Preto   White   Black

Brazil*   United States

*Brazilian percentages calculated excluding 2.2 million families (6.9 percent of total) for whom family head was not specififed.

Sources. Brazil: *Pesquisa nacional, 1987,* 1, table 20, p. 26. United States: *Black Population, 1988,* table E, p. 8.

the United States, and racial differentials in marriage were now greater in the United States than in Brazil. In the area of median age as well, the relative relationship which had existed in 1950 appeared close to reversal by the end of the 1980s, as American racial differentials fell from the peak recorded in 1960 and Brazilian differentials continued to rise.

Education

Brazil and the United States share very different historical traditions of public education. In the United States the provision of education has been one of the primary obligations of state and local governments. Only since World War II, however, have Brazilian governments assumed extensive responsibility for educating the nation's citizenry. The result, when combined with Brazil's lower levels of economic development, has been that Brazilians have had much more restricted access to classroom instruction than has been the case in the United States.[32] While most adult Americans, black or white, are high school graduates, the average white adult Brazilian has completed less than four years of schooling, and the average nonwhite less than two (Figure 4). Since the absolute levels of education in the two countries are thus quite different, racial disparities in education will be measured not by subtracting black rates from white, as in

Table 9
Percentage Literate by Race, Brazil and the United States, 1910–1987

	Brazil[a]			United States[b]	
	White	Pardo	Preto	White	Black
1910	N.A.	N.A.	N.A.	95.0	69.6
1930	N.A.	N.A.	N.A.	97.3	83.7
1940	52.8	29.3	20.9	N.A.	N.A.
1950[c]	59.3	31.1	26.7	98.0	89.0
1987	87.7	71.0	70.5	N.A.	N.A.

[a] Percentage of population aged 10 and over.

[b] 1910, 1930: percentage of population aged 10 or over; 1950 (1947): percentage of population aged 14 or over.

[c] United States data from 1947

Sources. Brazil: 1940, Recenseamento, 1940, table 17, pp. 28–29; 1950, Recenseamento, 1950, table 17, p. 20–21; 1987, Pesquisa nacional, 1987, 1, table 2, p. 4. United States: 1910, Negro Population, 1790–1915, table 1, p. 404; 1930, Fifteenth Census of the United States, 1930 (Washington, 1933), Volume 2, table 4, p. 1223; 1950 (1947), Black Population, 1790–1978, table 68, p. 91.

previous sections, but by looking at black rates as a proportion of white rates. (This same procedure will be used in the next section when we examine racial differentials in earnings.)

Indicative of the differences in educational attainment in the two countries is the fact that the achievement of basic literacy remains a serious problem in Brazil. As recently as 1950 forty percent of the white population, and the great majority of nonwhites (69 percent of pardos and 73 percent of pretos), were illiterate. By 1987 literacy rates had improved substantially for both groups, but brown and black illiteracy was still about 30 percent, more than double the rate for whites.

Brazil's 1987 literacy figures were roughly comparable to those for the United States in 1910, when 95 percent of whites were literate, and 70 percent of blacks. By 1947, the last year in which the Census Bureau gathered racial data on literacy, the black literacy rate was 90 percent of the white rate. In Brazil at that time, as we have seen, the pardo literacy rate was slightly over half the white rate, and the preto rate was 40 percent of the white rate.

Brazil lacks historical data by race on school enrollment and number of years of schooling completed. The 1950 census did, however, include information on the numbers of blacks and whites completing high school and college. These data confirm that secondary and baccalaureate degrees had been obtained by only a small minority of whites, and a minute number of blacks. The rate of high school completion was almost ten times higher for whites than for pardos, and the number of pardo and preto college graduates (3,568 and 448, respectively, in all of Brazil) was too small to generate even a one-decimal-point percentage rate (Table 10).

In the United States at the same time, the proportion of whites completing high school was 2.6 times greater than the proportion of blacks; the proportion of whites completing college was almost three times greater than the proportion of blacks. By 1987, however, black/white differentials in rates of high school graduation had been almost eliminated. Whites were still almost twice as likely as blacks to graduate from college; but blacks had almost quintupled their rate of college completion since 1950, and were now graduating at rates higher than those of Brazilian whites (as had also been the case in 1950).

Absolute rates of increase in the number of *pardos* and *pretos* graduating from high school and college were even more rapid in Brazil than in the United States. Nevertheless, the proportion of white high school graduates in 1987 was still almost 75 percent greater than the proportion of *pardo* graduates, and over two-and-a-half times greater than the proportion of *pretos*. The disparities were even more extreme at the university level, which whites were completing at a rate four-and-a-half times higher than *pardos*, and over nine times higher than *pretos*.

Most Brazilians, however, regardless of race, never get as far as high school. Education for most stops in the fourth grade or before, though even at this level whites receive on average twice as many years of schooling as nonwhites (Figure 4). In the United States that disparity, as of 1987, was three-tenths of a year. This low US differential in years of schooling completed reflects the absence of racial disparities in school enrollment: by 1987 essentially the same proportion of blacks and whites were receiving classroom instruction (Figure 5). In Brazil, rates of enrollment were much lower, especially at the high school and college levels. And a discouraging forecast of the future was the fact that racial disparities

Table 10

Percentage of Population Aged 25 or Over, by Race, Which Had Completed High School or College, Brazil and the United States, 1950, 1987

| | Brazil[a] | | | United States | |
	White	Pardo	Preto	White	Black
1950					
High school	4.9	0.5	0.2	29.0	11.0
College	1.2	0.0	0.0	6.4	2.2
1987					
High school	13.9	8.0	5.3	56.4	52.8
College	9.2	2.0	1.0	20.5	10.7

[a]For 1950, percentage of population aged 15 or over.

Sources. Brazil: *Recenseamento, 1950,* table 20, p.24; 1987, *Pesquisa nacional, 1987,* 1, tables 4–5, p. 7–10. United States: 1950, *Census, 1950,* 2, 1, table 44, p. 1-96; 1987, *Statistical Abstract, 1989,* table 212, p. 131.

Figure 4

Median Years of Schooling, Population Aged 25 or Over, United States, 1950–1987, and Brazil, 1987

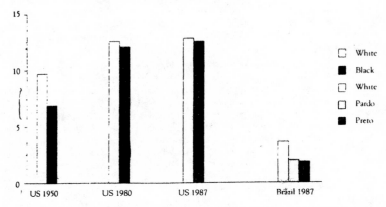

Sources. United States : 1950, *Census, 1950,* 2, 1, table 44, p. 1–96; 1980, *1980 Census,* 1, C, 1, table 83, pp. 21–23; 1987, *Statistica Abstract, 1989,* table 212, p. 131. Brazil: see Table 10.

Figure 5

Percentage of Population Aged 5–24 Enrolled in School, by Race, Brazil, 1987, and the United States, 1980

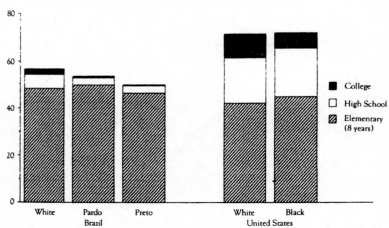

Sources. Brazil: *Pesquisa nacional, 1987,* 1, tables 5, pp. 9–10. United States: *1980 Census,* 1, C, 1, table 123, p. 1–97.

between the white and *pardo* groups were even greater among students currently enrolled (Figure 5) than among past graduates (Table 10). While whites aged 25 or over were 74 percent more likely than *pardos* to have graduated from high school, and 4.6 times more likely to have graduated from college, whites under the age of 25 were 88 percent more likely than *pardos* to be enrolled in high school, and 4.8 times more likely to be enrolled in college. The *preto* population had achieved relatively higher rates of representation among students currently enrolled than among past graduates. But their rates of matriculation still lagged behind those of the *pardos*, which were already quite low.

The United States has a considerable distance yet to go before it can claim full racial equality in the education of its citizens. Racial disparities in test scores, drop-out rates, and college enrollment continue to pose serious obstacles to black upward mobility, as do harder-to-measure differences in the quality of primary and secondary schooling received by blacks and whites.[33] Despite these shortcomings, there is no question that the United States not only provides higher levels of education to its black and white citizens than does Brazil, but has also achieved greater racial equality in the provision of that education.[34]

Jobs and Earnings

Table 11 tabulates changes in rates of economic activity (i.e., participation in the civilian labor market) from 1940 through 1987. The major trend evidenced by those rates, in both countries and among all racial groups, is one of gradually declining participation by males in the labor force, and sharply increasing participation by females. In both countries declines in male participation were greater among nonwhites than among whites and were especially pronounced among Afro-American men, who by 1987 were either employed or seeking work at rates significantly below their white counterparts.[35] In Brazil in the same year, by contrast, rates of labor force participation among white, *pardo*, and *preto* males were more or less equal, with *pretos* only slightly lower than *pardos* and whites.

Increases in female labor force participation in both countries have more than compensated for male withdrawal from the labor market, resulting in increased total rates of participation for all five racial groups. Since 1950, *preta* women in Brazil have taken part in the labor market at rates roughly six percentage points higher than white or *parda* women. In the United States, the gap between black and white female employment, which was almost 10 percentage points in 1950, had been reduced to two percent by the late 1980s, the result of white women entering the labor force in large numbers. By 1987 more than half of black and white women in the United States were either employed or seeking employment, a proportion considerably higher than among Brazilian women.

This higher rate of female labor force participation in the United States, and the greater ability of Afro-American women (as compared to Afro-Brazilians) to obtain jobs and earnings comparable to those of white women, prove to be key factors in explaining how racial inequality in employment and earnings has changed over time in the two countries. Tables 12 and 13 tabulate vocational data from the Brazilian and American censuses of 1950 and 1980 and then use that data to calculate indices of dissimilarity between each racial and gender group (e.g., for Brazil, dissimilarity between whites and *pardos*, whites and *pretos*,

Table 11

Percentage of Civilian Population Economically Active, by Race and Sex, Brazil and the United States, 1940–1987

Brazil[a]

	Total	White Male	Female	Total	Pardo Male	Female	Total	Preto Male	Female
1940	47.6	80.8	14.6	48.6	82.4	16.4	48.9	82.9	16.6
1950	46.1	80.1	13.1	45.6	80.8	11.8	50.2	82.3	19.7
1980	48.8	72.0	27.2	48.2	71.9	24.6	53.0	72.9	33.3
1987	56.9	76.6	38.6	56.8	76.7	37.5	60.2	76.3	44.5

United States[b]

	Total	White Male	Female	Total	Black Male	Female
1940	51.4	78.8	24.1	58.1	79.8	37.3
1950	54.3	81.4	28.9	57.9	79.2	38.5
1980	61.9	75.7	49.3	58.8	65.6	53.1
1987	65.8	76.8	55.7	63.8	71.1	58.0

[a]Percentage of population aged 10 or over.
[b]For 1940, percentage of population aged 14 or over; for 1950–1987, percentage of population aged 16 or over.

Sources. Brazil: 1940, Recenseamento, 1940, table 30, pp. 36–37; 1950, Recenseamento, 1950, table 23, pp. 30–31;1980, special tabulation of the 1980 census provided to the author by IBGE; 1987, Pesquisa nacional, 1987, table 6, p. 11. United States: 1940–1980, 1980 Census, 1, C, 1, table 86, p. 1–26; 1987, Black Population, 1988, table F, p. 9.

white males and pardo males, white males and preto males, white females and parda females, and white females and preta females).[36]

In 1950 the overall index of dissimilarity between black and white workers in the United States was 30.1, almost two-and-a-half times the indices yielded by Brazilian data from that year. When one divides the labor force into gender groups, however, one finds inequality to be twice as high among women as among men. Most of the disparity between white and black women is accounted for by two areas of the labor market: the service sector, where black women were overwhelmingly concentrated; and the white-collar administrative sector, where white women were most heavily represented. Not coincidentally, these two sectors accounted for two-thirds of the overall difference between the black and white racial groups.[37]

By 1980 the index of dissimilarity for the American labor force as a whole had fallen by almost half, and was now lower than the Brazilian indices for that year. This was the result in part of a significant reduction in inequality between black and white males. But even greater progress had been made in the female sector of the labor market, where racial inequality was now approximately one-third what it had been in 1950. Service and clerical jobs remained the areas of greatest disparity. But by 1980 a larger proportion of the black female labor force worked

Table 12

**Percentage Distribution, Civilian Labor Force by Race and Sex,
United States, 1950, 1980**

	Total	White Male	Female	Total	Black Male	Female
1950						
Professions	9.3	7.8	13.3	3.4	2.1	5.6
Administration	22.9	18.3	35.2	5.1	5.0	5.3
Sales	7.6	6.9	9.4	1.2	1.1	1.4
Non-agricultural manual	39.8	46.3	22.2	40.0	52.4	16.8
Service	8.0	5.2	15.3	30.3	14.3	60.2
Agriculture	11.1	14.3	2.8	18.5	23.5	9.1
Other/Unknown	1.3	1.1	1.8	1.5	1.5	1.6
Index of Dissimilarity	—	—	—	30.1	24.8	51.2
1980						
Professions[a]	15.5	14.1	17.6	11.2	7.6	15.0
Administration	27.9	19.6	39.9	22.3	14.6	30.4
Sales	10.5	9.5	11.9	5.0	3.9	6.2
Non-agricultural manual	31.7	44.3	13.7	37.1	53.9	19.5
Service	11.4	8.1	16.1	22.3	16.5	28.3
Agriculture	2.8	4.2	0.9	2.0	3.3	0.6
Other/Unknown	0.0	0.1	0.0	0.1	0.1	0.0
Index of Dissimilarity	—	—	—	16.3	18.0	18.1

[a]Includes technical personnel

Sources. 1950, *Census, 1950,* 2, 1, table 128, pp. 1-276-278; 1980, *1980 Census,* 1, D, 1, table 281, pp. 1-274-285.

in white-collar positions than in service jobs, and the percentage of black men and women working in office jobs had quadrupled since 1950.[38]

Brazil, by contrast, moved in a quite different direction between 1950 and 1980. The country's vocational structure was unmistakably "modernized" during those years: professional and administrative employment expanded exponentially, while agriculture declined sharply in importance. Both those changes, however, redounded disproportionately to the benefit of the white population, which exited agriculture at a much more rapid rate than nonwhites, and seized the new opportunities in white collar office work in much greater numbers than nonwhites. Indeed, in every area of the labor market except for sales and nonagricultural manual labor, racial disparities in employment were greater in 1980 than they had been in 1950.[39]

While those disparities had grown for both *pardos* and *pretos*, the increase was greater among the *pretos*. Gender differences within the *preto* racial group were less pronounced than in 1950, when indices of dissimilarity had been almost three times higher for *preta* women than for *preto* men. But racial inequality was still almost twice as high for *preta* women as for *preto* men, and, as in the United States in 1950, was caused mainly by their over-representation in domestic

Table 13

Percentage Distribution, Civilian Labor Force by Race and Sex, Brazil, 1950, 1980

1950	White			Pardo			Preto		
	Total	Male	Female	Total	Male	Female	Total	Male	Female
Professions	0.7	0.7	0.8	0.1	0.1	0.4	0.1	0.0	0.2
Administration[a]	2.0	1.9	2.4	0.9	0.9	0.5	0.7	0.9	0.1
Sales	8.4	8.8	5.7	3.4	3.6	2.1	2.2	2.5	0.9
Non-agricultural manual	21.3	21.4	20.6	18.3	18.7	15.9	19.6	21.8	11.1
Service	9.3	5.9	29.1	8.9	3.9	41.5	15.2	3.9	59.7
Agriculture	54.8	59.4	27.7	66.8	71.6	35.1	60.6	69.4	25.9
Other/Unknown	3.6	1.9	13.7	1.6	1.2	4.5	1.6	1.4	2.1
Index of Dissimilarity	—	—	—	12.1	12.2	19.8	11.8	10.5	30.6
1980									
Professions[b]	9.0	5.6	17.3	3.8	1.8	9.6	2.5	1.3	5.1
Administration	16.7	15.3	20.1	6.7	6.1	8.5	4.2	4.3	4.0
Sales	9.0	9.0	9.0	6.5	6.3	7.1	4.0	4.2	3.6
Non-agricultural manual	26.0	30.5	14.6	25.6	29.6	13.8	27.9	36.1	10.3
Service	10.7	5.0	24.9	13.0	4.9	37.0	22.6	6.3	57.9
Agriculture	22.7	27.8	9.8	38.6	44.8	20.3	31.5	38.9	15.7
Other/Unknown	6.0	6.7	4.2	5.8	6.5	3.8	7.2	8.9	3.4
Index of Dissimilarity	—	—	—	18.3	17.0	22.5	23.9	20.2	38.9

[a]State administration only; includes public school teachers
[b]Includes technical personnel

Sources: 1950, Recenseamento, 1950, table 23, pp. 30–31; 1980, special tabulation of the 1980 census, provided to the author by IBGE.

service and under-representation in office work. Statistical rates of vocational inequality in 1980 were actually fairly similar among Afro-American and Afro-Brazilian men, and among Afro-American women and *parda* women. But *preta* women clearly suffered extreme disadvantage in the Brazilian labor market, and it is their much higher rates of inequality vis-à-vis white women which put the *preto* racial group as a whole at such disadvantage as compared to whites and *pardos*.

Published data on salary inequality by race have only been available for Brazil since 1976; our discussion of this topic is therefore less historical in character and more focused on current conditions. We begin by contrasting salary data from the American and Brazilian censuses of 1980 (Table 14).[40] As might be expected from the preceding discussion of vocational distribution, the levels of salary inequality revealed in those documents were higher in Brazil than in the United States. Again one is struck by the degree of parity which Afro-American women had achieved with respect to white American women, in contrast to the disparities between white and nonwhite Brazilian women.[41] It is true that, within vocational groups, Afro-Brazilian women tended to earn salaries closer to those of their white counterparts than did Afro-Brazilian males. But this reflects the fact that in both countries gender inequality in earnings was greater than racial inequality, which resulted in lower earnings for white women than for nonwhite men in the same vocational category. And since *parda* and *preta* women were so heavily concentrated in low-paying agricultural and service occupations, their total median earnings lagged far behind even those of white women.

Salary inequality among males was somewhat similar in the two countries. In the United States in 1980, Afro-American men earned on average 69 percent of the salaries earned by white males; in Brazil, *preto* males earned 63 percent of the salaries received by white males, and *pardo* males earned 60 percent. For both *pardo* and *preto* men, inequality was most pronounced in white-collar employment: the professions, administrative positions, and sales. A similar pattern obtained in the United States, where, except for agriculture, salary inequality was greatest for black men in the professions, managerial positions, and sales. But Afro-Americans in these positions still earned, on average, a higher proportion of white median earnings than did nonwhite males in Brazil.

Table 15 extends the salary comparison into the late 1980s, presenting total nonwhite median earnings as a fraction of white median earnings, for the racial group as a whole and by gender. For the period 1980–1987, the data show quite similar increases in earnings inequality among nonwhite males in both Brazil and the United States. *Parda* and Afro-American women also lost ground during this period, while *preta* women improved their relative position vis-à-vis white women. In terms of the nonwhite racial groups as a whole, salary inequality remained more or less constant for the *pardos* and *pretos* of Brazil, while increasing slightly for Afro-Americans.

A final economic indicator on which comparative data are available is the proportion of families living in poverty (Figure 6). In the United States this indicator is determined by a formula which takes into account the size and composition of families. The Brazilian government does not make such calculations, but it does designate a "minimum salary" which in theory represents an income

Table 14
Median Earnings[a] by Race, Sex, and Vocational Category, Brazil 1980, and the United States, 1979

Brazil

	White		Pardo		Preto	
	Male	Female	Male	Female	Male	Female
Professions[b]	$509	$181	.48	.52	.42	.67
Administration	312	176	.62	.70	.50	.72
Sales	198	101	.58	.72	.49	.78
Non-agricultural manual[c]	141	90	.82	.68	.83	.89
Service	109	51	.81	.78	.82	.90
Agriculture	64	0	.79	[d]	.85	[d]
Total	$140	$ 97	.60	.53	.63	.55

United States

	White		Black	
	Male	Female	Male	Female
Professions/Technical				
Professions	$20,181	$11,034	.73	1.09
Technical	16,317	9,443	.83	1.08
Administration				
Managerial	21,694	11,113	.72	1.06
Clerical	14,732	8,107	.78	1.07
Sales	15,454	4,739	.65	1.02
Non-agricultural manual				
Skilled	15,525	8,273	.77	.97
Semi-and unskilled	12,508	6,922	.82	1.00
Service	8,393	3,828	.88	1.26
Agriculture	8,073	3,499	.72	.85
Total	$15,126	$ 7,251	.69	1.00

[a]For both countries, white median earnings expressed in current U.S. dollars; nonwhite median earnings expressed as a fraction of white median earnings for the same vocational category and gender group. U.S. figures are annual earnings; Brazilian figures are monthly earnings

[b]Includes technical personnel

[c]Industry and construction only

[d]Nonwhite females' median earnings in agriculture: *pardas*, U.S. $19 per month; *pretas*, U.S. $28 per month.

Sources. Brazil: Special tabulation of the 1980 census, provided to the author by IBGE. United States: *1980 Census*, 1, D, 1, table 281, pp. 1-274-285.

Table 15

Nonwhite Median Earnings as a Fraction of White Median Earnings, by Sex,
Economically Active Population, Brazil and the United States, 1980, 1987

| | Brazil | | | | | | United States | | |
| | | Pardo | | | Preto | | | Black | |
	Total	Male	Female	Total	Male	Female	Total	Male	Female
1980	.57	.60	.53	.57	.63	.55	.78	.69	1.00
1987	.57	.56	.52	.58	.58	.58	.76	.63	.98

Sources. Brazil: 1980, see previous table; 1987, *Pesquisa nacional, 1987*, 1, table 9, p. 14.
United States: 1980, see previous table; 1987, *Black Population, 1988*, table H, p. 14.

sufficient to support a working-class family. It is well known in Brazil, however,
that the minimum salary is inadequate for that purpose. I have therefore doubled
that figure to produce an approximate indicator of what, by American standards,
would still constitute acute poverty.[42]

The absolute racial differentials in the number of families living in poverty
are quite similar: in the United States the difference between the proportion of
black and white families falling below the poverty line is 22 percentage points;
in Brazil the racial disparity is 20 percent between white and *pardo* families,
and 22 percent between white and *preto* families. But as Figure 6 indicates, the
proportion of all families living in poverty is much greater in Brazil than the
United States. If we adopt the proportional method used above to compare

Figure 6

**Percentage of Families Living in Poverty, by Race,
Brazil and the United States, 1987**

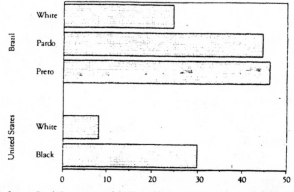

Sources. Brazil: *Pesquisa nacional, 1987*, 1, table 21, p. 27. United States: *Black Population, 1988*, table 1, p. 16.

earnings, we find that black families in the United States are 3.6 times more likely than white families to suffer poverty status. This is double the figure for Brazil, where *pardo* families are 1.8 times more likely than whites to live in destitution, and *preto* families 1.9 times more likely. Thus while racial inequality in labor force earnings is greater in Brazil, racial inequality in rates of poverty is greater in the United States. However, Brazil's greater equality in this area is in some senses a purely negative achievement, reflecting the much higher likelihood that Brazilian whites, in comparison to American whites, will spend some part, or all, of their lives in poverty.

Conclusions

From 1890 to 1960, racial differentials in the United States exceeded racial differentials in Brazil on almost every indicator for which data are available: regional distribution, life expectancy, fertility, median age, and vocational distribution. The only areas in which racial disparities were lower in the United States than in Brazil were marriage (1890, 1950) and educational achievement (literacy, and rates of high school and college graduation, 1950).

By 1980 the statistical comparison of racial differences in the two countries no longer favored Brazil. Indicators of educational achievement (literacy, enrollment, and graduation), which had shown Brazil to be more unequal than the United States in 1950, showed the same relationship in the 1980s. More strikingly, almost all of the indicators on which in 1950 the United States had ranked as a more unequal society than Brazil—regional distribution, life expectancy, fertility, and vocational distribution—had reversed direction, now showing greater inequality in Brazil. Only in marriage patterns did the reversal of indicators between 1950 and 1980 work to Brazil's advantage, indicating greater inequality in the United States.

Several new indicators (i.e., indicators for which comparative data were unavailable in 1950) also showed lower inequality in Brazil than in the United States. These included urban residential segregation, family structure, and poverty. They were balanced, however, by other new indicators—school enrollment, median years of schooling, and earnings—which showed greater equality in the United States.

Clearly a major transition had taken place between 1950 and 1980. While most measures of racial inequality had declined markedly in the United States, the same measures in Brazil had tended either to remain stable, or in some cases—most notably vocational distribution—actually to increase. As a result, by 1980 the two countries had reversed position, with the United States now ranking as the more racially equal of the two societies. Several of the comparative observers of the 1940s, 50s, and 60s had predicted a gradual convergence of Brazilian and American race relations in the second half of the century.[43] None had foreseen, however, that the two countries might pass the point of convergence and then continue on their separate ways, the United States toward less inequality and Brazil toward more. What caused this transition? Several factors appear to have been operating, some revealed by the comparative analysis in this essay, some suggested by other research on the two countries.

Migration, or the lack thereof, from economically backward regions to regions offering greater opportunities for education, employment, health care, etc., played a central role in either reducing or maintaining racial disparities in the two countries.[44] Afro-Americans' long-term movement out of the underdeveloped, segregationist South into the industrial cities of the North contributed directly to the improvements in black earnings and educational and vocational achievement registered since the 1930s. In Brazil, by contrast, the racial characteristics of interregional migration were quite different. *Pardos* did move out of the Northeast to the South and West, but at lower rates than whites, with the result that by 1980 Afro-Brazilians were far more likely than Euro-Brazilians to suffer the ill effects of the Northeast's continuing poverty.

A second factor contributing to the transition has been the character of economic growth in the two countries, and the income-concentrating effects of such growth in Brazil. As we have seen, Brazil experienced remarkable economic expansion between 1950 and 1980, from which all sectors of Brazilian society benefitted to some degree.[45] But those benefits tended to flow disproportionately to the top 20 percent of Brazilian society: the upper and middle classes, which were overwhelmingly white in composition. The absence of published racial data on earnings from 1950 or 1960 makes it impossible to say whether racial differentials in income increased during this period.[46] But vocational inequality clearly worsened, and racial disparities in education remained very high. These formed unlikely conditions for closing the racial gaps documented in 1950; and indeed, by 1980 those gaps had tended either to remain stable or to widen.

In the United States, by contrast, income inequality remained at significantly lower levels than in Brazil, and actually declined somewhat between 1950 and 1975.[47] This more equitable distribution of the wealth generated by the United States' postwar expansion formed an environment much more conducive to black social and economic advancement, which was already underway in the 1940s and 1950s.[48]

Further promoting that advancement was a third and final factor distinguishing the Brazilian and American experiences: state action at the Federal level to combat racial discrimination. In 1950 most Afro-Americans still lived in the segregationist South; and even those living in the North and West faced systematic and pervasive discrimination. A series of court decisions in the 1950s and 1960s mandating desegregation in education and public facilities, and the passage of the Civil Rights and Economic Opportunity Acts of 1964, struck directly at these racist practices in American life, enabling blacks to take part in postwar economic growth to a degree unprecedented in American history. Not only did racial differentials in income and earnings, education, and vocational achievement decline substantially during this period; analysis by economists and demographers suggests that the role of discrimination in causing the remaining differentials declined as well. Discrimination by no means disappeared during those years (see the studies cited in note 8), but by 1980 its importance as an obstacle to black advancement had been greatly reduced as compared to 1950.[49]

As with migration and income concentration, Brazil's experience with discrimination, and its official response to discrimination, diverge sharply from trends in the United States. While statistical analyses of black/white income inequality in the United States from 1960 to 1980 show discrimination declining in importance as a determinant of such inequality, similar work on Brazil shows just the opposite. In both countries, research of this sort measures the proportion of the income gap which can be explained by "compositional" differences in the black and white populations—differences in age, education, family background, region of residence, etc.—and attributes the unexplained residual to racial discrimination. In 1960 17 percent of the disparity between white and nonwhite incomes in Brazil was left unexplained by "compositional" differences; by 1980, that proportion had risen to 32 percent, suggesting that the role of discrimination in creating racial differentials in earnings had almost doubled during those twenty years.[50]

These data support predictions made by several observers in the 1950s and 1960s that Brazil's apparently harmonious race relations were likely to deteriorate as growth and modernization generated more opportunities for upward mobility and thus for more intense social and economic competition among Brazilians seeking to seize those opportunities. The intensity of the competition created strong incentives for some whites, particularly within the middle class, to attempt to use racial barriers as a means of barring Afro-Brazilians from the contest, thus reserving opportunities for upward mobility for themselves and their children.[51]

Afro-Brazilians responded to the rising discrimination of the 1960s and 1970s by demanding equal access to education, employment, and the other goods created by modern industrial society—by demanding, in short, that Brazilian society live up to the national ideology of racial democracy By 1980 middle-class Afro-Brazilians, angered by the racial exclusion which they were confronting in their efforts to move upward in Brazilian society, had joined together to create a political movement inspired in part by the American civil rights and black power movements.[52] Noting the impacts of anti-discrimination legislation in the United States, black activists focused their efforts on enacting similar laws and programs in Brazil. They pointedly criticized the anti-discrimination statute of 1951, the Afonso Arinos Law, which, mainly because of its lack of enforcement provisions, has been notoriously ineffective in combatting even well-publicized cases of bias in employment, education, and public services.[53] Some black politicians also lobbied for equal opportunity and affirmative action legislation of the sort enacted in the United States during the 1960s.

The black movement's proposals generated some scattered response at the state level, particularly in Rio de Janeiro, where Governor Leonel Brizola was elected to office in 1982 on a program of *socialismo moreno* (literally, "brown socialism"). But they have been rejected at the Federal level, and denounced both as "reverse racism" and as an imported, alien concept inappropriate for Brazil.[54] The official ideology of racial democracy, and Brazilian elites' deep-seated resistance to redistributive policies of any sort, explain much of the resistance to the movement's demands. But it is also instructive to note how differences in the two countries' structural situations in the 1960s and 1980s helped determine their respective responses to calls for equal opportunity and affirmative action.

Those programs were enacted in the United States after twenty years of robust economic growth, with the promise of more to come. The resulting mood of prosperity and expansion made it possible for white Americans to acquiesce in the broadening of opportunity to the nation's racial minorities, who at that time constituted less than one-eighth of the national population. Nonwhites in Brazil, by contrast, compose almost half of the national population. And the Brazil of the 1980s, unlike the United States of the 1960s, was in the grip of a profound economic crisis which has continued unabated into the 1990s.[55] In such a setting of scarcity and widespread anxiety, whites have little incentive to accept proposals for them to share the limited opportunities available with that near-majority of the population which is nonwhite. The Brazilian pie is seen as simply too small to be parcelled out among a greatly expanded number of would-be consumers.

Of course such feelings are by no means limited to Brazil. By 1980 American voters and politicians were also questioning the concept of affirmative action, as well as socially redistributive policies more generally. The result, following the presidential elections of that year, was a sharp redefinition of Federal policy which reversed previous governmental efforts to reduce racial inequality.[56]

Recent structural changes in the American economy have also worked against the further reduction of black/white disparities. The movement of Afro-Americans out of the South and into Northern cities, which in any case had come to an end by 1970, lost its previous positive effects as urban economic conditions deteriorated in the 1970s and 1980s. Reductions in manufacturing employment struck hard at black male workers, and especially young black males, whose levels of employment and earnings dropped far below those of their white counterparts.[57]

Declining industrial employment, and declining real wages at lower skill levels of the economy, were part of a larger trend obstructing further reduction in racial disparities: the concentration of wealth and income which took place in American society during the 1980s. After dropping slightly from 1950 through 1975, income concentration in the United States began to increase in the late 1970s and then jumped sharply in the 1980s.[58] As in Brazil, such increases had a particularly negative effect on the black population. In employment, earnings, and even higher education, the rate of reduction in racial inequality had slowed appreciably during the second half of the 1970s; it came to a halt, and on some indicators—most notably earnings and life expectancy—was actually reversed during the 1980s.[59]

Factors which had made major contributions to the reduction of American racial inequality between 1950 and 1980—migration and urbanization of the black population, non-income-concentrating economic growth, Federal policy in the area of race—were either no longer in place by the 1980s, or had exhausted their positive effects. Further reductions in such inequality therefore seem unlikely in the 1990s, and the possibility of widening racial disparities is very real.

Forces tending to reduce racial inequality are even less in evidence in Brazil than in the United States. A contrarian view, however, would note that Brazil has yet to experience the positive effects of reductions in regional, class, and urban/rural inequality. Should future governments succeed in reducing some of the severe disparities between Northeast and Southeast, between city and countryside, between rich and poor, the indirect impacts on racial inequality would be substantial. And should future governments undertake as well to confront racial discrimination in employment and education, Brazil would almost certainly resume its pre-1950 position as the more racially equal—or perhaps better put, the less unequal—of the two societies. But until such changes occur, the United States will provide more convincing evidence of racial democracy than will Brazil.

Department of History
Pittsburgh, PA 15260

ENDNOTES

The author wishes to acknowledge helpful criticisms of earlier drafts of this paper by Seymour Drescher, John Komlos, Peggy Lovell, Peter Stearns, Roye Werner, and an anonymous JSH reviewer.

1.   George M. Fredrickson, "Comparative History" in Michael Kammen, ed., *The Past Before Us: Contemporary Historical Writing in the United States* (Ithaca, 1980), p. 465.

2.   Stanley B. Greenberg, *Race and State in Capitalist Development: Comparative Perspectives* (New Haven, 1980); George M. Fredrickson, *White Supremacy: A Comparative Study in American and South African History* (New York, 1981); John W. Cell, *The Highest Stage of White Supremacy: The Origins of Segregation in South Africa and the American South* (Cambridge and New York, 1982); George Reid Andrews, "Comparing the Comparers: White Supremacy in the United States and South Africa," *Journal of Social History* 20, 3 (1987), pp. 585–599.

3.   E. Franklin Frazier, "A Comparison of Negro-White Relations in Brazil and in the United States," *Transactions of the New York Academy of Sciences*, Series 2, 6, 7 (1944), pp. 251–269; Frank Tannenbaum, *Slave and Citizen* (New York, 1981); John W. 1946); Marvin Harris, *Patterns of Race in the Americas* (New York, 1964); Pierre van den Berghe, *Race and Racism: A Comparative Perspective* (New York, 1967); Carl Degler, *Neither Black nor White: Slavery and Race Relations in Brazil and the United States* (New York, 1971); Thomas Skidmore, "Toward a Comparative Analysis of Race Relations since Abolition in Brazil and the United States," *Journal of Latin American Studies* 4, 1 (1972), pp. 1–28; Robert Brent Toplin, *Freedom and Prejudice: The Legacy of Slavery in the United States and Brazil* (Westport, CT, 1981); I. K. Sundiata, "Late Twentieth Century Patterns of Race Relations in Brazil and the United States," *Phylon* 48, 1 (1987), pp. 62–76.

4.   Slavery was abolished in 1865 in the United States, and in 1888 in Brazil.

5.   See for example Evaristo de Moraes, *Brancos e negros nos Estados Unidos e Brasil* (Rio de Janeiro, 1922); Tannenbaum, *Slave and Citizen*; Donald Pierson, *Negroes in Brazil: A Study of Race Contact in Bahia* (Chicago, 1942); Leslie B. Rout, "Sleight of Hand: Brazilian and American Authors Manipulate the Brazilian Racial Situation, 1910–1951," *The Americas* 29, 4 (1973), pp. 471–488.

6.   Luis de Aguiar Costa Pinto, *O negro no Rio de Janeiro* (São Paulo, 1953); Roger Bastide and Florestan Fernandes, *Relações raciais entre negros e brancos em São Paulo* (São Paulo, 1955); Fernando Henrique Cardoso and Octávio Ianni, *Côr e mobilidade social em Florianópolis* (São Paulo, 1960); Florestan Fernandes, *A integração do negro na sociedade de classes* (São Paulo, 1965); Florestan Fernandes, *The Negro in Brazilian Society* (New York, 1969); Florestan Fernandes, *O negro no mundo dos brancos* (São Paulo, 1972); Degler, *Neither Black nor White*; Carlos Hasenbalg, *Discriminação e desigualdades raciais no Brasil* (Rio de Janeiro, 1979); Pierre-Michel Fontaine, ed., *Race, Class and Power in Brazil* (Los Angeles, 1985); George Reid Andrews, *Blacks and Whites in São Paulo, Brazil, 1888–1988* (Madison, 1991).

7.   Frazier, "Comparison," pp. 268–269; Degler, *Neither Black nor White*, pp. 267–287; Claudia Mitchell-Kernan, "Foreword," in Fontaine, *Race, Class and Power*, p. ix.

8.   Joe R. Feagin, "The Continuing Significance of Race: Antiblack Discrimination in Public Places," *American Sociological Review* 56, 1 (1991), pp. 101–116; Ian Ayres, "Fair Driving: Gender and Race Discrimination in Retail Car Negotiations," *Harvard Law Review* 104, 4 (1991), pp. 817–873; George Galster, "More than Skin Deep: The Effect of Housing Discrimination on the Extent and Pattern of Racial Residential Segregation in the United States," in John Goering, ed., *Housing Desegregation and Federal Policy* (Chapel Hill, 1986); "When Blacks Shop, Bias Often Accompanies Sale," *New York Times* (April 30, 1991), pp. A1, A14; "Study Finds Bias in House Hunting," *New York Times* (September 1, 1991), p. 14.

9.   Brazil's 1990 census was postponed to 1991; its results were therefore not available for use in this article.

10.   "To attain a situation of complete racial equality, it is necessary that the two [white and nonwhite] racial groups be equally distributed along the social and economic hierarchy." Carlos Hasenbalg and Nelson do Valle Silva, *Estrutura social, mobilidade e raça* (Rio de Janeiro, 1988), p. 140.

11.   Werner Baer, *The Brazilian Economy: Growth and Development* (New York, 1989), p. 68; United States Bureau of the Census (hereafter USBC), *Historical Statistics of the United States: Colonial Times to 1970* (Washington, 1975), pp. 238–240.

12.   Instituto Brasileiro de Geografia e Estatística (hereafter IBGE), *Estatísticas históricas do Brasil 3* (Rio de Janeiro, 1987), table 4.7, pp. 111–112; George Thomas Kurian, *The New Book of World Rankings* (New York, 1984), p. 199.

13.   US data from USBC, *Statistical Abstract of the United States: 1990* (Washington, DC, 1990), table 695, p. 428; Brazilian data from Baer, *Brazilian Economy*, p. 102; Inter-American Development Bank, *Social and Economic Progress in Latin America: 1989 Report* (Washington, 1990), table B-1, p. 463. Per capita GNP in 1988 was $2,449 in Brazil, $19,810 in the United States.

14.   Charles H. Wood and José Alberto de Magno Carvalho, *The Demography of Inequality in Brazil* (Cambridge and New York, 1988).

15.   Simon Kuznets, "Economic Growth and Income Inequality," *American Economic Review* 45, 1 (1955), pp. 1–28; Kuznets, *Modern Economic Growth* (New Haven, 1966); Montek S. Ahluwalia, "Inequality, Poverty and Development," *Journal of Development Economics* 3, 4 (1976), pp. 307–342; Peter H. Lindert and Jeffrey G. Williamson, "Growth, Equality, and History," *Explorations in Economic History* 22 (1985), pp. 341–377.

16.   Jeffrey G. Williamson and Peter H. Lindert, *American Inequality: A Macroeconomic History* (New York, 1980), pp. 82–94; Kevin Philips, *The Politics of Rich and Poor: Wealth and the American Electorate in the Reagan Aftermath* (New York, 1990), pp. 8–25, 185–209; Andrew J. Winnick, *Toward Two Societies: The Changing Distribution of Income and Wealth in the U.S. since 1960* (New York, 1989).

17.   The relative decline in the US white population accelerated between 1980 and 1990. By 1990 the US population was 80.3 percent white, 12.1 percent black, and 7.6 percent "other." "Census Shows Profound Change in Racial Makeup of the Nation," *New York Times* (March 11, 1991), pp. A1, B8. It is worth noting that the Afro-Brazilian population is considerably larger than the Afro-American population. In 1980, the year of the last Brazilian census, Afro-Brazilians numbered 53.3 million, versus 26.5 million Afro-Americans. Afro-Brazilians constitute the second-largest black population in the world, exceeded in size only by Nigeria.

18. Table 1 employs data from the United States census of 1860 for two reasons. First, because of unsettled conditions in the South following the Civil War, the census of 1870 suffered from large undercounts of both the black and white populations in that region. Second, the 1872 Brazilian census and the 1860 United States census are the last enumerations of those countries' national populations while slavery was still in existence.

19. IBGE, Recenseamento geral de 1940. Censo demográfico: Estados Unidos do Brasil (Rio de Janeiro, 1950), table 4, pp. 6–7; IBGE, Recenseamento geral de 1950. Censo demográfico: Estados Unidos do Brasil (Rio de Janeiro, 1956), table 5, p. 5. Between 1940 and 1950 the analogous preto cohort declined from 4.2 million to 3.0 million, a rate of decline far beyond that expected for such a young population. Had the preto cohort declined at the same rate as the white cohort during this period, it would have contained 800,000 more people than the number indicated in the census of 1950—a shortfall almost equivalent to the increase in the pardo cohort.

20. Charles H. Wood, "Categorias censitárias e classificações subjetivas de raça no Brasil," in Peggy A. Lovell, ed., Desigualdade racial no Brasil contemporâneo (Belo Horizonte, 1991).

21. USBC, Negro Population in the United States, 1790–1915 (Washington, 1918), pp. 207–209.

22. Degler, Neither Black nor White, p. 224. See also Harris, Patterns of Race, pp. 54–94; Gilberto Freyre, The Mansions and the Shanties: The Making of Modern Brazil (New York, 1963), pp. 354–399.

23. Nelson do Valle Silva, "Black-White Income Differentials in Brazil, 1960" (Ph.D. dissertation, University of Michigan, 1978), p. 143. See also Nelson do Valle Silva, "Updating the Cost of Not Being White in Brazil," and Carlos Hasenbalg, "Race and Socioeconomic Inequalities in Brazil," in Fontaine, Race, Class and Power; Lúcia Elena Garcia de Oliveira et al., O lugar do negro na força de trabalho (Rio de Janeiro, 1985). A slightly dissenting voice is Peggy Lovell, who finds "crucial differences between blacks and mulattoes" in the Brazilian labor market. Nevertheless, she concludes that "the major dividing line [in salary inequality] falls between whites and nonwhites (hence confirming Silva's findings)." Peggy A. Lovell, "Racial Inequality and the Brazilian Labor Market" (Ph.D. dissertation, University of Florida, 1989), pp. 152–153.

24. The index of dissimilarity is a commonly used measure of inequality or difference between two populations. In the case of Table 2, it measures differences in the regional distributions of whites and non-whites; in Table 4 it measures racial differences in distribution among neighborhoods within cities; and in Tables 12 and 13 it measures racial differences in distribution among vocational groups. The index is calculated by summing the absolute values of the differences in distribution for each category (for Table 2, region; for Table 4, neighborhood; for Tables 12 and 13, vocational group) and dividing by two. It thus indicates the percentage of individuals in either racial group who would have to move from one category to another (in the case of Table 2, from one region to another) in order to produce complete equality. An index of 100 indicates total difference, or complete inequality; an index of 0 indicates no difference whatsoever, and therefore complete equality. See Henry S. Shryock and Jacob Siegel, The Methods and Materials of Demography (Washington, 1973), pp. 232–33; Reynolds Farley and Walter R. Allen, The Color Line and the Quality of Life in America (New York, 1987), p. 140.

25. IBGE, Pesquisa nacional por amostra de domicílios—1987. Cor da população (Rio de Janeiro, 1990), Volume 1, pp. 82, 90, 122, 130.

26. Gavin Wright, Old South, New South: Revolutions in the Southern Economy since the Civil War (New York, 1986), pp. 239–274.

27. Black workers in the South earned median incomes of $7,902, versus $9,391 for black workers in the North and West. The comparable figures for white workers were $12,109 in the South, $12,785 in the North and West (Southern earnings 95 percent of North and Western earnings.) These data, and those in text, from USBC, *Current Population Reports*, Series P-20, No. 442, *The Black Population in the United States: March 1988* (Washington, 1989), tables 6–7, pp. 25–29. Note that this publication's figures for years of schooling completed are somewhat lower than those reported in another Census Bureau publication, the *Statistical Abstract of the United States* (Figure 4).

28. In 1980, median per capita monthly income for the Brazilian population aged 10 or over was $36 per month in urban areas, and $0 in the countryside. IBGE, *Censo demográfico—Mão de obra—Brasil, 1980* (Rio de Janeiro, 1983), table 1.6, p. 28. In urban areas the median number of years of schooling completed was 3.1; in the countryside the median number of years is impossible to determine from published data, because most ruralites (57 percent) are indicated as having received "no instruction or less than one year." IBGE, *Censo demográfico—dados gerais, migração, instrução, fecundidade, mortalidade—Brasil, 1980* (Rio de Janeiro, 1983), table 1.5, p. 12. In 1987 81 percent of urban residents lived in homes with piped running water, and 96 percent had electricity. In the countryside, only 29 percent had running water, and 45 percent had electricity. IBGE, *Pesquisa nacional—1987*, 1, table 25, pp. 38–39.

29. For more discussion of residential segregation in the two countries, see Edward E. Telles, "Contato racial no Brasil urbano: Análise da segregação residencial nas quarenta maiores áreas urbanas do Brasil em 1980," in Lovell, *Desigualdade racial*; Douglas S. Massey and Nancy A. Denton, "Trends in the Residential Segregation of Hispanics, Blacks, and Asians, 1970–1980," *American Sociological Review* 44 (1987), pp. 802–824.

30. On declining black marriage rates since 1970, see Reynolds Farley, *Blacks and Whites: Narrowing the Gap?* (Cambridge, MA, 1984), p. 135. On the heated debate over the causes of that decline, see Gerald David Jaynes and Robin M. Williams, Jr., eds., *A Common Destiny: Blacks and American Society* (Washington, 1989), pp. 526–546.

31 "A group of two persons or more, related by birth, marriage, or adoption and residing together." *Black Population, 1988*, p. 34; Jaynes and Williams, *Common Destiny*, p. 519.

32. On education in Brazil, see Robert J. Havighurst and J. Roberto Moreira *Society and Education in Brazil* (Pittsburgh, 1965); and Cláudio de Moura Castro, "What Is Happening in Brazilian Education?" in Edmar Lisboa Bacha and Herbert S. Klein, eds., *Social Change in Brazil, 1945–1985: The Incomplete Transition* (Albuquerque, 1989).

33. Jaynes and Williams, *Common Destiny*, pp. 329–389; Farley and Allen, *Color Line*, pp. 188–208.

34. On the question of race in the Brazilian educational system, see *Raça negra e educação, Cadernos de Pesquisa (Fundação Carlos Chagas)* 63 (1987); and Carlos A. Hasenbalg and Nelson do Valle Silva, "Raça e oportunidades educacionais no Brasil," in Lovell, *Desigualdade racial*, pp. 241–262.

35. Conservative analysts (e.g., Charles Murray, *Losing Ground: American Social Policy, 1950–1980* [New York, 1984]) have argued that declines in black male economic activity were caused by the expanded social programs and transfer payments of the 1960s and 1970s; their critics (e.g., William Wilson, *The Truly Disadvantaged: The Inner City, the Underclass, and Public Policy* [Chicago, 1987]) stress structural changes in the American economy and declining employment opportunities for less educated, lower-skill laborers. On this debate see Jaynes and Williams, *Common Destiny*, pp. 301–312; Farley and Allen, *Color Line*, pp. 241–250; James P. Smith and Finis R. Welch, "Black Economic Progress after Myrdal," *Journal of Economic Literature* 27, 2 (June 1989), pp. 548–551.

36. As indicated in note 24, this index indicates differences in distribution among the various vocational categories.

37. The index of dissimilarity between whites and blacks in 1950 was 30.1; 20.1 of those points are accounted for by the differences in black and white representation in administrative and service occupations.

38. On changes in vocational distribution in recent decades, see Jaynes and Williams, *Common Destiny*, pp. 272–277; Farley and Allen, *Color Line*, pp. 256–282; Smith and Welch, "Black Economic Progress"; and Bart Landry, *The New Black Middle Class* (Berkeley, 1987). Racial differentials in vocational distribution remained more or less stable during the 1980s; the index of dissimilarity for 1987 was 16.1. "Household Data Annual Averages," *Employment and Earnings* 35, 1 (1988), table 21, p. 180.

39. The Brazilian national household survey of 1987 provides additional, more recent data on vocational distribution. However, it did not canvass rural areas in the northern states and thus lacks nationally comprehensive data for agricultural workers, who, as the census of 1980 indicates, are still a major component of the Brazilian labor force. This precludes the calculation of indices of total vocational inequality for that year; but indices restricted to vocational categories other than agriculture show further slight increases between 1980 and 1987 for both *pardo*/white and *preto*/white inequality.

40. As indicated in Table 17, white median earnings for both countries are expressed in current (1980 or 1979) US dollars; non-white median earnings are then expressed as a fraction of white earnings for the same vocational category and gender group.

41. Farley and Allen's analysis of wage data from the 1980 census "suggest[s] that black women no longer suffer from racial discrimination in wage rates . . . Black women . . . did not receive lower rates of return than white women. Their wages may be limited once because they are women, but they are not penalized a second time because their skin color is black." Farley and Allen, *Color Line*, p. 340.

42. In September 1987, when the national household survey of th it year was taken, the minimum salary was equivalent to US $41 per month. See also Helga Hoffman, "Poverty and Prosperity in Brazil: What is Changing?", in Bacha and Klein, *Social Change in Brazil*, p. 218, which uses two minimum wages as an indicator of poverty.

43. See note 7.

44. On the United States, see Farley and Allen, *Color Line*, pp. 103–136; Smith and Welch, "Black Economic Progress," pp. 539–547. On Brazil, see Hasenbalg, *Discriminação*, pp. 134–193.

45. Note for example the improvement in black life expectancy during this period, which increased faster in both absolute and relative terms than did white life expectancy (Table 5).

46. Peggy Lovell, working with public use samples from those censuses, argues that such differentials remained constant between 1960 and 1980, with nonwhites earning between 56 and 57 percent of white earnings in both years. Peggy A. Lovell, "Development and Racial Inequality: Wage Discrimination in Urban Labor Markets, 1960–1980" (unpublished paper presented at The Peopling of the Americas Conference, Veracruz, Mexico, 1992). However, her samples are limited to urban male wage-earners and therefore do not take into account the increased disparity (by 1980) between white and nonwhite employment in agriculture, and increased female participation in the labor force. Both these factors would tend to increase overall white/nonwhite earnings inequality.

47. Gini indices of inequality for family income in the United States are as follows: 1950,

.379; 1960, .364; 1970, .354; 1980, .365. USBC, *Current Population Reports*, P-60, 137, *Money Income of Households, Families and Persons in the United States: 1981* (Washington, 1982), table 17, p. 47.

48. Smith and Welch, "Black Economic Progress"; Jaynes and Williams, *Common Destiny*; Farley and Allen, *Color Line*.

49. For statistical analyses of discrimination, see Farley and Allen, *Color Line*, pp. 277–280, 320–342; on the implications of reduced discrimination, see William Julius Wilson, *The Declining Significance of Race in American Life* (2nd edition, Chicago, 1980).

50. Lovell, "Development and Racial Inequality"; for similar findings, see Silva, "Updating the Cost." Compare these findings to Farley and Allen, *Color Line*, pp. 335–342, who report both decreasing disparities between black and white earnings in the United States between 1960 and 1980, and the decreasing importance of discrimination in explaining those disparities. For a description of how discrimination functions in the Brazilian labor market, see Andrews, *Blacks and Whites*, pp. 166–174.

51. Van den Berghe, *Race and Racism*, pp. 70, 74–75; Roger Bastide and Florestan Fernandes, *Brancos e negros em São Paulo* (3rd edition, São Paulo, 1971), pp. 168–169; Degler, *Neither Black nor White*, pp. 284–285; Fernando Henrique Cardoso, "Le préjugé de couleur au Brésil," *Présence africaine* 25 (1965), pp. 120–128.

52. Lélia Gonzalez, "The Unified Black Movement: A New Stage in Black Political Mobilization," in Fontaine, *Race, Class and Power*; Michael George Hanchard, "Orpheus and Power: The Movimento Negro of Rio de Janeiro and São Paulo, Brazil, 1945–1988" (Ph.D. dissertation, Princeton University, 1991), pp. 178–236.

53. Hasenbalg, *Discriminação*, pp. 271–281; Peter R. Eccles, "Culpados até prova em contrário: Os negros, a lei e os direitos humanos no Brasil," *Estudos Afro-Asiáticos* 20 (1991), pp. 135–164. A strengthened version of the Afonso Arinos Law was incorporated into the Constitution of 1988, but the same problems concerning enforcement persist.

54. Andrews, *Blacks and Whites*, pp. 191–207, 221, 226, 241–243.

55. Inflation ran at annual rates of 934 percent in 1988, 1,765 percent in 1989, and 1,795 percent in 1990. "Inflation," *Latin America Weekly Report* (December 26, 1991), p. 6.

56. For an analysis of that redefinition and its impact on a single city, Atlanta, see Gary Orfield and Carole Ashkinaze, *The Closing Door: Conservative Policy and Black Opportunity* (Chicago, 1991). These changes in Federal policy provoked comment in Brazil: see "A volta (discreta) do racismo," *Jornal do Brasil* (September 23, 1987).

57. Jaynes and Williams, *Common Destiny*, pp. 294–312; Smith and Welch, "Black Economic Progress," pp. 541–545.

58. See the sources cited in Figure 1 and note 16.

59. Jaynes and Williams, *Common Destiny*, pp. 271–379 passim; William P. O'Hare et al., *African Americans in the 1990s* (Washington, 1991), pp. 2–4 and passim; "Growing Gap in Life Expectancies of Blacks and Whites," *New York Times* (October 9, 1989), p. A6; "Life Expectancy for Blacks in US Shows Sharp Drop," *New York Times* (November 29, 1990), p. A1.

Turning Weakness Into Strength

The Internationalization of Indian Rights

by
Alison Brysk

Social movement activists of the 1980s urged their constituencies to integrate grass-roots activity and international consciousness with the slogan "Act locally—think globally." But movements to support the rights and better the conditions of indigenous peoples of the Americas have followed the opposite path. A movement that epitomizes "local knowledge" and consciousness has engaged in extensive international activity with surprising success; the anthropologist Stefano Varese has described this as "Think locally, act globally" (NACLA, 1991). How has a movement representing the most marginalized within its own societies been empowered by acting globally? What can a study of the Indian rights experience tell us about social movements and transnational relations?[1]

International relations are an increasingly important determinant of domestic social change, while transnational alliances play a growing role in social movement activity (Alger, 1988). Yet most treatments of social movements are still framed in terms of implicit levels of analysis that subsume domestic protest and reform under relations with the state. These questions assume particular significance in Latin America. Historical patterns of U.S. domination have so thoroughly colored the region's international relations that many scholars treat Latin American international relations as a version of inter-American relations in a way that takes the claims and agenda of the

Alison Brysk is an assistant professor of politics at Pomona College. Her book *The Politics of Human Rights in Argentina* was recently published by Stanford University Press. This article is based on research presented at the 1992 Latin American Studies Convention in Los Angeles. An important source for the research is a series of 22 formal interviews and a number of extended conversations with international Indian rights advocates, adjudicators of international arenas, and allied organizations in New York, Washington, and Boston during May 1992. The essay also draws on attendance and interviews at the United Nations Working Group on Indigenous Peoples in Geneva during July 1993. The author acknowledges the assistance of these informants and the financial support of Pomona College. She thanks Jane Jaquette, Rodolfo Stavenhagen, Melina Selverston, Thomas Risse-Kappen, and Michael Kearney for collegial support and insightful comments. Marc Serrano of the Claremont Graduate School provided much-appreciated research assistance.

LATIN AMERICAN PERSPECTIVES, Issue 89, Vol. 23 No. 2, Spring 1996 38-57
© 1996 Latin American Perspectives

38

state at face value (Brysk, 1992). Within the structure of the current world system, transnationalization represents a contradictory but ultimately constructive strategy for many social movements. Although there has been an explosion of literature on Latin American social movements, few studies explore their transnational dimension.[2] The Indian rights movement, which is highly internationalized, is a promising arena for examining this new kind of relationship. Furthermore, the movement has become internationalized largely through truly transnational relationships with intergovernmental and nongovernmental organizations, creating networks of nonstate actors which operate relatively autonomously of state interests.

Beyond recognizing and documenting the existence of transnational politics for social movements, we must begin to analyze patterns and mechanisms of transnational social change. Why and how do some social movements act globally, and why do some do so more than others? Which characteristics of the international system and the movements themselves influence receptivity to social movement appeals and alliances? Here too, the Indian rights movement is illuminating—in this case, because it presents a paradox. Indian rights represent a *least* likely case for internationalization of a social movement, since Indian peoples are generally powerless and marginalized within their own states. Such a movement faces other obstacles (language, transport, resources, sanctions) that challenge the resource-mobilization perspective that has long dominated analyses of social movements (Tilly, 1978; Gamson, 1975). We will see that the internationalization of Indian rights occurred precisely *because* indigenous social movements were weak domestically; some of their domestic weaknesses actually facilitated transnational alliance building and effectiveness.

The Indian rights movement was able to act globally because it acted as a new social movement based on identity and consciousness rather than objective material position. The new-social-movement perspective depicts social movement activity as the mobilization of identity rather than material resources (Alvarez and Escobar, 1992; Cohen, 1985; Frank and Fuentes, 1990; Kriesi, 1988; Mainwaring and Viola, 1984; Melucci, 1989). A new-social-movement approach thus accounts for the transnational success of conventionally weak movements through a focus on their use of information and images to create and project identity (Brysk, 1993). The current debate within indigenous movements on class versus ethnicity must be informed by a deeper examination of the international power of ethnicity *as a form of information* that has empowered a movement rich in identity but poor in everything else. Transnational mobilization of ethnic group or panindigenous identity could often overcome fragmented and even contradictory local identities based in village, clan, or class (Kearney and Nagengast, 1990).

THE EMERGENCE OF THE INDIAN RIGHTS MOVEMENT

There are about 40 million ethnically indigenous people in Latin America, making up anywhere from less than 1 percent of the population in Brazil to a clear majority in Bolivia or Guatemala. In addition, large numbers of Latin Americans have an indigenous heritage but do not identify themselves as culturally indigenous or live in Indian communities.[3] While these 40 million differ extensively from each other in identifying characteristics such as language, culture, mode of production, urbanization, and degree of assimilation into Latino society, they tend to share a positive identity of cultural difference and a negative status of extreme social marginality.[4] Objectively, Latin American Indians are the poorest, sickest, most abused, and most defenseless members of their societies. Subjectively, peoples with diverse backgrounds and environments share a sense that their relative deprivation is a result of a historical process of ethnic conflict that has disenfranchised a formerly autonomous and nurturing community (Burger, 1987; Martínez Cobo, 1986; Urban and Scherzer, 1991).

Indian peoples have physically resisted Latin domination since the conquest; in Bolivia, Peru, and Guatemala, for example, there have been hundreds of rebellions against minority rule, often involving extensive disruption and attendant casualties (Smith, 1990). But uprisings had generally dwindled to local events by the national period. The Indian rights movement has increasingly reclaimed this history of "500 years of resistance," including the subtle daily contestation of dominant cultural practices through language, religion, dress, and artistic expression (Nash, 1989; Howe, 1991). During the 20th century, Indians' most significant political role had been participation in revolutionary coalitions in Mexico and Bolivia—though even this participation was defined primarily in terms of economic role as peasants rather than indigenous ethnic identity. A formal social movement for Indian rights did not arise until the late 1960s and early 1970s (Stavenhagen, 1988; Chiriboga, 1986; *Cultural Survival Quarterly*, 8[4].)

By the late 1970s a variety of actors had begun to mobilize seeking improvements in the rights and conditions of Latin American Indians. At the local level, a handful of indigenous groups such as the Shuar of Ecuador had formed grassroots associations to promote and defend their interests. In some cases, Indian activists were brought together as they sought relief for local problems through state structures: Peruvian and Colombian activists met in capital city land ministries (interviews July 27 and 29, 1993), while the Brazilian Yanomami shaman Davi Kopenawa Yanomami met the future leader of Brazil's national indigenous movement through Brazil's government Indian agency (interview, July 18, 1993). Internationally, indigenist groups such as the World Council of Indigenous Peoples and Cultural Survival were founded (respectively by and on behalf of indigenous peoples) to address global threats to ethnic identity and group survival. International fora such as the International Labor Organization and transnational nongovernmental organizations such as the World Council of Churches systematically examined indigenous issues within the organizations' wider mandates and brought together Indian activists. For example, Peruvian (and later pan-Amazon) organizer Evaristo Nugkuag stated that the 1980 Russell Tribunal showed him that indigenous problems were global (interview, July 27, 1993).

Since indigenous advocacy developed in a variety of settings and was reacting to a panoply of external threats, specific demands were diverse. But as Indians themselves participated more in the movement, situational goals coalesced around the concept of self-determination. Land rights and access to natural resources were usually a prominent theme, as was relief from human rights abuses. The overarching theme of self-determination encompassed these goals within a framework of local autonomy, cultural survival, and "ethnodevelopment": empowered and informed self-management of cultural and social change (Bonfil Batalla, 1982). Cultural survival in the sense of the preservation of precontact, low-technology indigenous cultures is neither viable nor desired by most groups. Most indigenous people in the Americas have already encountered and been influenced by Western culture; in any case, Indian cultures are not static or primordial but evolve like all others. Even isolated lowland groups generally seek a buffer in their contact with Latino settlers, missionaries, and other intrusive outsiders rather than cultural autarky. The question then becomes who 'manages the pace and content of development so that indigenous peoples can exercise self-determination.

At the same time, Indian political participation has grown in a variety of venues over the past generation, from peasant federations to guerrilla movements to Latino-dominated political parties. Within the Indian community—especially among Andean and urbanized groups—debates rage over the class or ethnic basis of Indian subjugation and thus over the proper political response (Diskin, 1991; Díaz Polanco, 1987; Freeland, 1989). But indigenous rights activism has been more cohesive, effective, and internationally salient than other forms of Indian political participation, in part because of the diversity of peoples such a movement aspires to represent, from hunter-gatherer lowland groups to highland peasants (with varying systems of land tenure) to somewhat acculturated urban marginals to indigenist intellectuals—and even some proletarians. The reduced role of class-based activism by

Indians in Latin America is also due to several issues historically problematic for marxism that are central to Indian identity: land, language, and religion (Nimni, 1991).

The Indian rights movement, then, does not include all forms of political participation by Indians but rather is confined to groups working for principled change in the status and conditions of Indians as a distinct cultural group. This will include local federations such as the Kuna of Panama, cultural reassertion movements like Bolivia's Movimiento Indio Tupac Katari (Tupac Katari Indian Movement—MITKA), peasant movements for which culturally defined land rights are a primary focus (as in Colombia), national indigenous organizations like Brazil's União das Nações Indígenas (Union of Indigenous Nations—UNI), transnational indigenous federations such as the Coordinadora Indígena de la Cuenca Amazónica (Indigenous Coordinator for the Amazon Basin—COICA), and these groups' non-Indian "indigenist" allies (such as the advocacy group Cultural Survival or Brazil's Comisão Pro-Indio).

THE INTERNATIONALIZATION OF INDIAN RIGHTS

The social movement network supporting Indian rights in Latin America is transnational and consequential. Many social movements draw on international resources, alliances, or opportunities; indigenous advocacy differs in degree but not kind from other social movements. The degree of international support for grass-roots social movements is sometimes a politically sensitive point, since target governments often attempt to discredit dissident groups with the claim that they are not authentically indigenous and have been mobilized by "outside agitators." However, nationalist claims of this sort inaccurately depict the domestic political system as closed when historically the state and dominant social groups themselves have usually drawn on significant outside resources. In the case of Indian movements, local Latino elites historically dominated Indian populations through monopoly of access to markets, transport, state services, and other channels of contact with "outsiders" (Evans-Pritchard, 1990). Some Latin American Indian groups first gained access to their own governments through international organizations; the 1940 conference establishing the Organization of American States Inter-American Indigenous Institute mandated the formation of national Indian agencies throughout the Americas. As recently as 1993, indigenous activists attending a Latin American regional caucus at the United Nations Working Group on Indigenous Peoples appealed to their states' diplomatic corps to facilitate access to state agencies at home.

Transnational social movement mobilization is also an appropriate response to increasingly transnational social problems, from development projects sponsored by multinational corporations and multilateral development banks to increasing cultural penetration by missionary groups. Peru's local federation of the "isolated" Amazonian Aguaruna and Guambisa was organized as a direct response to the disruption of indigenous groups by German director Werner Herzog during the filming of *Fitzcarraldo* (interview, July 27, 1993). A group of Ecuador's Amazonian Cofan have recently blockaded multinational oil facilities demanding better compensation and environmental monitoring—led by their designated tribal authority, the son of North American missionaries.

Many if not most indigenous peoples' organizations receive international funding (in Latin America, Cultural Survival, OXFAM America, and the Inter-American Foundation have been important sources). Large numbers of foreign actors converge on particular local situations and conflicts. For example, a 1992 meeting to assess the plight of Ecuador's Huaorani involved representatives from 13 nongovernmental organizations and briefs from 15 others. The United Nations Working Group included delegates from Earth First, the Nature Conservancy, the Indian Law Resource Center, Cultural Survival, the South and Meso-American Indian Information Center, Survival International, the International Working Group on Indigenous Affairs, the Anti-Slavery Society, and the International League for the Rights of Man. Representatives of millions of indigenous peoples regularly mobilize through global, regional, and transnational organizations: the United Nations Working Group on Indigenous Peoples, the COICA, the global Rainforest Peoples Movement, and the 500 Years of Resistance [Anti-Quincentenary] Campaign, among others.

Even the resources donated by foreign supporters to Indian organizations are increasingly resources for transnational activity. International organizations arrange foreign tours by South American Indian leaders (the UN has established a voluntary fund to sponsor indigenous representatives' participation in international meetings). The U.S.-based Indian Law Resource Center has published a handbook for Indian rights activists explaining the organizations, mechanisms, and requirements of the international human rights regime (Indian Law Resource Center, 1988). A coalition of European indigenist advocacy groups regularly lobbies the European Community on investment and human rights issues in indigenous areas. International activists routinely summarize and distribute information through the Indigenous Peoples' Network, a proliferation of newsletters, catalogues, and even Internet electronic bulletin boards. A representative of the World Council of Churches described its early support for indigenous movements in highly international terms: the Council helped indigenous groups through funding international meetings, making groups aware of international opportunities and UN mechanisms, and assisting them in formating information in an internationally effective manner (interview, June 30, 1992).

Indeed, it is often difficult to define the traditional boundaries of a domestic social movement as distinct from its international supporters. The World Council of Churches sponsored the 1971 Barbados Conference that launched the international indigenous rights movement. The movement developed further through a series of conferences for nongovernmental organizations sponsored by the United Nations; Bolivia's Movimiento Revolucionario Tupac Katari was founded after such a conference in 1978. As one scholar of indigenous movements has noted, it is striking that many movements initially developed from local to international before a corresponding national level of organization was established (Stavenhagen, 1988: 153). This pattern extends further: a number of domestic Indian rights groups were established with significant international support (Willetts, 1982). Transnational religious groups (such as the Salesians in Ecuador and the Brazilian Bishops' Conference) have played a prominent role in establishing a number of Indian rights organizations (Stavenhagen, 1988: 149). Both the indigenous advocacy group Cultural Survival and OXFAM America have explicitly identified "institution building" as a program goal: Cultural Survival supported the development of national Indian federations in Brazil, Ecuador, and Peru in one year alone (*Cultural Survival Quarterly* 8[4]). Another indigenist advocacy group, the International Work Group on Indigenous Affairs, advised the World Council of Indigenous Peoples (IWGIA) during its formation (International Work Group on Indigenous Affairs, 1988: 29). Bolivia's Indian federation Central Indígena del Oriente Boliviano (Indigenous Organization of the Bolivian East—CIDOB) was organized with the help of anthropologists and has received support from Cultural Survival, the Inter-American Foundation, the South and Meso-American Indian Information Center, and the National Wildlife Federation (*Cultural Survival Quarterly* 11[4]).

In addition to resource flows and the historical role of international actors in movement formation, the transnational network has developed a mode of operation in which local and international action interpenetrate. For example, the National Wildlife Federation works directly and simultaneously with a local indigenous group (the Yuqui of Bolivia), their national-level federation (CIDOB), and the regional confederation of national Indian organizations from the Amazon Basin (COICA) (interview, May 19, 1992). International actors have taken an explicit role in linking local groups: one of the major functions of the IWGIA is the publication and dissemination of materials documenting the experiences of local South American Indian groups *for other South American Indian groups* (the "South-South Project"). Similarly, Cultural Survival has reformulated its role for the 1990s as intermediary between increasingly internationalized South American Indian leaders and their own increasingly distant rank and file (interview, May 14, 1992). Initiatives for transnational penetration come from the indigenous organizations as well as the advocacy groups. Indigenous activists in Brazil asked the rock musician Sting to establish a U.S.-based foundation on their behalf (the Rainforest Foundation). The foundation then sponsored a visit by Brazilian Indians to Japan to consult on their common medical crisis of mercury poisoning, caused by gold mining in Brazil and toxic dumping in Japan (*Rainforest Foundation Newsletter,* Winter 1992, 5).

Finally, indigenous groups around the world have now established their own transnational organizations. Within the hemisphere, the International Indian Treaty Council and the South and Meso-American Indian Information Center link natives of North and South America. The Canada-based World Council of Indigenous Peoples brings together groups from throughout the world, as does the Rainforest Peoples Movement. Within Latin America, regional confederations exist for South America (Consejo Indio de Sud América [Indian Council of South America—CISA]), Central America (Coordinadora Regional de Pueblos Indios de Centroamérica [Regional Coordinator for Central American Indians—CORPI]), and the Amazon Basin (COICA).

This transnational social movement network is not merely an interesting sociological phenomenon but a politically consequential force for social change. The Indian rights network has reformed international organizations: the United Nations declared 1993 the Year of Indigenous People, and the new international organization Indigenous People's Fund was created at a summit meeting of Latin American presidents with support from the Inter-American Development Bank. Transnational movement mobilization has changed domestic state policies, most notably in Brazil with the demarcation of a Yanomami reserve strongly resisted by powerful domestic interests. Activism continues to build international networks and raise international consciousness—Amnesty International reassessed the application of its mandate and prisoner-of-conscience model to indigenous peoples and launched a year-long special campaign on their behalf (Amnesty International, 1992). Unfortunately, these changes barely begin to address the multiple, urgent needs of the continent's indigenous peoples and certainly do not meet most of the goals of the Indian rights movement, but they demonstrate that a transnational coalition can achieve social change and that a transnational movement network has accomplished more in one generation than previous (purely domestic) efforts had in centuries.

Although the importance of internationalization must be assessed on a case-by-case basis, it has clearly helped the movement. In general, domestic reform has been strongest where international and transnational actors have played a prominent role. Paths of international influence can be identified in specific cases such as the establishment of reserves in Brazil, Ecuador, and Nicaragua. Even the selection of target situations has been heavily determined by international as much as local priorities. International supporters chose to focus on Brazil's Polonoroeste road-building and colonization project as a paradigm of World Bank planning problems (Le Prestre, 1989: 180), while a *Cultural Survival* article urged supporters to focus on the situation of Brazil's Wauja in order to maintain international attention and optimism for a clear small victory (Ireland, 1991: 57). As we shall see, this degree of internationalization has also had its costs for movement development.

Why has the Indian rights movement internationalized so quickly, thoroughly, and successfully? In large part, indigenous peoples turned to the international system out of domestic powerlessness. Contrary to the implicit assumptions of a levels-of-analysis model, international activity required fewer resources than domestic mobilization and was more amenable to information politics. In some cases, characteristics that were domestic handicaps became international strengths.

TURNING WEAKNESS INTO STRENGTH

The central defining characteristic of indigenous peoples—cultural and racial difference—produced domestic marginality but international recognition. The image of Indian as Other was read differently by Latin American policymakers and international publics. To their compatriots, Indians' appearance made them threatening, subhuman, or simply invisible; to North Americans and Europeans, it marked them as fascinating, exotic, and romantic. Several indigenous rights advocates spoke frankly of their initial attraction to the exoticism of Indian cultures and the resonance of this attraction within their organizations—though each added that ethical and effective advocacy must ultimately be based on a recognition of Indians as pragmatic partners (interviews, May 1992). A journalist for a national radio network who decided to focus on the indigenous representatives at an international conference stressed that the decision was largely based on the media appeal of the exotic languages being spoken (interview, April 15, 1992). An anthropologist and indigenous activist who works with Central American Indians pointed out that (with the exception of Guatemala) they have received much less media attention than similarly situated and less numerous but "more colorful"

Amazonian peers (interview, April 18, 1992). In general, less acculturated lowland groups are domestically weaker but more internationalized than highland Indians (Jackson, 1991: 135).

The very marginality of domestic Indian groups is also sometimes an advantage with the media. One journalist explained his coverage of "the indigenous angle" with the comment that "the underdog is a good story"(interview, April 15, 1992). But ethnic marginality is more internationally salient than other forms. Within the European advocacy groups, several key figures are themselves members of minority ethnic groups (Scottish, Catalan, Flemish). Similarly, a North American indigenist activist who has held U.S. government posts explained that he consciously decided to focus on the Brazilian Indian leader Paiakan rather than the mestizo rubber tapper Chico Mendes because Paiakan's image was more ethnic and "less politicized" (interview, May 21, 1992).

South American Indians have also reached out internationally to compensate for weak local alliances and alliance possibilities. With some exceptions, Indian-Latino political partnerships have been hindered by geographic and cultural isolation, the class-based character of opposition forces, and lack of interest in resource-poor Indians in other sectors of civil society.[5] Indian leaders from Brazil to Honduras stated that they sought international help because "we had no real support at home" (interviews, July 24 and 28, 1993). As one Northern environmentalist noted, it is (physically and politically) easier for his South American Indian contacts to communicate with him than with (often urban-based) environmentalists in their own country (interview, May 19, 1992). Conversely, when Indian groups have had access to state-sponsored coalitions (as in Mexico) the Indian movements have been much less internationalized and generally less effective.

Another initial handicap which ultimately increased and shaped the internationalization of Indian rights was the early absence of "peer lobbies" (Brysk, 1993). Although other domestically weak social movements have benefited from the influence of better-positioned ethnic, functional, or ideological peers in more powerful countries (fellow writers or Protestants or mothers), the lack of an early, sustained alliance with North American Indians pushed South Americans toward non-Indian Northern partners. Lacking a natural channel of contact, North and South American Indians often met only at international conferences. Historical differences led mainstream North American Indians to emphasize spiritual and cultural issues rather than the political and class ones of concern to their Southern peers. At one point, the American Indian Congress even issued a resolution rejecting international involvement. As one North American Indian activist recounts, the potential coalition was initially impeded by North American Indians' images of South

American Indians as primitive and "not worthwhile allies" (interview, May 22, 1992). Recently, this alliance has grown through 1992 anti-Quincentenary activities, but it was not available to South American Indians during the critical formative stages of their movement.

Many indigenous peoples had nothing left to lose—except their identity. Lacking material or organizational resources, South American Indians were able to develop and project this identity internationally through a politics of information. In a way that illuminates the emerging shape of transnational politics, South American Indians went from oral history to sound bites in one generation.

FROM PREMODERN TO POSTMODERN POLITICS

Until the formation of an Indian rights movement, Indian political participation was generally premodern in both form and content. Literacy and status limitations on the franchise excluded Indians from citizenship in even the most narrow, formal sense into the 1960s. Lowland groups of the Amazon Basin were physically isolated from the dominant state and generally lacked formal internal political structures. Andean and Mesoamerican Indians were incorporated into their states through quasifeudal clientelistic relationships. Resistance was often reactive or apocalyptic, seeking ancestral rights or relief from taxes rather than state power. By the 1980s the Indian rights movement had transformed these premodern demands into a modern vocabulary of nationalism: the hinge between tribe (or empire) and modern state system.

But just as Indians were the last to enter their domestic political systems, Indian nationalism entered the world system as modern structures were again transforming: the state was simultaneously "withering, widening, and wavering" (Rosenau, 1990). In postmodern international relations, states were wavering largely because they had lost monopoly power over information. The link between premodern identity and postmodern information politics was expressed succinctly by shaman Davi Yanomami, winner of the United Nations' Global 500 award: "Because I am Yanomami, I explain to other countries who we are and our problems" (interview, July 28, 1993).

Nonstate actors such as social movements can use images, models, facts, and messages as forms of power in the international system. An indigenous rights activist who has held a variety of posts in the U.S. policymaking apparatus explained, "Of course we look for international levers, and when they are there we use them. But when they're not, we've still got media and information" (interview, May 21, 1992). As the Kayapo leader Paiakan put it, "In the old days, my people were great warriors. Now, instead of war clubs, we are using words" (Whittemore, 1992: 4).

276

Activists consciously use the press to present their case internationally; several described off-the-record incidents in which they had "planted" a story to pressure target states—or even other nongovernmental organizations (interviews, May 1992). A 1989 conference at Altamira, Brazil, marked a turning point in media relations for the movement, drawing almost as many journalists as participants. Local Indian groups that may lack access to physical roads or basic needs such as health care have often acquired cheaper and more transferable high-technology communications—the high road to the global village. Most national Indian federations have fax machines and electronic mail, and a number of local groups have access to camcorders to document their own conditions. A recent Cultural Survival grant to the most significant regional group, COICA, was earmarked for the development of telephone, fax, and electronic mail capabilities (Aranda, 1990: 87). The recent development of radio modems powered by solar-cell batteries will allow villages without electricity or phone lines access to the Internet.

The Indian rights movement has engaged in extensive and effective image projection and political theater. Throughout 1989 Sting toured with the Brazilian Indian leader Raoni, lending his own image to the distant cause of Amazonian land rights. In 1991 Paiakan's image entered millions of American homes when he was featured on the cover of *Parade* magazine. His appeal for Indian rights was framed as a call to planetary ecological consciousness: "Help me to save lives—ours and yours" (Whittemore, 1992). At around the same time, Cultural Survival's president, David Maybury-Lewis, created and narrated a nationally broadcast eight-part public-television series on tribal cultures, *Millennium*. The 1992 Nobel Laureate Rigoberta Menchú has maintained traditional clothing to dramatize the culture and plight of Guatemala's Maya, even donning the garb of groups other than her own to project their image. At the 1992 Rio Earth Parliament (the nongovernmental organizations' alternative to the UN Conference on Environment and Development), photographs of Amazonian Indians were featured in the international press daily for several weeks—including one memorable front-page image of South American Indians with the Dalai Lama (both representatives of stateless nations).

More extensive and situated uses of political theater and symbolic protest also abound. In a 1985 incident, Cinta Larga Indians protesting developers' failure to construct a promised road occupied a plant and then called CBS and offered an exclusive interview—and the road was built (Junqueira and Mindlin, 1987). Traditionally garbed Indians from several groups filled the observers' gallery throughout the deliberations of Brazil's 1988 Constituent Assembly. Upon adopting a new constitution incorporating substantial improvements in Indian rights, the members of the assembly turned to the gallery and applauded the Indian observers (Allen, 1989). Similarly, when the Kayapo leaders Paiakan and Kube-I and the North American anthropologist Darryl Posey were put on trial for subversion by the Brazilian government following international lobbying efforts, Kayapo massed outside the courthouse in traditional battle regalia and engaged in symbolic "war games" (Posey, 1989). The trials generated extensive international attention, and the case was thrown out by an appeals court. During the Earth Summit, the local Indian leader Marcos Terena organized the construction of an intertribal village bringing together dozens of groups as witnesses to the simultaneous negotiations of their states under UN auspices. As a result of the publicity this generated, Maurice Strong, the organizer of the UN Conference on Environment and Development, met with the Indian leaders present and considered their demands (Latin American Database #017109).

The fact that the transnational movement network had a conscious communications strategy does not discredit the movement; all political actors consciously or unconsciously learn to represent themselves in the way that is most effective, and indigenous representatives drew their demands and representations authentically from the repertoires of their own cultures. It does, however, highlight an inherent irony of identity-based movements that has been particularly keen for indigenous peoples. Movements do not merely defend identities but also develop them. A movement for cultural identity faces the paradox that identity is not primordial; it changes as you use it. Thus, in an illustrative situation, a Brazilian Indian group that defines its identity strongly in terms of land and location was forced to move its village to the borders of a proposed reserve in order to defend its identity by staking out its boundaries (Rainforest Foundation, n.d.). This intrinsic irony can be resolved only by a focus on self-determination rather than concrete cultural content.

In this regard, the projection of information also facilitates international learning as isolated and culturally disparate groups provide potentially transferable models of self-determination and autonomous development. One of the first-generation organizations—the Shuar Federation of Ecuador—has founded its own press to share several decades of experience and has been widely studied by other indigenous groups. Similarly, indigenous and indigenist groups have closely followed the autonomy agreements negotiated in 1987 by Nicaragua's Miskito. Recently, a Guatemalan Indian leader called for autonomy on the basis of the Miskito model (Latin American Database #018480). The Wauja of Brazil say that their 1991 campaign for land rights was inspired by the example of their Kayapo compatriots (Ireland, 1991). Panama's Guaymi have modeled their organization and desired reserve on those of the Kuna (interview, July 22, 1993). More concretely, a forestry management arrangement for the Quechua of Ecuador has involved training by indigenous veterans of similar projects—including the Kuna of Panama and Peru's Yanesha—as well as Northern nongovernmental organizations (MacDonald, 1992: 21).

Besides models and images, information also involves facts. Generation, processing, and projection of facts by local Indian groups was initially weak for both logistical and cultural reasons. This was another determinant of the movement's internationalization and transnational evolution; a de facto division of labor developed in which Indians presented the images and advocates presented the facts. But a shortage of facts also delayed the involvement of potential allies that depended heavily on factual information (such as many human rights groups).

Two developments have changed the role of facts in Indian rights movements' information politics. First, indigenous peoples—especially a remarkable group of bicultural leaders—have learned which elements of their experience are internationally salient and how to gather and format factual material. After several frustrating experiences with the UN Working Group, indigenous leaders began to organize preparatory conferences in Geneva in which they taught each other to present information effectively within the UN system. Second, Northern allies have realized new value in Indian groups' "local knowledge." Opponents of multilateral development bank activities saw Indian experiences as important evidence to supplement the nongovernmental organizations' environmental critique. These activists realized that indigenous knowledge of fragile rainforests could help make the case for conservation and/or suggest alternative resource uses for sustainable development (Aufderheide and Rich, 1988; *Cultural Survival Quarterly* 8[4]; Schwartzman, 1991; Rich, 1990).

The Indian rights movement turned local knowledge to global power in a way that sometimes bypassed state-level structures of domination. But the global power of a transnational social movement was ultimately limited, fragile, and even self-contradictory.

TURNING STRENGTH INTO WEAKNESS

The internationalization of Indian rights has exacerbated a generic problem of social movements that is particularly salient for ethnic organizations: the question of representation. Social movements often lack authoritative, hierarchical structures of representation. It is inherently difficult for culturally distinct communities to designate leaders who are both representative of the group's values and effective in the wider political arena. This creates cleavages within indigenous groups (which often coincide with generational splits) between traditionally designated and internationally recognized authorities (Barros Laraia 1985). Those with the skills to lead internationally may be the least "representative": for example, one extremely effective Indian leader encountered at the UN Working Group was a law student, another was a former Congressional representative in his country, and a third was one of his people's eight college graduates. Conversely, one of the few truly grass-roots delegates at the UN—an Andean peasant woman—was ultimately unable to deliver her prepared statement.

The transnational evolution of the movement that was a source of its strength also perpetuated and reinforced this problem. Fluid, transnationalized information politics are widely accessible and do not require a mandate through institutionalized mechanisms of representation. Indian organizations developed simultaneously on several different levels: as local grass-roots organizations, ethnic federations, peasant groups, and wider indigenist movements marked by an ideology of cultural reassertion (Smith, 1984). In any particular situation, traditional tribal leaders, local grass-roots organizations, ethnic federations, peasant groups, indigenist supporters, journalists, missionaries, ecologists, and anthropologists could and did claim to speak for Indians on the ground.

For the relatively unacculturated Huaorani of Amazonian Ecuador, this has led to several levels of confusion in seeking "informed consent" for development. Different groups and families within the same administratively defined tribal area hold different views on proposed development projects that do not necessarily correspond to the views of their local, national, or regional Indian federations (Kane, 1993). At the other end of the spectrum of cultural mobilization, competitive internationalization of the conflict between Nicaragua's Miskito and the Sandinista government illustrates the potential for divisiveness in the absence of clear and accountable representation. Miskito have belonged to a plethora of organizations with various domestic and external patrons (Molieri, 1986). As the Miskito-state conflict developed, membership in different organizations brought distinct international treatment. Those repatriated by the UN High Commission on Refugees received aid not available to voluntary returnees. The OAS aided members of Brooklyn Rivera's YATAMA ("Mother Earth") who demobilized under Chamorro but ignored similarly situated Miskito who had laid down their arms under the Sandinistas (*Latinamerica Press,* March 14, 1991).

The crisis of representation in Indian rights movements has also alienated potential allies and, ironically, strengthened the role of advocacy groups as gatekeepers for messy local political factions. For example, Ecuador's Confederación de Nacionalidades Indígenas del Ecuador (Confederation of Indigenous Nations of Ecuador—CONAIE) is the national-level Indian federation, but regional subgroups have more extensive international representation; the regional Organización de Pueblos Indígenas de Pastaza (Indigenous Peoples' Organization of Pastaza—OPIP) has three permanent representatives in Europe, while the highland regional Ecuador Runacunapac Riccharimui (Ecuador Awakening—ECUARUNARI) attended the UN Working Group in the absence of any formal CONAIE delegation. A North American activist from a major human rights organization spoke candidly about the group's frustration in trying to assess the "legitimate representatives" of Indian peoples, concluding that the human rights group tended to leave the field to the more specialized advocacy movements (interview, April 1992). Governments, too, turn to indigenist organizations as intermediaries in controversial situations. The Agency for International Development has subcontracted projects to Cultural Survival in Peru and Ecuador, a development that may improve particular projects but complicates Cultural Survival's role as an advocate for Indian rights. As governments, funders, and international organizations increasingly turn to indigenist organizations and other international allies instead of Indians themselves, the internationalization of Indian rights becomes fraught with the potential for a new, postmodern form of dependency (Hastrup and Elsass, 1990; Smith, 1987; Kajese, 1987).

CONCLUSION

Latin America's Indian rights movement has empowered marginalized people by creating a transnational alliance based on information and identity—turning weakness into strength. Although this alliance has improved the conditions and political access of indigenous peoples, it has not overcome the larger power relationships in which it is embedded. Ironically, the crisis of representation reflects the democratization of transnational relationships—once social movements escape state-based structures, they lack definitive arbiters.

The Indian rights experience of transnationalization parallels a process at different stages for the human rights, ecology, and feminist movements in Latin America. In each case, nonstate actors seeking principled social change have reached beyond state boundaries to gain international support. As Latin American states themselves seek regional integration and international diversification and international organizations gain new influence, the space for transnationalism should grow. To fill that space, we can learn much from Indians' "global knowledge."

NOTES

1. Terminology to describe native Americans is currently in a state of flux. Until recently, the term "Indian" was avoided because of its historical inaccuracy and pejorative connotations (especially in Spanish). However, the term has now been reclaimed by some Indian activists in the Americas, and it avoids the potential confusion in using "indigenous," which can equally well designate pre-Columbian cultures or modern Latino cultures as distinguished from North American models. The label "Native Americans" is technically accurate but has become so strongly associated with the original inhabitants of North America that it is not commonly applied to South America. Therefore, I will use the terms "Indian" and "indigenous" interchangeably and with an attempt to achieve maximum clarity in a particular context (e.g., "Indian rights" more clearly designates the Americas).

2. An important exception to these trends and a potential model for research that takes transnationalism seriously may be found in various analyses of the changing role of the church in Latin America.

3. There are complex debates on the proper definition of indigenous peoples within the indigenous movement, national Indian agencies, and international organizations. Consensus elements of these definitions include historical continuity with preconquest populations, self-identification, recognition by an indigenous community, (often) use of a non-Latin language, and (usually) social marginality. A helpful summary is provided in an appendix to Serafino (1991). The negative status of Indians in most Latin American societies complicates the measurement of indigenous populations and leads to fluctuations in self-identification. Most parties to the debate employ cultural rather than racial definitions, since racial identity is difficult to determine, subject to abuse, and socially superseded by cultural identity in any case. But most activists resist a strictly ethnic definition in favor of a recognition of Indian populations as peoples or nations.

4. The most fundamental distinction among indigenous peoples of South America is that between highland and lowland groups, which differ systematically in their geographic situation, mode of production (agricultural versus hunter-gatherers), degree of contact with Latino societies, and pre-Columbian political heritage (empires versus egalitarian clan or village decisionmaking). Varese highlights the last factor in his classification of *macroetnias* and *microetnias* (Varese, 1989)

5. Exceptions include the Peoples of the Forest alliance with Brazilian rubber tappers (Schwartzman, 1991). Indian advocacy groups of lawyers, church activists, and local environmentalists have also played a limited role in Brazil. Revolutionary movements throughout Latin America have often attempted to appeal to rural Indians as peasants but have generally slighted ethnic identity. The seeming exception and most prominent success is the Zapatista movement in Mexico.

REFERENCES

Allen, Elizabeth
    1989 "Brazil: Indians and the new constitution." *Third World Quarterly* 10(4): 149-165.
Alvarez, S. E., and A. Escobar (eds.)
    1992 *The Making of New Social Movements in Latin America.* Boulder: Westview Press.

Aranda, Esther
   1990 "Cultural survival projects, 1990." *Cultural Survival Quarterly* 14(4): 83-87.
Amnesty International
   1992 *Indigenous Peoples in the Americas Campaign.* New York: Amnesty International.
Aufderheide, Pat and Bruce Rich
   1988 "Environmental reform and the multilateral banks." *World Policy Journal* 6: 302-321.
Barros Laraia, R.
   1985 *New Trends in Brazilian Indian Affairs.* London: Signal Press.
Bonfil Batalla, Guillermo
   1982 *Etnodesarrollo y etnocidio.* Santiago: Facultad Latinoamericana de Ciencias Sociales.
Brysk, Alison
   1992 "Beyond hegemony: U.S.-Latin American relations in a 'New World Order'?" *Latin American Research Review* 27(2): 165-176.
   1993 "From above and below: Social movements, the international system, and human rights in Argentina." *Comparative Political Studies* 26(3): 259-285.
Burger, Julian
   1987 *Report from the Frontier: The State of the World's Indigenous Peoples.* London: Zed Books.
Chiriboga, Manuel
   1986 *Del indigenismo a las organizaciones indígenas.* Quito: Abya Yala.
Cohen, Jean
   1985 "Strategy or identity: new theoretical paradigms and contemporary social movements." *Social Research* 52(4): 663-717.
Díaz Polanco, Héctor
   1987 "*Neoindigenismo* and the ethnic question in Central America." *Latin American Perspectives* 14 (Winter): 87-100.
Diskin, Martin
   1991 "Ethnic discourse and the challenge to anthropology: the Nicaraguan case," in G. Urban and J. Sherzer (eds.), *Nation-States and Indians in Latin America.* Austin: University of Texas Press.
Evans-Pritchard, Ambrose
   1990 "The reconquest." *Wilson Quarterly* 14 (Summer): 54-57.
Frank, Andre Gunder and Marta Fuentes
   1990 "Civil democracy: social movements in recent world history," pp. 139-180 in Samir Amin et al. (eds.),*Transforming the Revolution: Social Movements and the World-System.* New York: Monthly Review Press.
Freeland, Jane
   1989 "Nationalist revolution and ethnic rights: the Miskitu Indians of Nicaragua's Atlantic Coast." *Third World Quarterly* 10(4): 167-189.
Gamson, W.
   1975 *The Strategy of Social Protest.* Homewood, IL: Dorsey Press.
Hastrup, Kirsten and Peter Elsass
   1990 "Anthropological advocacy: a contradiction in terms? *Current Anthropology* 31: 301-311.
Howe, James
   1991 "The struggle over San Blas Kuna culture," in Greg Urban and Joel Scherzer (eds.), *Indians and Nation-States in Latin America.* Austin: University of Texas Press.
Indian Law Resource Center
   1988 *Indian Rights, Human Rights: Handbook for Indians on International Human Rights Complaint Procedures.* Washington, DC.

International Work Group on Indigenous Affairs
    1988 *Yearbook.* Copenhagen.
Ireland, Emilienne
    1991 "Neither warriors nor victims, the Wauja peacefully organize to defend their land."
    Cultural Survival Quarterly 15(1): 54-59.
Jackson, Jean
    1991 "Being and becoming an Indian in the Vaupés," in Greg Urban and Joel Sherzer (eds.),
    Nation-States and Indians in Latin America. Austin: University of Texas Press.
Junqueira, Carmen and Betty Mindlin
    1987 *The Aripuana Park and The Polonoroeste Programme.* Copenhagen: IWGIA.
Kajese, Kingston
    1987 "An agenda of future tasks for international and indigenous nongovernmental organi-
    zations: views from the South. *World Development* 15: 79-85.
Kane, Joe
    1993 "Letter from the Amazon: with spears from all sides." *The New Yorker,* September 27,
    54-79.
Kearney, Michael and Carole Nagengast
    1990 "Mixtec ethnicity: social identity, political consciousness, and political activism."
    Latin American Research Review 25(2): 61-91.
Kriesi, Hanspeter
    1988 "The interdependence of structure and action: some reflections on the state of the art,"
    pp. 349-368 in Bert Klandermans, Hanspeter Kriesi, and Sidney Tarrow (eds.), *International
    Social Movement Research.* Greenwich, CT: JAI Press.
Le Prestre, Pierre
    1989 *The World Bank and the Environmental Challenge.* London: Associated University
    Press.
MacDonald, Theodore
    1992 "The Quichùa of eastern Ecuador," in S. Davis (ed.), *Indigenous Views of Land and
    the Environment.* Washington, DC: World Bank.
Mainwaring, Scott and Eduardo Viola
    1984 "New social movements, political culture, and democracy: Brazil and Argentina in the
    1980s." *Telos* 61: 17-52.
Martínez Cobo, José
    1986 *Study of the Problem of Discrimination Against Indigenous Populations.*
    E/CN.4/Sub.2/1986/7/Add.4. New York: United Nations.
Melucci, Alberto
    1989 "Getting involved: identity and mobilization in social movements," pp. 329-348 in B.
    Klandermans, H. Kriesi, and S. Tarrow (eds.), *International Social Movement Research.*
    Greenwich, CT: JAI Press.
Molieri, Jorge Jenkins
    1986 *El desafío indígena en Nicaragua: El caso de los Miskitos.* Managua: Editorial
    Vanguardia.
NACLA (North American Council on Latin America)
    1991 *The First Nations, 1492-1992: Report on the Americas.* 25(3).
Nash, June
    1989 "Cultural resistance and class consciousness in Bolivian tin-mining communities,"
    pp. 182-202 in S. Eckstein (ed.), *Power and Popular Protest.* Berkeley: University of
    California Press.

284

Nimni, Ephraim
    1991 *Marxism and Nationalism: Theoretical Origins of a Political Crisis.* London: Pluto Press.
Posey, Daryl
    1989 "From warclubs to words." *NACLA Report on the Americas,* May, 13-18.
Rainforest Foundation
    n.d. *Program Statement.* New York.
Rich, Bruce
    1990 "The emperor's new clothes: the World Bank and environmental reform." *World Policy Journal* 7(2): 305-329.
Rosenau, James
    1990 *Turbulence in World Politics.* Princeton: Princeton University Press.
Schwartzman, Stephan
    1991 "Deforestation and popular resistance in Acre: from local social movement to global network." *Centennial Review* 35(2): 397-422.
Serafino, Nina (ed.)
    1991 *Latin American Indigenous Peoples and Considerations for U.S. Assistance.* Washington, DC: Congressional Research Service.
Smith, Brian
    1987 "An agenda of future tasks for international and indigenous nongovernmental organizations: views from the North." *World Development* 15 (suppl.): 87-93.
Smith, Carol
    1990 *Guatemalan Indians and the State.* Austin: University of Texas Press.
Smith, Richard Chase
    1984 "A search for unity within diversity." *Cultural Survival Quarterly* 8(4): 6-14.
Stavenhagen, Rodolfo
    1988 *Derecho indígena y derechos humanos en América Latina.* Mexico City: Instituto Interamericano de Derechos Humanos/El Colegio de México.
Tilly, Charles
    1978 *From Mobilization to Revolution.* Reading, MA: Addison-Wesley.
Urban, Greg and Joel Sherzer (eds.)
    1991 *Nation-States and Indians in Latin America.* Austin: University of Texas Press.
Varese, Stefano
    1989 "Movimientos indios de liberación y estado nacional," pp. 215-232 in S. B. Devalle (ed.), *La diversidad prohibida: Resistencia étnica y poder de estado.* Mexico City: El Colegio de México.
Whittemore, Hank
    1992 "A man who would save the world." *Parade,* April 12, 4-7.
Willetts, Peter
    1982 *Pressure Groups in the Global System.* New York: St. Martin's Press.

THE REASSERTION OF INDIGENOUS IDENTITY:
Mayan Responses to State Intervention in Chiapas[*]

June Nash

City College of the City University of New York

In the early hours of 1994, a few hundred men and women of the Ejército Zapatista Liberación Nacional (EZLN) blocked the Pan American Highway between Tuxtla Gutiérrez, the state capital of Chiapas, and San Cristóbal de las Casas and the road to Ocosingo, declaring war on Mexico's ruling Partido Revolucionario Institucional (PRI). This move signaled to the world that indigenous populations intended to make themselves heard at home and abroad as Mexico restructures its economy according to the neoliberal model promoted by President Carlos Salinas de Gortari. The rebels captured and briefly held the municipal buildings in San Cristóbal, Altamirano, Las Margaritas, and Ocosingo. Speaking for the rebels, Subcomandante Marcos declared that their war was "a final but justified measure": "We have nothing, absolutely nothing. Not a decent roof, nor work, nor land, nor health care, nor education."[1]

The rebellion brought to the forefront long-standing complaints that peasants and workers in this southernmost Mexican state have been making for decades. Every peaceful demonstration was suppressed with massive military action and arrests. But because of the recent passage of the North American Free Trade Agreement (NAFTA) in late 1993, a rebel-

*Research funds from the National Science Foundation permitted me to carry out field investigations in the summers of 1990 and 1991. I benefited from the presence of students participating in the Research Experience for Undergraduates, some of whom accompanied me to the townships in the region. Some students also collaborated in articles cited herein, among them Pedro Farías, Robert Martínez, Gina Peña Campodónico, Kathleen Sullivan, and Luz Martín del Campo. I am also grateful for the inspiration in the field of Melissa Castillo, Brenda Currin, Liliana Fasanella, Courtney Guthrie, and Christine Kovic, who participated in an exchange program I directed in the spring of 1993, supported by the International Studies Program at City College. Earlier versions of this article were improved by critiques from participants in the discussion group on indigenous movements, including Hugo Benavides, Gina Peña Campadónico, and Hernán Vidal. Kay Warren also provided helpful comments, and I have relied on her publications as well as those of Ricardo Falla, Susanne Jonas, Beatriz Manz, Carol Smith, and others to explicate the Guatemalan indigenous presence in Chiapas.

1. Tim Golden, "Rebel Attack Hits Four Towns in Mexico," *New York Times*, 1 Jan. 1994, p. A4.

7

lion that otherwise would have been noted only briefly has remained the focus of analysis by specialists on world economics and politics.

Many of the issues the rebels have raised recall those fought for by Emiliano Zapata, the national hero of the Mexican Revolution in the early decades of the twentieth century. Like the farmers who joined Zapata's forces, the rebels are demanding access to land and just wages to counteract growing discrepancies in wealth. The gains of the Constitution of 1917 were never realized in many regions of Chiapas, where large landowners succeeded in blocking land reform and where educational and medical services have remained minimal. The demands of the modern-day Zapatistas, however, go far beyond those of the earlier revolution in calling for recognition of ethnic distinctiveness and dignity as well as participation in the democratic process as the Mexican economy becomes integrated into global markets. Subcomandante Marcos announced that the rebels chose to initiate their war on the eve of implementation of NAFTA as a warning to the Mexican government not to leave indigenous peoples out of decisions that threaten their very survival as distinct ethnic groups.[2] The rebels also called for annulling a government elected fraudulently and installing a transition government to ensure democratic voting procedures in the 1994 presidential elections. Although the rebels recognize that their marginalization has resulted partly from free-market trends, they are not rejecting international exchange but are calling instead for participation by all sectors in decisions related to these changes.

Official attempts to link the rebels to Central American revolutionary groups have failed to counter the growing evidence that most of the rebels are Mexicans. The Unión Revolucionario Nacional Guatemateca (URNG) and the Salvadoran Frente Farabundo Martí de Liberación Nacional (FMLN) have both denied relationships with the insurgents, and only one Guatemalan was found among the captives.[3] Ties have been suggested with the Unidad Popular de Trabajadores y Campesinos Revolucionarios based in Oaxaca and the Partido de los Pobres, which was active until the mid-1970s on the Pacific Coast.[4] But the youthful members of the revolutionary directorate have an agenda that is different, although related to issues endemic in the rural sector. They insist that they seek not to seize power but to open a path for democratic processes. The military command of the rebellion is made up of Tzeltales Tzotziles, Choles, Tojolabales, Mames, and Zoques. All of these groups speak indigenous languages of the region, including Mam-speaking Guatemalans

2. Guillermo Correa, Julio César, and Ignacio Ramírez, "Estallido que estremece a México," *Proceso*, no. 897, 10 Jan. 1994, pp. 6–21.
3. Tim Golden, "Mexico Offers an Amnesty to Rebels as They Retreat," *New York Times*, 7 Jan. 1994, p. A8.
4. Tim Golden, "Mexican Troops Battling Rebels, Toll at Least 57," *New York Times*, 3 Jan. 1994, p. A1.

8

who have lived on the Mexican side of the border for generations. Media interviews and reports have confirmed that the rebels are indigenous persons, many of them monolingual.

The rebellion attests to the extraordinary durability of distinctive cultures in Middle America. Anthropologists have attributed this persistence variously to indigenous withdrawal into zones of retreat (Aguirre Beltrán 1979), exploitation in the form of internal colonialism (González Casanova 1970), and Catholic traditions imposed by the conquerors to encumber native groups with debts for religious celebrations (Diener 1978; Harris 1964). These earlier theories stressed one side or the other of the dominant-subordinate hierarchy, with those maintaining the essentialist position emphasizing primordial cultural characteristics and those arguing domination from above emphasizing that forced acculturation has conditioned indigenous responses. Structuralists attacked the functionalism of those emphasizing the rational basis for distinctive indigenous characteristics (Stavenhagen 1965; Wasserstrom 1983), while their opponents challenged economic determinists for failing to recognize the preconquest ideological constructs manifested across wide regions (Gossen 1974; Vogt 1976b).

Protagonists on both sides of this older debate have shown that the persistence of distinct beliefs and practices among indigenous populations of the Americas arises from internal resources and from pressures exerted by the dominant group. Current debates are taking into account the combined force of antagonistic but interpenetrating relationships between *indígenas* and *ladinos* as they generate and sustain ethnic diversity. While this conjuncture of forces has provided a basis for subordinate groups to mobilize claims on the state for resources (Ehrenreich 1989; Hill 1989; Selverston 1992) and to resist exploitation and repression (Nagengast and Kearney 1990; Smith 1984b), it has also reinforced relations of subordination and domination (Díaz-Polanco 1992). By looking inward at "narrative strategies for resisting terror" (Warren 1993), evoking dialogue between ancient and present traditions (Gossen and Leventhal 1989), and assessing the economic opportunities that condition their survival (Cancian 1992; Collier 1990; Nash 1993, 1994a), researchers are constructing a theory that recognizes both the structural imperatives of the colonial and postcolonial systems encapsulating indigenous peoples and their own search for a base from which to defend themselves and generate collective action.

The new social movement theorists who would separate these ethnic movements reasserting their identity from the economic conditions that give rise to their actions (Laclau and Mouffe 1985) miss as much of the dynamic as do those who would reduce these movements to class relations. The rebels themselves justify their recourse to war in both economic and cultural terms. According to Subcomandante Marcos, the

9

rebels are well aware that they have been excluded from power because as Indians, "We have always lived amidst a war that, up til now, was against us."[5] But today, their claims for dignity and autonomy are coupled with demands for land, schools, and medical services.

Revindicación étnica—the reclaiming of indigenous rights and autonomy—is the rationale being advanced for action based on the equation of shared poverty with indigenous identity from the colonial period to the present.[6] Growing differences in wealth among indígenas within corporate communities that have accommodated to the state power structure now contradict the communal basis for identification more apparent in the collective activity in colonizing areas in the new frontiers. In the face of internal divisions and external repression, reassertion of ethnic identity is finding distinct expressions among Mayas in highland communities and settlements on the border as they react to economic encroachment and violence that threaten their culture and their lives.

My purpose here is to compare reassertive actions by highland Mayas in corporate communities with those of colonizers and Guatemalan exiles in the Lacandón jungle area and the southern frontier of Mexico in order to clarify some of the distinct processes involved in ethnic rebellion. Despite the many differences among communities of both regions, more contrasts can be found in the histories that constituted ethnic awareness and the ways in which indígenas were integrated into the ladino-dominated economy and polity in these regional groupings than if one were to compare any of the language groups.[7]

---

5. Guillermo Correa, Julio César López, and Ignacio Ramírez, "La capacidad de convocatorio de organización de divisos políticos en el origen del estallido," *Proceso*, no. 897, 10 Jan. 1994, pp. 22–25.

6. The primary difference between Mayas who are rebelling and those who are not committed is that the former are aware that as Indians they have been marginalized by the state and experience discrimination in the markets they enter as sellers of labor and products.

7. Alicia Castellanos (1988) contrasted ethnic *revindicación* in two subregions of highland Chiapas that express distinct "forms of insertion in capitalism according to socially differentiated degrees produced within the groups" as well as distinct "forms in which groups have internationalized the dominant ideology and customs." The first subregion includes Simojovel, Huitiupan, Pantelhó, and the department of Chilón. Except for Oxchuc and Cancuc, these communities are found at lower altitudes where lands are more productive and indigenous communities live near the large landholders engaged in cattle herding and agroindustry. The second subregion includes San Martín and San Miguel Mitontic, Chalchihuitán, San Pedro Chenalhó, Tenejapa, and Chamula, communities that had greater autonomy. In the first group, indigenous groups united with poor mestizo cultivators in the struggle for land, but in the second, communities tended to construct their ethnic struggles according to "corporative tactics" shaping the formation of indigenous caciques. This categorization, however, ignores too many anomalous cases (particularly Oxchuc and Cancuc) to be satisfying. Cancian and Brown (1994) compare two communities in their analysis of the uprising, Zinacantán and Pantelhó, thus avoiding ambivalent cases. Yet the narrower scope also means that one misses the particular historical circumstances that shape events.

10

ETHNICITY IN HIGHLAND CHIAPAS CORPORATE COMMUNITIES

Resistance to culture change forced during the colonial and independence periods required daily organization of life to enable indígenas to retain some degree of control over earning their livelihood, socializing their children, and exercising social control. The nexus for this social reproduction was provided by semi-subsistence cultivation of small plots organized by patriarchal households in which women were responsible for maintaining the domestic unit while men migrated seasonally in search of wage work. To sustain this structure, however, indígenas needed access to land, political channels, markets, and education to defend themselves in the nonindigenous world. Historically, this access was achieved by Spanish establishment of corporate communities with communal lands and autonomy in internal affairs run by a nonindigenous president and secretary assigned by the crown (MacLeod 1973; Wolf 1957). After independence, administrators maintained this pattern of control with some modifications up to the present day (Tax 1937; Wolf 1957).[8] Access to land and other resources was so limited that indígenas had to sell their products and labor power to the dominant ladinos, Spanish-speaking bearers of European culture who were often of mixed ancestry.

General Porfirio Díaz presided over the fragmentation of corporate landholdings of the Catholic Church and of state and local governments during his presidency (1875–1910). Better lands were seized or sold to large landowners, and most indigenous men were forced to work several months each year on coastal plantations (Wasserstrom 1983) or as transporters (Cancian 1992) and wage workers. Women maintained their families unassisted while men were working on distant plantations, and women transmitted cultural identification by socializing their children in the distinctive Maya patterns of work and beliefs, even taking over leadership of the *cargo* (the burden of supporting the annual cycle of fiestas for the saints) (see Rosenbaum 1993; Wasserstrom 1983). Indígena semi-subsistence farmers and artisans have also provisioned urban ladinos with corn, beans, and other staples as well as artisan products in ceramics, textiles, and woodwork, first as tribute and then as cheap commodities.

Following the Mexican Revolution, the Land Reform Act (Article 27 of the Constitution of 1917) allowed restitution of communal lands of

8. Recognition of these boundaries should not be interpreted as a denial of the integration of corporate communities within regional, national, and even international markets where they are subject to pressures from the capitalist enterprises in which they are bound. Researchers who have carried out long-term fieldwork are impressed with the perceptiveness of *indígenas* regarding the boundedness of their horizons even while they are involved in political, commercial, and ritual relations with ladinos and indígenas in other towns (Cancian 1965, 1992; Collier 1975, 1990; Gossen 1984; Nash 1970, 1993). The persistence of traditions like the twenty-day ceremonial calendar and beliefs about the four-path way of the world (Gossen 1984; Gossen and Leventhal 1993) is invoked not as part of pan-indigenous political identity but rather as an affirmation of distinct identity in separate communities.

11

indigenous communities lost during the liberal period and opened up national land for *ejidos* (collectively owned and individually cultivated plots allotted to cultivators who established residence in colonies). Land reform had a mixed effect in Chiapas, however. Some indigenous communities acted on it late, twenty years after land reform was enacted in the central plateau, while other communities never got state support to challenge large landowners. The few communities that managed to get title to ejido lands (as in Amatenango del Valle) were outnumbered by those that lacked good cultivable lands within municipal boundaries (as in San Juan Chamula) or fought unsuccessfully to win their claims, gaining only a fraction of eligible land (as in Venustiano Carranza).

Long considered the most backward and isolated of Mexico's thirty-one states, Chiapas lacked roads connecting indigenous villages, potable water, and electricity. Ladino mayors and secretaries mediated relations between indigenous communities and the state government, while a local hierarchy of civil and religious officers presided over town affairs. Until Lázaro Cárdenas became president, Chiapas had neither schools nor health services. This backwardness resulted from both neglect and planning: the lack of interest in promoting indigenous peoples, still feared because of their potential rebelliousness, combined with the desire to exploit their labor led to policies excluding them from the dominant culture while ensuring a labor supply for harvest seasons on the coastal coffee plantations (Fábregas Puig 1988).

The integration of indigenous communities into the "modern sector" of the economy as anything more than severely exploited wage laborers began in 1950 with the founding of the Instituto Nacional Indigenista (INI). Bilingual education programs and health clinics employing indigenous *promotores* (change agents) were introduced to villages, some not even connected by roads to the highland commercial center of San Cristóbal. The INI also promoted cooperatives to provision local stores and other enterprises serving an indigenous clientele.

Reinterpreting these innovations provides a key to how indigenous societies have managed to change in ways that preserved their cultural integrity. I discovered this pattern in Amatenango del Valle, where I carried out fieldwork first in 1957–1958 and each summer from 1963 to 1966. No nonindigenous people lived in the town center other than the schoolteachers, a couple with three daughters who later taught in the schools in the 1960s. The schoolmaster, retired from the Mexican army, often threatened those who menaced him with an arsenal of old army rifles. In previous years, two Mexican anthropologists had been asked to leave. My research team members were tolerated, the indigenous president told us after two months residence in the town, because we never said we wanted to civilize the indigenous people. Until the late 1960s, the town rejected the ladino pattern of modernization. Many Amatenanguero

12

families tried to keep their children out of the local school and ignored extension agents representing the INI and the Banco Ejidal. Some of the men who had gone to the boarding school in Chamula during the Cárdenas era were among the first cohort of indígenas to serve in the town offices, first as president in 1957 and then as secretary the following year. These posts were formerly occupied by ladinos from the neighboring town of Teopisca.

On returning in 1963 for another extended field period, I found that members of the community had organized several cooperatives based on the model of the INI store to promote liquor distilleries and bars where electrically amplified music attracted customers. The objective in organizing the cooperative of five or six owners was less to share the risk of loss than to share the risk of success, given that new opportunities for income excited the envy and potential charges of witchcraft by villagers lacking such revenues.

Innovation was adapted selectively to the prevailing ways of life. For example, when potable water was introduced by capturing spring water in pipes that went directly to the householders willing to pay a small fee, the u'uletik (curer-diviners) who bathed their patients in the spring water objected. An agreement was worked out whereby a stream of the spring water was diverted into a pool to providing access for curative bathing without contaminating the pipes carrying potable water. The son of the chief diviner-curer was trained as a paramedic, and father and son shared patients and consultations, yielding to modern medicine in cases where it had proved effective (as in immunizing against contagious diseases and antibiotic injections for common infections), while calling on the elder curer for diseases caused by witchcraft. Wheat was introduced to allow continuous cultivation of milpa because wheat replaced soil nutrients used up by the corn. Bilingual education was introduced into schools with native speakers of the Maya dialects acting as promotores. In some areas, these modernizing changes eliminated institutions that were subsequently reintegrated when the changes seemed to threaten traditional reciprocity between humans and the ecological system. For example, the religious office of alférez (captain of religious celebrations) was abandoned in 1971 after young men objected to the high costs of time and money for these posts, but it was resumed two years later when intervening droughts were blamed on the failure to celebrate saints' days.

The Amatenangueros' selective responses to innovation and abandonment of old traditions derived from a pragmatic assessment of what worked for them within their own cultural design. The Mexican development model in the 1950s and 1960s promoted existing techniques without highly capitalized and intensive agricultural techniques. Working with indigenous promotores, INI introduced bilingual education in grade schools (de la Fuente 1989), crop rotation rather than expensive fertilizers, and

13

other "green revolution" techniques as well as collective forms of capital accumulation in cooperatives (Nash 1966).

These changes, modest as they were, stirred antagonisms within the community. During my field research from 1963 to 1966, the major opposition to these signs of modernization came from the dual hierarchy of curer-diviners. Having literate indigenous young men as officeholders replacing the ladino president and secretary who had mediated relations with the regional and national government threatened control by the elder *principales* (men who had served in all the posts in the civil-religious heirarchy) over the curers, whose power was based on age and authority and backed by the principales. The curer-diviners' decline in power and authority was marked by an outbreak of witchcraft accusations and homicide in the late 1960s as young curer-diviners, lacking the authority of their predecessors, vied for position in the eroded civil-religious hierarchy.

This involuted revolution led to reconstitution of an indigenous civil and religious hierarchy of offices that validated the modernizing processes undertaken in the previous decade. Young men served in the positions in which they confronted ladino authorities in San Cristóbal, while older men occupied the posts of judges and principales without threatening the people's identification as *batzil winiketik*, true men who upheld traditions expressed in rituals related to a particular history and often dramatized in Catholic religious events. By deferring to elder statesmen on ceremonial occasions and ensuring the flow of funds into the celebrations, youthful authorities did not subvert the age-ordered hierarchy, and growing differences in wealth were tolerated as long as richer members of the community accepted the more expensive cargos in the cycle of fiestas. Anthropologists working in Zinacantán (Cancian 1965) and San Juan Chamula (Gossen 1974; Rus and Wasserstrom 1980; Rus n.d.) demonstrated the key role played by the civil-religious hierarchy in validating authority while modernization processes were eroding the old bases of community integration: shared poverty and gerontocracy.

The compromises achieved in this wedding of tradition and modernization did not come about without strife in the highland communities. Periodic outbursts have occurred with increasing frequency throughout the 1990s as dissidents within these communities have objected to the corrupt tactics of their leaders. Earlier accusations of witchcraft have been updated as political parties and state development agencies have encroached on the community, but the contest for legitimation in relation to ethnic traditions continues. The Zapatista uprising fueled latent resentment against corporatist control by the PRI.

An important element in this fictive or imagined representation of a distinct ethnic identity is the gender specialization in responsibility for

14

adhering to custom.[9] Women in most highland communities still wear the distinctive *huipil* (blouse) along with skirts that identify their community of origin and sometimes the onset of menses (as in San Juan Chamula). Because marriage occurs within townships, women's dress identifies marriageable partners. It also situates the woman who wears a hand-loomed and brocaded or embroidered garment in the universe. Marta Turok captured the textual significance of huipiles in Santa María Magdalena, where the richly brocaded central panel forms a great cross over the shoulders, breast, and back (Turok 1988, 47–52). According to her informant, a diamond-shaped design in the center represents the cosmos containing the world within it, which resembles a cube with three levels, with earth in the center between the sky and the underworld. The colors of the huipil—red, black, yellow and white—represent grains of corn and cardinal points in the diamond world, while symbols of death—bat, *zopilote* (turkey buzzard), and worm—represent the pueblo. A Magdalena woman wearing her huipil thus situates herself in her cultural and natural world.

Amatenango women are less articulate about the symbolism of their dress. But extrapolating from their vision of the universe as a set of contained squares from a sacrificial hole in their houses (representing the house itself, the milpa, and the world), anthropologists can perceive them situating themselves in that universe when they wear the broad bands of red and gold forming a square around the neck. The significance of this orientation occurred to me when my *comadre* reacted with horror on seeing a Protestant proselyte offering free clothing from U.S. Goodwill dump sites to townspeople. Women's clothing in Amatenango became even more richly embroidered with silk threads on backstrap-loomed cotton from Venustiano Carranza as Amatenangueros acquired more income from pottery production for tourists in the 1980s. Women prayer-makers serving the Virgin Lucia replaced her ladino-style satin and lace garments with indigenous clothing in the 1970s as they gained greater autonomy when the pottery cooperative was functioning.

Indigenous men of the highland region tend to be less traditional in their everyday clothing than women. In the thirty-year interval be-

9. The stereotype of women as culturally conservative carriers of tradition has been attacked in feminist revisions of Latin American history, and I have tried to show how this stereotyping falsifies female participation in the labor force over time (Nash 1982). This critique of the stereotype should not obscure the fact that at certain moments in history and in many parts of the world, women are indeed charged with conserving their culture. For example, indigenous women in Mexico and Guatemala preserve the artisan traditions that identify them as distinct cultures in cooking, weaving, and pottery (Nash 1993). This tendency is in part a response to impoverishment of the domestic economy but is also a conscious priority in daily practice and in socializing children. Paradoxically, women are also in the forefront of radical adaptive change when they become the preferred labor force in transnational factories (Safa 1981) or when they engage in selling "traditional" artisan products in global markets (Nash 1993).

15

tween my visits to Amatenango, men stopped wearing the distinctive backstrap-loomed cotton shirts and wrapped pants in their everyday life, although they still use the *kotonchu* (tunic, literally "heart covering"), which is made in San Juan Ixcoy in Guatemala and imported clandestinely, for ceremonial occasions. The men of Zinacantán and San Juan Chamula differ from most men in highland communities in the increasing elaborateness of their tunics, which are hand-loomed by women. In these communities, where men are forced to seek income in areas farther and farther away, elaboration of their distinctive tunics may represent an attempt by the women to "brand" their men.

In the 1970s, the gender-specific integration of men in commercialization and transport of products while women were cut off from the burgeoning public realm of indígena-ladino encounters began to change as women's artisan production started to attract a wider market and higher earnings. The INI, prodded by women from artisan-producing communities, promoted the organizing of marketing cooperatives. Through these cooperatives, women gained increasing control over the money they made from pottery and weaving, which were now being sold to tourists and, through museum outlets, to a national and even international public (Nash 1993). But when Petrona, leader of the pottery cooperative in Amatenango del Valle, used the political contacts she had made through the cooperative to run for political office, her male opponent hired a killer to gun her down. She was obviously attacked as a political leader and organizer, even though many other motives related to her nontraditional behavior as a woman were advanced. After Petrona challenged the male-dominated power structure and her accusation that her opponent had misappropriated funds given to the town led to her death, other active leaders fled the town. No one dared revive the cooperative until 1995, when women in the Partido Revolucionario Democrático (PRD) gained support from the new party challenging the PRI monopoly of power through caciques (an Arawak word for leader carried to New Spain by Spaniards and now applied to indigenous authority figures).

Thus although women are becoming educated, acquiring Spanish language and writing skills, and venturing directly into markets, they are still more restricted to the home than men. The level of control exercised by men over women varies considerably in highland communities, from San Juan Chamula, where women are enjoined to walk barefoot "with their heads bowed" (Rosenbaum 1993), to Venustiano Carranza, where they reputedly browbeat men. It is clear nonetheless that their adherence to custom gives men the security to venture farther into the ladino world. Women did not vote until 1994, when the PRI, stung by accusations of fraud in the 1988 elections, insisted that the law requiring all citizens to vote be upheld. In indigenous villages co-opted by the PRI, the fine for failing to vote had been ignored with impunity

16

by patriarchal *caciques*. Petrona's fate made clear the danger for women in seeking public office.

Cooperatives of weavers in Chenalhó, Tenejapa, Oxchuc, and San Andrés Larainzar have often been undermined by the very development projects designed to promote their efforts. Credit from the Inter-American Development Bank remains channeled through the Desarrollo Integral de la Familia (DIF), whose titular leader is the wife of the governor of Chiapas. This agency purchases stock for its artisan retail outlets from individual producers, thus bypassing the cooperatives that provided an independent power base for women. This practice also makes it possible to keep prices low for work commissioned with individuals, given the lack of a bargaining agent to defend the women's interests.

The convoluted mixture of indigenous and Hispanic beliefs and practices that makes up "tradition" is manifested in the celebrations of Christian saints identified with the community. This custom is manifested most grandly from Carnival to Easter week in San Juan Chamula, the largest township in the region and the one closest to the ladino-dominated city of San Cristóbal de las Casas. Although the population of more than eighty thousand is distributed in many separate villages, all inhabitants have retained distinctive dress, woven of wool sheared from the flocks tended by women. All villagers contribute money for the communal festivals related to the saints' celebrations, and officials rent houses in the center during their term of office. This sacrifice of time and money guarantees them entry into positions in the civil-religious hierarchy that validates the authority of traditional caciques. During the religious celebrations between Carnival and Easter, the younger men, watched over by the elder officials, reenact at least seven historical events that Victoria Rifler Bricker (1981) has identified with conquest and independence uprisings. The most outstanding one is the "Caste War" (1867–1870), when Chamulans threatened to invade the governing center of San Cristóbal.[10] The costume worn by dancers reenacting the Chamulan rebellion is that of the French grenadier, a ladino officer in Maximilian's imperial army who allied himself with the Chamulans. During the nineteenth-century rebellion, religious devotees of a cult promising reinstatement of indigenous rule crucified a youth as their own martyred Christ in a vain attempt to gain the power of Catholic overlords (Bricker 1981). The rebellion failed, but its memory is kept alive in the drama reenacted each year. The entire event was ignored in Mexican history books and has only recently been recognized officially in school texts as an attempt to overcome the brutal repression of indígenas by ladinos.

10. Jan Rus (n.d.) questioned the official interpretation of the war as a "caste rebellion" of Indians versus ladinos because the aggression was initiated by ladinos and indigenous self-defense turned into a rebellion against intolerable oppression.

17

In other communities as well, religious dramatizations served as a venue for acting out subversively the latent antagonisms that have characterized relations between indígenas and ladinos, often beneath the gaze of church and state authorities who were unaware of the actors' latent intent. These "traditions" have changed along with the ethnic relations on which they were scripted. For example, in Amatenango del Valle, I witnessed the Holy Week pageant of the jailing and crucifixion of Christ in 1966 and again in 1993. I perceived a shift in dramatization from a hostile encounter between polarized ethnic groups to a hilarious contest between indígenas and specific "change agents." In 1966, after the *mayordomos* attended to the crucified Christ, Judas was hung from the church belfry on Saturday in order "to show the world that he killed Christ." On the surface, the attack on his swinging body seemed to enact vengeance for Judas's role in killing Christ, as it had just been described in the sermon presented by the ladino priest. But the indigenous portrayal of Judas—wearing sun glasses, a cigarette dangling from his lips, and dressed in a somber jacket, shirt, pants, boots, and cowboy hat—could also be read as a caricature of a ladino *ranchero*, one they might even have worked for. When the effigy was cut down from the gallows on Sunday, the mayordomos (caretakers of the saints) beat it with sticks in mocking castration of a clearly hated figure. Later it was carried around town on horseback—itself an ironic act because in early colonial times only ladinos were allowed to ride horses (Colby 1966)—while the mayordomos collected money from the curers to buy liquor. Finally, the assembled audience tore the figure apart, saving the wooden mask but burning the straw body. This sequence seemed to me a subversive attack on the dominant ladinos, mimicking the indígenas own desire to kill their opponent (the ladino oppressor) (Nash 1968).

The overt hatred and intense attack on the effigy in the earlier ritual were absent when I witnessed the same occasion twenty-seven years later. In 1993 Judas was dressed in a red shirt, jogging pants, and Nikes, sporting a blue helmet like those worn by engineers in the field and carrying a plastic attaché case. When I asked the meaning of this costume, the mayordomo told me with a smile that it represented a forestry agent. Known for their penchant for soliciting bribes from town officials for violating any one of a hundred rules on cutting trees, these agents now symbolize the quintessential corrupt representative of the government. The scene was a hilarious spoof of ethnic encounter, now focused on particular agents: boys accompanied the Judas on horseback, led by a mayordomo on a tour of the town center. Much joking and laughing ensued when the men dismantled the figure and burned the straw. They were no longer handling a figure of fear but rather a comical interloper whom they humiliated rather than attacked.

During the lengthy interval between my visits, relations between

18

indigenous groups and ladinos had changed. Indigenous men were competing in local elections as members of the ruling PRI, the opposition Partido Revolucionario Democrático (PRD), or the Partido de Acción Nacional (PAN). They had become familiar with populist tactics of co-optation and knew how to reap rewards within that system. Most of the men elected as president had garnered enough money from the allotments for public works to buy television sets, trucks, or cattle. Now they were making demands on a system that had been glad to co-opt them into the corporatist framework of government. These officeholders knew how to bribe officials in the numerous overlapping agencies dealing with indigenous affairs in the Comisión de Reforma Agraria, the Secretaría de Agraria y Recursos Hidrólicos (SARH), and the agency directly concerned with indigenous affairs, the Oficina de Asuntos Indígenas. Thus the participants acted in the ladino scenes with self-assurance rather than the temerity combined with outbreaks of rage that characterized their demeanor in the past. The same men were increasingly using their power while in office to take advantage of members of their own village, allotting the best ejido lands to themselves and using state government funds for their own purposes.

In the 1970s and early 1980s, the PRI increased control over caciques and their local communities through freewheeling spending by the Programa de Desarrollo para Chiapas (PRODESCH). In the absence of strict accounting controls, these expenditures were little more than payoffs to local caciques to deliver the vote to the PRI. In Amatenango a group of bilingual teachers who were indígenas from other communities opposed the local caciques, men belonging to an extended family whose members had taken advantage of funds funneled through PRODESCH to buy themselves trucks and expand their own commercial activities. The teachers demanded the removal of one cacique whom they had identified as the assassin of Petrona, the president of the pottery cooperative. In retaliation, the caciques killed the older, most-venerated educational promotor, a native of the community. The teachers' attempt to bring the suspect to justice failed because PRI-dominated state officials were unwilling to intervene as long as the caciques continued to support the official party.

The reaction against corrupt local officials peaked in 1994. On 14 July, more than a thousand Zinacantecos seized and beat the mayor and four other Indians whom they charged with misappropriating government funds for community projects.[11] The same month, Chenalhó townspeople openly accused PRI-backed officials, and even in the PRI stronghold of San Juan Chamula, townspeople criticized the mayor's expulsion of compatriots and circulated rumors that he would be forced to resign. Amid the growing critique of PRI politics following the Zapatista upris-

11. *Tiempo*, 15 July 1994, 16, no. 2256 (published in San Cristóbal de las Casas, Chiapas).

19

ing, the tactics used to co-opt local leaders (detailed in Cancian 1992) were no longer acceptable.

President Salinas de Gortari had introduced more efficient accounting practices when he took office in 1988, funneling international aid and discretionary public funds from the newly created PRONASOL (Programas Nacionales de Solidaridad) to reward local power brokers and curb rebellious constituencies (Nash and Kovic n.d.). During his *sexenio*, money tended to be expended where protest was greatest—except in the jungle area where there were no polling booths and the settlers never voted.

Caciques in many indigenous villages who had won control of political offices during the decade of co-optive giveaways developed a new tactic for enriching themselves: they began to expel Protestants and others whom they claimed were not following "traditions," seizing their lands, homes, and animals. The wealth gap within indigenous communities has also widened due to the rise of trucking and other commercial ventures. Moreover, it had become clear that the growing population could not be sustained by subsistence crop production, especially in Chamula, where good farm land is even more scarce than elsewhere. Starting in 1972, the caciques instigated massive expulsions of more than fifteen thousand locals charged with being Protestants or not following tradition (Tickell 1991). Those expelled now live in the *"cinturones de miseria"* (poverty belts) on the outskirts of San Cristóbal or on land along the Pan American Highway bought by Protestant churches. Women are bearing the burden of these expulsions because they are often abandoned by their husbands after fleeing to the city and attempting to earn a living by selling artisan products of their own or those purchased wholesale (Sullivan 1992).

Urban exiles organized to protest the violation of their rights to land in their own communities in a peaceful demonstration in San Cristóbal de las Casas in 1992. In response, the Chamulan caciques threatened to fine each head of household a week's wages unless members of the community went to the city and confronted the urban exiles with a counterdemonstration in their barrio, La Hormiga. When violence resulted, some in the crowd were injured by stones thrown, and arrests were made. This failure by the municipal authorities in San Cristóbal to punish aggressors follows a stance historically justified in terms of the autonomy of indigenous peoples, a right mainly recognized when only indígenas are the victims. Although these expulsions violate religious freedom as sanctioned by the Mexican Constitution, PRI state officials have not responded to the appeals of the expelled.

The most recent group expelled consisted of 485 men, women, and children forced to flee several Chamula hamlets in September 1993. Unlike their predecessors, however, these exiles did not establish homes in

20

the urban "poverty belts" but took up residence in the vacated offices of the Oficina de Asuntos Indígenas. They also acquired weapons, and when the Chamula authorities came after them in August 1994, the Protestants fired on them and killed two. After months of trying to negotiate with the interim governor of Chiapas, the families finally returned to their homes in August 1994, just before the elections. Although the leaders had not succeeded in gaining any guarantees of safety from state or local officials, they reasoned that if they waited until after the elections, they would have to wait six more years to call attention to their plight. Their situation is now being monitored by civil rights advocates and national and international media, and they have not vacated their homes as yet, even though two were killed in September. Although the interim governor of Chiapas did not provide legal guarantees or seek compensation for the exiled Protestants, his willingness to enter into negotiations with their leaders was unprecedented for a PRI official.

The involution of the political struggle in Amatenango, Chamula, and other established communities involves a class and gender struggle masked as religious and cultural "purification." Sometimes this struggle takes the form of abuse of women, alcoholism, and homicide directed against individuals in the same village (Eber 1994; Nash 1970, 1993; Rosenbaum 1993). But increasingly, it has resulted in wholesale expulsions of thousands of compatriots, as in Chamula where more than twenty thousand have been expelled since 1972. Frequently, the targets of the repression are poorer members of the community who have protested control by the caciques. Women like those who left Chamula only to be abandoned by their husbands once they had established residence in San Cristóbal or those from Amatenango who were forced to flee when their cooperative leader was assassinated have now become activists in changes that are disrupting domestic units as well as communities (Nash 1993; Sullivan 1992).

This dominance by a few leaders in the center has engendered resentment on the part of community members who are excluded from the indigenous power structure within their own township. Sometimes this resentment has been channeled in the opposition of center versus the peripheral hamlets and *aldeas*, as in Amatenango. At other times, it is expressed in the opposition of wealthy families who have taken funds and resources coming into the municipio versus the poor who do not have access to offices or public funds, as in Zinacantán. This opposition is now expressed in party affiliation as the highland villages, inspired by the Zapatista uprising, seek redress for the many injuries and abuses they have suffered. Following the elections in August 1994, PRD militants seized town halls in fifty-seven communities in the state of Chiapas where they had strength and declared the right to autonomy in the choice of authority guaranteed in Article 39 of the constitution.

21

Amatenango was one the municipios where PRD followers took over the town hall two days after PRI officials assumed office in the formal ceremony on New Year's Day, which began with a mass in the church and continued with the keys being handed over to the new officials and a procession with banners across the plaza. The town offices of president and *sindico* have always been held by residents of the nucleated center, with residents of the aldeas holding only judgeships and police duties. These officials are paid less and have no access to funds coming into the township. Following the takeover, a plebiscite was held, and women's participation was encouraged by both parties. The resulting vote (892 for the PRI to 1,095 for the PRD) was closer than in August, when the PRI got slightly over one-half of the votes. Although PRI officials chose to consider all PRD supporters as "outsiders" or members of the hamlets, I recognized many center residents. PRD supporters characterized the opposition as being under the sway of Protestants, although they were not a numerically predominant force, despite the conversion of the mayor.

Amatenango's rebellion reflects the currents of change affecting the corporate communities due to the unsettled conflict in the jungle. New cohorts are demanding a voice within as well as outside the boundaries erected to defend ethnic divisions. Women, who constituted the majority (600 of 1,095 votes for the PRD), may become a decisive force as male power blocs seek their support. The stimulus for change emanating from the uprising is being channeled through ancient divisions as the new course of action is being set.

One of the few townships where the classical struggle between *campesinos* and large landowners has continued to rage since the eighteenth century is Venustiano Carranza, where large landowners prevented implementation of land reform long after the revolution. Unlike the lands belonging to indigenous communities at higher altitudes, the lands in the township are more fertile and are irrigated by the rivers running through the town. The Organización de Campesinos "Emiliano Zapata" (OCEZ) staged protests there and also dramatized the campesinos' plight with a hunger strike in San Cristóbal and the state capital of Tuxtla Gutiérrez, all to no avail.

Shortly after the Revolution of 1910, the caciques who were to dominate the town for the next half-century seized the best land and ruled the civil government, preventing the passage of revolutionary reforms. When Indians tried to seize land according to the agrarian reform in 1923, the town mayor imprisoned the ejido commissioner. This violent pattern was repeated in 1929, when leaders of land seizures were killed, and again in 1945. In May 1976, soldiers were sent in UNICEF vans comandeered by the government to put down a protest, and in September, soldiers using these vans photographed campesinos in the Casa del Pueblo.

22

They were forced to kneel and make a victory sign while holding machine guns placed in their hands to prove that they were part of an armed uprising (Guzmán 1977). In 1974, the Departamento de Asuntos Agrarios y Colonización had notified cattlemen to abandon lands officially granted to Indians, but the order was ignored. Construction of the Angostura hydroelectric dam reduced the land available for peasants, who received seven million pesos (equaling seven thousand new pesos). Fifteen campesinos were killed in a fight in August 1984, and others were tortured while in prison.[12] Throughout the governorship of Castellanos and his successor, Patrocinio González Garrido, conflicts over land embroiled hundreds of campesinos and resulted in scores of deaths.

My direct knowledge of the conflict began in June 1991, shortly after I visited the town. At that time, the cane growers of the township of Venustiano Carranza confronted the new owners of the sugar refinery in Pujiltic (a settlement within the township) over failure to pay adequate prices for the growers' sugar, and they were fired on by a detachment of military police sent from barracks just outside San Cristóbal. The refinery had been denationalized in 1986 in the wave of privatizations required by the International Monetary Fund to renegotiate the national debt, and the new owners, a consortium of Japanese and Mexican owners, retained ownership just long enough to sell the reserve sugar supplies in the warehouses. Meanwhile, government efforts to stabilize the regional economy by offering subsidies to local farmers in the form of low-interest loans and low-cost fertilizers and pesticides were stopped. These events all contributed to the sense of injustice arising among indígenas as they watch the area's rich resources being confiscated by the government, which has consistently favored wealthy businessmen and large landowners in its neoliberal reforms.

Reforms in government spending brought an even greater threat to local autonomy: the so-called reform of the Reforma Agraria. Corporate landholdings guaranteed by Article 27 of the Constitution of 1917 are again being threatened, as they were during the Porfiriato, by changes in the agrarian law. A new law passed in 1992 allows for the sale of ejido (collectively held) lands as well as for joint ventures with private enterprises. The law was modified in the negotiations that took place while the act was being discussed, adding guarantees that indigenous ejido lands would not be alienated, but most indigenous groups are aware that if *ejidatarios* are not able to repay loans made in joint enterprises on communal lands, banks could take the lands.

Breakdown of the fragile balance between co-optive spending and outright repression in Mexico came with the 1994 New Year's guerrilla

---

12. See the "Declaración de los Presos Políticos en Chiapas, al Governador Absalón Castellanos Domínguez, Tuxtla Gutiérrez, 25 de agosto 1984," documents in INAREMAC.

23

insurrection that challenged the legitimacy of the ruling PRI. By resorting to armed force, Mayas in Mexico seemed to be paralleling the developments in Guatemala since the 1970s (Carmack 1984; Jonas 1984). Subsequent developments in the conflict zone, however, indicate that this apparent similarity obscures different premises and an alternative path to achieving political goals.

ETHNIC CONSCIOUSNESS IN LOWLAND CHIAPAS

Indigenous culture survives more easily in situ. The Mayan landscape reveals shrines built to ancestors and Christian saints that often mask an indigenous deity identified with a Christian counterpart. During the annual cycle of religious festivals, rituals carried out at these shrines imprint their significance on each succeeding generation. For example, on the third day of May, the Day of the Cross in the Christian calendar, Amatenangueros accompany the captains of the fiesta cycle to the hill of the ancestors. They are believed to live in a cave there, coming out to climb a precipitous rock spire in order to keep vigil over the town and make certain that no evil enters it (Nash 1970). Zinacantecos worship at altars set out in the open at each water hole, from which they derive a spiritual relation to the lineage ancestors and the spirits inhabiting the environs. Each cave and hill are the potential residence of spirits who must be propitiated to ensure survival (Vogt 1976a). Inhabitants of Chenalhó, for example, can identify much of their mythic history in the surrounding landscape (Arias 1985).

This kind of situational identity is lost in migrations that upset the sense of living in a sacred environment. Yet ethnic identification persists even in the inhospitable areas of the Lacandón jungle and on the rocky hilltops, which were previously considered unfit for occupation until purchased by dissident Protestants forced to flee their communities. But the meaning of such situational identity has been transformed for both the bearers and the state. Mexican and Guatemalan Mayan migrants into the lowlands of the Lacandón jungle and the border area have found a new basis for identity that relies on communalistic norms forged in the reconstituting of their ethnicity.

Mexican Colonizers in the Lacandón Jungle

The jungle began to be colonized soon after independence as private companies started to exploit the land for lumber and oil and to introduce cattle and coffee. Few indigenous settlers arrived until after World War II, when indígenas from nearby townships in the department of Ocosingo who were seeking land were followed by Tzeltales from Palenque. Four colonies were established—Nueva Esperanza, El Lacan-

24

dón, 11 de Julio, and Ricardo Flores Magón—during the presidencies of Adolfo López Mateos and Gustavo Díaz Ordaz, both of whom emphasized ejidos over large landholders to promote basic production of subsistence crops (Arizpe, Paz, and Velázquez 1993, 82). Colonizers after 1970 came from Guerrero, Puebla, Oaxaca, Michoacán, and Chiapas. After being granted fifty hectares of land, the ejidatarios received cattle credits and a promise that the state would buy the wood they cut. These policies promoted devastation of the forest at a rate so alarming that the situation attracted world attention. In 1972 the Mexican government decreed that more than six hundred thousand hectares would be ceded to sixty-six Lacandón heads of families, knowing that it would be easier to bypass controls if concessions were mediated by indígenas. Simultaneous delineation of a biosphere reserve in the central-west jungle impeded the sale of lands in a restricted area. Despite the fact that colonizers have experienced increasing aridity and heat accompanied by high winds and torrential rains as the jungle disappeared, some still resent the government's urging them to save the forest (Arizpe, Paz, and Velázquez 1993, 123).

The experience of the colony named Marqués de Comillas in the department of Ocosingo encompasses most of the problems affecting indígenas in their new environment. Four ejido plots located in the Montañas de Oriente on the banks of the Usumacinta were carved out of the jungle in 1963. Hemmed in by the large Lacandón land grants and the Reserva Biosfera Montes Azules, new immigrants are now encroaching on colonies established prior to 1972, when the first land grant was made. The region now includes Choles, Zoques, Nahuas, Chinantecos, Tojolobales, Tzeltales, and Tzotziles along with mestizos and ladinos who have settled on ejido land.

The lack of clear policies on forest exploitation and other natural resources has occasioned many political conflicts in the Lacandón jungle. Contradictory goals are being pursued in the colonies settled by indigenous inhabitants versus those where mestizo settlers predominate. Arturo Coutino Ferrera (1987) found that in the indigenous colonies, indígenas in Flor de Cacao and Nueva Unión show a strict respect for the forest reserves, while mestizos are cutting the forest with chain saws for commercial sales or burning woodlands for cattle *fincas* in their settlements. The presence of employees of PEMEX (Petroleros Mexicanos) distorts market prices for local buyers. Also, indigenous colonizers have often gotten into disputes with the cattle ranchers, oil explorers, and the state.

The ambiguities and contradictions inherent in government policies led to a protest march in 1991 by hundreds of colonizers in Marqués de Comillas. The government ruled that trees could be cut but could not be sold for lumber. When colonizers cut down the trees to plant their crops, government trucks arrived without warning, loaded up the wood, and carried it off to sell. Many of the various groups colonizing the area

25

objected, and more than 150 individuals began a march to Mexico City to protest the corruption of the government. They were met by 700 military troops stationed in the area, and men, women, and children were imprisoned in Palenque and Tuxtla Gutiérrez jails and held incommunicado for several days, without the food offered by relief agencies. The coincidental meeting of a United Nations group in Mexico at the time of the jailing led to a declaration calling for their release. Despite this experience, the same group re-formed several months later to protest the government's failure to uphold the terms of the agreement (Nash and Sullivan 1992).

Such protests have demonstrated the political potential of these communities. Despite the diversity of Mayan linguistic groups in this new setting, they have shown a greater ability to coordinate political action than the corporate communities they left behind. The general poverty of the colonists contrasts with the growing differences in wealth in corporate communities, where "tradition" is invoked to validate the arbitrary rule of caciques, and the shared poverty creates a class solidarity that reinforces ethnic identity as indígenas rather than as members of distinct communities.

The change in Article 27 regarding claims to land is affecting the colonizers in the Lacandón jungle more than the indígenas in corporate communities. For those who lacked title, it dashed the hope that they would ever obtain legal rights to land some had occupied for decades, the same land promised when they migrated there twenty years ago. Colonizers who have titles to their lands are now more prone to sell because they became indebted while trying to establish their new homesteads. The new law also re-creates the conditions for *latifundismo*, thus breaking the social contract established by the Mexican Revolution. José Luis Calvo claims in *La disputa para la tierra* that via corporations operating through contracts with communities, the maximum amount of land held can be multiplied up to twenty-five times above the legal limit of a hundred hectares of irrigated land per person.[13] With titleholders being able to include allotments for children and spouses as part of a single domain, cattlemen in the Lacandón rain forest have been able to increase their holdings to as many as 250 hectares of irrigated land, 20,000 hectares of wooded land, and up to 300,000 of pasturage.

Neil Harvey (1994) summarized the policies of President Salinas that precipitated the rebellion: the withdrawal of subsidies in the form of credit; cutbacks or discontinuation of government programs providing technical aid and marketing assistance; privatization of nationalized companies that often sustained regional economies; and the elimination of price subsidies. In Chiapas, these policies had negative effects on output as well as the environment because campesinos tried to increase the

13. For a review of this work, see *Proceso*, no. 905, 7 Mar. 1994, p. 18.

26

cultivated area to make up for their losses, thus contributing to deforestation and soil depletion (Harvey 1994, 12). Nor did increased expenditures of PRONASOL money in the jungle on social welfare programs, which grew by 130 percent in 1989–1990, make up for the losses in production caused by neoliberal policies (Harvey 1994, 18).

The population of 200,000 settlers in the vast tract that was once the Lacandón *selva* is now split between the majority of those who support the Zapatistas and those who are neutral. The cattle ranchers have opposed all colonizers even before the uprising and have tried to drive them out or kill them by hiring *guardias blancas*. None have taken a stand against the Zapatistas, although thirty families who had converted to Protestantism went into self-exile in Guatemala in June 1994. Others have retreated to refugeee camps in towns near the conflict zone, such as Altamirano and Las Margaritas. The 60,000 inhabitants of the "conflict zone" (where the Zapatistas have a majority of supporters) are clearly identified with the movement and are encircled by the army, which limits their movements beyond the military outposts. Their ability to sell their crops has also been hurt: they were forced to sell their cash crops like coffee and fruits from the last harvest at a tenth of the normal retail price that settlers receive.

In June 1994, I visited Flor del Río, a Tojolobal town in the *municipio* of Las Margaritas in the territory held by the Zapatistas, with María Eugenia Santana who has worked there in an applied anthropology program for the past four years. The colonizers arrived in 1972. The elders speak Tojolobal, but the younger members have lost their Mayan language. They farm their land in common, with men and women working side by side cultivating and harvesting their crops, which are then distributed collectively or sold in common. The houses were even more miserable than those of the Guatemalan refugees I visited, and the public buildings clearly had not benefited from PRONASOL funding. Like most of the jungle colonies, the community has no clinic, and medical service in the neighboring town offers few medicines and only sporadic visits by a doctor. The high power lines visible overhead send no feeder lines into the village. The school has one teacher for over a hundred children and was closed due to his absence when we arrived, a situation described to me as typical.

Even more poorly served was Pathuitz, a community about two hours by car from Ocosingo (in Zapatista territory), which we visited on election day. The schoolhouse and town offices were more wretched than those in any of the communities of Guatemalan exiles after twenty-five years of settlement. We saw no signs of traditional artisan production in the houses or yards, although the wooden houses were thatched in the same manner as reconstructions of housing in Classic Maya sites. Most of the women were monolingual. Disarming in their bright synthetic dresses

27

and aprons, with rows of metal barrettes flashing like ammunition clips in their hair, these young women were clearly constituents of the Zapatista army arrayed at the Convención Nacional Democrática. Their camera-shyness related more to the ongoing danger that they would be identified by army security forces than to the sense of *vergüenza* (shame) cultivated among women in Hispanic society.

When the Zapatistas opened the area for the convention held 6–9 August 1994, more than 5,000 delegates and 600 press representatives witnessed the impoverished conditions and experienced them firsthand when they camped on the ground cleared for the occasion. The introduction by Subcomandante Marcos of the "army" brought tears along with applause as a few hundred of the "soldiers" marched on the cement walkway bordering the grandstand, painstakingly constructed by the colonizers for their guests. The few soldiers in uniforms of a sort, masked and bearing weapons, were followed by young men and women often bearing sticks. The last group to file by had tied white binding on the barrels of their rifles, a symbol of their search for peace. Women, many of whom had babies in carrying cloths, wore aprons over printed cotton or synthetic dresses much like those described by B. Traven in his novel of the jungle written in the 1930s, *El puente en la selva*. The flimsy nylon kerchiefs masking their faces and wooden sticks carried like arms symbolized their new status as revolutionaries. Except for the roads constructed for the benefit of cattle ranchers and oil explorers, the villages have no more amenities in the mid-1990s than those found by B. Traven while living among indígenas in the wilderness sixty years ago.

In an impassioned speech, Subcomandante Marcos invoked patriotism, the desire of the Zapatistas to become full citizens in civil society, and their commitment to peaceful negotiations. The discussions by participants in the Convención Nacional Democrática that preceded the trip to the jungle in San Cristóbal introduced the themes of cultural autonomy and the tolerance of differences, dignity, and justice. The verbal messages contained nothing new, but the articulation of many different groups who made up the convention and the interaction taking place at the discussion tables in San Cristóbal and later in the jungle presented an alternative political process. Given the PRI's monopoly on power, little hope existed that the issues could be resolved in the convention or in elections on 21 August, but the spirit of compromise, unity, and democracy keynoted by Pablo González Casanova in his speech in the natural amphitheater gave listeners hope for fundamental change. The Convención demonstrated the possibility of incorporating all ethnic groups into the democratic agenda, an objective never attained by the revolutions of the past three centuries.

The uprising has already affected the Mexican political process. Even before the negotiations in March, President Salinas de Gortari agreed

28

to provide economic aid to the region, recognize human rights provisions for the insurgents and their supporters, and limit campaign spending in the coming elections. As a step toward overcoming discrimination against indígenas in the region, he dismissed acting governor Elmar Setzer Marseille and his predecessor Patrocinio González Garrido, who had held the post of interior minister in the nation's capital until recent events revealed the depth of resentment against his suppression of protest movements while he was governor. The state and federal governments also agreed to assist agriculturalists adversely affected by NAFTA and promised a series of economic and social improvements to include increased medical attention, electrification, and improved bilingual schooling. But the PRI has not yet addressed the issues of land redistribution and title to land allocated to colonizers that has been encroached on with impunity by oil, lumber, and cattle enterprises. Negotiations have not been resumed. After the elections, the Zapatistas warned that violence would erupt again if new governor Eduardo Robledo Rincón, whom they claim was fraudently elected, did not step down.[14] Later, on 18 September 1994, they announced that the Mexican army had doubled its troops in Chiapas. This claim was denied by the Mexican Departmento de Defensa, which stated that troops had not been increased above the 20,000 stationed there since January.[15] By October, it was evident nevertheless that troops had indeed been increased,[16] and Mexican paramilitary troops were rumored to be infiltrating the Zapatista area.

Guatemalan Exiles along the Southern Mexican Border

Chiapas was part of the province of Guatemala throughout the colonial period, and the choice by elites to align the region with Mexico was made years after independence from Spain in 1821. The resulting border divides Mayas who have more in common with each other than with Mexico's indigenous peoples to the north. They also share a similar history in their relations with the national government. After independence, liberal policies pursued in both Guatemala and Mexico were aimed at promoting export production and a free market by breaking up corporate landholdings. Because of their limited resources, however, neither government could overcome the power of regional caudillos (military leaders) for half a century. Díaz Ordaz's counterpart in Guatemala was General Justo Rufino Barrios, who became president after the liberal revolution in 1871. He permitted indigenous communities to retain limited allotments of communal lands because cultivation of small plots allowed

14. Anthony DePalma, *New York Times*, 8 Sept. 1994.
15. Anthony DePalma, *New York Times*, 18 Sept. 1994.
16. Tim Golden, *New York Times*, 18 Oct. 1994

29

them to survive while forcing them to work for the abysmal wages paid in the coffee and fruit plantations (McCreery 1990; Smith 1984a, 1984b).

Mayas in the border area have always moved back and forth across the artificial line separating them. During the Mexican Revolution of 1910, many indigenous Chiapanecos fled to Guatemala. The flow reversed starting in the 1920s, as 10,000 to 20,000 Guatemalans crossed the border periodically to work in coffee harvests. After the coup in 1954 by Carlos Castillo Armas, their numbers swelled to 60,000 (Hamilton and Chinchilla 1991). Some of these indigenous and mestizo workers settled in Chiapas, blending into Mexican society or retaining their distinctive cultures (Hamilton and Chinchilla 1991). The seasonal exodus of indígenas leaving Guatemala for Mexico increased in the late 1970s and reached a flood in 1981 and 1982, as political exiles augmented the flow. In a startling reversal in June 1994, 30 families of Mexican Mayas, most of them Protestant converts, joined Guatemalan exiles who had returned to their country because they were unwilling to face the dangers of living in the conflict zone in the Lacandón selva.

Increased settlement in the frontier regions on the Guatemalan side of the border paralleled that on the Mexican side in the 1970s as Mam-speaking indígenas began to colonize the jungle area of the Ixil triangle. Pressure on land had been growing since the coup led by Castillo Armas in 1954, after which lands granted under the Land Reform Act of 1946 were returned to their previous owners and all peasant cooperatives were dissolved (Kinzer and Schlesinger 1981). With households becoming more dependent on the market, few of them could grow more than half of their own food needs. Most relied on seasonal wage labor on export-oriented plantations and artisan production (Smith 1984b, 147). Rural Guatemalans with no land were forced to work in highly exploitative conditions.

Attacks on indigenous peoples intensified in the late 1970s, peaking under General Romeo Lucas García (1978–1982) and his successor, Efraín Ríos Montt (1982–1983). The purpose of disarticulating the populations that served as the social basis for the insurgents became increasingly clear during the Lucas García presidency, when 5000 indigenous Guatemalan campesinos were captured and assassinated. Ríos Montt launched a scorched-earth policy from April to November 1982, destroying harvests and entire villages in some thirty collective massacres (Jonas, McCaughan, and Martínez 1984, 1). In the ensuing conflict, the Guatemalan army forced more than a hundred thousand peasants off land they legally owned, and thousands of activists were assassinated by paramilitary groups organized by the Guatemalan army with the help of U.S. counterinsurgency forces (Jonas, McCaughan, and Martínez 1984). Indígenas were displaced from their homes and forced into "model villages" under militarized regimentation. Patrols of the countryside initiated under Ríos Montt continued under President Oscar Humberto Mejía Victores

30

(1983–1985), especially in the Ixil triangle in the department of El Quiché (adjacent to Chiapas), where 400 hamlets were destroyed (Warren 1993). Those who claim that indígenas are the unwitting victims of two armies—the Guatemalan military and the guerrilla—ignore or reject the evidence of researchers intimately associated with the region.[17] According to Carol Smith, massacres "were carried out by the state against unarmed, non-politicized, rural people located either in zones planned for future capitalist development or in zones thought to have considerable potential commercial development" (1984b, 151). Quoting S. Davis and J. Hodson, she adds that anyone perceived as Indian, especially an Indian traditionalist, was also targeted.

Thus when class divisions were beginning to fragment the indigenous populations in Mexico, the extreme poverty and genocidal policies of the Guatemalan government forced more than 150,000 indigenous Guatemalans to flee into exile in the border states of Mexico. The alternative, as Beatriz Manz indicated, was to be relocated by the Guatemalan national army in militarized communities or risk death (Manz 1988, 145ff). The political refugees who tried to enter Mexico in 1980 were not accepted until the end of 1982, when they gained the cooperation of the Mexican government, the Catholic Church, and international agencies who assisted the families in relocating along the border. Some joined Mexican communities in the jungle area.

Multiple massacres and destruction of aldeas and communities by the Guatemalan army disarticulated the indigenous communities (Green 1992). But this outcome had the unplanned consequence of overcoming the diversity of indigenous communities (Escalona and Nava 1992, 202) and reactivated the communitarian and regional exchanges that had also been part of their tradition as they adapted to the new setting (Watanabe 1992). Re-creating a community requires space to build its houses and cultivate crops, undertakings in which communities were assisted by Mexican and international agencies, but it also requires a basis for rebuilding their identity. Some Guatemalan indígenas brought marimbas and introduced their religious festivals into the communities where they settled. Often they named the camps after aldeas or cooperatives of origin or the linguistic group to which they belonged (Escalona and Nava 1992, 203). With funding received from international sources, they soon outpaced their Mexican neighbors in the health and education services organized by promoters among the refugees. Agents of the Comisión Mex-

17. Stoll's (1993) image of indigenous Guatemalans caught between two armies is not reflected in the narratives of Guatemalans who fled into exile starting in 1981. Manz recounts their stories of gruesome killings, unheard-of torture, and destruction of entire villages by the Guatemalan army (Manz 1987, 146). The Guatemalan Ejército Guerrillero de los Pobres arose as an alternative course for resisting genocide. Analysts with divergent theoretical leanings concur on the precipitating causes of the violence (Smith 1984a; Warren 1993).

31

icana para la Ayuda de los Refugiados (COMAR) drew on skills of the Guatemalan refugees in bicultural education and artisan programs and were impressed with the creative results (Manz 1988, 148).

I witnessed this remarkable reconstitution in 1991 in Pozas Ricas and Porvenir, two border communities. Pozas Ricas includes hundreds of exiled Guatemalans who are living peacefully with Mexican indígenas and ladinos. They work in the milpas of both ethnic groups at half the minimum wage of five U.S. dollars a day. Guatemalan merchants travel throughout the area regularly, selling Guatemalan artisan products like traditional tie-dyed skirts from Totonicapan and other commercial craft items. Pozas Ricas is unusual in having a clinic staffed by dedicated doctors and health care agents who serve the surrounding area, including those Guatemalans who risk crossing the border illegally to use the clinic. Exile communities like Porvenir that received aid from UN and Catholic relief agencies have built their own schools and churches, where lay people conduct classes and religious services. Their programs started to reflect issues of ethnic revindication and a search for their own cultural roots as they began to make themselves the subject of the histories they taught the children.

More than 20,000 of the 150,000 Guatemalan Mayas who fled across the border have remained in Chiapas, even after relocation of the exiles in Quintano Roo and Campeche in 1984 and the repatriation movement led by Rigoberta Menchú in January 1993. Their presence sharpens competition for resources and in the labor force but has also led to some positive exchanges. In their struggle to overcome the alienating experience of military repression and exile, the Guatemalan indigenous exiles have certainly reinvigorated the Mexican Mayan sense of a distinct identity. Ana Maria Garza Caligaris has studied ejidatario attitudes in Nuevo San Juan Chamula, Nuevo Huixtán, and Nuevo Matzam regarding Guatemalan exiles in their midst (Garza Caligaris 1992). Mexican ejidatarios view themselves in a similar position vis-à-vis the expansion of capitalism in the south of Mexico. Like the Guatemalans, they too are trying to escape having to work on the plantations, and they too find themselves harassed by military and immigration agents who treat them little better than the Guatemalans (Garza Caligaris 1992, 207). The suspicion that Guatemalans living in sanctuary in Chiapas may have instigated the uprising (a claim denied by the Zapatistas) has exacerbated the prejudicial treatment of both groups by the augmented troops in the area (Earle 1994). This shared persecution has undoubtedly sharpened indigenous awareness of the common problems they face as Indians. Once the Guatemalans arrived with the permission of the Mexican government, the Mexicans already settled in the area accepted them in their midst. Few Mexicans were taken in by the claim that the new arrivals were guerrillas and have judged them instead by their willingness to work and their cooperativeness in communal affairs.

32

CONCLUSIONS

Cultural autonomy, defended throughout five hundred years of conquest and colonization, is a powerful resource in providing the ideological context in which indígenas are framing their new world. Theoreticians who focus exclusively on identity forget the struggles for bread and land in which it was forged and thus bring a Eurocentric perspective to their analyses of such movements (see Laclau and Mouffe 1985; Laclau 1990; Slater 1992). Theories that emphasize culture and identity (especially Hall 1986; Escobar 1992) amplify understanding of how and why individuals and groups become actors in history, but their success also derives from the contextualization in the reality that indígenas endure. As subordinated groups within the capitalist framework of production and exchange, indígenas need protection for their land against further privatization in order to allow the collective strategies with which they have defended themselves to flourish (Stephen 1994)—but they also need the credit, technology, and modern techniques that will enable them to sustain growing populations with limited land resources (Collier 1993). They need access to information and the skills to use it for their own ends—but they also need a democratic arena where their distinct aims and values will be tolerated by ethnically distinct groups.

Appeals to ethnic cohesiveness may be effective in times of political crisis, but the distinctive histories of Chiapas Mayas work against the possibilities of pan-indigenous movements at this time. The contrast between highland Mayan communities and the settlers in the lowland jungle and frontier areas illustrates the different experiences of these diverse Mayan populations that have shaped future regional alliances in terms of ethnic identity. Highland communities split by growing class differences have used alliances with the ruling PRI to take advantage of their own townspeople, expelling some in the name of a specious tradition and seizing public funds for private use. These wealthier individuals are the beneficiaries of gains from the Revolution of 1910, from which other Mayan populations—especially those who have colonized the jungle—are being systematically excluded. Wealthier highlanders enjoy a degree of local autonomy and are governed by officials indigenous to the community, while many selva communities are governed by cattlemen who are mestizos or ladinos. Moreover, highland communities' access to public funds has made those in power insensitive to the rebels' claims and less committed to regional movements for land. In the lowland areas, indigenous and mestizo campesinos participate to a greater extent in regional associations such as the Central Independiente de Obreros Agrícolas y Campesinos (CIOAC), the Unión de Ejidos Kiptikta Lekubtesel Unidos por la Fuerza en Chiapas, and the Unión de Uniones Ejidales y Grupos Campesinos Solidarios de Chiapas (UU). These associations operate indepen-

33

dently of the PRI-controlled Confederación Nacional de Campesinos (CNC). Simojovel in the northern highlands and Venustiano Carranza in the central highlands, which contain good agricultural lands held by large landowners, manifest the same willingness as settlers in the selva to participate in regional movements for revindication.

At this point in history, Guatemalan Mayas in exile have found accommodation within Mexican colonies in the selva. Mexican Mayas, like the cattlemen and plantation owners along the border and in the Lacandón selva, are taking advantage of this very cheap labor force. But unlike the powerful landowners, Mexican Mayas have problems in common with the exiles due to their marginalization from the centers of political and economic power. Like Guatemalan Mayas, they have separated themselves from invidious ranking systems operating in and among highland Maya communities. Whereas highland indígenas farm ejido lands individually and even scheme to expel compatriots to take advantage of their plots, lowland Mayas in the colonizing area have adapted communalistic forms of work and redistribute harvests in the jungle. They have initiated peaceful protests over the past decade, calling for legalized claims on land, an end to corruption in government, and resistance to new laws that permit privatization of communal land and resources. All these protests have met with armed repression. Encounters with armed troops and police agents ordered into action by the former governor of Chiapas, General Patrocinio González Garrido, and his predecessor, General Absalón Castellanos Domínguez, aggravated the frustration that erupted in the uprising on the eve of 1994. Mexican Mayas consequently are sympathetic to the protests of Guatemalan Mayas against state policies in both countries that have excluded them from meaningful participation in decisions regarding the global processes affecting their lives.

Despite these similarities, the goals of the Zapatistas are not phrased in terms of pan-Indian political revindication, as are those of some leaders of Guatemalan Mayas who are involved in repatriating exiles to their country (Menchú 1992). The support of international agencies in sponsoring the return of the exiles to Guatemala (Manz 1988) and gaining the release of Mexican Mayas jailed in past protests (Nash and Sullivan 1992) will undoubtedly reinforce a tendency (seen especially in South America) in which indígenas seek recognition as nations within the new world order. Indigenous commitment to a worldview distinct from that of ladinos still animates Mexican and Guatemalan Mayas, but few Mexican Mayas have entrusted their destiny to international movements.

The absence of this kind of rhetoric is notable in the official reports from the Convención Nacional Democrática called by the Zapatistas. In their search for alternative paths of development, the delegates emphasized the need for changes in national political processes in rhetoric in-

34

voking patriotism and commitment to revolutionary goals in the Mexican tradition. Although the discussions preceding the meeting in the jungle called for local autonomy, dignity, and justice for persons of distinct cultures, they did not echo the clamor for hemispheric resistance set forth in the pamphlet *Quinientos años de resistencia indígena* at the 1991 meeting preparing for the quincentennial year in Guatemala.[18] The Zapatistas' new vision of federalism is that of a multinational state with territorial autonomy for indigenous peoples as part of the Mexican nation. The cultural autonomy they call for would make a living reality of the bicultural policies now part of the rhetoric of the Secretaría de Educación Pública (SEP). But their perspective remained tied to the national context. Native Americans from the United States attending the National Democratic Convention held by the Zapatistas in August 1994 complained privately that the convention lacked an orientation toward a distinctive indigenous mobilization for change.

Clearly, individualized production on small ejido plots, which formerly enabled Mayas to carry on their distinctive cultures, is not viable in an increasingly integrated world market. Neoliberal policies have removed the subsidies that promoted entry for indigenous producers in commercial enterprises in past sexenios. Mayas have demonstrated a talent for reclaiming collective cultural practices amid far-reaching development processes in Mexico (Collier 1990, 198; Nigh 1992) and in the face of massive military attacks in Guatemala (compare Smith 1984b and Warren 1992). Mayas are now generating innovative solutions as they change enough to remain identified as Mayas. The new "associative corporations" that provide collective control over commercialization, technical assistance, and redistribution of profits (Nigh 1992) are providing a new model that allows the combined efforts of household labor engaged in a community-wide collective enterprise to deal with the vagaries of the market.

But even with their more modest agenda, the Zapatistas represent the threat that subsistence systems might pose to global trade agreements heading policy agendas in Mexico and around the world. The generally favorable attention that the strike has attracted in the world press attests to the development of a global moral community that may set standards for more egalitarian redistribution of profits from production.

Theorists studying European movements exclude such "Third World

18. Resolutions of the Comisión sobre la Posición de los Pueblos Indígenas ante el V Centenario 1992 opposed modernization, privatization, subordination to U.S., Israeli, Japanese, and European imperialism (meaning seizure of lands or natural resources), and the imposition of multinational companies "converting us into exploited workers of industrial enterprises and plantations." Dedicating itself to the struggle for agrarian reform and rights to education and health services, the group appealed to the United Nations to recognize the right to self-determination of indigenous communities.

35

struggles . . . between more clearly demarcated camps" (Laclau and Mouffe 1985, 166). But their emphasis on the significance of the symbolic function of such movements as they experiment "with direct practice of alternative frameworks of meaning" (Melucci 1988, 248, as cited in Escobar 1992, 405) strikes a resonant chord in analyzing this first postmodern movement in the Third World. As the Zapatistas have shown, despite their lack of military force to win an armed struggle, the space they have occupied in international news media has magnified the stage on which they are symbolically enacting guerrilla warfare (Nash n.d.). Their firearms—no more than wooden sticks or plastic toys for some of the soldiers—evidence the desperation of their actions, and yet their very existence has caused the Mexican stock market to plunge and has brought about more reform in the Mexican political process than has been witnessed in the past sixty-five years of PRI dominance.

New social movement theorists remind anthropologists of the cultural context of political and economic struggles that is intrinsic to good ethnography, which many have acknowledged even when the discipline was mired in colonialism. But new social movement theorists also err in making the same universalizing premises that its proponents criticize in Marxism. Some have rescued the best of Marx, specifically his emphasis on particular historical contexts demonstrated in *The Eighteenth Brumaire*, by inventing some changes to make it acceptable to the new discourse. The proposition by John and Jean Comaroff that ethnicity emerges out of specific historical forces that are simultaneously structural and cultural situates the experience of ethnicity in a field of forces that allows analysis of the many distinct manifestations of ethnicity in an area like Chiapas (Comaroff and Comaroff 1992, 50). Comparison of these experiences in highland corporate communities, where caciques have until recently been reinforcing their appropriation of diminishing resources by brandishing their claims to ethnic traditions, with those of lowland small plot farmers and laborers opposing powerful agroindustrial interests in their midst, indicates that both groups are engaged in ethnic reassertion. But while highland caciques reinforce the power of entrenched political and economic interests, lowland smallholders and laborers demonstrate an alternative to ethnic stratification. For the campesinos of indigenous origin who have moved into the jungle, ethnicity is not the irreducible substratum for action but an identification that provides collective strength and a sense of self denied by the dominant ladinos. The indígenas work with poor mestizos who share common problems, and their ultimate goals are pluri-ethnicity within democratic structures. As highland Indians join the forces in rebellion against the monopoly of power by the PRI, they are upsetting the old power structures and creating new forms of democratic participation. They thus present one of the few alternatives that offer hope in this postmodern world.

36

REFERENCES

AGUIRRE BELTRAN, GONZALO
1979   Regions of Refuge.Washington, D.C.: Society for Applied Anthropology.
AMERICAS WATCH COMMITTEE
1985   Guatemala Revised: How the Reagan Administration Finds "Improvements" in Human Rights in Guatemala. New York: Americas Watch Committee.
ARIAS, JACINTO
1985   San Pedro Chenalhó: Algo de su historia, cuentos y costumbres. Tuxtla Gutiérrez, Chiapas: Subsecretaría de Asuntos Indígenas.
ARIZPE, LOURDES, FERNANDO PAZ, AND MARGARITA VELAZQUEZ
1993   Cultura y cambio global: percepciones sociales sobre la deforestación en la selva lacandona. Mexico City: Centro Regional de Investigaciones Multidisciplinarias.
BRICKER, VICTORIA REIFLER
1981   The Indian Christ, the Indian King: The Historical Substrate of Maya Myth and Ritual. Austin: University of Texas Press.
CANCIAN, FRANK
1965   Economy and Prestige in a Maya Community. Stanford, Calif.: Stanford University Press.
1992   The Decline of Community in Zinacantán: Economy, Public Life, and Social Stratification, 1960-1987. Stanford, Calif.: Stanford University Press.
CANCIAN, FRANK, AND PETER BROWN
1994   "Who Is Rebelling in Chiapas?" Cultural Survival Quarterly 18, no. 1 (Spring):22-25.
CARMACK, ROBERT
1987   Harvest of Violence: The Maya Indians and the Guatemalan Crisis. Norman: University of Oklahoma Press.
CASTELLANOS, ALICIA
1988   Notas sobre la identidad étnica en la región Tzotzil Tzeltal de los altos de Chiapas. Iztyapalpa: Universidad Autónoma Metropolitana Iztyapalpa.
COLBY, BENJAMIN N.
1966   Ethnic Relations in the Chiapas Highlands. Santa Fe: Museum of New Mexico Press.
COLLIER, GEORGE A.
1975   Fields of the Tzotzil. Berkeley and Los Angeles: University of California Press.
1990   Seeking Food and Seeking Money: Changing Productive Relations in a Highland Mexican Community. UNRISD working paper. New York: United Nations Research Institute for Social Development.
1994   "Roots of the Rebellion in Chiapas." Cultural Survival 18, no. 1 (Spring):14-18
COLLIER, GEORGE A., WITH ELIZABETH LOWERY QUARATIELLO
1994   Basta! Land and the Zapatista Rebellion in Chiapas. Oakland, Calif.: Food First.
COMAROFF, JOHN, AND JEAN COMAROFF
1992   Ethnography and the Historical Imagination. Boulder, Colo.: Westview.
COUTINO FERRERA, M. ARTURO
1987   "Incendios forestales, conflictos agrarios, colonización sin freno y atosigamiento de PEMEX." Perfil 1, no. 5 (Nov.-Dec.):22-23.
DAVIS, S., AND J. HODSON
1982   Witnesses to Political Violence in Guatemala. Boston, Mass.: Oxfam America.
DE LA FUENTE, JULIO
1989   Educación, antropología, desarrollo de la comunidad. Fourth edition. Mexico City: Instituto Nacional Indigenista (first published in 1964).
DIAZ-POLANCO, HECTOR
1992   "Indian Communities and the Quincentenary." Latin American Perspectives 19, no. 3:6-24.
DIENER, PAUL
1978   "The Tears of St. Anthony: Ritual and Revolution in Eastern Guatemala." Latin American Perspectives 5, no. 3 (Summer):92-116.
DISKIN, MARTIN, ED.
1983   Trouble in Our Backyard: Central America and the United States in the Eighties. New York: Pantheon.

37

EARLE, DUNCAN
  1994   "Indigenous Identity at the Margin: Zapatismo and Nationalism." *Cultural Survival Quarterly* 18, no. 1:26–31.
EBER, CHRISTINE
  1994   *Before God's Flowering Face: Women and Drinking in a Tzotzil Maya Community.* Austin: University of Texas Press.
EHRENREICH, JEFFREY DAVID
  1989   "Lifting the Burden of Secrecy: The Emergence of the Awa Biosphere Reserve." *Latin American Anthropology Review* 1, no. 2 (Winter):49–54.
ESCALONA, JOSE LUIS, AND NORMA NAVA Z.
  1992   "El derecho a ser." In FREYERMUTH ENCISO AND HERNANDEZ CASTILLO 1992, 200–205.
ESCOBAR, ARTURO
  1992   "Culture, Practice, and Politics: Anthropology and the Study of Social Movements." *Critique of Anthropology* 12, no. 4:395–432.
FABREGAS PUIG, ANDRES
  1988   "La antropología social en la frontera sur." In *La antropología en México: Panorama histórica*, edited by Andrés Fábregas Puig. Mexico City: Colección Biblioteca del Instituto Nacional de Antropología e Historia.
FALLA, RICARDO
  1994   *Massacres in the Jungle: Ixcan, Guatemala, 1975–1982.*
FREYERMUTH ENCISO, GRACIELA, AND AIDA ROSALVA HERNANDEZ CASTILLO, EDS.
  1992   *Una década de refugios en México: Los refugiados guatemaltecos y los derechos humanos.* Tlalpán, Chiapas: Centro de Investigaciones Ecológicas y Estudios Superiores en Antropología del Sureste (CIESAS), Instituto Chiapaneco de Cultura.
GARZA CALIGARIS, ANA MARIA
  1992   "La violencia: Guatemala es el ejemplo." In FREYERMUTH ENCISO AND HERNANDEZ CASTILLO 1992.
GONZALEZ, JORGE R.
  1992   "De panzos a el aguacate: Sobre la ruta del Quinto Centenario." In FREYERMUTH ENCISO AND HERNANDEZ CASTILLO 1992, 119–69.
GONZALEZ CASANOVA, PABLO
  1970   *Sociología de la explotación.* Mexico City: Siglo Veintiuno.
GOSSEN, GARY
  1974   *Chamulas in the World of the Sun: Time and Space in a Maya Oral Tradition.* Cambridge, Mass.: Harvard University Press (new edition published in 1984 by Waveland Press, Prospect Heights, Ill.).
  1986   *Symbol and Meaning beyond the Closed Community: Essays in Mesoamerican Ideas.* Albany: State University of New York Press.
GOSSEN, GARY, AND RICHARD LEVENTHAL
  1989   "The Topography of Ancient Maya Religious Pluralism: A Dialogue with the Present." In *Lowland Maya Civilization in the Eighth Century AD: A Symposium*, edited by Jeremy A. Sabloff and John S. Henderson. Washington, D.C.: Dumbarton Oaks.
GREEN, LINDA
  1992   "Shifting Affiliations: Mayan Widows and Evangélicos in Guatemala." In *Rethinking Protestantism in Latin America*, edited by Virginia Garrard Burnett and David Stoll. Philadelphia, Pa.: Temple University Press.
GUITERAS HOLMES, CALIXTA
  1985   *Los peligros de alma: Visión del mundo de un tzotzil.* Mexico City: Fondo de Cultura.
HALL, STUART
  1986   "The Relevance of Gramsci for the Study of Race and Ethnicity." *Journal of Communication Inquiries* 10:5–22.
HAMILTON, NORA, AND NORMA STOLTZ CHINCHILLA
  1991   "Central American Migration: A Framework for Analysis." *LARR* 26, no. 1:75–110.
HARRIS, MARVIN
  1964   *Patterns of Race in the Americas.* New York: Walker.
HARVEY, NEIL
  1994   *Rebellion in Chiapas: Rural Reforms, Campesino Radicalism, and the Limits to Sali-*

38

nismo. La Jolla: University of California Ejido Reform Research Project, Center for U.S.-Mexican Studies, University of California, San Diego.

HILL, JONATHAN D.
1989   "Demystifying Structural Violence." *Latin American Anthropology Review* 1, no. 2 (Winter):42–48.

JONAS, SUSANNE, EDWARD MCCAUGHAN, AND ELIZABETH SUTHERLAND MARTINEZ
1984   *Guatemala: Tyranny on Trial: Testimony of the Permanent People's Tribunal*. San Francisco, Calif.: Synthesis.

KINZER, STEPHEN, AND STEPHEN SCHLESINGER
1981   *Bitter Fruit: The Untold Story of the American Coup in Guatemala*. Garden City, N.Y.: Doubleday.

LACLAU, ERNESTO
1990   *New Reflections on the Revolutions of Our Time*. London: Verso.

LACLAU, ERNESTO, AND CHANTAL MOUFFE
1985   "Beyond the Positivity of the Social: Antagonisms and Hegemony." In *Hegemony and Socialist Strategy: Towards a Radical Democratic Politics*, 93–148. London: Verso.

LAURELL, ANA CRISTINA
1982   "Democracy in Mexico: Will the First Be the Last?" *New Left Review*, no. 194:33–53.

MACLEOD, MURDO
1973   *Spanish Central America: A Socioeconomic History, 1520–1720*. Berkeley and Los Angeles: University of California Press.

MANZ, BEATRIZ
1981   "Refugees: Guatemalan Troops Clear Petén for Oil Explorations." *Cultural Survival Quarterly* 5, no. 3 (Fall).
1983   "Guatemalan Refugees: Violence, Displacement, and Survival." *Cultural Survival Quarterly* 7, no. 1 (Winter).
1988   *Refugees of a Hidden War: The Aftermath of Counterinsurgency in Guatemala*. Albany: State University of New York Press.

MCCREERY, DAVID
1990   "State Power, Indigenous Communities, and Land in Nineteenth-Century Guatemala, 1820–1920." In *Guatemalan Indians and the State, 1540–1988*, edited by Carol Smith, 96–115. Austin: University of Texas Press.

MELUCCI, ALBERTO
1985   "The Symbolic Challenge of Contemporary Movements." *Social Research* 52, no. 4:789–816.

MENCHU, RIGOBERTA
1992   "The Quincentenary: A Question of Class, Not Race." *Latin American Perspectives* 19, no. 3:96–100.

NAGENGAST, CAROL, AND MICHAEL KEARNEY
1990   "Mixtec Ethnicity: Social Identity, Political Consciousness, and Political Activism." *LARR* 25, no. 2:61–91.

NASH, JUNE
1966   "Social Resources of a Latin American Peasantry." *Social and Economic Studies* 15, no. 4:353–67.
1968   "The Passion Play in Maya Indian Communities." *Comparative Studies in Society and History* 20, no. 3:318–27.
1970   *In the Eyes of the Ancestors: Belief and Behavior in a Maya Community*. New Haven, Conn.: Yale University Press.
1982   "Implications of Technological Change for Household-Level and Rural Development." In *Technological Change and Rural Development*, edited by P. M. Weil and J. Eltereich, 75–128. Newark: University of Delaware Press.
1993   *Crafts in the World Market: The Impact of Global Exchange on Middle American Artisans*. Albany: State University of New York Press.
1994a   "Global Integration and Subsistence Insecurity." *American Anthropologist* 96, no. 2:1–31.
1994b   "Press Reports on the Chiapas Uprising." Paper presented to the American Anthropological Association, 24 Nov.–3 Dec. Atlanta.

39

NASH, JUNE, WITH CHRISTINE KOVIC
   n.d.   "The Challenge of Trade Liberalization to Cultural Survival on the Southern
           Frontier of Mexico." In *The Challenge of Globalization*, edited by James Mittleman.
           Boulder, Colo.: Lynne Rienner, forthcoming.
NASH, JUNE, AND KATHLEEN SULLIVAN
   1992   "Return to Porfirismo: The View from Mexico's Southern Frontier." *Cultural Sur-
           vival Quarterly* 16, no. 2 (Spring):13–16.
NIGH, RONALD
   1992   "La agricultura orgánica y el nuevo movimiento campesino en México." *Nueva
           Epoca Antropológica* 3.
ROSENBAUM, BRENDA
   1993   *With Our Heads Bowed: The Dynamics of Gender in a Maya Community*. Austin:
           University of Texas Press.
RUS, JAN
   n.d.   "The 'Comunidad Revolucionaria Institucional': The Subversion of Native Gov-
           ernment in Highland Chiapas, 1936–1968." Colección Chiapas, Centro de Estudios
           Ecológicos del Sureste, San Cristóbal de las Casas.
RUS, JAN, AND ROBERT WASSERSTROM
   1980   "Civil Religious Hierarchies in Central Chiapas: A Critical Perspective." *American
           Ethnologist* 7, no. 3:466–78.
SAFA, HELEN
   1981   "Runaway Shops and Female Employment: The Search for Cheap Labor." *Signs* 7,
           no. 2 (Winter):418–33.
SELVERSTON, MELINA
   1992   "Politicized Ethnicity and the Nation-State in Ecuador." Paper presented to the
           Latin American Studies Association, 24–27 Sept., Los Angeles.
SLATER, DAVID, ED.
   1985   *New Social Movements and the State in Latin America*. Amsterdam: CEDLA.
SMITH, CAROL A.
   1984a   "Labor and International Capital in the Making of a Peripheral Social Formation:
           Economic Transformations in Guatemala, 1850–1980." In *Labor in the Capitalist
           World-Economy*, edited by Charles Bergquist. Vol. 7 of *Political Economy of the World
           System*. Beverly Hills, Calif.: Sage Publications.
   1984b   "Local History in Global Context: Social and Economic Transitions in Western
           Guatemala." *Comparative Studies in Society and History* 26, no. 2:193–229.
STAVENHAGEN, RODOLFO
   1965   "Classes, Colonialism, and Acculturation." *Studies in Comparative International De-
           velopment* 1, no. 6:53–77.
STEPHEN, LYNN
   1994   "Accommodation and Resistance: Ejidatario, Ejidataria, and Official Views of
           Ejido Reform." *Urban Anthropology* 23, nos. 2–3:233–65.
STOLL, DAVID
   1993   *Between Two Armies in the Ixil Towns of Guatemala*. New York: Columbia University Press.
SULLIVAN, KATHLEEN
   1992   "Protagonists of Change." *Cultural Survival Quarterly* 16, no. 4 (Fall):17–20.
TAX, SOL
   1937   "The Municipios of the Midwestern Highlands of Guatemala." *American Anthro-
           pologist* 39, no. 3:423–44.
TEICHMAN, JUDITH
   1992   "The Mexican State and the Political Implications of Economic Restructuring."
           Latin American Perspectives 19, no. 2 (Spring):88–104.
TICKELL, OLIVER
   1991   "Indigenous Expulsions in the Highlands of Chiapas." *International Work Group
           on Indigenous Affairs Newsletter*, no. 2: 9–14.
TORIELLO GARRIDO, GUILLERMO
   1984   "On the Role of the U.S. and Israel." In JONAS, MCCAUGHAN, AND MARTINEZ 1984,
           24–30.

40

TUROK, MARTA
1988   *Como acercarse a la artesanía.* Mexico City: Plaza y Valdiacies.
VOGT, EVON Z.
1976a   "Some Aspects of the Sacred Geography of Highland Chiapas." In *Meso-American Sites and World View*, edited by Elizabeth P. Benson, 119–42. Washington, D.C.: Dumbarton Oaks.
1976b   *Tortillas for the Gods: A Symbolic Analysis of Zinacanteco Rituals.* Cambridge, Mass.: Harvard University Press.
WALLACE, ANTHONY F. C.
1956   "Revitalization Movements." *American Anthropologist* 58:264–81.
WARMAN, ARTURO
1970   "Todos santos y todos difuntos: crítica histórica de la antropología mexicana." In *De eso que se llaman antropología mexicana.* Mexico City: Colegio de México.
WARREN, KAY B.
1992   "Transforming Memories and Histories: Meanings of Ethnic Resurgence for Maya Indians." In *Americans: New Interpretive Essays*, edited by Alfred Stepan, 189–219. Oxford: Oxford University Press.
1993   *The Violence Within: Cultural and Political Opposition in Divided Nations.* Boulder, Colo.: Westview.
WASSERSTROM, ROBERT
1983   *Class and Society in Central Chiapas.* Berkeley and Los Angeles: University of California Press.
WATANABE, JOHN M.
1992   *Maya Saints and Souls in a Changing World.* Austin: University of Texas Press.
WOLF, ERIC
1957   "Closed Corporate Peasant Communities in Mesoamerica and Central Java." *Southwestern Journal of Anthropology* 13 (Spring):1–18.

41

Ironies of Citizenship: Skin Color, Police Brutality, and the Challenge to Democracy in Brazil*

MICHAEL J. MITCHELL, *Arizona State University*
CHARLES H. WOOD, *University of Florida*

Abstract

Despite the transition from authoritarian rule to a democratically elected government in 1985, there remains in Brazil a persistent gap between the formal principles and the actual practices of democracy. The gap is particularly manifest in the daily contacts between citizens and representatives of state authority, especially regarding the treatment of Afro-Brazilians. Analyses of the "regulated" and "relational" character of citizenship in Brazil, as well as observations about the attitudinal dispositions of the members of the criminal justice system, suggest that Afro-Brazilians are likely to benefit from fewer protections compared to whites and are more likely to suffer discrimination at the hands of the police. Analyses of the 1988 National Household Survey (PNAD-88) support both hypotheses: Net of statistical controls for key socioeconomic indicators, Afro-Brazilians are more likely than whites to be the victim of assault, and they are more likely to be assaulted by the police. The findings show how the perceptions of class, color, and criminality produce differential protections and treatments inconsistent with the attributes of universal citizenship. Our analysis points more generally to the formidable institutional and cultural challenges that confront the attempt to fully consolidate a democratic regime in Brazil.

The demise of authoritarian rule in Argentina, Bolivia, Brazil, Chile, Ecuador, and Uruguay represents a critical watershed in the contemporary political history of Latin America.[1] Yet, for all of the attention that these events have received, it appears that the fundamental dilemmas posed by the wave of regime changes that took

* Thanks are due Suzana Cavenaghi for programming assistance, to Jeff Needell and Elisa Maranzana for substantive comments and editorial assistance, and to the anonymous reviewers of the original manuscript. Correspondence should be directed to Charles H. Wood, Center for Latin American Studies, PO Box 115530, University of Florida, Gainesville, FL 32611-3225.

Social Forces, March 1998, 77(3):1001-1020

place during the 1980s are only beginning to be understood. The unqualified enthusiasm that once greeted the "transition to democracy" has given way to a more sober appreciation of the problems associated with the "second transition," described as the movement from a democratically elected *government* to a truly democratic *regime* (O'Donnell 1994:56). The challenges of the second transition involve the formidable task of dismantling the legacies of authoritarian rule and creating the institutional and cultural bases for equal representation and universal citizenship. But nothing guarantees that the second transition will occur. The emergent and fragile democracies may regress to authoritarianism, or they may stall at varying points along the road to a consolidated and fully institutionalized democratic regime (Karl 1991; O'Donnell 1994).

The dilemmas of the second transition are arguably "longer and more complex than the initial transition from authoritarian rule" (O'Donnell 1994:56). In the posttransition stage, countries face the problem of reconstructing state institutions and of transforming civil society in a manner that successfully closes the gap between formally defined democratic rights and the everyday practices of politics and power. Central to the task is the (re)construction of the political entities, such as the congress, political parties, and the judiciary. Democratic consolidation occurs when contending social classes and political groups come to accept that a set of formal rules and informal understandings "are the most appropriate way to govern collective life in a (given) society" (Linz & Stepan 1996:6).[2] Equally important is the formidable job of strengthening a "culture of citizenship" inasmuch as people must embrace beliefs and practices that are suitable to the notion of democracy if they are to learn how to act within the renewed institutional system (Jelin 1996:102).

The posttransition period in Brazil illustrates the configuration of social and political obstacles that confront the institutionalization of a democratic regime. Following twenty-one years of military rule, the civilian government inaugurated in 1985 set out to reform the country's conspicuous authoritarian properties. A milestone in the process was the enactment of a new constitution in 1988, which sought to (re)establish the institutional bases for political representation and the legal premises of universal citizenship rights. But these guarantees notwithstanding, there remains in Brazil a persistent breach between the formal content of democracy and the de facto exercise of state authority.

Brazil is hardly unique in this respect since the task of institutionalizing the practice of democracy is a problem shared with all other countries that have undergone the transition from authoritarianism. Nonetheless, the particular character of the dilemmas confronted by elected governments are specific to a country's history, institutions, and culture. In the case of Brazil, the persistent gap between the principles and the practice of democracy has been attributed to various factors. Karl (1991:179) points to the unique character of the transition from authoritarianism: Because the military exerted almost complete control over the transition — and was therefore neither prepared nor compelled to fully compromise — the new civilian governments that followed "remained controlled by authoritarian elements." For O'Donnell (1994), it was not the mode of succession that mattered but rather the inability to solve the deep social and economic crises that civilian governments inherited from their predecessors, which produced a quasi-authoritarian form of "delegative democracy." Either way, the result was a partially institutionalized democracy that retained many of the authoritarian and exclusionary practices of the past.

Our objective here is to descend from the macrosocial terrain claimed by Karl and O'Donnell to unravel the specific institutional and cultural arrangements that are notable obstructions to the democratic project. Of particular relevance are the organizational, procedural, and attitudinal elements that fashion the interactions that take place at the critical interface between the population (and its various subgroups) and the exercise of state authority as manifested by the judiciary and the street-level behavior of the police. By focusing on this uneasy juncture — especially as it concerns the fate of Afro-Brazilian sectors of the population — we can render salient the processes that manifest differential privileges and protections inconsistent with a respect for human rights and with the attributes of universal citizenship. We use data from the 1988 National Household Survey to produce empirical findings that support the popularly held perception that Brazilians of African descent receive less protection from the police and are more likely than their white counterparts to be victims of police brutality. More generally, our analysis shows how the complex and highly nuanced interplay of race, class, and criminality presents formidable organizational and cultural challenges to a fully institutionalized democratic regime. We introduce this argument with an overview of the historical and political evolution of the concept of citizenship and its applicability to the analysis of democratization in contemporary Brazil.

The State and the Culture of Citizenship in Brazil

In the narrow sense, citizenship refers to formal membership in a nation and the individual rights and obligations that go along with it, such as that of voting and military service. Citizenship conveys the notion of rights held by individuals and protected by a state whose authority is exercised within explicit boundaries that cannot be exceeded without violating a state's legitimacy. But democratic citizenship also encompasses the broader sense of public, and hence collective, participation in exercising the right to change the way resources are allocated. "Citizenship is, from this perspective, always negotiated since, by their participation, citizens can change their rights and obligations and, equally, governing elites may seek to limit or influence these changes as a means of consolidating their power" (Roberts 1995:184). The concept of citizenship forms the basis of political participation, representation, and accountability and provides the ideological premise for collective claims on the state's capacity to distribute resources, administer justice, and promote economic well-being (Navarro 1994; Waters 1989; Schlaefer et al. 1994; Garrison & Landrum 1995; Roche 1992). Hence, the concept of citizenship is often invoked as a means to challenge exclusionary practices and to press for equal representation in contestations about human rights, immigration policy, and the treatment of subnational ethnic groups (Van Steenbergen 1994; Paoli 1992; Turner 1993).

Studies of Brazil have treated citizenship as the cornerstone for social movements that seek to widen the scope and content of civil society (Garrison & Landrum 1995; Navarro 1994; Schlaefer et al. 1994). Citizenship, in this view, becomes the basis for making claims for social justice and other concerns thought to lay outside an elite political agenda. To overcome the obstacles imposed by existing power configurations, movements of workers, women, and ethnic groups couch their demands in terms of universal rights and privileges putatively accorded all members of the nation. The perspective assumes that claims flow, implicitly if not outright, from the constitutional specifications of citizenship rights which social movements strategically use to make appeals based on guarantees of universal citizenship.

The degree to which the political system delivers full and universal rights of citizenship, both in terms of codified laws and in the daily contacts between citizens and representatives of the state, is a measure of the progress made toward institutionalizing a democratic regime. Our understanding of the historical trajectory of democracy owes much to T.S. Marshall's (1965) seminal work on the progression that generated the attributes of modern citizenship in the United Kingdom. Marshall noted a development that began with the extension of civil rights in the eighteenth century (e.g., freedom of speech, the right to property and justice), followed by the granting of political rights in the nineteenth (e.g., the right to vote), and ending in the contemporary period with the increasing recognition of social rights (e.g., the right to a modicum of economic welfare and security). Despite recent critiques of his work (Sommers 1993; Mann 1987), Marshall succeeded in moving the treatment of citizenship out of the arid legalistic terms in which the concept had been mainly cast, to position the study of citizenship in the dynamic context of nation building and historical development.

With Marshall's contribution as background, Brazilian writings on the question of citizenship have taken several forms. A prominent example is presented by the political scientist Wanderley dos Santos (1979), who views the state as the primary obstacle to the creation of a developed citizenry able to function independently of the encroachments and domination of the state. Dos Santos explains why citizenship continues to convey notions of privilege and state sponsorship by proposing the concept of the "regulated" citizen, which takes as its starting point the semicorporatist and the semiauthoritarian traditions in Brazil.

Whereas Marshall observed that the modern welfare state in England (the last stage in the progression) was predicated on a foundation of preexisting independent rights, in Brazil the welfare state came first, in response to the political imperatives of the modernization project adopted in the 1930s. In the social charter of the 1934 constitution, for example, certain occupational categories received guarantees while others — rural labor and certain urban occupational categories, such as transient laborers — were left out altogether. The result was a hierarchy of citizenship categories based on occupational prestige and a national labor code that regulated and severely circumscribed the behavior of labor unions. By providing differential treatment according to earnings, the state "consecrated in practice the inequality of welfare benefits given to occupationally defined stratified categories of citizens" (Santos 1979:77). Using this and coercive measures to forestall labor conflicts, the modern state in Brazil adeptly preempted other citizen demands and placed itself in a position to dictate the purview of the rights accorded. Social rights were presented as a "gift" from above, given to those below, rather than as a result of working-class struggles (Caldeira 1996:200). Regulated citizenship in Brazil thus emerged, not from the independent claims of a mobilized citizenry (as they presumably did in the United Kingdom), but from the state's need to control the process of economic growth and development.

Anthropologist Roberto da Matta (1987) shares with dos Santos the premise that Brazilian citizenship is partial and contingent, but he adopts a different focus, noting the degree to which, in the course of everyday life, the respect for individual privileges heavily depends on the individual's social standing relative to others involved in a particular interaction. For da Matta, Brazilian citizenship is imbued with multiple and contradictory meanings and practices, resulting in what he calls the "relational" citizen, whose rights are defined by the power relationships present in a given circumstance (Da Matta 1987:313-16). Evidence of relational citizenship is readily demonstrated in the routine interactions with agents of the state. For example, the police in Brazil, who are generally regarded as having low social status, regularly deal with individuals of higher social standing in the process of enforcing ordinary codes of behavior, such as traffic and parking ordinances. High-status individuals can expect the police to overlook an infraction. Low-status individuals will experience the full force of the law. In a situation of unequal status, the common Brazilian question "Do you know who you are talking to?" carries a powerful message of domination that is likely to meet with fearful silence.[3]

Dos Santos and da Matta's observations highlight the degree to which rights and responsibilities are embedded features, not only of institutional arrangements (as in the case of regulated citizenship), but also of the fundamental cultural assumptions that organize and inform daily life (as in the case of relational citizenship). Moreover, subordinated social sectors routinely consider their exclusion as "normal," and the relationship with the state is expressed more often in terms of clientelism or paternalism than in terms of citizenship rights and obligations. Although Brazil has experienced a rich and complex history of popular struggles for the expansion of citizenship rights, the culture of subordination — especially as it concerns racial, ethnic, and class differentiations — has a deep and significant historical continuity (Jelin 1996:107). As a result, these phenomena do not necessarily disappear with the transition to an electoral system but, as we will argue, tend to linger, often gaining rather than losing strength.

The legacy of regulated and relational forms of citizenship pose significant obstacles to the extension of equal rights. In a context in which privileges have been selectively bestowed from above by a controlling elite, and in which "equal rights" themselves are perceived as contingent on social standing, it is unsurprising that the criminal justice system presents a critical arena in which privileges of full citizenship are differentially apportioned across class and color boundaries. We can therefore look to the courts and to the behavior of the police for concrete examples of the processes that separate the de jure provision of equal rights and their implementation in practice.

Color, Class, and the Criminal Justice System

How a criminal justice system identifies those who fall within its purview and the degree to which routine procedures adhere to the principles of due process reflect the state's institutional ability to guarantee citizenship rights. In its dealings with the public, a criminal justice system may follow a codified set of objective protocols or, as in the case of Brazil, it may impose its force with considerable latitude, to the point of tolerating extralegal conduct in the pursuit of its mandate. The practical realities of citizenship in Brazil are thus revealed in the discretionary prerogatives open to the criminal justice system, whose functioning is contingent on the perception of numerous factors, including the skin color and social class of the individuals with which it interacts.

Even though Brazilian law endorses an explicit commitment to due process, criminal proceedings are structured in a manner that subverts this principle. In contrast to the style characteristic of the courts in the U.S., where a (presumably) impartial judge monitors the adversarial relationship between the prosecution and the defense, judges in Brazil function in an inquisitorial manner, behaving more like interrogators than neutral arbiters. Charged with fact finding in criminal cases, judges possess considerable latitude in the conduct of direct examinations of the accused and of witnesses. In effect, the judge's task is to reconcile as nearly as possible the facts presented by the police with the information presented by the parties involved.

The inquisitorial treatment of defendants — which tends to subordinate the rights of the accused to the interests of the state — is, in Roberto Kant De Lima's (1995:244) view, the contemporary manifestation of the ecclesiastical origins of

Portuguese secular criminal laws, which were embedded in "pre-republican hierarchical conceptions of society." This cultural legacy and the manner in which the "facts of the case" are determined in the Brazilian courts result in a system in which judges lend substantial credence to the physical and emotional demeanor of the accused, making determinations that are highly responsive to the defendant's comportment and appearance of truthfulness. The historical legacy of Brazil's legal system thus disposes it to potential bias against some defendants, particularly those who are poor and nonwhite.

That perceived social status is a defining characteristic of citizenship is further evident in popular attitudes about crime and punishment. In her analysis of Brazilian public opinion regarding the issues of crime and punishment, Alba Zaluar (1993) concluded that attitudes toward criminal justice appear to be rooted in particular constructions of citizenship. In response to violent crime, Zaluar found a clear preference for retributive measures, such as the death penalty and forced labor during incarceration. Preferences for retributive justice, moreover, were linked to social class. Upper-income and highly educated respondents in her survey supported the death penalty and other measures of retributive justice more than did others. Similarly, retributive justice was endorsed less for the nature of the crime than for the perceived attributes of the citizens who commit the crime. Low-status individuals apparently deserve different treatment from the criminal justice system compared to those of high status.

Zaluar's respondents rarely if ever expressed the idea of citizenship as the embodiment of rights before the law, favoring instead a conception that viewed citizenship as a set of obligations, such as voting, paying taxes, and performing military service. In a manner akin to dos Santos's regulated citizen, the full scope of rights is extended to those who hold higher-status jobs and to those who fulfill their obligations to the state. Such notions resonate with the commonly held image of the "criminal," which is constructed through a combination of elements. "At the most general level, people of all classes stereotypically associate criminals with the poor, with black people, with migrants from the northeast of Brazil, with sons of single mothers, with consumers of drugs, with promiscuity, and with cortiços (tenements) and favelas (shantytowns)" (Caldeira 1996:201). The association between criminality and dark skin color is a special case of the widespread prejudice and discrimination against blacks.[4]

Police behavior is similarly influenced by an institutional framework and a normative culture that are prone to the discriminatory exercise of power. As Paul Chevigny (1993:25) notes, the very posture and perceived mission of the police foster a culture in which the police regard themselves as "waging war" against criminals. The stance places a premium on eliminating the criminal class and a lower priority on protecting the rights of citizens. Police regularly invade shanty towns (favelas) in Rio de Janeiro to extract vengeance from suspected killers. The deaths of innocent bystanders notwithstanding, such actions are regarded as legitimate attempts to deter crime through intimidation. Chevigny captures the essence of this culture in a telling statement made by a former secretary of public safety for the state of São Paulo: "We [go into the streets] to protect the public and we are greeted with bullets by the criminal class. In those instances the police must respond with force and not with roses" (10; authors' translation). The secretary's comment is consistent with the way Zaluar (1993:65) sums up her interpretation of popular attitudes about criminality and its relationship to employment status: "Those who kill must die; those who do not work must [also] die."

Two recent incidents reveal the extent to which the wartime metaphor encourages extralegal behavior: the killing of street children on the steps of the Church of the Candelária in Rio de Janeiro in 1993, and the brutal quelling of a disturbance at the Carandiru Prison in São Paulo in 1992 (Scheper-Hughes 1994; Pieta & Perreira 1993; see also Dimenstein 1991 and Marques et al. 1993). In the Carandiru incident, the military police, in an action apparently designed to quell a fight between gangs in the prison, used machine guns at close range to kill 111 prisoners.[5] In both the Candelária and the Carandiru episodes, the exercise of extreme violence was justified, not on the basis of evidence that crimes were committed or that lives were in danger, but on the assumption that the primary mission of the police force was to eliminate obvious members of the criminal class. A survey conducted by the newspaper *O Estado de São Paulo* shortly after the prison massacre reported that 44% of the city's population endorsed the police action (cited in Caldeira 1996:198). In fact, crowds of people took to the streets to demonstrate in favor of the police and against human rights activists who criticized police behavior.

In the "war against crime," race and class play a prominent role, a phenomenon that has its historical roots in the evolution of a professional police force that in the colonial period confronted the task of controlling black slaves in an urban environment. As Thomas Holloway (1993) notes, in a context where slaves enjoyed a degree of freedom, anonymity, and distance from their masters, the need for efficient social control was the primary motivation for the establishment of a standing police force in Rio de Janeiro. Charged with the mandate to preserve the racial hierarchy of a slave society, the police assumed responsibility for the full procedural range of a criminal justice system. When slaves were thought to have violated a strict code of conduct (e.g., they were prohibited from wearing shoes), it was the police who apprehended, judged, and punished them. A contemporary legacy of this historical tradition is evidenced in a statement made by a former lawyer for the military who noted that "the military police believe they have permission to kill when their victim is poor, Black and a thief" (Chevigny 1993:19; authors' translation).

Color, Victimization, and Police Brutality

Although the idea that Brazilians of African descent are more likely than their white counterparts to be the targets of police brutality has received considerable attention in analyses of the historical record and in reports that make headline news, the absence of high-quality crime statistics has made it difficult to subject this hypothesis to rigorous testing or to estimate the magnitude of the phenomenon. A partial solution to this problem can be found by analyzing the information on skin color and crime victimization contained in the 1988 National Household Survey (Pesquisa Nacional por Amostra de Domicílio, PNAD). The PNAD is administered once a year by the Brazilian Census Bureau (Instituto Brasileiro de Geografia e Estatística, IBGE). The IBGE uses a stratified random selection design and a large number of cases (around 80,000) to construct a data set that is, with the exception of rural areas in the Amazon, representative of the country as a whole.

The PNAD questionnaire consists of two parts. The first, which consists of the "core" questions that are repeated each year, elicits sociodemographic information, such as the respondents' age, sex, skin color, and education, as well as data on employment experience, such as hours worked, occupation performed, and wages earned. The second part of the questionnaire targets a particular topic, which varies in content from one year to the next. When we join the responses of the socioeconomic questions contained in the core to the items contained in the supplement, the result is a generalizable sample survey of exceptional scope and quality.

In 1988, the supplement addressed the issues of "social and political participation" by asking questions about memberships in unions, voluntary associations, and political parties. An additional item asked whether the respondent had been the victim of an assault within the previous year. Victimization rates derived from this item serve as a proxy measure of the degree of protection the police provide to the public. A follow-up question inquired about the identity of the perpetrator, thereby providing a direct measure of the frequency of police brutality.

The 1988 PNAD used the same method as the decennial demographic censuses to classify the population by skin color. The method, based on self-reports, asks respondents to classify themselves as white (*branco*), brown (*pardo*), black (*preto*), or yellow (*amarelo*). The yellow category, which refers to people of Asian descent, represented only .7% of the population and was dropped from the analysis.[6] For males 18 years of age and older, the 1988 survey found 58.8% white, 35.6% brown, and 4.9% black.

The precise meaning of this classification has been the topic of considerable debate (see Harris et al. 1993; Andrews 1991:app. B; Wood & Carvalho 1995). Both the census and the PNAD data explicitly refer to a respondent's perceived skin color rather than to the person's biological race, which in any case would be difficult to establish. But the notion of skin color itself is subject to multiple definitions in Brazil, a highly miscegenated country in which people recognize, and have a rich vocabulary to describe, the subtle gradations that lie between white and black. The three-category scheme used by the IBGE is therefore a gross simplification of a highly nuanced system of color classification.[7]

Table 1 shows that for men 18 years of age and older the probability of being assaulted in Brazil during the yearlong reference period before the 1988 survey was 101 per 10,000 (column 1). The highest rate was in the south (136), followed by the north (127) and the southeast (100). Unsurprisingly, the assault rate was substantially higher in urban compared to rural areas (118 and 56, respectively) and tended to decline sharply with increases in age. The observed rise in victimization rates with increases in education and income seems counterintuitive, yet this relationship results from the fact that the upper-income and more highly educated population lives in the south, where assaults are far more common.[8]

The breakdown by skin color, shown in columns 2-4, reveals a fairly consistent pattern. In all regions except the northeast the victimization rate was higher for brown men than for white men, and it was highest among blacks. The same general pattern held in urban areas and where the rates were classified by the respondent's level of education, income, and age (exceptions appear only in the lowest education and income strata). Even after controlling for key socioeconomic indicators, men 18 years of age and older who described themselves as brown, and especially those who described themselves as black, were more likely than white men to be victims of assault. In nearly every row in Table 1 the white-brown differences were substantially smaller than the brown-black differences. In other words, the shade of skin color matters: nonwhite men are at greater risk of assault than white men, but the risk is greater still for those at the darker end of the color continuum.

Table 2 presents the results of a multivariate analysis that simultaneously controls for all of the independent variables. The figures in the table refer to the relative odds of being assaulted, net of the effects of the other variables in the equation. The odds are derived from the coefficients of logistic regressions that use as the dependent variable whether the respondent suffered an assault in the previous year (yes = 1; no = 0). Values above 1.00 indicate a higher probability of being victimized relative to the omitted reference category.

Model 1 introduces dummy variables for region of the country and rural-urban residence. The results confirm some of the conclusions derived from the previous table: the odds of assault were greatest in the south (1.305) and substantially greater in urban compared to rural areas (1.944). After controlling for region and place of residence, the relative odds for skin color, presented at the bottom of the column, show that, compared to white males, brown men were 1.199 times more likely to be assaulted, and black men 1.552 times more likely.[9]

TABLE 1: Probability of Being Assaulted for Men 18 Years of Age and Older, by Skin Color and Selected Variables, Brazil, 1988 (per 10,000)

Independent Variables	Total (1)	White (2)	Brown (3)	Black (4)
Total	101	101	96	137
Region				
North	127	121	129	133
Northeast	83	86	79	117
Southeast	100	94	110	129
South	136	129	153	227
Center-west	88	80	90	185
Residence				
Urban	118	113	120	165
Rural	55	59	51	62
Education				
None	81	79	76	124
1-4 yrs.	113	104	117	166
5-8 yrs.	160	154	168	197
9+ yrs.	128	125	140	135
Income[a]				
0-1 mw	88	105	71	135
1-2 mw	99	93	100	132
2-3 mw	95	95	94	100
3-5 mw	105	107	100	115
5-10 mw	110	106	105	196
Age				
18-29	179	171	180	253
30-39	136	121	148	230
40+	103	103	102	113

Source: Pesquisa Nacional por Amostra de Domicílio (PNAD) 1988

[a] Monthly household income, in minimum wages

The second model introduces age, income, and education into the equation.[10] A comparison of the odds in Models 1 and 2 points to the effects of simultaneously controlling for geographic location and socioeconomic status. The odds associated with the south and with urban residence remain statistically significant and even increase somewhat. The results further indicate that young men are at much greater risk compared to men over 39 and that (in contrast to the pattern shown in Table 1) the probability of assault declines with increases in education and income.

TABLE 2: Odds Ratios for Probability of Being Assaulted for Men
18 Years of Age and Older (Logistic Regression)

Independent Variable	Model 1	Model 2
Intercept	−4.883	−5.095*
Region		
Southeast	.908	.942
South	1.305*	1.321*
Center-west	.866	.878
Northeast[a]	—	—
Residence		
Urban	1.944*	2.090*
Rural[a]	—	—
Age		
18-29		1.764*
30-39		1.397*
Age 40+[a]		—
Education		
None[a]		—
1-4 yrs.		.967
5-8 yrs.		.973
9+ yrs.		.737*
Income[b]		
0-1 mw[a]		—
1-2 mw		.975
2-3 mw		.992
3-5 mw		.886
5-10 mw		.864
10+ mw		.605*
Skin color		
White[a]	—	
Brown	1.199*	1.093
Black	1.552*	1.419*
χ^2	94.632	185.879
Cases	75,430	75,430

Source: Pesquisa Nacional por Amostra de Domicilio (PNAD) 1988

[a] Reference category

[b] Household income, in multiples of minimum wage

* $p < .05$

With respect to skin color, it is apparent that some of the effects noted in Model 1 result from differences in socioeconomic standing, as evidenced by the decline in the odds of being assaulted when we introduce additional controls. When age, education, and income are added to the regression in Model 2, the odds of brown males being assaulted (1.093) were not significantly different from those of whites (the reference category). The coefficient for blacks nonetheless remains large and statistically significant even after introducing all of the variables into the equation. The results of Model 2 indicate that, other things being equal, black men were 1.419 times (or 41.9%) more likely to be assaulted than white men.

We can obtain further insights into the covariates of assault by turning to the follow-up question contained in the supplement to the 1988 PNAD, which asks about the identity of the perpetrator — whether a relative, acquaintance, stranger, or policeman.[11] Unlike the previous analysis, in which the dependent variable is a dichotomous (yes/no) response, in this case four outcomes are possible. When a response has more than two categories, the appropriate statistical procedure is a multinomial logistic regression. The results presented in Table 3, where nonvictims are used as the reference or base category, show the odds that the assault was committed by a relative, acquaintance, stranger, or policeman.[12] The findings show no statistically significant differences between white and brown men with respect to the identity of the perpetrator. The results for black males, however, are striking. For blacks, the odds of being assaulted by an acquaintance were 1.945 times greater than for whites. Similarly, the odds of being assaulted by a policeman were 2.401 times greater.

In summary, analyses of the PNAD data offer important insights into risks of physical assault in Brazil in 1988. With respect to skin color, the findings provide striking evidence to support the popular perception that, independent of social status, black men in Brazil are far more likely than white men to be the target of physical assault. The results further support the intensely debated contention that — net of the effects of region, place of residence, and social status — black men are far more likely than white men to be the victims of police aggression.[13]

Conclusion

The transition from authoritarian to elected governments in 1985 represented an important step toward the institutionalization of democracy in Brazil. Today, official barriers to political participation have been lifted and political rights have been formally protected. The most recent Brazilian constitution (like the ones before it) denies status privileges and restrictions and reaffirms the inviolability of private property and the equality of all citizens before the law. Yet the transition to an elected government is not a sufficient condition for the creation of an institutionalized democratic regime. The latter involves the reconstruction of state

TABLE 3: Odds Ratios for Probability of Being Assaulted for Men 18 Years of Age and Older, by Identity of the Perpetrator (Multinomial Logistic Regression)

Independent Variable	Relative	Acquaintance	Stranger	Policeman
Intercept	.002*	.004*	.002*	.001*
Region				
Southeast	1.628	.780	.967	.967
South	1.754	1.685*	.931	1.194
Center-west	1.018	.896	.867	1.158
Northeast[a]	—	—	—	—
Residence				
Urban	1.443	1.885*	3.244*	2.001*
Rural[a]	—	—	—	—
Age				
18-29	1.678*	1.487*	1.788*	5.729*
30-39	1.087	1.282	1.305	2.495*
40+[a]	—	—	—	—
Education				
None[a]	—	—	—	—
1-4 yrs.	.549*	1.292	.930	1.087
5-8 yrs.	.401*	1.280	1.263	1.060
9+ yrs.	.123*	.816	1.116	.608
Income				
0-1 mw[a]	—	—	—	—
1-2 mw	.759	.815	.951	.837
2-3 mw	.762	.504*	.846	.846
3-5 mw	.695	.524*	1.090	.776
5-10 mw	.649	.506*	1.187	1.108
10+ mw	.233*	.374*	.967	1.088
Skin color				
White[a]	—		—	—
Black	.945	1.945*	.968	2.401*
Brown	1.023	1.204	.982	.998
χ^2	2,241.100			
df	5,976			
Cases	79,197			

Source: Pesquisa Nacional por Amostra de Domicílio (PNAD) 1988

[a] Reference category

institutions and of civil society and the dismantling of antidemocratic forms of exercising power, which may be authoritarian, corporatist, or plainly coercive in nature. It requires a change in the rules that govern the distribution of power, as well as a recognition of rights and the legitimation of social actors. Moreover, it requires a change in the behavior of political leaders, who must abandon their recourse to arbitrariness and impunity, and the adoption of norms and values consistent with a culture of citizenship (Jelin 1996:102).

Despite the transition to elected governments, there remains in Brazil a substantial gap between the formal principles and the actual practices of democracy. The gap is particularly manifest at the critical interface between people and the exercise of state authority by street-level agents of the state. The breach between principle and practice has its origins in a host of institutional and cultural factors that come into play in complex ways. Some stem from the exclusionary practices of Brazil's corporatist tradition (regulated citizenship), while others have their roots in the tendency in Brazil to associate rights with social position (relational citizenship).

Aspects of regulated and relational forms of citizenship find concrete expression in our analysis of the judiciary and the behavior of the police, particularly with respect to the treatment of the Afro-Brazilian sector of the population. Because of strong prejudices against dark skin color, and because the majority of Afro-Brazilians are found among the ranks of the poor and unemployed, the treatment of Afro-Brazilians in the criminal justice system and at the hands of the police illustrates how the practice of democracy is compromised by the interplay of institutional organization, cultural attitudes, and social class. More specifically, the vulnerability of Afro-Brazilians has its roots in a highly complex set of issues, the more significant of which include a political tradition in which citizenship rights are contingent on social standing; a criminal justice system prone to bias against individuals who are either poor or nonwhite (or both); a police force that sees its members as soldiers in an unbridled war against crime; a populace that endorses extreme action against criminals, whose threat to the public is seen as proportional to the darkness of their skin; and a cultural tradition in which the individual's relationship to the state is more often based on clientelism or paternalism than in terms of citizenship rights.

Notions regarding the contingent nature of citizenship, and the wide discretion open to street-level agents of the state in defining the boundaries of citizenship rights, imply that Afro-Brazilians are less likely to enjoy protection from, and a more likely to receive harsher treatment by, the police. These two hypotheses are empirically supported in our analysis of the data from the 1988 National Household Survey. Afro-Brazilians are more likely than whites to be the victims of assault, and they are more likely to have been assaulted by police. The effects of skin color — which remain statistically significant even after controlling for key indicators of social and economic standing — exemplify the differential protections and exclusions that are inconsistent with a respect for human rights and with the attributes of universal citizenship. More generally, our analysis highlights the institutional and cultural factors that profoundly challenge the attempt to establish a fully consolidated democratic regime in Brazil.

Notes

1. To this list of recent democratic tendencies in the region we can add the grudging political liberalization taking place in Mexico and the election of civilian presidents in Guatemala, El Salvador, Honduras, and Nicaragua. If over two-thirds of Latin America's people were living under military rule in 1979, by 1993 not a single military regime remained in Central or South America.

2. Different institutional and procedural forms are compatible with "democracy" so long as certain basic conditions are met. For Loveman (1994) these include the following: alternation in government offices as a result of free and fair elections; broad public contestation (without repression of opponents) both to fill government offices and to debate public policy; freedom of the press and other mass media to permit dissemination of opposing views; widespread respect for and implementation of civil liberties and rights and the rule of law; operation within specified legal limits by those with authority to govern; and provision for government accountability.

3. In his elaboration of some suggestions of da Matta (1987), O'Donnell notes that an Argentinian would respond to the same question with "Who cares?" whereas an American would take offense, asking, "Who do you think you are?" (cited in Reis 1996:134).

4. Studies by Silva (1978) on labor markets and Hasenbalg (1979) on social mobility were among the first national-level publications to empirically document the disadvantages Afro-Brazilians experienced compared to the whites with the same human capital. These findings are consistent with the results of more recent analyses of such varied topics as residential segregation (Rolnik 1989; Telles 1991), child mortality (Wood & Lovell 1992), wage discrimination (Lovell 1993, 1994), and educational inequality (Hasenbalg & Silva 1987, 1992). Evidence that the Brazilian public is aware of the existence of racial prejudice is found in a poll conducted by DATAFOLHA, the polling arm of the Brazilian newspaper *Folha de São Paulo*. The results of a poll carried out in April 1995 found that more than 80% of respondents agreed that racial prejudice was a fact of life in Brazil. A significant majority (61%) affirmed that racial prejudice in Brazil was intense. Surprisingly, the latter varied only slightly by the respondents' skin color (white, 60%; brown, 60%; black, 64%).

5. The prison massacre was not an isolated event. In 1991, 1,171 people died in São Paulo during confrontations with the police, compared to 27 in New York City. The following year, 1,470 people were killed, including the 111 prisoners (Caldeira 1996). Extralegal vigilante groups, mostly composed of off-duty policeman, are similarly responsible for scores of deaths each year (U.S. Department of State 1997).

6. Three observations are relevant to our use of the "skin color" variable in the survey: (1) We translate the Portuguese word *pardo* as brown. This translation is more intelligible to English readers than the word "gray," which is one of the meanings in Portuguese. It is also less risky than the use of other terms such as "mulatto," which in Portuguese has connotations that cloud the issue. (2) Given the nature of the question in the survey, and in light of the social construction of the concept, we consistently refer to "skin color" rather than to "race," except in those instances were the reference is to arguments or cultural traits that make use (correctly or otherwise) of the term "race." (3) Because the terms refer explicitly to socially recognized differences in skin color (and not to biological races), we lowercase "white," "brown," and "black."

7. The interpretation of data on skin color is further complicated by the tendency in Brazil for color identity to be confounded by social status. Compared to dark-skinned individuals who are poor, equally dark skinned people who are wealthy are likely to describe themselves, and to have others describe them, using a term that is closer to the white end of the continuum. The social basis of identity means that the concept of skin color in Brazil is mutable. The mutability of racial identity and its association with social status, moreover, mean that the cultural system allows upwardly mobile blacks to "whiten" as they rise in position. One study (Wood & Carvalho 1995) found that between 1950 and 1980 — a period of considerable upward mobility in Brazil — approximately 38% of the men and women who classified themselves as black in the first census reclassified themselves as brown thirty years later. The results indicated that the boundary between black and brown was quite "porous." The same was not true of the boundary between brown and white, however. The special character of color identity in Brazil imposes potential caveats on the interpretation of results based on PNAD data (as noted above).

8. Support for this interpretation is evidenced in Table 2. Once we simultaneously control for region, place of residence, and age, the positive association with education and income no longer persists.

9. The findings in Table 2 can be understood to mean that, independently of an individual's geographic location and social status, black skin color is associated with a higher probability of being assaulted. In light of the observations in note 7, it must further be noted that the size of the population that classified itself as black is likely to have been reduced over time by the number of successful black men who define themselves as brown. If skin color independently increases the probability of assault, then the coefficent for the brown population is likely to be somewhat inflated by virtue of including black men in the brown designation. To explore this issue, we performed a simulation that exaggerated the reclassification phenomenon by randomly selecting 15% of upper-status blacks, recoding them as brown, then rerunning the logistic regression. The ratio of the black-to-brown coefficients dropped from 1.29 (with no simulated reclassification) to 1.24 (with simulated reclassification). In other words, if the reclassification phenomenon is present in the data, it is likely that the reported difference between brown and black odds is underestimated (compared to the results that would obtain if no black men classified themselves as brown).

10. Given the nonlinearities observed in Table 1, the measures of age, education, and income have been coded as dummy variables.

11. The category "policemen" includes the small number of assaults perpetrated by private security guards.

12. A different choice for the reference category is possible. Rather than using nonvictims as the reference, an alternative is to restrict the analysis to the 1,068 individuals who experienced an assault and to use one of the responses (e.g., "stranger") as the reference category. When we performed this analysis, the results hardly differed from the odds reported in Table 3. For example, the odds of black men being assaulted by an acquaintance or policeman were 1.927 and 2.446 times greater than their being assaulted by a stranger. The comparable odds in Table 3, using nonvictims as the reference category, are 1.945 and 2.401, respectively.

13. The data set used in this analysis was collected in 1988, which was in the early stage of democratic consolidation in Brazil. Although we cannot say with certainty that the same relationships exist in the more recent period, subsequent human rights reports suggest that the observed patterns may not have changed. Reports issued in 1997 and 1998 by the U.S. Department of State have routinely noted the link between color and human rights abuses.

References

Andrews, George Reid. 1991. *Blacks and Whites in São Paulo, Brazil, 1888-1988*. University of Wisconsin Press.

Caldeira, Teresa P. R. 1996. "Crime and Individual Rights: Reframing the Question of Violence in Latin America." Pp. 197-211 in *Constructing Democracy: Human Rights, Citizenship and Society in Latin America*, edited by Elizabeth Jelin and Eric Hershberg. Westview.

Chevigny, Paul. 1993. *Violência Policial Urbana no Brasil*. Translated by Olaya Hanashiro. New York and São Paulo: America's Watch and Nucleo de Estudos da Violência, Universidade de São Paulo.

Da Matta, Roberto. 1987. "The Quest for Citizenship in a Relational Universe." Pp. 307-335 in *State and Society in Brazil*, edited by John D. Wirth, Edson de Oliveira Nunes, and Thomas A. E. Bogenschild. Westview.

Datafolha. 1995. *O Racismo Cordial*. São Paulo: Ática.

De Lima, Roberto Kant. 1995. "Bureaucratic Rationality in Brazil and the United States: Criminal Justice Systems in Comparative Perspective." Pp. 241-69 in *The Brazilian Puzzle*, edited by David Hess and Roberto da Matta. Columbia University Press.

Dimenstein, Gilberto. 1991. *Brazil's War on Children*. Translated by Chris Whitehouse. London: LAB.

Dos Santo, Wanderley. 1979. *Cidadania e Justiça*. Rio de Janeiro: Campus.

Garrison, John W., II, and Leilah Landrum. 1995. "Harvesting the Bounty of Citizenship: The Fight against Hunger and Poverty in Brazil." *Grassroots Development* 19:38-48.

Harris, Marvin, et al. 1993. "Who Are the Whites? Imposed Census Categories and the Racial Demography of Brazil." *Social Forces* 72:451-62.

Hasenbalg, Carlos A. 1979. *Discriminação e Desigualdades Raciais no Brasil.* Rio de Janeiro: GRAAL.

Hasenbalg, Carlos A., and Nelson do Valle Silva. 1992. "Raça e Oportunidades Educacionais no Brasil." Pp. 79-1000 in *Relações Raciais no Brasil,* edited by Nelson do Valle Silva and Carlos Hasenbalg. Rio de Janeiro: Rio Fundo Editora.

Holloway, Thomas H. 1993. *Policing Rio de Janeiro: Repression and Resistance in a Nineteenth-Century City.* Stanford University Press.

Jelin, Elizabeth. 1996. "Citizenship Revisited: Solidarity, Responsibility, and Rights." Pp. 101-19 in *Constructing Democracy: Human Rights, Citizenship and Society in Latin America,* edited by Elizabeth Jelin and Eric Hershberg. Westview.

Karl, Terry Lynn. 1991. "Dilemmas of Democratization in Latin America." Pp. 163-91 in *Comparative Political Dynamics,* edited by Dankwart Rustow and Kenneth Erickson. Harper Collins.

Linz, Juan, and Afred Stepan. 1996. *Problems in Democratic Transition and Consolidation.* Johns Hopkins University Press.

Lovell, Peggy. 1993. "The Geography of Economic Development and Racial Discrimination in Brazil." *Development and Change* 21:83-101.

―――. 1994. "Race, Gender and Development in Brazil." *Latin American Research Review* 29:7-35.

Loveman, Brian. 1994. "'Protected Democracies' and Military Guardianship: Political Transitions in Latin America, 1978-1993." *Journal of Interamerican Studies and World Affairs* 36:105-89.

Mann, Michael. 1987. "Ruling Class Strategies and Citizenship." *Sociology* 21:339-54.

Marques, João Benedito de Azevedo, et al. 1993. *Execuções Sumárias de Menores em São Paulo.* São Paulo: Órdem dos Advogados do Brasil.

Marshall, T.H. 1965. *Class, Citizenship and Social Development.* Anchor/Doubleday.

Navarro, Zander. 1994. "Democracy, Citizenship, and Representation: Rural Social Movements in Southern Brazil, 1978-1990." *Bulletin of Latin American Research* 13:129-53.

O'Donnell, Guillermo. 1994. "Delegative Democracy." *Journal of Democracy* 5:55-69.

Paoli, Maria Celia. 1992. "Citizenship, Inequalities, Democracy and Rights: The Making of Public Space in Brazil. " *Social and Legal Studies* 1:143-59.

Pieta, Eloi, and Justino Perreira. 1993. *Pavilhão 9: O Massacre de Carandiru.* São Paulo: Página Aberta.

Reis, Fábio Wanderley. 1996. "The State, the Market, and Democratic Citizenship." Pp 121-37 in *Constructing Democracy: Human Rights, Citizenship and Society in Latin America,* edited by Elizabeth Jelin and Eric Hershberg. Westview.

Roberts, Bryan. 1995. *The Making of Citizens: Cities of Peasants Revisited.* Arnold.

Roche, Maurice. 1992. *Rethinking Citizenship: Welfare, Ideologyand Change in Modern Society.* Polity Press.

Rolnik, Raquel. 1989. "Territórios Negros nas Cidades Brasileiras." *Estudos Afro-Asiáticos* 17:29-41.

Scheper-Hughes. 1994. "Kids Out of Place." *NACLA: Report on the Americas* 27:15-23.

Schlaefer, Carlos F., Viana, Garcia Rodigues, and Serintino Moretti. 1994. "Community Development and Social Movements: An Experience of Solidarity and Citizenship in Brazil." *Community Development Journal* 29:329-36.

Silva, Nelson do Valle. 1978. "Black-White Income Differentials: Brazil, 1960." Ph.D. dissertation, University of Michigan.

Silva, Nelson do Valle, and Carlos Hasenbalg. 1992. *Relações Raciais no Brasil Contemporâneo*. Rio de Janeiro: Rio Fundo.

Sommers, Margaret. 1993. "Citizenship and the Place in the Public Sphere: Law, Community and Political Culture in the Transition to Democracy." *American Sociological Review* 58:587-620.

Telles, Edward. 1991. "Contato racial no Brasil: análise da segregação residencial nas quarenta maiores áreas urbanos do Brasil em 1980." Pp. 341-65 in *Desigualdade Racial no Brasil Contemporâneo*. Belo Horizonte: UFMG/CEDEPLAR.

Turner, Bryan (ed.). 1993. *Citizenship and Social Theory*. Sage.

U.S. Department of State. 1997. Brazil Country Report on Human Rights Practices for 1996. Available from http://www.state.gov/www/issues/human_rights/1996_hrp_report/brazil.html. Internet; accessed Feb. 27, 1997.

———. 1998. Brazil Country Report on Human Rights Practices for 1997. Available from http://www.state.gov/www/issues/human_rights/1996_hrp_report/brazil.html. Internet; accessed Mar. 25, 1998.

Van Steenbergen, Bart (ed.). 1994. *The Condition of Citizenship*. Sage.

Waters, Malcolm. 1989. "Citizenship and the Constitution of Structural Social Inequality." *International Journal of Comparative Sociology* 30:159-80.

Wood, Charles H., and José Alberto Magno de Carvalho. 1995. "Census Categories and Racial Identity in Brazil." Paper presented at the annual meetings of the Population Association of America (PAA), San Francisco.

Wood, Charles H., and Peggy Lovell. 1992. "Racial Inequality and Child Mortality in Brazil." *Social Forces* 70:703-24.

Zaluar, Alba. 1993. "Urban Violence, Citizenship, and Public Policies." *International Journal of Urban and Regional Research* 17:56-66.

Acknowledgments

Yashar, Deborah. "Contesting Citizenship: Indigenous Movements and Democracy in Latin America." *Comparative Politics* 30, no. 1 (1998): 23-43. Reprinted with the permission of the editors of Comparative Politics.

Smith, Carol. "Race-Class-Gender Ideology in Guatemala: Modern and Anti-Modern Forms." *Comparative Studies in Society and History* 37, no. 4 (1995): 723-749. Reprinted with the permission of Cambridge University Press.

Fry, Peter. "Politics, Nationality, and the Meanings of "Race" In Brazil." *Daedalus* 129, no. 2 (2000): 83-118. Reprinted with the permission of Russell Sage Foundation.

Stephen, Lynn. "Culture as a Resource: Four Cases of Self-Managed Indigenous Craft Production in Latin America." *Economic Development and Cultural Change* 40, no. 1 (1991): 101-130. Reprinted with the permission of the University of Chicago Press.

Chiswick, Barry, Harry Anthony Patrinos, and Michael Hurst. "Indigenous Language Skills and the Labor Market in a Developing Economy: Bolivia." *Economic Development and Cultural Change* 48, no. 2 (2000): 349-376. Reprinted with the permission of the University of Chicago Press.

MacIsaac, Donna and Harry Anthony Patrinos. "Labour Market Discrimination against Indigenous People in Peru." *Journal of Development Studies* 32, no. 2 (1995): 218-233. Reprinted with the permission of Frank Cass & Co. Ltd.

Johnson III, Ollie. "Racial Representation and Brazilian Politics: Black Members of the National Congress, 1983-1999." *Journal of Interamerican Studies and World Affairs* 40, no. 4 (1998): 97-118. Reprinted with the permission of the University of Miami, Graduate School of International Studies.

Van Cott, Donna Lee. "A Political Analysis of Legal Pluralism in Bolivia and Colombia." *Journal of Latin American Studies* 32 (2000): 207-234. Reprinted with the permission of Cambridge University Press.

Korovkin, Tanya. "Weak Weapons, Strong Weapons? Hidden Resistance and Political Protest in Rural Ecuador." *Journal of Peasant Studies* 27, no. 3 (2000): 1-29. Reprinted with the permission of Frank Cass.

Andrews, George Reid. "Racial Inequality in Brazil and the United States: A Statistical Comparison." *Journal of Social History* 26, no. 2 (1992): 229-263. Reprinted with the permission of the *Journal of Social History*, Carnegie Mellon University.

Brysk, Alison. "Turning Weakness into Strength: The Internationalization of Indian Rights." *Latin American Perspectives* 23, no. 2 (1996): 38-57. Copyright 1996 by Sage Publications Inc. Reprinted by permission of Sage Publications Inc.

Nash, June. "The Reassertion of Indigenous Identity: Mayan Responses to State Intervention in Chiapas." *Latin American Research Review* 30, no. 3 (1995): 7-41. Reprinted with the permission of *Latin American Research Review*.

Mitchell, Michael and Charles Wood. "Ironies of Citizenship: Skin Color, Police Brutality, and the Challenge to Democracy in Brazil." *Social Forces* 77, no. 3 (1998): 1001-1020. Reprinted from *Social Forces*. Copyright The University of North Carolina Press.